Wendy
Orange

Simon & Schuster
New York   London   Toronto   Sydney   Singapore

Coming Home to Jerusalem

A Personal Journey

SIMON & SCHUSTER
Rockefeller Center
1230 Avenue of the Americas
New York, NY 10020

Designed by DEIRDRE C. AMTHOR

Manufactured in the United States of America

1   3   5   7   9   10   8   6   4   2

Library of Congress Cataloging-in-Publication Data
Orange, Wendy, date.
Coming home to Jerusalem: a personal journey / Wendy Orange.
    p.   cm.
1. Orange, Wendy.   2. Jews, American—Jerusalem—Biography.
3. Journalists—Israel—Biography.   4. Arab-Israeli conflict—1993–
5. Israel—Ethnic relations.   I. Title.
DS113.8.A4O736 2000
915.694'420454—dc21   ISBN 0-684-86951-9   00-022579

"A Guest in Jerusalem," from *Asleep in the Garden* by Stanley Moss (New York: Seven Stories Press, 1997), p. 21, reprinted by permission of the publisher.

Excerpts from "The End and the Beginning," from *View with a Grain of Sand* by Wislawa Szymborska, copyright © 1993 by Wislawa Szymborska, English translation by Stanislaw Baranczak and Clare Cavanagh, copyright © 1995 by Harcourt, Inc., reprinted by permission of the publisher.

"Tourists," from *The Selected Poetry of Yehuda Amichai*, edited and translated by Chana Bloch and Stephen Mitchell, copyright © 1996 by the Regents of the University of California, reprinted by permission of the publisher.

In memory of my loving dad:
Harold Basser, 1919–1982, and
in loving tribute to:
Yitzhak Rabin, 1922–1995

Gone too soon

Contents

PART III. AFTER THE HANDSHAKE   131

PART IV. LOSING THAT WILD EARTH   209

PART V. THE WORLD IS UPSIDE DOWN   247

One of Wallace Stevens' most beautiful poems is called "Thirteen Ways of Looking at a Blackbird." Israel presents at least as many possibilities; it is a modern state, a biblical anachronism, a socialist experiment, a colonial outpost, a homeland, an oppressor, a democracy, an occupying power, a small country with a narrow coastal strip, the centre of the world, an orange, a machine gun, a gathering ground for migrating birds, a holiday destination, the last resort, the Holy Land, Palestine, Israel.

—Clive Sinclair, *Diaspora Blues*

Prologue:
In the Beginning

Certain moments stand out, imprinted on our memories, however innocuous they seem when lived: On a Sunday morning in late autumn 1990, I was walking down a deserted street in Cambridge, Massachusetts, walking into a familiar alienation.

The first signs of winter were coming on. The last tattered leaves were dropping from the oaks, maples and elms under a gray November sky. Since childhood this sight had thrown me into mysterious dejections, a sense of exile. Certain that I could not rise above this recurring mood, I looked down and studied a grayish stretch of sidewalk. And it came to me, starkly, that I was homesick.

In the New York suburb where I grew up, there were similar sidewalks, nearly identical streets and trees, this same hushed quiet. There, too, the action took place in that American agora—the mall—which in the 1950s was the shopping district at the center of town. As I walked along, I realized that I was homesick for a place where I'd rarely felt at home—a thought that filled me with numb wonder.

What I found estranging when growing up in Woodmere, Long Island, was the town's obsession with appearances, clothes, homes and cars, a materialism that seeped even into children's lives. My best friend, Lizzie, for example, had a mother who wouldn't allow her to go outside, not even to elementary school, on days when her hair frizzed.

This focus on externals was the rule, not the exception. Yearly, *everyone* went into a high-voltage shopping frenzy as the Jewish High Holidays approached. Mothers and daughters crammed the stores, searching (not in quiet, but in boisterous desperation) for the right outfits. At ten, I'd already discovered that shopping was a lacerating ordeal from which it took hours to recuperate. Though objectively there was little wrong with my appearance, I loathed the mirror reflections, the pressures to look good, the thingifying of it all. Especially, I dreaded the outings for holiday dress-up clothes, all-important occasions in which I had no vote about whatever was purchased. That momentous decision was left to my mother, who, along with a particularly mousy saleswoman, conferred and then plucked crinolines, stockings, crepe skirts and Pappagallo shoes for me to wear. For all the difference my presence made, I might have stayed home and left it to them to outfit me. Unfortunately, this thought never occurred—and if it had, I'd have spent hours in that store anyway.

What I loved to do, as much as I dreaded shopping, was to talk on the phone with my friends for hours and then (a leap of no small proportions) retreat up to my bedroom where, surrounded by books, I'd read obsessively about the Holocaust. Such an immersion, which lasts to this day, surely began (I speak here as a parent) when I was far too young.

Decades later, I can view the split-level irony of those evenings: I'm upstairs tripping the light fantastic into Treblinka while my parents, below, are bustling about their living room, creating their private tribute to the nascent Jewish state. Gold-plated menorahs, silver mezuzahs, enlarged photographs of David Ben-Gurion and Chaim Weizmann were placed (and replaced) among rows of books on Mideast history, which held all I thought I'd ever glimpse of the state of Israel. Squeezed among these volumes and artifacts were the burgundy prayer books that we dusted off twice a year before heading out to Temple.

Once inside our high-ceilinged synagogue, I tried to follow the Hebrew text, rising and sitting and rising again as instructed. But soon only boredom was rising in me, usually less than an hour into the day-long service. Though some adults in the room were audibly snoring, if I began fidgeting, my mother would dig her long red nails into my skinny arms, putting an end to all thoughts of dashing out to the hallway for a break. So I restlessly listened to the English part of the service and then to the rabbi's long lecture, which invariably focused on Israel. He'd remind us that Israel was a country in dire need of our devotions, our prayers and our money as well—lots of it, everything we could muster.

The adults, presumably, sent in checks. We children slid all our spare change—nickels, dimes, quarters—into pre-packaged envelopes, with scooped out coin-sized slots. These packets were then shipped halfway around the world. Months later, we received "deeds" to our very own Israeli trees—commodities whose value wasn't clear to us; after all, we lived in a town full of them. Yet we spent many Sundays collecting those coins because our parents and Hebrew teachers demanded we do so, and because (as became clear over time) for most adults in our town Judaism played a distant second to Woodmere's primary religion, which was Israel. Or so it seemed to one over-earnest ten-year-old.

Overheard everywhere were fever-pitched discussions about the new Jewish state. The din of these voices was as striking as the silence about the events occurring prior to Israel's birth. The silence and the commotion, as I was later to learn, were entwined because many in my hometown had family members who had been murdered by the Nazis.

Reading in my bedroom led me to identify ever less with Israel's blue star, ever more with that yellow *Jude* armband worn by Europe's doomed millions. My room burgeoned with books I found in the local library, not only popular ones like Anne Frank's *Diary* but also obscure titles, any that mentioned the death camps. The more I read, the more Israel's flag seemed a flimsy cover for an immense darkness.

At night, seemingly safe in the suburbs, I often dreamed of the Nazis, of concentration camps or the cattle cars. I'd wake drenched in sweat, heavy-hearted, suffering dream hangovers. In my pink-and-gray-striped bedroom I'd sit up and try to dispel these night visions while listening to the thunderous Long Island Railroad trains whose tracks cut through our small backyard. At eight-minute intervals the commuters, as we called them, rattled our dishes and shook the photos on our walls, deafening all conversation. As they chortled past, I heard echoes of those other trains, traveling along their terrifying trajectories.

By the time I entered high school, Israel had formed a peculiar shape in my mind, odd as its contours on the map. I alternately pictured that faraway country as another Long Island suburb or as a barren desert populated by grim, regimented pioneers. Whichever image dominated, for me Israel had become the antithesis of hip, emblematic of the suburbia I longed to escape. And I did escape—the suburb and talk of Israel—the day my parents drove me to Manhattan to enroll in college. On New York's Upper West Side, for the first time in my remembered life, I felt the enchantment of being rightly placed.

In the spring of 1967, I married a sweetheart of a guy named Julian. Only days after our wedding, I received a phone call from my father. Speaking even more softly than usual, he said, "Sit down, sweetie. *Are* you sitting? Bad news. Very bad. Your grandpa Phil just died."

I sat in a daze as my father recounted how *his* father had been staying home to rest after his heart attack. "But today, he'd defied doctors' orders. When he heard that a war in Israel had broken out, he left his bed and rushed to a fundraiser at the Waldorf-Astoria. His doctor and your grandmother were grabbing onto his coat but he shook them off, racing up onto the stage. There he gave one of his speeches. He was shouting 'the very survival of Israel is at stake' when he had his fatal attack."

"Grandpa Philip died on a hotel stage?" I asked, amazed.

"Talk about fundraising! Your grandfather raked in at least twenty ambulances with *that* performance," my dad said wryly, as was his way. This was all I knew or cared about the '67 war.

And then, within three years, as the sixties and my marriage were both coming to an end, and just after finishing my Ph.D. in clinical psychology, I accepted a job in Boston. It was a prestigious position I thought too good to turn down, even though the hospital contract stated clearly that returning to live in New York would be impossible for years.

The week I arrived in Boston, I knew I had just made one colossal, irrevocable mistake. Though I came to love my work, clients and new friends, the town of Cambridge, where I leased an apartment, shuttled me emotionally right back to Woodmere—different as I knew these places to be. It was as if my years in Manhattan were a fleeting mirage.

Since no one else I knew disliked the Boston area, I tried to ignore the memory flashbacks which the physiognomy of the town evoked. Yet despite reminding myself that I was always hyper-sensitive to *place,* despite continual attempts to ignore my feelings, I couldn't. Living in Cambridge gave rise to an inner suffocation not dissimilar to the claustrophobic awareness that you've just married the wrong person.

I quickly sought out a supervising analyst at my hospital, a Jewish woman with whom I'd developed a slight rapport. We set up a session where I talked about the disconsolate moods that could strike without notice, triggered by anything at all—the shape of a multiplex theater, a shadow cast on a wall, an angle of winter light.

The analyst studied me, her eyebrows raised in surprise. I couldn't be this superficial, she suggested. After all, we were both psychologists. We knew, better than most, how we take ourselves with us wherever we go. "There is no *wrong place,*" she asserted before changing the subject to ask if I remembered my dreams. I nodded, flashing on a dream that recurred regularly, usually in autumn. I prefaced it by saying that I'd studied Buddhist meditation for the last few years. Then I walked her through the dream's tableaux: *It's the Jewish High Holidays but I'm at a Buddhist retreat. Meditation ends; I drift toward a run-down section of town where I enter a dissolute tavern. That's when I hear Hebrew melodies. They grow louder, obliterating the Buddhist chants and gongs. When the sad cantorial sounds fade away, I sidle up to a degenerate guy and am, at the dream's end, madly trying to kiss him, even though he's more or less drowning in his beer.*

"That's an easy one," the analyst responded. "This dream points to your neglected Judaism. It's telling you to search for your ethnic roots. I suggest you start with the writings of Martin Buber. Read his essays. Tonight would not be a minute too soon. Your dream shows that you're 'drunk' on the wrong religious practices. Study the great Jewish scholars now. One day, with luck, you'll get to Israel. There you'll find your true heritage. In the meantime, I encourage you to stop this nonsense about sidewalks and trees. Hit yourself [here she handed me a thick rubber band] the minute you think a negative thought about this quite lovely place."

Was she Freudian or Jungian; a behavioral psychologist or just dull-minded? I didn't know. What I knew was that my Buddhist dabblings were in no way an alternative religion. And that, given the volumes on psychoanalytic technique we had to read every night, I couldn't find time for Martin Buber as well. Once out of her office, I rehashed her airtight "dream interpretation," one I found so simplistic that as I drove away it crossed my mind that my mother, living on Long Island, had somehow managed to give this woman a ring before I arrived.

It was a Saturday in September 1973. Specifically, it was the afternoon of Yom Kippur and I was driving to visit my grandmother—a fragile woman, now long widowed—who still lived in the Orthodox Jewish neighborhood of Far Rockaway, Queens. On this day she was too weak to attend synagogue (which was fine with me). Instead, we lounged together on twin beds in the home she'd shared with my grandfather for over fifty years. Sounding wistful, she said, "It's like Phil's still in the bathroom—just shaving or washing up." I asked how she kept Philip alive in her mind years after his death, a comment that evoked a sharp look of pity. My grandmother rightly intuited I would never love anyone for half a century. She then asked about Julian—what had happened; why the divorce?

I explained about evading the Vietnam draft, about emigrating to Canada. I told her how, at the last possible moment, we returned to New York where Julian, miraculously, or sort of miraculously, received a psychiatric discharge. "On what grounds?" my grandmother wanted to know. She leaned forward, her face frowning. I relayed the strange truth: that after Julian pretended to be crazy to avoid the draft, he actually went crazy. My grandmother, all ears, was thinking out loud: "That boy is lost. If only he'd moved to Israel! There, he'd have something to fight for. In Israel, he'd have become a man." I listened to her, wondering how a *country* could heal anyone's primal wounds, a simple fact of life if you asked anyone in my family.

I drifted into reveries about whom to date next while my grandmother checked her clock. *Shabbat* was over so she was free to turn on her radio. At first the room filled with loud static. But soon the station cleared and we heard the shocking news that, just a few hours before, Israel had been the target of a surprising, deadly Arab attack. I looked at my grandmother. After twisting in agony on her bed, she pushed an ear *into* her high-topped old radio. Both of her arms were curled around it, as if for comfort. Occasionally, she'd wag a gnarled, arthritic hand over at me, motioning me to stay quiet, even though I hadn't said a word. She was obviously in a state of alarm about Israel's fate. What alarmed me was *her* fate. She was so weak; I certainly hadn't forgotten what the last Israeli war had done to my grandfather.

Soon my grandmother became exhausted and needed sleep. I brought water to her bed, smoothed her covers and kissed her good night. As I was turning off her radio, she waved her arm in agitation again. "Leave it on; I need the news. . . . Another war," she mumbled in a small, tired voice.

"Try not to worry," I said. "Remember, I'll be here first thing tomorrow morning."

"Come early," she whispered hoarsely.

I did. At 7:30 A.M., I was standing with my parents on her front porch, carrying bagels and lox. Her door was still locked. "Good. She's sleeping late," my father said, relieved that his mother was getting rest. He, too, was terribly distracted by the war raging in Israel. My mother retrieved our hidden key and we walked inside to find my grandmother lying in the exact position I'd left her nine hours ago. Except that now she was dead. In the heightened eeriness of that moment, the only sounds filling her too-silent bedroom were bulletins from Israel's battlefields.

Despite this second wrenching loss, I developed no more interest in the Yom Kippur War than I had in the '67 Six-Day War. As Franz Kafka wrote in a journal: "My family draped themselves over the map of the world, leaving me free to inhabit only the places they left untouched." In a less dramatic (and less acerbic) vein, the same was true for me: Israel belonged, had always belonged, to my family.

The next events happened in quick succession when my parents were still in their fifties: In the early 1980s each was diagnosed with a terminal illness. After two years of constant worry and travel to help my mother, she died. A month to the day after her funeral, my father began his equally urgent, non-stop medical crises. Chemotherapy and dialysis, heart attacks and emergency rooms, bedpans and pain were our daily fare. And then, as if suddenly, he too was gone.

Soon after losing them, I remarried, this time to a happy man, a bit *too* happy I might say, and happiest of all in the most remote spot imaginable— *rural* Jamaica, West Indies—an unusual place for a Long Island Jew, which he was, to call home. And then, within a year or so, I was offered a job as a college professor and we agreed to relocate to Burlington, Vermont. After the initial rush of joy with our new home, work and friends, I often sank into a Sunday ennui, one which could spread, low grade, over an entire week. In such moods I had the sensation of being only randomly or arbitrarily placed—or felt, as a friend put it, that I was living in an *anywhere* but not a *somewhere*.

Our marriage ended eight years later. By then I had an infant daughter. Where should I raise her? By now, I felt too Jewish for Vermont, too cerebral for Jamaica, too hooked on natural beauty for Manhattan, too eccentric for Cambridge. So I traveled with my baby from one place to another, aware that time and money were running out and that Eliza would soon be old enough to realize that not everyone lives in planes, trains and cars. The year she turned four I "settled down"—an injunction that anyone who knew me, for even ten minutes, emphatically advised. Cambridge was the sensible choice: a kid-friendly, academic town where I still had close friends and a professional identity. Yet mere months after returning there came that homesick moment on the sidewalk. And then, two months later, in January 1991, the Gulf war broke out.

I was glued to the television in my small Cambridge living room, watching CNN. On the screen, an Israeli reporter was struggling, none too successfully, to position a gas mask over his face. Once in place, it made him look like a huge rodent. His voice trembled and his knees were buckling as the building he reported from began shaking. Later, we learned that this was the first Scud missile to hit Tel Aviv. But at the time, a news bulletin, shortly retracted, announced that a missile had just dropped poisonous chemicals over central Israel.

My association was as instant as it was historic; once again Jews were being gassed! On the screen I watched a slow-moving caravan of cars exiting Tel Aviv and heading up to Jerusalem—a place considered safer because Saddam Hussein was unlikely to bomb the holy Muslim sites there (though his aim was proving less than accurate). Watching that cold metallic war, I realized I had no idea where Jerusalem was located. I didn't know how far it was or in what direction from Tel Aviv. In fact, I had no sense of Mideast geography, none at all. Yet those Israeli telecasters as well as the Israelis on the streets being interviewed all felt familiar. They looked and dressed like me and my friends, were the same age, had the same verbal intonations as they spoke. Something was rising up in me, an idea as solipsistic as it was prescient—prescient about me, not about Israel. The thought went like this: If my parents and grandparents were alive, they'd be riveted by this war. But they are dead. So who is taking care of Israel now? Maybe it's my turn.

A month later I happened upon a brochure advertising a peace conference for "American, Israeli and Palestinian intellectuals." It was scheduled for the coming June in Jerusalem. By then, as was accurately predicted, the Gulf war would be over. I scrutinized this pamphlet with its list of speakers and assorted topics. Mostly, I studied that word "Jerusalem," a city whose name suddenly carried resonance, a city to which I'd never given three thoughts before. Jerusalem was stirring in my imagination: I'd walk around Cambridge, visualizing lemon and orange trees. I'd dream of a desert and wake wondering if this was what the Middle East looked like. It was as though I was somehow able to picture that distant, wild earth.

I brought the conference's pamphlet to my close friend—my twin soul—Michael Koran. He'd lived in Israel for a few years, decades ago. He still had friends there and knew the country well. Immediately, he understood my hallucinatory response to the idea of going to see Jerusalem. "You will be amazed. You will be transformed. Definitely, we'll go together," he said, adding, "You'll never forget this trip." The next day we both signed up.

But in June, at Boston's Logan Airport, *after* we'd passed through intensive security and were standing at the open door to the 747 El Al jet, I panicked. I was worn down from single-parenting my five-year-old daughter, yet dreaded being separated from her. I'd never left her for more than an afternoon and I already missed her fiercely. In addition, I was certain that I'd have nothing, zip, to contribute to a conference of intellectuals steeped in Mideast history, Israeli politics, the nuances of peacemaking. The entire region again loomed as someone else's domain; Israel reverted to seeming too geographically and psychologically remote.

"Come on. You'll pour water for the geniuses," Michael joked.

"But I can't fly," I blurted. Which was true. After thirty-odd years of flying (my first flight was at age nine) I'd never gotten through a single plane ride without the certainty that *this one* was doomed. Strong liquor, in-flight hypnosis, fear-of-flying workshops—all had been to no avail. On every flight, as I told Michael, I ended up mangling the arm of whoever sat beside me. Just then, El Al security resolved my dilemma. A tall man sternly demanded that we take our seats.

From that moment, though braced for the familiar flood of macabre images—wings falling off or engines bursting into flame—not only did I fail to conjure visions of destruction but, on the contrary, I felt extraordinarily at peace. The longer the plane hummed along, the greater my sense of well-being. I was comforted by the voices of Jewish pilots talking in Hebrew over the loudspeakers, by the sight of religious Jews davening (bending back and forth in prayer) at the rear of the jet. The poised Israeli flight attendants, the friendly, nonstop conversations, the chaos and indifference to airline etiquette, all relaxed me. I was thrust into a rare meditative calm, a sense of homecoming that brought me close to my parents and grandparents. They seemed to surround me in an angelic (almost psychedelic) welcome to the Holy Land.

Toward the end of the long flight, I looked down at my hands and saw reflections of my father's fingers. As we prepared for landing, I heard echoes of my grandma Rose's voice: "Yes, at last! To Israel!"

Part I
Among the Israelis

My family was, I suppose, a rather typical middle-class American Jewish family. . . . I was sent to Hebrew school five days a week as a young boy, but after age . . . thirteen, the synagogue interested me little; I was a three-day-a-year Jew. [I took a trip] to Israel.

That trip would change my life. . . . I don't know if it was just the shock of the new, or a fascination waiting to be discovered, but something about Israel and the Middle East grabbed me in both heart and mind. I was totally taken with the place, its peoples and its conflicts. Since that moment, I have never really been interested in anything else. Indeed, from the first day I walked through the walled Old City of Jerusalem, inhaled its spices, and lost myself in the multicolored river of humanity that flowed through its maze of alleyways, I felt at home. . . . It may have been my first trip abroad . . . but I knew then and there that I was really more Middle East than Minnesota.

—*Thomas L. Friedman,* From Beirut to Jerusalem

CHAPTER ONE

Trains in the Distance

Once off the plane Michael hails a taxi to drive us up to Jerusalem. Our driver turns out to be a man with whom Michael once studied Hebrew, a man named Shuki. They talk as I look out the window at our sandy surroundings. In less than an hour we're checking into the King David Hotel. After stashing his bags in an adjoining room, Michael enters my room and starts pacing back and forth, though I'm already in bed, exhausted. I'm half asleep when he suggests that we leave Jerusalem immediately, that we take a tour of the country.

"Tour the country?" I ask, incredulous. "Michael, we just got here."

I'm sinking back into sleep when he shakes me awake. He's feeling sick, he says. I sit up and see that he looks pale. His legs are shaking. I suggest we call a doctor, but he says something about having weird feelings, a panic attack, and in a flash, after grabbing his backpack, he's out the door. "I need to get out of here," I hear him say as he goes, leaving me wide awake. I've never seen Michael act like this and now I'm completely alone in this foreign land.

Having never traveled such a distance, I know nothing about jet lag. I become mystified by the mood that overtakes me—a high wakefulness laced with a free-floating fear. Luckily, the conference isn't scheduled to begin for six days. Cornered by my own anxiety, I venture only as far as the hotel's gift shop, where I buy Thomas L. Friedman's *From Beirut to Jerusalem*.

For the next three days the sun shines brightly. Not a cloud passes overhead. But too shy to go outside by myself, I stay in the hotel, devouring Friedman's depictions of Israeli and Palestinian realities. I read in bed, on the balcony, in the dining room. I don't brave leaving the hotel until I've nearly memorized Friedman's words. Yet I know I haven't come halfway around the world to read a book.

So, on the fourth luminous morning I force myself to go out. Five steps away I spot a line of taxis. "You want tour?" a driver asks. "I take you Yad

Vashem," he says, referring to the Holocaust memorial. I nod, climb into his backseat and remain mute as we head uphill. We pass modern stone buildings and drive up curving hilltops with views of desert vistas. Then we take a winding urban route and pass overflowing cafes filled with animated crowds. What I see from this cab window is nothing like my imagined Israel. Jerusalem looks exotic, yet feels familiar in ways I can't explain to myself. I'm awed by the beauty of this country that I've so studiously avoided all these years of my life.

As I gaze out the window, my driver shouts to me in English, "A few years back . . . Thugs. Nazis called. 1930s. They kill all Jews. Dead and dead everywhere! This guy, named Hitler . . ." I tune him out, mumbling, "I know about *that*," wondering who in the world doesn't, while mesmerized by the Jerusalem that's passing before me. Soon I ask him to let me out of the car, and I wander haphazardly through neighborhoods that seem inviting.

I enter dark alleyways which open onto sunny courtyards. I stroll past stone houses terraced with colorful plants and flowering bushes. If I ask people for directions, we often end up playing Jewish geography ("You from New York? Know Abe Grossman?"). The Israelis I meet act as if there's all the time in the world for such chatting. Almost everyone greets me as a family member, though I notice that unlike Americans, Jewish Israelis are firmly planted on their land, in their country's politics and history. They may be shrill, but they're not suffering from any estrangement, I notice. That night I get into bed suffused with the day's physical and human warmth, impatient for my next excursion.

Part of Jerusalem's allure is purely visual. In the days that follow I study the birds and the oddly juxtaposed trees: pines and palms, lemon and eucalyptus, firs and figs blossom everywhere. Whether lacy or aromatic, they fill the courtyards, encircle each home, towering above the stones that turn rose, lavender, yellow, white and gray under the oscillating summer light. I study these transformations as if deciphering my destiny. Or I move to another neighborhood where I contemplate each scene, costume and character as if I'm gazing at an Old Master's artwork.

In the Jewish Quarter of the Old City, I see ultra-Orthodox men and boys garbed in black from hat to shoe racing toward a yeshiva, side curls (*peyot*) flying in the breeze, cigarettes dangling from their lips. Nearby, wizened old men in the Muslim quarter sit with their heads swathed in checkered scarves, known as kaffiyehs, relaxing and smoking hookahs (water pipes) at outdoor tables. They seem oblivious to the Jews rushing past. Back at my hotel in modern Jerusalem, I'm surrounded by casually dressed Israelis, uniformed in T-shirts and jeans, smoking, talking, gesturing vivaciously. Wherever I walk, whoever comes into view, I've yet to see a set of dulled eyes.

One morning near the Damascus Gate, an archway leading into the Old

City, I watch six Greek Orthodox priests walking abreast of each other, so close they seem to occupy one body. When a wind blows their long black robes, each one billows like an umbrella, while their gold crucifixes catch the sun while swinging back and forth on their chests. With the Judean mountains in the background and with so many religiously attired figures around me, I feel as if I've wandered far from the post-modern world onto a page torn from the Bible. At the same time, my sense of alienation is evaporating, as is the Sunday sadness (in Israel, Sunday is a weekday) that's assaulted me everywhere else. Instead of withdrawing from life, I feel an easy intimacy with the people, with the place and with myself, wherever I go.

When I finally lie down to sleep, I can't wait for morning, for the dawn sun rising over the Old City in brilliant red, for the sounds of Hebrew and Arabic prayers mixing in the air. Before reading the day's newspapers or opening one of my books on Mideast history, I sit on my small balcony and look out at the Judean desert hills and beyond, all the way out to the horizon. By 8 A.M., every mosque and synagogue shines golden under a sun that's guaranteed a full six months here. These sights and sounds all wake me to an alertness so intense, it almost replaces coffee.

Whether I walk through Mea Shearim (the eighteenth-century replica of a Jewish shtetl) or on crowded Ben Yehuda (in central downtown), or to the neighborhood of Abu Tor with its moonscape park, the Tayelet, every sight draws me out of myself and into this waking dream. The city's old stones have a warmth that seems historical, evocative of recent generations in my family, my most intimate link to the vast chain of Jewish history. I've long known that our subjective moods can "create" external reality; now I learn that the converse is true: that an outer world of meanings can shift the sense of who we are. I'm no longer identified with that wicked child of the Passover service, the one who says, "What happened to *you* in the land of *your* forefathers?" Here, I wonder naturally, "What happened to *us?*" The fact that I feel so at home in a place where everything is reversed—the alphabet, the calendar, the Celsius weather reports, the books that read from right to left, the rhythms of the Jewish holidays—confirms the notion that my feelings of displacement are being reversed as well.

I belong in Jerusalem. This inner refrain arises not only from the exotic landscapes, constant sunlight or the dynamism of human connections. What most enlivens me is the Jewishness of it all—a multicultural, bohemian, cosmopolitan Jewish expressed in English, Hebrew, French, Russian and Aramaic, languages spoken everywhere in this city of immigrants.

On my sixth night I meet an Israeli intellectual who's sipping Turkish coffee in the hotel lobby. He invites me to join him, tells me that he's driven the two hours from Haifa, and is also waiting for the conference to begin. (Men seem like cousins here. There's no sexual subtext coloring every encounter, though there's plenty of free-floating flirting.) Uri is a scholar and, as I soon learn, is not part of the peace movement. He's here to check out Americans and Israelis who are pro-peace and is wary of us all. He knows Torah as well as the minutiae of Israel's history. He quizzes me on what *I* know, barking questions like the stern professor he is. He asks me about the Bible, about recent politics and distant history—a test I fail miserably. Yet it's easy to be direct with him.

"Look," I say, "I know next to nothing; I'm here to learn."

"At least you're honest," Uri says, shaking his head. "American Jews aren't usually aware of their ignorance about us. Why do you people *always* superimpose your fantasies on *our* reality?" I shrug. That he even thinks I *have* fantasies about his country shows he hasn't caught on to how little I yet know about Israel.

As night wears on, we can't stop talking in this ornate lobby. Or rather, he can't. I become the rapt listener. Somewhere near 2 A.M., I realize that despite Uri's erudition (his lived Zionism, his yeshiva education begun at age five, continuing into his mid-fifties), he needs me as an audience or sounding board for the argument he's having with himself. I watch as he moves through the tunnels of his mind vis-à-vis the "Arabs" (the word he, like most Israelis, uses when discussing the Palestinians). He's trying to envision a "two-state solution" and at one point almost talks himself into one, though he continues to sprinkle his monologue with racist epithets against Arabs—a people he thoroughly distrusts. And, as he lets me know, he finds pro-peace Americans not much better. "Naive, unsophisticated, arrogant" is what he calls us over and over. Nor does he lose any love on the Sephardim—Jews from Arab countries. He's elitist, sexist, certainly a Jewish chauvinist. But as he keeps smiling at me, I intuit how much he welcomes a neutral mind onto which he can work out his zigzagging thoughts about peace, its possible solutions.

"I hate even the *thought* of losing the biblical sites on the West Bank," he says. Like a good therapist, I nod, saying nothing. "But we can't afford any more of our soldiers dying while trying to control those terrorist kids with their stones." As he says this, his face goes rigid. Yet around the next curve in his mind, he's wrestling with more liberal ideas—ideas he'd never entertain if I'd suggested them. "You know nothing. It's amazing! Nothing!" he says, which is true, after all. Yet he seems unaware that it's my ignorance that frees him to speak opposing thoughts out loud. After a few hours he winds down. Immediately, as if he's waking from a trance, he says, "But none of this is any of your business."

"Sure, it's my business," I say, thinking less of American Jewish money poured into this country and more of the *hours* I've just spent listening to each twist and turn of his complex mind. "Why else would we be talking if it's not my business? As you said, all Jews are connected through 'birth and persecution,' " I repeat his words back to him calmly. I don't need to be defensive, however dismissive and rude he is. Because, for once in my life, I know I belong to this story.

The next morning, the conference begins. More than four hundred American Jews have flown over to attend. In the mornings and evenings we're joined by Israelis who by day must go to work. On the schedule is a highly anticipated panel featuring four Palestinians. But I see no Palestinians at all during our daily sessions. What I see is how we Americans appear to the Israelis, especially those among us who talk with authority, sounding arrogant, a tone that's never lost on the sabras, native-born Israelis.

Yael Dayan, daughter of famed Israeli military hero Moshe Dayan, and a firebrand in her own right, a woman who will soon become a member of the Knesset (Israel's parliament), steps to the stage, gives a passionate speech. She outlines the Israeli peace movement's strategies, their plans to counter Likud Prime Minister Yitzhak Shamir's intransigence against even modest compromises with the Palestinians. She finishes to wild applause. Following her to the podium is the newly elected senator from Minnesota, Paul Wellstone. His talk is long, earnest and abstract. As he finishes, he looks at Dayan, who's sitting in the front row of this packed auditorium. "I so appreciate that you've taken the time to come here tonight. How generous of you to interrupt your busy life and to share your thoughts," he says.

Dayan leaps from her seat. "*Mamash!* [Really!] Maybe in the States you say such things. But not here, not to us Israelis, not to *me*. We, sir, do not attend your meetings out of 'generosity.' Peace work is no hobby for us. Don't you understand? Coming here is not altruism; it's our life! Who are *you* to thank *me?*" The Israelis smile during her outburst. The Americans do not. They seem taken aback by her directness, which I find energizing, even if rude. In fact, I'm overcome by a sense of freedom at this Israeli bluntness and the permission it gives us all to speak our minds truthfully.

The next morning I join hundreds of Americans who are sitting around an outdoor amphitheater at Hebrew Union College. Try as I do to concentrate on the scholars' talks on the Bible or Jewish spirituality, on class schisms in Israel or the possible pathways to peace, I keep getting distracted by a clump of cypress trees in the corner of the yard. Each tree seems a testament to a hundred years of Zionism. I force myself to concentrate by taking notes, but soon I'm off on another reverie, marveling at "Jewish" birds flying in a "Jewish" sky, trying to remember all those words about Israel I so assiduously tuned out since childhood. I'm preoccupied with sorting out my long-held prejudices about Israel from this wild place all around me.

At the mid-afternoon break an American woman asks if I'll join her for a meal. I like her voice, her homey manner, the way left-leaning American Jews can be so casual and unpretentious. But to my surprise, over lunch not a word is said about the conference. We focus on her problems: a mastectomy years back, her mother's death two decades ago. She talks about being fat, saying that it's obvious to everyone that she has problems.

"Well, don't we all?"

"But *your* problems aren't obvious," she responds. I show her my bitten nails. She shrugs. "That's nothing, just fingers," she says. When our meal is over, we walk to the Wailing (Western) Wall, touch the ancient stones, move a few feet back to stare at them and then touch them again. Nothing stirs in me; I'm a bit numb. Rather than forcing a feeling, I study the people who are praying here, separated into men's and women's sections. Many have prayer books open and are davening back and forth, muttering in Hebrew. Several women nearby are sobbing openly. Others are crying quietly. I open my notebook and write a letter to God. I give gratitude for being in Jerusalem and ask for grace for all those I love—the living and the dead. Following the common custom, I then press the note into the cracks of this massive stone wall. We then head back to the conference.

But not before making a detour to sit in the cafe adjacent to Jerusalem's Cinémathèque, the film center here. It's gorgeous out on this stone ledge. We can see the Sultan's Pool, the David Museum, the Dome of the Rock, the hills of Palestinian Silwan. Again I feel emanations of history coming at me, exactly what the Wailing Wall did not evoke. When I try to talk about my sense of being placed, my companion can't respond; she's staring down at a near-invisible stain on her dress that she wants me to agree is obvious. It isn't.

We arrive back at the conference just in time to catch a poetry reading. Someone is introducing the famous Israeli poet Yehuda Amichai: "They call this the Holy Land. But what's really holy are the connections between people." Amichai reads from his poems, including one called "Tourists," which is a minor synchronicity because his words capture what I was thinking only an hour ago at the Wailing Wall:

> *Once I was sitting on the steps near the gate at David's Citadel and I*
> *put down my two heavy baskets beside me. A group of tourists stood*

there around their guide, and I became their point of reference. "You see
that man over there with the baskets? A little to the right of his head
there's an arch from the Roman period. A little to the right of his head."
"But he's moving, he's moving!" I said to myself: Redemption will come
only when they are told, "Do you see that arch over there from the Ro-
man period? It doesn't matter, but near it, a little to the left and then
down a bit, there's a man who has just bought fruit and vegetables for his
family."

The following session is standing room only (the audience is entirely American). Taking place in a large auditorium, it's billed simply as "The Palestinians." Faisal Husseini and Sari Nusseibeh, two men from prominent East
Jerusalem Arab families, are on the program. As are Hanan Ashwari (who's
not yet a household name) and Zahira Kamal (a West Bank lawyer and activist). But three of the four on the program do not show up. Only Zahira Kamal arrives, along with a young male associate. She's a wisp of a woman,
smart and soft-spoken. With reserve, she begins speaking about Palestinian
work going on in the territories, about the long vigil her people endure, of Israeli occupation with "its unspeakable record of human rights abuses." She
explains what the Intifada (the Palestinian stone-throwing uprising) has
meant, not to Israelis, but to the structure of Palestinian family life. She tells us
how women's roles have been altered; that they now have more power and authority in their communities. She talks about the psychology of Palestinian
kids, of the consequences they face when choosing to either fight in the Intifada or not.

After her speech, to my horror, Kamal is bombarded by questions thrown
out at her like . . . stones. These harsh queries are voiced by the most vocal
among us—mostly by American men in the audience. They question Palestinian disorganization, making aggressive comments that dispute her "Israel-
bashing." They voice suspicions about her people's "martyrdom." She's asked
if the Palestinians' stoic stance is a public relations stunt. Seated in the front
row, I watch Zahira Kamal field these queries with seeming aplomb. But I can
feel her disappointment, her weariness. Finally a man stands up and speaks
sternly.

"Imagine what it would be like to be a Jew addressing a large group of
Palestinians," he says. "Would that be easy? Wouldn't you want respect?
Wouldn't you hope for the audience to learn about your reality rather than in-
stantly challenging every word you said? Who among us would reveal internal
Jewish schisms to Palestinian strangers? What do you expect of these two who

were gracious enough to show up?" When he sits, the group is quiet. The two Palestinians make a hasty exit into a world about which I *really* know nothing.

Days pass as I tour the country, make new acquaintances, visit homes where I have meaningful, even revelatory conversations. Occasionally I go to hear the scholars speak at the conference. But more often I take day trips (with Michael's taxi friend Shuki) to the Dead Sea or to Tel Aviv. On the streets, especially in Jerusalem, I frequently hear anti-Arab slurs, just what the conference is attempting to reverse. But during these days, neither politics nor the future really grips me in the way that the architecture, trees, smells and random conversations do. I feel swept away by this zestful place, by wave after wave of extroverted Mediterranean energy—an energy that seems to feed on itself.

Every day I hear stories of the past from those who lived it. In a restaurant a man shares the tale of how he survived the Holocaust. An elderly gentleman sits me down at the Dead Sea spa and tells me at length of his role in 1948's War of Independence. At cafes in Tel Aviv and Jerusalem, I hear about Israel's history from the people who created it. Israelis of all ages pull up chairs to regale a foreign Jew with personal accounts—of making *aliyah* (the "ascent" to live permanently as a citizen in Israel), of fighting wars or growing up as sabras. I'm surprised at their openness, at how readily Israelis talk of the most personal matters—comrades lost in past wars, buried children, friendships, even marriages, formed (or riven) by politics. They are equally free with advice about how to navigate life here—the traffic, the best place to exchange money, what movies to see.

I relish the way Israelis lean into my life, asking, "Where's the child? You come so far and without your girl? No husband? How can you afford the expensive hotel?" I do not experience these interchanges with strangers as intrusive; rather, in no time, "strangers" seem like aunts, grandparents, cousins. The more I talk to Israelis, the less American I feel, and this all occurs so quickly that I question my own perceptions. Each time I go to the conference, by contrast, I feel the psychological distance that exists between us American Jews, even though the speakers' political and biblical explications are usually brilliant. I seem to come alive only when out on the streets, wrapped inside Israel's shifting, ambiguous realities.

One evening a group of Israeli intellectuals takes over the stage—writers, activists, politicians, poets. I resonate with the masculine men and the no-nonsense, straightforward women. A. B. Yehoshua, a famous Israeli novelist, takes his turn at the microphone, announcing that, unlike those who preceded him, he'll give his lecture in Hebrew. The crowd groans, but he says that this reborn ancient language should be known by us all. And off he goes—on and on in Hebrew. Oddly, while few can understand him (and I do only because bits of his speech are translated for me by an Israeli who's sitting nearby) the group seems to rise up along with Yehoshua's energy. Somehow his talk is more powerful than all the other speeches put together, as though language is no barrier.

The gist of his exhortation is: "Come to live in Israel. Other Americans, the ultra-religious, the right-wing settlers, *they* come in droves. But you! You intellectuals. You peaceniks. You only visit. That's wrong! Don't you realize that *you* could help create a new Israel? Help create social justice here. Help make peace with the Arabs. Even rid us of Shamir! But no, you give your opinions, not your lives. I say to every one of you: *Make aliyah; not conferences!*"

Can I do this? Move here? I approach him after his talk while busy calculating the logistics. I do have enough money to live for a year without full-time work. My child hasn't entered kindergarten yet. Surely, she'll pick up Hebrew "like a sponge," as all young children do with foreign languages. Yehoshua eventually turns to me. It's as if he can see through me and is convinced I will be the rare American to heed his call, to move here. This is one of those moments when something speaks through you and you listen, more than a little surprised. Yehoshua is pulling these thoughts from me as he puts an arm paternally around me, casually jotting down his home phone number. "You'll call; we'll talk," he says, as though the case is closed and I'll be back soon.

Excited and disoriented, I look around only to spot Michael. He must have just returned from the Negev or from wherever he disappeared to. He hugs me apologetically, says that he knows he deserted me, is sorry. I can't forgive him until he explains what happened. As soon as we entered Jerusalem, he says, he was flooded by painful memories, searing flashbacks. That's why he had to escape this "so powerful place."

"Jet lag," we quip and then we stare at each other. I tell Michael that he looks stronger and more virile here. He swears I already look like an Israeli. He can see my soul rising into my face.

A group of Israeli, American and English Jews joins our reunion and we all head to a nearby cafe for hummus, pita and olives. Around the long table, Israelis describe what it was like living through the Gulf war. They talk of wearing gas masks, of the sealed rooms essential in every home. One woman passes around photographs of her children lying on cots, under thick sheets of tarpaulin. We take turns studying their small faces strapped into huge masks; they look like children in emergency rooms or in intensive care.

"It must have been terrifying," an Englishman observes, but the Israelis laugh it off. The war's over; very few were killed. Their mood remains cheerful even as our talk turns to the Palestinians. We ask why only one activist showed up at the conference, rather than the four expected. An Israeli explains about the latest political rift. He says that cultural tensions these days are not due only to Shamir's rigidity. They also result from recent Palestinian actions, the way so many danced on their rooftops, cheering on Saddam Hussein. This, he tells us, has ripped apart the small Israeli and Palestinian peace cultures, disrupting decades-long friendships between those who work together.

An American asks, "But isn't it obvious that the enemy of your enemy is a natural ally? Isn't that the reason why Palestinians took the side of Iraq?"

The Englishman says, "Your Israeli government didn't help matters. How could they refuse to distribute gas masks to those living in the territories?" An Israeli argues with them. He believes the Palestinians only showed their true feelings with such actions—that they simply hate all Israelis. Despite these opposing views, the group energy at our table remains high-spirited and open-hearted. During a lull I mention that my lifelong sense of estrangement has disappeared since my arrival. An Israeli named Chava turns to study me. "No one told you that Israel cures alienation?"

"No," I say, as everyone stops talking to look at me in disbelief. They find my ignorance about Israel astounding. Each then describes how he or she first came here, under what circumstances that long romance with this place began. An Israeli man who arrived here as a youngster from Europe is sitting next to his South American–born wife. He says neither of them can imagine living in the States. Whenever they visit there, life seems too fractured and lonely. To my surprise, all the Americans at the table nod in agreement. Each claims that the only reason he or she has not moved to Israel is because of family or work obligations in the U.S. One after another insists that, if possible, in a New York minute, they'd come here to stay for good.

I casually mention that I *can* stay, that nothing is keeping me in the States except that I don't know Hebrew. This comment draws a chorus of, "You'll learn . . . You're *so* lucky . . . Hebrew's no big deal . . . Do it!" Someone says I'll be welcomed because I'm a good listener. "And who listens here?" they ask each other, laughing.

Long after midnight Michael and I leave the cafe. As we walk back to the hotel, I tell him how seductive I find these conversations. I ask if he's noticed that the Israelis we meet all seem happier than our friends back home. He nods; yes. I ask if life here really is more richly textured or is that just my beginners' fascination? He says, "Of course it's more meaningful. For sure."

●   ●   ●

I've kept a clock on my night table set to Boston time, seven hours earlier than Israel's. At first I called Eliza daily. Since then, less often. Now, two days before I'm scheduled to leave, I step away from a lively conversation going full tilt out on my terrace to phone her. It's 2 A.M. here, dinner time in Boston. "Mom," she says in sweet, babyish intonations, "it's raining here all day. So come and get me tomorrow, okay?"

"Sweetheart," I say, "it's the day *after* tomorrow. Are you going to be all right?" But she's already handed the phone to her babysitter, who assures me that Eliza is doing fine. I hang up, thinking of my daughter with a longing laced with dread. In some essential way I've forgotten our American life and its rhythms, so immersed have I been in this Jerusalem adventure, the whole new world that's opened up for me. I walk back to my guests: British filmmakers and others from the media. They're talking about the conference, the Palestinians, about British anti-Semitism. I'm only half listening; am looking up at the crystalline stars and mulling over Eliza's word "rain."

"Rain," I muse, as if this word refers to some rare meteorological anomaly, as if I haven't experienced a dreary day of rain in years. God, how awful, I think, gazing around at the balmy Jerusalem night. I know that I've been the proverbial wandering Jew, looking for place in all the wrong places. For over the past days the initial sense of homecoming has grown so strong that with a rapture I'd previously attributed only to the deeply pious, with my voice intoning like a crazed TV evangelist, I've taken to saying out loud, "Thank you, Lord. Thank you, Lord," while leaping two red-carpeted hotel stairs at a time. I regularly belt out the *S'chma Yisroel,* one of the few Hebrew prayers I know, thanking God or Whoever for delivering me from my own Egypts, that life-long sense of exile.

Though the conference has days to go, I arrived early and must leave before everyone else: Eliza is waiting for me. Michael drives me to the airport. In the car he jokes that, in Jerusalem, God is a local call. I've heard this comment before and always considered it flaky. But now I wonder if miracles do occur more easily here. I tell him that my instant ease in Jerusalem has given me the sense that though I *have* an American body, I *am* an Israeli soul. And if that's so, I ask him, then shouldn't I return here to live, as soon as possible? We hug and then I dash up the airport steps to catch my plane. At the top stair I turn to wave. Michael is standing tall in the midst of a carnival of lively Israelis. With his arms raised and his face beaming up at me, he's shouting, "Yes!"

If I have second thoughts on the flight back to the States, it's because the logic of making *aliyah* has no logic. I have no religious life, speak no Hebrew, have only a beginner's grasp of Mideast cultures and politics. To live in

Jerusalem, I'll have to give up my work as a psychologist and professor. I'll have to learn Hebrew. I'll be uprooting my already vulnerable daughter, who's been moved about too often in her short life. She's excited and ready to enter kindergarten with her new Cambridge friends. Tearing her away from all she knows simply because I like myself and this world I've briefly glimpsed gives me pause. Maybe I am suffering from what psychiatrists call Jerusalem madness, an affliction that's common among travelers to the Holy City, those who in no time believe that they're Jesus or Moses. Except that my delusion, if that's what this is, is that in Jerusalem I've become *myself*.

Wrestling with such doubts in the airplane, I'm also reading Saul Bellow's *To Jerusalem and Back*. I soon find his sensibilities are antithetical to mine. "How can the Israelis bear living with such intensity?" he writes, as I wonder, How can I live without that? I put down his book, pick up an essay by Israeli author Amos Oz, in which I've already underlined ". . . suppose this hysterical Jewish bond were severed. . . . Could I give up this drug, this addiction to collective excitement, these tribal ties? . . . If I could kick the habit, what would I have left? Are we really capable of living ordinary, peaceable lives? Could any of us?" *That* I understand.

When we land at JFK in New York, I enter depressive shock. Though Manhattan's multiplicity and anonymity once enthralled me, the city now seems too huge, as if everyone here is fated to remain strangers, to live inside a giant disconnect. I fiercely miss the family feeling I've just left and head for a newspaper and magazine stand, longing for something—for *anything*—to read that will keep Israel alive. Fiction, nonfiction, history, current news. But what I discover all over this shop are headlines heralding Donald Trump's latest sexcapade.

In this tiny moment my decision begins to take shape. Because these headlines are such a contrast to Israeli news, which never *centers* on reports about the vagaries of the rich, but on life-and-death issues that connect everyone in a country-wide intimacy, despite all the famed religious and political schisms. I think back to the bold print of the *Jerusalem Post* on my first morning in Jerusalem. The headline, one large word, read *"GEVALT"* (*Oy vay*, or My God). This memory gives rise to an overpowering urge to return to a place where politics are personal, where people are bonded by public shorthand.

As I wander around New York's airport it's as if I lived in the States only briefly, forty-odd years ago, and have been in Israel ever since, rather than the other way around.

Within five weeks I've packed up eight cardboard boxes, filled with toys, clothes and books (on Judaica, Israeli history and politics). I'm ready to travel six thousand miles for what I intend to be the rest of my life. When friends ask why I'm going, I can't answer coherently, not at first. Only gradually do I see that the powerful familial ties I felt instantly in Israel were connected to that fate I didn't suffer, a fate I lived in my imagination as a child. Was my youthful belief that my true origins were closer to the forties' death trains than to the fifties' 'commuters' one reason why Israel's stories affected me as if they were my own?

I'm not sure. What I know is that while obsessing on the Holocaust, I missed the next chapter in Jewish history, the birth of Israel. I know now where I'm traveling—to a complex world, rich with many subcultures I've barely glimpsed. That richness nearly takes my breath away.

On our line at JFK Airport, an Israeli family is standing directly behind us. The mother asks casually, "Why are you going to Israel? How long will you be vacationing there?"

Instead of answering, I look down at Eliza's sad face. It's now I see, with naked clarity, that I'm taking us both away from friends, school, work and, most of all, from an English-speaking world to live in a culture that, if I can face this fact, I've been exposed to—in its entirety—for *thirteen* days.

The line inches forward. I turn back to the Israelis and say, "We're not going to visit. We're moving there."

CHAPTER TWO

Into the Heart of Jerusalem

At Ben-Gurion Airport an El Al guard asks, *"Ma zeh?"* (What's this?), while staring at our eight bulging boxes. "You have family here?"

"Most of my family is dead," I say.

"Well, here in Israel we're one big family," he responds, protectively ushering Eliza and me through customs, helping as first one, then another, unwieldy carton slips off our pushcarts.

Once outside, everything I see—the tumult, the talking, the desert—looks enchanting. But not to Eliza, who stands immobilized. She takes a long look around at desert shrubs, at the people hugging and shouting, at two swarthy cabdrivers who are looming over her. When they shout in Hebrew for us to follow them, she starts howling. Her mouth opens so wide, she looks like a character from a "Peanuts" cartoon.

"Why are we here?" she cries. Hiccoughing sobs, she lists the reasons we shouldn't have come, ending with the wail, "And now you're taking me away from all my friends!" I sink into a familiar mood of maternal inadequacy and lift Eliza up. I'm praying for something to say that will console her. I remind her that Jackie, her "very favorite person on earth," will be arriving any minute from the Caribbean. That she's going to live here with us. Eliza leaps down and turns to face the mechanized glass doors that are spewing passengers. She won't take her eyes off them as she scouts for Jackie. And here she comes.

Eliza races to her. After a year's separation they're delirious, jumping up and down, hugging. I watch Jackie, who's now a sophisticated seventeen-year-old wearing a silk dress and high heels. I see the same ebullient girl whom I've raised since she was seven, who lived with me before and after Eliza was born. Only this past year were we forced to separate.

The three of us are sitting at the airport's curb under a blazing August sun, straddling our boxes. We're waiting for Shuki—Michael's old friend, my favorite tour guide in June. He's promised to meet us. "We're a family again," I say to the girls, thinking how right it is to have brought them to a place where family life has primacy, when I spot Shuki's Toyota. I point out his taxi numbers to the girls: 5665. They repeat, "5665, 5665," over and over, as if singing scales.

He pulls up and leaps from his car. He's wearing his usual garb—jeans, a white T-shirt and silky black blazer. He strongly resembles the young Al Pacino (though he's in his forties), a likeness I haven't registered before. The girls stare up at him. Eliza, usually shy, pipes up: "You're 5665, and I'm five." He bends to hug her while Jackie checks him out. She sees a slim, dark-haired man whose raven eyes can shift in a flash from edgy to confident.

He hugs Jackie, too, then gracefully maneuvers our odd-shaped boxes into his trunk, easily strapping two that don't fit onto his roof rack. I hop up front; the girls settle into the backseat as Shuki drives away from the airport. "Hi, hi," he says to me, telling the girls that when I called from Cambridge to say we were returning to make *aliyah,* he was so surprised he almost fell off his chair.

"Fell off his chair," Eliza repeats. "My mom called and he *fell off his chair,*" a phrase she finds uproarious. I turn and see she's punch-drunk from jet lag. Shuki continues, "Everyone I show around Israel is going to move here tomorrow, immediately, next month. *Everyone.* But do you know who does? Almost no one. And within weeks? *Never.*" As he speaks, we catch his spirit of adventure, aware that this ride up into Jerusalem is the beginning of a new life.

Shuki's radio is blaring. Trying to please us, he presses buttons like mad, searching for words or music we'll understand. We hear snippets of lilting Arab tunes, wailing prayers, barking Hebrew news, hip Israeli rock 'n' roll. I tell him to give up radio surfing, that I've come to be *here* and don't need familiar American sounds.

On the last mile into Jerusalem we navigate a steep mountain road, the main entrance into this spiritual city. Below us, cragged cliffs and sculpted valley beds lie in shadow. Ahead, the afternoon sun casts an apricot hue over stones and sand. This beauty gives rise in me to a mental clarity, a sensation of coming home.

We pull into the apartment-hotel where I've arranged to stay until we find something permanent. Greeting us at the door of the Lev Yerushalayim (Heart of Jerusalem) is a bone-thin young Israeli with olive skin and hazy brown eyes. After checking us out, he sighs, "Thank God, you're not one of *them.*"

"Them, who?" I ask, assuming he means Arabs.

"The religious. Those *ultras,*" he sneers as we walk inside. "We can't stand them," he says within earshot of several large religious families clustered in the lobby. The young boys are all wearing *peyot* and *kippot*—Hasidic side curls and skullcaps. "These religious nuts dictate our lives," he proclaims, as if they can't hear him, or more likely, so that they will. No one looks his way—not a glance, not even a blink. "You'll see," he snarls, "these people close down everything on *Shabbat*: buses, restaurants, movies. They want to run—no, make that *ruin* our lives."

Jackie and Eliza are baffled by his outburst. But now our volatile receptionist-doorman turns formal and announces that he'll escort us up to our "reserved suite." None of these words—"reserved," "escort," "suite"—remotely suggests what awaits us behind the locked door. The room is drab and tiny, with cement walls that are stained brown. A smell of mildew assaults us. We see double-decker beds with mattresses thin as playing cards, so wide that they flop over the bedsprings. The floor is uneven; the windows are smudged.

I'm sinking in disappointment. This room is a far cry from the suite I had at the commodious King David Hotel, a place I decided was too expensive for this extended stay. I walk to open a window, but it's sealed. Looking through the grime, I try to catch a view, but there are no views, no vistas of the Old City—no vistas at all. We face into another tall building. Below us, two streets converge at a busy intersection. "Our two main streets. Ben Yehuda and King George," the bellman says. "They're always filled with crowds."

But what I notice are the cars. They zoom forward, honking wildly *before* a light turns green. One small Fiat passes so fast that it almost knocks down an elderly man who's caught halfway across the street. I'll hear the statistic often: "More dead on our roads than in all our wars together." It's a comment everyone repeats but no one seems to analyze. On my way outside I remark on this insane traffic to an Israeli standing in the lobby. He shrugs. "This is Israel. Go figure."

Walking outside into commercial Jerusalem, I'm surrounded by crowds, noise and graffiti and can see all that was invisible when, as a tourist, I was staying mere blocks away. Immediately I know what hadn't registered on the plane: that visiting Israel and moving here to live are poles apart. I'm viewing exactly what Saul Bellow describes in *To Jerusalem and Back*: ". . . small dead-end streets, littered with the customary fallout of orange peels and excrement, eggshells and bottle tops."

Four days later I'm busy rummaging around our room with its half-unpacked boxes, which are flung everywhere. I'm in shock, am already the archetypal immigrant: disoriented, excited, riding an emotional roller coaster. One hour I suffer an attack of dissociative fear so strong I can hardly breathe. The next, I'm euphoric. Either way, it seems as if we've landed not in a foreign country, but on a foreign *planet*. Shuki drops over unannounced to see how we're doing. After chatting, he offers to help me unpack. "No, just sit," I say, "that is, if you can locate a chair in this mess." He plops down on Jackie's bed and spends the next hours rustling through newspapers, exactly as if he's my dad returned from the dead, as if we're family.

It's not only Shuki. People begin visiting us, even those I hardly know, without phoning ahead. I've yet to see a single appointment book. Israelis I met last June call me every day, eager to ease our transition. They do. Their attention cushions us as a small community forms around us, much faster than I expected. I find this Israeli friendliness exhilarating, in such contrast to the distancing I take for granted in the cities of North America. Again, anyone who speaks English lingers to chat after translating a street sign or pointing us in the right direction. They share stories or inquire about us. Such dependable camaraderie makes this labyrinth of strangeness seem more like a lucky pilgrimage than a terrifying mistake.

The girls, sisters again, discover a favorite playground, Liberty Bell Park *(Gana Palmach),* where they rush every morning to roller-skate, eat Israeli ice cream or play with neighborhood kids. Jackie's extroverted personality brings Eliza (and half of Jerusalem) into lively spirits, leaving me free to wander for hours around the neighborhoods that make up this city. It's like browsing the pages of a long, magic-surreal novel. I catch vivid scenes, but am unable to discover the overall plotlines, much less any subplot. What's most eye-catching is how Israeli life plays in fast-forward. There's a hyper-intense fluidity, rarely captured in writings about Jerusalem, a racing intensity, a pandemonium and chaos on the streets that makes this small city feel unusually alive.

On TV, I glimpse what may fuel this collective mania. Unpacking boxes, I catch a CNN segment that shows heavily clad Arabs assembled for a conference in Qatar. The sheikhs take turns at the microphone. One, filled with hatred for Israel, keeps referring to us as "that Zionist entity." Another sternly quotes UN resolutions by number, demanding that Israel comply with them. The cool demeanor and resolute tones of these men frighten me. I begin to worry about the anti-Semitism all around us—a fear I've never entertained as a Jew in America. Suddenly, I can't fathom why I've chosen to throw in my lot with a country where, six months ago, I'd have been terrified under the siege of Saddam Hussein's Scuds. Trying to quell my anxiety, I turn off the TV and pace the room. But my fears multiply. In growing hysteria, I picture Israel as the site of the next Jewish holocaust and only calm down when I remember that I'm not alone with this paranoia, that such ideas fill the air here and are communal.

Another day unpacking; another broadcast on CNN. This one features President George Bush at a press conference. He announces that he's sending Secretary of State James Baker to Jerusalem. He warns the Israeli government that they won't receive U.S. loan guarantees if Shamir, "our" prime minister—

I already think of myself as Israeli—continues building Jewish settlements on what many believe is Arab land. I agreed with this . . . or thought I did. But even a presidential address sounds different when heard from Jerusalem. Referring to the Jewish lobbyists in Washington, Bush remarks, "Hey, I'm just one lone guy down here," words that invoke ancient notions of Jews as too powerful, as subverters of international policy. This subtext is one I'd have missed completely, or simply ignored, from Cambridge.

A week later, with our boxes still strewn all about the room, I find myself standing and reading Alan Dershowitz's *Chutzpah*. The gist of his book is that Jewish Americans need more naked ambition and less fear of the goyim. More ambition?! His words throw me back to the Woodmere of my youth, to the boys with their thick hair and thick ambitions. Or we girls focused on appearances, on which colleges to attend, all keenly sensitive to status, highly competitive. What a different world from the teenagers we met earlier today, children of the Mendes-Flohrs—a couple I met in June who invited us for afternoon tea. Their son and daughter, high school students, seemed attuned to politics; their ideas were treated with more respect than kids their age are given elsewhere. They weren't tentative when voicing their convictions, nor self-conscious about their bodies, no doubt because they're fused with the body politic, prepared to enter the army soon.

Sitting with them, I pictured Eliza, hair down to her waist, gun strapped over her shoulder and dressed in a khaki uniform. This vision struck me as a healthier, maybe even a safer, life than what she'd face as a teen in America—surrounded by random violence, all sorts of temptations, with no collective purpose. There are things worse than war, I was thinking, easy enough to believe when her feet didn't reach halfway to the floor while sitting at the Mendes-Flohrs' table. Leaving our new friends, we walked away from their home in the German Colony, the most picturesque neighborhood I've yet to see here. At dusk, we passed small stone houses set back from the road under aromatic bushes and abundant trees. For all the world, it felt as if we were strolling through a fairy tale.

Back at Lev Yerushalayim, Jackie and I talk about these kids' maturity and self-assurance while standing on line for our communal shower. In the dimly lit hallway we are right behind a family of Ethiopian immigrants. They smile shyly at us and warm to Jackie, who tousles the kids' hair, offering to braid them. The parents whisper together, then invite us to visit in their room down the hall. After showering, we enter their suite, one identical to ours, and are greeted with an almost comical formality, in such contrast to the casual Israeli way.

We sit on their bunk beds as the mother brews tea for us. The father and children (ages eight to eighteen) speak a poor pidgin English. I'm straining to understand them, and gather they are having problems with money and the language here, having just recently arrived. I remember watching Operation Solomon on TV a year ago, that airlift of Ethiopian Jews into Israel. During their sudden exodus I saw African Jews lighting bonfires on a seatless El Al jet, cooking meals as if they were living in the Stone Age. I wondered then, and do so even more now, how these Jewish Ethiopians have managed to span centuries in a single plane ride.

The mother, especially graceful, if wordless, begins serving tea. She's lean and copper-skinned, with petite hands. Her long dark hair is entwined in a yellow scarf. She seems unusually calm and is beautiful, as is everyone in this family—fine-boned, with an ethereal air about them. I realize why the new Russian immigrants envy the Ethiopians, who've arrived in smaller numbers at this same time. The Africans are soft and otherworldly. The Russians seem angry and gruff. Little wonder that the Ethiopians get more attention from Israel's social services, more flattering portraits in news reports.

The mother suddenly bursts into wracking sobs, hiding her face behind her small hands. What happened? Last week, her son explains, a nephew who came to Israel a year ago, committed suicide in the army. The mother becomes increasingly convulsed and we're politely asked to leave. The three of us, embarrassed because they are, back out their door and continue walking backward, single file, down the darkened hallway. Once in our room, the awful thought occurs: Maybe everyone is so hospitable to us because life in Israel is far more dangerous than we've imagined.

Upset after this visit, Jackie and I allow Eliza to stay up later than usual, what's normal for Israeli kids whom we see out on the streets, running in and out of stores until midnight. We head to a cafe on Ben Yehuda, a street that's described as a pedestrian mall, though there's nothing mall-ish about it, not in the American sense of the word. It's cobblestone and steeply inclined, lined with small shops and large cafes. Since no cars are allowed, there's a swell of crowds drifting up and down the street. Sitting outdoors, I see people talking, gesticulating, kissing madly or engaged in loud, but not angry, debates. This liveliness is a dose of pure optimism after meeting our ill-at-ease, grief-stricken neighbors.

I'm studying the typical Israeli night scene. Religious and secular Jews and a handful of Arabs parade by without detectable boundaries, without anyone drawing stares or evoking hostility. I ask the girls if they notice how friendly everyone is here. They don't respond; they are busy drawing on paper place mats. So I sit silently, taking in the crowds, seeing no vigilance, no rampant or even subtle mistrust in evidence. On the contrary, the ambiance is easygoing. Middle Easterners of every age, ethnicity and dress pass by, taking seats at sidewalk tables, circling musicians who are playing in the center of the street, inspecting artisans' makeshift stalls filled with handmade jewelry, leather goods and wall hangings. Loud voices rise over the din of accordions, violins and guitars. This party atmosphere is in such contrast to my image of Israelis as danger-conscious around the clock.

The only sign of war is the ever-present Jewish-Israeli soldiers—girls and boys who amble up and down the street, coiled into groups. Their khaki uniforms look more hip than militaristic, as if purchased at the Gap. Each has a long gun slung casually over a shoulder, carried like a backpack, not a lethal weapon. It's hard to believe that *these kids* form the core of the famed Israeli military force.

I strike up a conversation with a couple at the next table, Holocaust survivors who came to Israel after the Second World War. They tell me not to be deceived by the gaiety on the street. That threats seem remote these days only because there have been no stabbings nor bombings in the last few months. They assure me that hardly a family here is untouched by death and war, whether *before,* in Europe, or *after* 1948, in Israel. Everyone they know has lost someone close. No, they answer me, they do not know any Arabs personally.

When their middle-aged, Israeli-born sons arrive, they pull their table close to ours and regale us with tales of who fought where in the "big" wars of '48, '56, '67 and '73. They don't respond when I ask about patrolling the Intifada or what it's like doing duty in the territories (where the Israeli military monitors every aspect of Palestinian life). That's the rare topic Israelis react to with silence. Absolutely everything else—intimate details of work, money, family, marital life—is openly discussed, with a hunger for connection.

Another afternoon; another marathon walk. When I return to our room, I look around and call out to Jackie and Eliza that I can't stand another hour in this squalid place. The small room with its dirty windows, the noisy streets below, the religious families screaming at hostile waiters about which pancakes are *glatt* (kosher) demoralize me. The realtor hasn't found us an apartment but assures me that she will *"chik-chak"* (quickly). So, impulsively, though not without a pang of guilt at my extravagance, I call the King David and make reservations. As soon as we check in, I feel elated, though going up to our room I have to wonder about my lifelong *supposed* bohemianism. Part of me is cut straight from Woodmere, I see, craving luxury—especially when stressed out.

The girls, who've never been here, run from window to window, exclaiming over the views, the bathroom, the high ceilings. After jumping on thick mattresses, they plunge into an oversized bathtub, where I leave them with instructions to begin unpacking as soon as they get out. ("Never," they call out, "we're *never* getting out of this tub.")

I head down for a swim in the hotel's large turquoise pool. Anticipating huge crowds in this summer-like September heat, I'm surprised to find myself virtually alone. There's no one around the pool and only one person swimming in it. I stand under a scorching sun and watch a woman doing laps. I'm about to jump in when she pulls herself out and grabs a towel. I squint, place a hand over my eyes to block the sun and move closer. Before me is . . . Daphie, the only Israeli I've ever met in America, the summer when we shared a communal house on Martha's Vineyard, over a decade ago. I've kept her phone number in my address book, but have put off calling her. I thought she wouldn't remember me. Now we're hugging; she greets me like a long-lost friend. Stepping back, she asks what in the world I'm doing here. Why didn't I call?

I ring up the girls on the house phone. Jackie refuses to leave the bathtub, but Eliza comes down and we three walk the few blocks to Daphie's apartment, in this same neighborhood of Rehavia. As we walk, Daphie engages Eliza. She says that she's a mother, too, and that her daughter, Tal, is almost Eliza's age. She tells me that she's been married for five years and is a professor, teaching elementary school teachers. She sure has a way with kids, I think, as Eliza takes her hand. When we reach her ground-floor apartment, Tal opens the door. The girls stare at each other as the adults in the room (Daphie's husband, Shimon; her mother, Alisa) comment on how alike they look. The girls are still staring, as if startled by a mirror reflection. They soon rush off to play in Tal's bedroom. We overhear them comparing their freckles in the bathroom mirror. When they start building a house for Tal's dolls, we know they're set to play for hours.

Out in Daphie and Shimon's garden, she tells her mother and husband how we met, about our summer in America, and of the shock she felt at seeing me, "the only one at the pool that's usually jam-packed," she says, still astounded that I'm here. In this garden, the scent of roses, the swirling stars and ease of conversation all relax me. Shimon begins telling me about his childhood. In slow, halting English, he describes what it was like growing up on a northern kibbutz during the 1950s.

He talks of his direct exposure to war as a child, how by twelve he was accustomed to finding bullet-strewn corpses, and carrying the dead on his shoulders. This happened during night patrol on his collective farm or while keeping vigil at the nearby Golan Heights. Intimate contact with death and war didn't strike him as unusual, he says, until he left the rural Galilee to live in Israel's cities. There, he met sabras who grew up in more protected circumstances. That's when he realized that his own childhood was unusual, even for an Israeli immigrant boy during Israel's first decade.

As Shimon finishes, I overhear Daphie and her mother gossiping about a friend, Judith Beiserman. I interrupt them to say that my maiden name was Basser. This non sequitur leaps from my mouth without any thought. Maybe I'm getting *too* relaxed here, I reflect, certain that they'll all look blankly at me, thinking, So what?

But as soon as Basser is blurted, Alisa stops talking to study my face. "Harold's daughter? Rose and Philip's granddaughter? Bernice's niece?"

"You know them?"

"Know them?! Your aunt was my roommate for four years at NYU. I spent every *Shabbat* at your grandparents' home in Far Rockaway. Had a mad crush on your dad. Know them? I bet I have a photo album of your whole family. Wait, don't move," she says, dashing off to her apartment around the corner. Daphie and I lock eyes. "So that's why you've always felt like a cousin," she says. It's true; we shared an effortless ease from our first days on Martha's Vineyard.

Before long I'm gazing at my immediate family who seem to be gazing back at me. The photographs, spread around Daphie's coffee table, are lit by candlelight. This ambient hue gives my parents', grandparents' and aunt's eyes a radiant glow. It's as if they're here in Israel too, a nearness that feels numinous—the same sensation I've had since my first flight. These photographs are especially compelling because I've never seen them before.

I study my parents at twenty—playing tennis, doing cartwheels, clowning around on a Catskills summer lawn. I look down at them, far younger than I am now, as I hear Alisa chatting away in the background. My grandparents' home was "something special," she's saying. My grandma Rose cooked wonderful meals, was all sweetness. My dad was "a cut-up, a catch." She recalls my mother perfectly, her beauty and regal poise. "But your mother; she could kill with a certain look."

I nod emphatically. Her recollections are as accurate as her photos. But I say nothing, am near tears at having my lost family resurrected in her words and snapshots. Not for the first time, I find myself wishing that my grandfather Philip had moved here, rather than to America, in 1904 because then (admittedly a highly irrational take on my life) I'd have been born an Israeli.

It's time to go. Already Tal and Eliza seem glued at the hip; they cry out that they don't want to separate. "This is incredible . . . my family is so small," I say. "Even the girls . . ." I nod my head over at the dark-haired, bright-eyed kids, too dumbfounded to finish my sentence.

Alisa, reading my mind, says, "You'll see. This is only the beginning. This is Israel. Coincidences happen here. They happen all the time."

CHAPTER THREE

Joining the Tribe

I'm sitting by the King David pool with Daphie and Rabbi Herb Weiner, a man I met years ago at a conference in Switzerland where I studied his book, *9½ Mystics*. That I know Herb and that he's Alisa's best friend is another coincidence which, as she predicted, happens regularly here. The group is discussing Bush's demands that Shamir stop building settlements. Many intellectuals are against these ever-expanding housing projects inhabited mainly by religious Jews. They're built over the Green Line—that demarcation left after Israel won the 1967 war, capturing the West Bank from Jordan, the Gaza Strip from Egypt. When the map was divided, the boundaries were drawn in green ink, which is how the line got its famous adjective. Many say, "It's the settlements that will make any political settlement impossible."

"What do *you* think?" I ask Herb.

"It's good and not good," he says in his rabbinical, reflective voice. "It's morally right to pressure Israel monetarily, but the American government's lack of sympathy with Israeli Jews—well, that's disturbing." Daphie surprises me. Once active in Peace Now, a political movement that advocates two states as the way to solve the Israeli-Palestinian stalemate, she denounces Bush and his attempts to stop Jewish developments. She says she *hates* Israeli dependence on U.S. money, *hates* being manipulated by anti-Semites, even if in an ethical direction. She says this with such anger that her soft Botticelli beauty—waist-length, curly red hair; pale green eyes—and her aura of goodness are momentarily eclipsed.

Another woman joins our circle on the grass and expresses the opposite viewpoint just as emphatically. The American pressure will cost Shamir the next election, she's sure. I listen and feel lucky. If she's right, my arrival here may coincide with a real peace process, something that, according to most I meet, has been dead in the sand for years.

• • •

The High Holidays, which I thought would bring me closer to my religion, do the opposite. With the entire city shut down and without a single car on the roads, Eliza, Jackie and I walk for miles to find the "hippie" synagogue that's been highly recommended. Though there's no dressing up at this casual place, no American formality, no paying for the best seats, the Hebrew is as indecipherable as ever and the service feels far too long. On Yom Kippur, I try fasting but by 3 P.M. I'm ravenous, and guiltily eat the cold food kept on reserve for the elderly at the hotel. Every hotel in Israel is, I learn, kosher, and not only on these High Holidays, but on every *Shabbat*. I'm disappointed that I don't respond to religious Judaism even here in Israel. But Daphie assures me that most of her friends don't either, that the great majority of secular Israelis take to the hills or to the beaches over the High Holidays.

The country shuts down not for the ten Days of Awe but for a full three weeks, until the end of Sukkot, the fall harvest festival. Right after Yom Kippur, Daphie suggests we take our kids down to the resort town of Eilat, the southernmost tip of Israel. During the twisting three-hour bus trip, I watch the landscape change. At first, we're surrounded by massive desert mountains whose monochrome facade is broken only by the occasional white Bedouin sheet fluttering above us or by a camel gone astray, its humps swathed in colorful fabrics. Then we cruise past the Dead Sea, said to be the lowest spot on earth, whose roads are clogged with tourist buses and with a sulphurous air, an odor that blows through the bus windows for miles. Next, we traverse a long desert stretch that's completely flat. There's little to see except sand and more sand. Finally, we enter Eilat.

This resort town sprawls along the Red Sea, whose waters glow turquoise by day, reflecting the rocks of the Adom (Red) mountains—brilliantly colored cliffs that seem to rise directly from the wide expanse of sea. We change into bathing suits and escape the heat by racing to the swimming pool. There, I imbibe a wild, all-embracing energy. Raucous music, children leaping into the water, adults rushing about—young and old create a mood of happy bedlam—everyone seems spontaneous, not at all preoccupied with how they appear to others. I feel instantly free in this atmosphere. Playing water tag with Eliza and Tal, I'm without a worry in the world, not a common state of mind.

Curiously, I feel most myself here where the Israelis vacationing are darkskinned Middle Eastern Jews from Arab countries, not those with European backgrounds. I remember a line that journalist Ze'ev Chafets wrote after he made *aliyah:* "All the Puerto Rican girls here are Jewish!" In this brutal heat, surrounded by wild crowds, his remark rings as more accurate than racist.

Nights later, after the girls are asleep, I wander down to the pool. Now I begin to see that what looks like Mediterranean abandon has an edge, a mania that's not really carefree. With rock music blasting in the background, I fall into a conversation with three voluble, fast-talking teenaged boys. They're here in Eilat to deep-sea dive, they tell me, as I pull up a chair at their table.

This is one of their last breaks before high school graduation, after which they'll serve time in the army. I listen to them calculating which units they hope to join. At first, they sound like kids in the States debating what colleges to attend. But soon, I hear an undercurrent of tension in their voices, see that what I took as free-flowing ease has a riptide, a sense of impending danger. They talk about "the Arabs," whom they've never directly met, but whose "mentality" is very dangerous, they assure me. They talk of the "next" war as inevitable. As they do, I begin to shift uncomfortably in my seat. I realize that we're really discussing the possibility that any, or all, of them could be facing death this time next year. Yet they're unquestioningly committed to serving in the army, to fighting wherever necessary.

Uri, the most astute, explains that virtually no one, except the ultra-religious, ("fake religious," another interjects) avoids the draft—that's unthinkable. They describe their burden as heightened, not diminished, by their parents' attempts to conceal all anxieties about what might happen to them, their sons. Our talk turns to older brothers, to fathers and uncles maimed or killed in past wars. I see how much is lost when a child has to bear such burdens; the gaiety around us begins to shift into slow motion. The hour grows late. The boys are becoming more expressive. They can't fathom why I find their lives or observations so compelling. Has no one listened to their reality? Is this highly conversational country somehow deaf to pain? At midnight, we part, after I agree to join them in the morning, to see a "tower" that is nearby.

By 9 A.M. the next day, we're walking along a stretch of beach in an already suffocating heat. A mile from our family hotel, we enter a white building that's right on the Red Sea. We climb its circular stairway five flights to the top. The boys lead me to a telescope, through which I can see Jordan, Egypt and Saudi Arabia. They want me to understand these countries are *that* close. I swivel the lens from west to east to southeast as the boys surround me, talking about Israel's loss of the Sinai to Egypt. Uri, sounding resentful and sad, says, "I don't understand why any Israeli would tour Egypt. I would *never* go there. Those Camp David Accords!" he says in disgust, referring to the peace treaty signed in the late 1970s. "Egypt got the Sinai and its oil. And what did we get? Enemies on our doorstep. As you can see."

We have tea downstairs in a cafeteria and then exchange phone numbers. The boys are leaving Eilat later today. They head out for one last swim while I sit at a table near large glass windows. I watch as they walk down the beach.

Each is holding his scuba gear, and as they recede in the distance, their lean bodies seem to grow smaller, as if they're walking back into childhood rather than toward instant adulthood. I gaze at them fondly, wondering what will become of them.

By late afternoon, the heat abates and it's safe to go outside. I rent a small car and within minutes am driving like the best of Israelis. I zigzag toward the bus station with Daphie sitting beside me and Tal in the back. They're bound for the 4 P.M. Egged (National) bus to Jerusalem. Early tomorrow Daphie has a job interview that could lead to a promotion at her university. She can't miss this bus. Heady with pride, I navigate these roads like a pro, paying no attention to the speed limit. As I'm approaching the bus station, I come upon a makeshift wooden barrier. Determined not to be delayed by what I assume is minor road repair, I swing right around it shooting blithely up the empty street. Daphie grabs my arm. "Listen!" she yells. I hear amplified words blaring from invisible loudspeakers. "KEEP AWAY! WE HAVE A SUSPICIOUS PACKAGE!" she translates from the Hebrew.

I screech to a halt and we leap from the car, leaving it parked on a diagonal in the middle of the empty street. Daphie grabs Tal's hand and they dash toward Eilat's bus station. She shouts over her shoulder not to worry, that bomb scares happen all the time. I'm not worried, I'm terrified. Racing up one street, running frantically down another, I can't find anyone who speaks English. I still don't know if it's a *bomb scare* or a *bomb,* a distinction I can't read on the faces around me. Then I get lost. By the time I figure out where I left my car, the street has been reopened; the car is blocking traffic. Six police or army officers (hard to tell who's who) are standing around it, calling to have it towed away.

I rush up to these men, spouting apologies. I assume they'll be sympathetic, as we would in the States after an averted catastrophe. In a jumble of non sequiturs, I explain . . . I'm an American . . . recently moved here . . . didn't understand their Hebrew announcements . . . ready to settle in for an amiable chat. But these uniformed men aren't interested in an amiable anything. They're furious at my carelessness. First in Hebrew, then in English, they yell at me, becoming more, not less furious at my carelessness: "We don't care where you're from! You live here now. Don't you ever pass a roadblock again!"

When I get into the car, I see that the backseat is a mess of bathing suits, toilet items, crayons and toys. The suitcases Daphie left were ripped open and searched. As I drive off, I see the officers in my rearview mirror; they're still making hostile hand gestures at me. I drive slowly, very slowly, back to the hotel. There I describe this mishap to a security guard. After he patiently hears me out, he walks me onto the beach. A few feet from my first-floor room, he shows me where, a year ago, a Jordanian terrorist hid a bomb in the sand. It exploded, killing a three-year-old child from Scandinavia. Now I notice plain-clothes security men and women combing the beaches day and night. From this moment, and for years to come, I scan every place I walk for suspicious packages, alerting the police to many a paper bag that turns out to be empty.

In Jerusalem, I rush to see a doctor who's more alarmed than I am at the hives breaking out on my arms, legs and face. "Foolish!" he exclaims, lecturing me about the dangers of the sun, about self-neglect. "You didn't use sun-screen in Eilat?" he asks, incredulous. I study my skin and see the eruptions as a warning or a metaphor that I've been too naive about self-protection here. After prescribing skin cream, Dr. Litman asks for my impressions of my new country, offering his own observations, including mean-spirited remarks about the "Arab mentality." His words are much like what I heard from the boys in Eilat. Pedantic yet kind, he draws me out, freezing only when I ask him about the "occupation."

"So you're on the left," he sputters. "I'll tell you about the 'left.' They *left* the country in droves to vacation in Greece or Turkey or God-knows-where during the Gulf war. You left-wing Americans [I'm left-wing because I used the word 'occupation'?] didn't even telephone from abroad during the Scud attacks. You didn't call, didn't care what happened to us. You have no idea what you are talking about; there are no territories. We're one country and it's all ours. How can *you* speak of an *occupation*?" This man is no right-wing fanatic; he's literate and cultured, has talked to me about Yehoshua's novels, of swimming daily with his good friend, the poet Yehuda Amichai.

I can't dismiss the doctor's words as simply retro or obtuse, though I agree with little he's said. He's devoted his life to this country, has fought in every Israeli war since fleeing Germany in 1938. He has earned his beliefs. He knows much that I don't.

Still mulling over this encounter, I squeeze onto a crowded bus that's careening up a hilltop toward Hebrew University. I'm going to hear a lecture by Emil Fackenheim, the world-acclaimed philosopher and theologian. When I enter the room I see an aged man who seems, by turns, dour or animated. Fackenheim, a survivor of Auschwitz, says, "Everyone asks why the Nazis did it." Long pause. "The answer? They killed us *because they decided to*." The hush that fills this classroom is palpable.

The professor then discusses the economic underpinnings of the Holocaust, which gives way, by some logic I can't follow, to a long speech on the Arab "mentality"—my second in as many hours. He lists "their" psychological attributes, conveying the impression that "they" share none of "our" values. I have to wonder how a billion Arabs (a billion anything) can be handily described in a tidy list of attributes. Yet this elderly scholar is no fool. He lives here. His children's and grandchildren's lives are on the line. Surely, *he'd* be motivated to rise above such easy stereotyping in the interest of a lasting peace. Maybe he's still living in that Nazi region of the mind where only other Jews can be trusted. But again, if he's so sure about the Arabs, what do I know?

Most of what I know comes from reading. I read while waiting on long lines: at banks, in the Super Sol grocery, at the drivers' registry. This pleasure-oriented country is anything but efficient, so I have plenty of time to read. The finest Israeli novelists—Amos Oz, A. B. Yehoshua and David Grossman—write essays or books about politics, too. These intellectuals argue for rapprochement with Palestinians. I follow their logic, but begin to wonder why their outlook is in such opposition to others' views. There's a huge schism between the two-state types and the get-rid-of-the-Arab proponents. Especially confusing, since everyone—from cabdriver to professor to grocer—sounds dead certain that his or her view is right. On this subject, I hear little ambiguity.

In truth, I see little evidence to support either side. The only Arabs I encounter are gardeners, construction workers or cleaning women employed by middle-class Israelis. Or I see others, packed in cars while heading out of Jerusalem; all wear stony, unreadable expressions. I'm advised to avoid those I pass on the streets. "You don't know who will be the next terrorist," Israeli friends caution me, warning me also to stay alert while driving: One wrong turn could land me in East Jerusalem, that dangerous Arab neighborhood behind the Old City, and just across the Green Line. Yet those who warn me most emphatically are the same friends who sound most nostalgic for the pre-Intifada days (before the Palestinian uprising began in 1987). They mention enjoyable visits to Arab villages, expeditions to the Old City or to Jericho, anecdotes about the time when crossing cultures was exciting, full of warm conversations, exotic feasts. I can't get a fix on these mixed messages.

I'm anyway far too busy looking for a rental apartment. Realtors show me small, ugly rooms whose owners quadruple the rent as soon as they hear my American English. Shuki, whom I've come to count on as a good friend, offers to help me find a place. One day as we're driving through the German Colony (an area I've loved since the night we visited with the Mendes-Flohrs). I point out a house I've noticed each time we pass it. It's charming, tucked away from traffic, with a well-tended garden. I mention this so he'll know what appeals to me. But Shuki takes me literally, swerving his car around and leaping out before I can stop him. He races up the stairs and rings the bell. An elderly Hungarian couple open the front door. "No, nothing to rent," the man says. "We'd never leave our home." But then these owners cheerfully beckon to me and insist that we both come in. We stay for hours. The wife invites us to join them for a long dinner, after which her husband, who's in his late seventies, gives me a tour of every nook and cranny of their home. He shows me his many sculptures and is equally proud of his wife's paintings.

Then he takes out a photo album and pats the seat next to him, motioning me to sit by his side, the better to catch the lamplight. He wants me to see his parents, sisters and brothers. We're laughing at their old-fashioned bathing suits, their modest styles, when he says dryly, "All dead in the ovens."

I reel out of their home and tell Shuki that I don't have enough emotional space for such harrowing moments. I don't have enough time to keep dropping in on strangers. Yes, I answer, I love meeting Israelis. Yes, I admit, I'm getting a great education about this culture of hospitality. But I must focus on finding a home first, I almost wail. Tour guide to the core, Shuki has a "great idea"—something that will relax me: We'll go to see the Great Synagogue, the largest and most elaborate in Jerusalem. This will revive my spirits. I shoot him a look of disbelief but he's already pulling into a parking space at the foot of a long stairway. I dutifully, if sulkily, climb the stairs to study the lavish front doors. Next to them is a huge gold plaque. I lean over it. Inscribed are these words: "TO THE MEMORY OF THE SIX MILLION JEWS WHO PERISHED, 1938–1945." Under which, in only slightly smaller letters, is written: "AND TO MILTON AND HELEN HIRSCH OF WOODMERE, NEW YORK, EXEMPLARY DONORS."

• • •

Soon after this night, I close on an eight-month rental behind the King David, in Yemin Moshe, a neighborhood with tiny stone houses whose roofs and terraces face the Old City walls. I enroll Jackie and myself in *ulpan,* the six-month intensive Hebrew course given to all new immigrants, and I find her a math tutor. Eliza, I've decided, will attend the Anglican School—the only English-speaking elementary school in Jerusalem. I don't want to stress her out by plunging her into a Hebrew-language *gan* (kindergarten) so soon. She seems wary of Hebrew, has yet to utter a simple *Shalom.* She'll pick up the language gradually in the afterschool she'll attend with Tal. I want her to catch on naturally, without being pressured all day long. By next fall, she'll be ready for full immersion in *kittah aleph* (first grade). Other foreign Jewish kids come to this school, though the majority are Christians and Muslims. I assume it has a cosmopolitan parent body; many of these parents are here to work at the United Nations or on various humanitarian projects.

The night before Eliza is due to start school, a week after classes have begun, I'm invited to a parents' meeting. Within minutes of arriving, I see that many here are less ecumenical than missionary—are evangelicals bonded by a dislike for Israelis. As I mill around a table full of sweets and coffee, I overhear one Ghanaian woman say, "Just ghastly, these people!" She's talking to a pregnant Irish woman, who responds wholeheartedly: "I never imagined they'd be so crude . . . so rude."

The Ghanaian, tall and dignified, her hair wrapped high in a colorful African sash, becomes more emphatic: "No manners. . . . They drive like madmen." She pauses. "They *are* far more barbarian than I was warned. And *I was* warned, my dear, many times." She shakes her head. This lilting recitation draws others into this conversation, including an upscale Arab couple whose name tags announce that they're from Cairo. Yet these people, so derisive about Israelis, seem, in other ways, perfectly decent.

I'm relieved to spot a bubbly American woman from Tennessee; she's heading my way from across the room. Nancy had dropped by my house earlier this week to tell me that our daughters are in the same class. As she weaves through the crowd, I sense I can trust her, that she'll have guessed that I'm Jewish, will sympathize with how I feel. But before she can reach me, the school's headmaster rings a bell and walks toward a small podium. He climbs up a few stairs to the microphone. Already feeling angry, I view him in the worst light, noting his dandruff-flaked hair, heavily slicked with something viscous and shiny. His boyish pants, which are hiked up, reveal the brightest yellow socks I've ever seen.

He begins talking, turning wild-eyed. His voice rises high, then higher—in praise of Jesus this, Jesus that. After forty-five minutes he's nearly speaking in tongues. "Give your sins to our Lord; he died on the cross for you," are his parting words.

I'm nearly catatonic in the corner of the room when Nancy finally manages to reach me. "What's with this place?" I ask. "The brochure said the school is open to all religions."

"I knew you were Jewish; you look just like my college roommate," she begins, then adds, "What can I say? The few Jewish parents here don't pay him any attention. He can't help himself; he's just evangelical to the bone." Then she calls out to Eliza's teacher, an elderly Filipino woman with white hair and a wide smile. This woman takes my hand warmly and claims that she, too, was upset by the headmaster's talk. "That belongs in church," she says matter-of-factly. She assures me that Jesus is "at most" one third of her curriculum, and that Judaism can be included too. Brightening, she invites me to visit the class. As the only Jewish mom in her small group, I'm welcome to come in and teach her kids about Judaism—about our holidays and traditions, our history and especially "your lovely Hebrew."

I don't know whether to laugh or cry at the absurdity of sending Eliza to a school in Israel dominated by Jesuit Holy Rollers, or by being designated as the point parent to teach the children what I, myself, don't yet know. My grandparents' Torah knowledge wasn't passed down to me. What could I possibly teach? Driving fast, talking fast, being funny, reading all the time—that pretty well sums up my Jewish identity as of now. When I move to the front door, I pass through more packed crowds, hear more contemptuous talk about Israelis. Here, on the spot, I decide Eliza will tough it out at a Hebrew *gan*, at *any gan*.

•   •   •

At *ulpan*, Jackie and I study hard, memorizing fifteen words each night. Yet strangely, we never hear a single phrase we've learned when out on the streets, with friends, or even on the nightly news. Hebrew phrases start reverberating in my mind, but I've no idea what I'm thinking. One day, *"Lo chashuv"* repeats so often that I ask a stranger at a bus stop to translate it for me.

"It's not important," he says.

"But it *is* important," I respond. "You see, I can't seem to master your language."

The man laughs. *"Lo chashuv means* 'not important.' "

"Oh," I say. We're both laughing as I jot down this phrase before I lose it. I mastered French and Spanish with lightning speed, and was sure Hebrew would be a cinch. But I retain few words and fewer idioms. Much of this strangely shaped language just slips through the crevices of my mind. So I drop out of *ulpan*, sure that I'll make better use of my energy and time by getting an education in Jewish history, in Torah. I enroll for three evening classes at Pardes Yeshiva.

My favorite is taught by Levi Lauer, the yeshiva's director. It's a study of the *Shoah* (Holocaust), its relation to Orthodox Judaism and to contemporary Israel. These three hours fly by, without a boring moment. Most of the other students are Americans in their early twenties. Levi Lauer and I are the only ones in our forties and so a small rapport develops between us. That is, until the fourth week of classes.

Having insisted that we must interrupt him if he mentions anything, but *anything*, we don't understand, Lauer catches a wave of confusion crossing my face as he alludes to the Amalek. He stops lecturing and pointedly asks, "Is that word unknown to anyone here?" Amalek has a familiar ring, but I can't place it precisely and begin to raise my hand. As I do, my classmates stare. Levi Lauer looks at me dumbfounded, his mouth literally dropping open. I lower my hand, blushing. Too late. I see that in the great Jewish chain of being, I'm about to become one lone, disconnected link.

"Amalek," Lauer says, repeating this word very slowly while glowering at me, "is an ancient and *extremely well-known* term for our enemies." Then he adds, "So late in life, so much to learn, yes?" But his semi-smile quickly downshifts as he asks, "Do you know Deuteronomy?"

Maybe I do; maybe I don't. I shake my head, no.

"Anything at all in the Bible?" he asks next, his voice dripping with disdain. I nod a tentative yes. My heart pounds as he mockingly questions, "Well, then, you do know how the story of Abraham and Isaac turns out?"

After the Amalek fiasco, my confidence is a little shaky. I can picture Isaac under Abraham's knife and that last-minute reprieve. But something is a little hazy about *why* God changed his mind. Under the kleig lights of the class's eyes, I'm quiet a second too long. Lauer jumps in: "Be sure, my friend. No one else in this room is sitting on the edge of her seat, wondering how that story ends."

Slouching out of class, I climb up Ben Yehuda, humiliated. I haven't learned what almost everyone in Israel takes for granted. I, who have lived to read, who've read more books than most of my friends, have never tackled the Bible. Yet the Old Testament intersects with every aspect of life here: with holidays, marriage vows, grounds for divorce, as the basis for legal actions and political battles, central to the imagery of everyday life and to the identity of every Israeli Jew, religious or secular.

I've been rightly put down. Yet it's also clear to me that being Jewish is more than Torah study or history; it's a cultural, even a biological resonance as well. Sometimes we European Jews look so alike that I imagine we all come from the same small shtetl, sharing ten distant forebears. Yet I take Lauer's challenge to heart. The farther I walk, the more his taunts begin to inspire rather than deflate me, mainly because the crowds I pass are, as usual, so energetic and friendly.

I walk into our new home, find Jackie and Eliza sitting at the kitchen table, groaning over the Hebrew alphabet. I sit down with them and admit that I'm doing no better than they are. My words alarm them both. So I quickly assure them that Hebrew is bound to get easier for all of us once we give it more time.

Eliza, who's developed a metaphysical bent lately, no doubt under the many new pressures, pipes up, "Mom, if it gets any harder, we'll all land in some serious hot water."

We laugh and talk before all three of us head upstairs to our adjoining bedrooms. I'm carrying the mail Jackie just handed me—what looks like Hebrew junk mail, though how to tell for sure? While wondering if I will ever penetrate this strange, vowel-less alphabet, I spot a letter from California. It's from my aunt Bernice, Alisa's friend, and is surprisingly thick. Once it's opened, I see that folded inside her friendly note is another letter, with legal forms.

The second letter is from an Israeli lawyer in Tel Aviv. One Mr. Abromowitz, Esq., welcomes me warmly to Israel. Writing in English, he says that he's so glad that a Basser has finally moved here because, as I'll see from the enclosed papers, my grandfather, Philip Basser, bought a parcel of land in what was then Palestine in 1929. He was planning to move here to live, a fact he's heard from his own grandfather. That's why he's sending me, via my aunt, this deed to the land that Philip Basser bought and where he had hoped to raise his family. The letter goes on to say that though it may not be worth much money, it should have sentimental value. For only at the last minute did my grandfather change his mind, fearing that his wife and three young children would find Palestine too radical a move from Far Rockaway, Queens, New York. Mr. Abromowitz ends by saying that this parcel of land now belongs to me and several cousins, that it's located in the town of Holon, near Tel Aviv.

I sit up and study the yellowing deed. I see it as my Israeli passport, as my birthright, as one reason I was moved to move here. There must have been some odd cross-generational transmissions at work, I think. Either that or a memory I don't remember, because this "almost" move to Israel is complete news to me. Too excited to sleep I go up to our rooftop, where I study the stars and wait for the sun to rise over the teeth of the Old City walls. By flashlight, I begin reading "The Thirteen-Petaled Rose," a short mystical text written by famed Rabbi Adin Steinsaltz, a renowned biblical scholar who happens to live around the corner. I'm reading of his notion that each Jew has a specific destiny, thinking that I'll easily find mine here and then become that Israeli I was always meant to be.

I can look back at this scene as if it happened to someone else. I see myself sitting up on that high roof, book and deed in hand, blissfully ignorant of all that will befall me.

CHAPTER FOUR

What We Talk About in Israel

A human tide is pushing us from Tel Aviv's seashore into King's Square, the largest park in this city. Sloganeering and chanting are going at high pitch. Daphie is beside me as we join the large rally, with people of all ages and from all over Israel. "Four hundred thousand," we've just heard over loudspeakers, "have already arrived." We're gathered today in support of this Israeli government's participation in the Madrid peace conference, scheduled to begin tomorrow. These will be the first face-to-face meetings between Israel, the Palestinians, and many Arab nations.

"This is the largest rally in Israel since the protests against the Lebanon War in 1982," Tzalli Rechef, a leader of Peace Now *(Shalom Achshav)*, announces. I learn that most here believe Prime Minister Shamir acts in bad faith; that he has no intention of trading "land for peace." His face, seen daily in the newspapers, *is* usually scowling. On TV, he seems magnetically attracted to one of the few Hebrew words I understand: *lo* (no).

The speeches by longtime peace activists, writers and members of Meretz—the new Peace and Justice party—all sound more sensible than hopeful. As translated for me by patient Daphie, I hear a substrate of despair. This, she tells me, is due to fifteen years of Likud rigidity, five years of the Palestinian Intifada. The slogan most often repeated is Amos Oz's famous dictum: "Make Peace, Not Love," a twist on the American anti-Vietnam refrain, "Make Love, Not War."

Though the speakers mistrust the government, each tries to lift the spirits of the many who have good reason to be demoralized. These crowds well know what I'm just glimpsing—that it's hard for Israelis in the peace camp to muster genuine optimism. I concentrate on what's positive, tuning out the undercurrent of anxiety, because I'm personally energized, so happy to be in Israel.

I'm more engrossed by my own reveries than I realize because when A. B. Yehoshua, the novelist I met last June, pushes through the crowds to approach me, his grip on my arm wakes me from my dreamy bliss. In a hearty voice he says, "You listened, eh? I told you we need more Jews like you here. You've come to stay? Eh? *Zeh tov meod!*" (That's very good). Then, he leads me and Daphie up onto the stage, introducing us to Amos Oz, Knesset member Shulamit Aloni and other luminaries. Daphie turns shy among these leaders. I'm not shy, mainly because I have no idea who these famous people are, though I see that meeting anyone from Israel's intellectual elite is effortless.

I also know that Yehoshua's enthusiasm isn't personal. It's a reaction to anyone of his political persuasion who chooses to move here. We few American or English *olim* (immigrants) who aren't here to settle the Greater Israel (land in the West Bank) are likely to vote for Meretz or Labor, against Shamir and a Likud Knesset in next June's elections. That's why we're welcomed into peace circles; we bring much-needed energy. Like every Jew, I can become an Israeli citizen. The process takes time, but once *aliyah* is official, I'll have, among other rights, the right to vote. I hope that long, bureaucratic process will be wrapped up by June. It's only late October now.

• • •

The morning after the rally, many Israelis, in Jerusalem and all around the country, steal hours away from work or school to watch the Madrid conference on television. I walk down a tiny alleyway off Yoel Salomon Street (itself an offshoot of Ben Yehuda), searching for a cottage owned by an acquaintance, an American-born woman named Sandy Schwartz. I've heard her story: She and her husband moved from rural New Hampshire to Jerusalem on a whim, with their two infants. Only weeks after they arrived, Sandy's husband had a heart attack and died. She stayed, raised her two babies and worked hard to master Hebrew. Eventually, she passed the Israeli bar and is now a well-known Jerusalem lawyer.

Entering her house, I see eight women (ex-American or Canadian professionals). Each is stretched out along one of Sandy's futons, drinking coffee and laughing. They greet me casually, as if we've already met and are continuing a conversation begun long ago. I think how this Israeli informality—the assumption of similarities—is a great way to greet anyone.

We're waiting for the Madrid conference to begin on television in this, the first neighborhood in Jerusalem that's been wired for cable. My ease with these women is quickly marred by a faux pas I made. Knowing as yet nothing about class schisms in Israel, I invited Shuki to come here too, after Sandy told me to bring along any of my friends. Shortly after I arrive, he arrives, along with four of his cab-driving buddies.

The women glare at them. The men return the bad vibes until they get distracted by cable TV, gaping at the vast number of stations available, which interests them more than the upcoming political conference. Sandy passes popcorn around; the men refuse. They also refuse to sit down, remain standing over us as the conference's opening formalities begin. We women are riveted by the obvious tensions being played out on the screen.

Under flashing cameras and rolling film, no participant passes up the chance to play to the public, to plug self-promoting views. Shamir begins rotely: "We pray this meeting will mark the beginning of a new chapter in the history of the Middle East. We hope that this conference will signal the end of hostilities and bring coexistence and peace." Then he faces the cameras and, with undisguised fervor, says: "We Jews are the only people who have lived in the Land of Israel without interruption for four thousand years. We are the only people for whom Jerusalem has been a capital. The Zionist movement gave political expression to our claims to the Land of Israel. In 1922, the League of Nations recognized the justice of this. . . . Regrettably, the Arab leaders, whose friendship we wanted most, opposed a Jewish state. . . ."

"*Oy,*" we women sigh as if in one voice, "*oy, vay, voy.*" This rare opportunity to talk *to* the Arabs is being wasted. Who is Shamir addressing? we wonder. Certainly not those sitting around Madrid's long table who are now openly glaring at him.

Next, Dr. Haidar Abdel Shafi, head of the Palestinian delegation, stands to speak. I'm drawn to this grandfatherly doctor from Gaza, a man with an angular, intelligent face. He rises, with effort, and begins a poetic speech: "We, the people of Palestine, stand before you in the fullness of our pain and in our pride and anticipation. For too long, we Palestinians have gone unheeded, silenced, denied. Our identity is too often negated . . . our present existence is poorer in every way because of the past tragedy of another people, those whom we tried not to harm."

But instead of turning to areas of mutual interest, he treats us to *his* litany: against Israelis who have tightly controlled the conditions for today's meeting. He derides the Israeli terms, which include demands that Yasser Arafat, PLO members and everyone from East Jerusalem be excluded from participation (this, at a time when any Israeli who meets a PLO member is breaking the law). Dr. Shafi is furious about these absurd preconditions, accusing the Israelis of being, as usual, intransigent. He says that it's unfortunate that Israel wielded power with the U.S. because that will make a sham of this meeting. (It *is* an open secret that those excluded are all the major Palestinian decision-makers.)

When I look around Sandy's living room, I see that an intra-Israeli version of Madrid's schisms is playing out right here. Shuki and his friends, still standing, make crude jokes. One points to an Arab headdress, another laughs at a sheikh's English accent. The four men escalate their ridicule; we women try to pay them no attention. We're bent forward, eager to catch every word of the speech being given by Hanan Ashwari, the woman who's now at center stage. A relatively unknown English professor from Ramallah, she has, as a result of the Israeli demands to exclude many Palestinians, become the lead spokesperson for their cause. She's using her command of English to great effect. She's fluent, brilliant, passionate and furious.

When the cameras pan to the Israeli delegates, they're frenetically writing notes, then passing them back and forth among themselves. We joke that they're scribbling, "Where the hell did she come from? Whose bright idea was this? Bring back Arafat!" The more we imagine such words, the more they fit the scene we are watching. Soon, we're laughing uproariously, infuriating Shuki and his friends, who begin to loudly deride an Arab head of state whose kaffiyeh is hanging lopsided, eclipsing half of his face. Sandy explodes: "*Maspeek! Di!*" (Shut up! Enough!).

I tune them out; I am busy scanning Madrid's long oval table. I see that it's dominated by countries that represent 220 million Arabs (whose numbers dwarf tiny Israel—a fact that's invoked here daily). But I notice that the Arabs outnumber not only Israel, but the Palestinian delegation as well. I remember reading that Arab nations bully the Palestinians living among them—that they exploit them, use them for menial labor, treat them like social pariahs. Yet the leaders of these same Arab nations harangue the world, the UN and every international conference with reports about the Palestinian "cause." Do they do this only to manipulate world opinion against Israel?

A woman sitting next to me says that in Kuwait, Saudi Arabia, Abu Dhabi, Qatar and even Jordan, the Palestinians are among the best-educated Arabs, but can be expelled at will. Another woman, who's studied this subject, agrees that everywhere in the Arab world, Palestinians are ghettoized. Sizing up the proportions visible at Madrid's table, I see the Palestinian delegates whispering among themselves—a small group situated between two powerful adversaries. What must it feel like, I wonder, with Israeli enmity on one side and Arab hostility on the other? I ask Sandy about this. Without taking her eyes off the TV set, she says, "Earth to Wendy: The Palestinians are persecuted by all other Arabs. They're the Jews of the Arab world." She speaks as if such information is too rudimentary to repeat. Yet her words inflame Shuki and his friends. They have no patience with such distinctions. "An Arab is an Arab is an Arab," one mutters. Another sharp dismissal from Sandy and they all bang out her door.

• • •

A few evenings later near the end of *Shabbat,* after a difficult week of job-hunting, I'm ambling around Jerusalem, savoring the quiet of this always quiet day. I'm also weary from interviews at psychology clinics, increasingly sure that I won't do clinical work here. What interests me most is the intersection of psychology and politics, two disciplines that seem inseparable in this city and country. Politics implode on everyone but are rarely acknowledged as being, in large measure, psychological.

I want to participate in that convergence, in the collective psychodramas. But how? Maybe I'll write essays. I have gotten requests from a New York editor who's read articles of mine on Vermont politics and on psychology. He's offered me a commission for an essay about Israel, about what uprooting myself from America has been like. If only I had something coherent and less purely personal to report about, I'd do that.

I'm so absorbed in thought that I barely notice that five feet away is a table where Shuki and some friends are drinking coffee, smoking and talking. This is Shuki's hangout—a cafe on a small street perpendicular to Ben Yehuda, a rare one that opens an hour before *Shabbat* ends. As soon as I spot Shuki, I warm to the sight of him, though I still have no idea why he was so obnoxious at Sandy's house the other day. He seems equally glad to see me, waving my way, patting the seat next to his for me to sit down.

Around his table is a group of men I've never met. Shuki tells his friends, "She's okay." The men look up, look me over, nod and return to their talk. Shuki asks them to speak in English and grudgingly, they do. I listen to them discuss gambling, love affairs, sports and, occasionally, their wives. Their repartee is teasingly familiar. Shuki tells me that this crowd grew up together in the same small neighborhood, which is not far from here, that they have been friends since kindergarten. "Give an Arab an inch, he'll take a mile" is repeated every few sentences. Am I the catalyst for these words? Their tone is so playful, it's hard to take such phrases seriously. I watch them instead. Each emanates that high enthusiasm and energy for life, what Israelis are famous for. I'm surprised by how openly they care about each other and how easily they show it.

Shuki gives me a running commentary as his friends talk. He tells me that all of them are members of the Likud, meaning that they're "right-wingers." I tell him that I gathered as much at Sandy's house. He seems embarrassed and laughs to cover his emotion. Then he says that he and his friends, like many Israelis from Arab countries, were born into the Likud party; they have a family obligation to vote the way their parents did.

"But why?"

The men tune in to our talk, turning their attention to me for the first time. Inadvertently I break up their lighthearted banter by asking about their origins, their politics. Instantly, all joviality dissipates. Each man—Ari, Joseph, Tzadik—is Israeli-born but from a family who emigrated from Morocco or Iraq "long before the other Sephardim came over in the 1950s," one says. They tell stories of their parents' treatment on arrival, saying that, even generations back, neither their parents nor their grandparents were welcomed into Israel. Instead, they were all treated as inferior to the "great European Jews." I'm told that Israeli grief over the *Shoah*'s victims, one that these men share, is complicated for them. The specter of the dead European millions adds to their (Sephardic) marginalization because *Shoah* victims are considered, even in death, superior to them.

They begin to tell bitter anecdotes. Soon each one is proving his point, interrupting the other, piling example upon example of the discrimination that they and their families faced and still do. The fault lies with the "upper class, elitist Ashkenazic [European] Jews. That's who runs this country," Tzadik, the sweetest of the group, assures me. Joseph, openly shaking, says, "How many generations do we have to live here for half of us to climb *halfway* to the top?"

Shuki's oldest friend, Ari, says, "Take Shuki. He's the best example. His baccalaureate scores were in the top two percent in the country. Yet, he couldn't get into an elite army unit or into a university either." I ask why. Ari says that it's because his family was too large (Sephardim have more kids than European Jews) and his home address was a giveaway. "We're all from the 'wrong' neighborhood—how do you say in America?—from the wrong side of the tracks."

I catch an expression of wistfulness crossing Shuki's face. Given his intuitive gifts and accurate radar about life, I can well believe that he scored high on exams. With his quick mind, he could have done far better than cab-driving, I realize. Shuki, who rarely admits to anything being amiss, says, in an atypically slow voice, how much he wanted to study law. But in those days, in the fifties, it was impossible to get into a university if you were not Ashkenazic. Less than one percent of the student population was Sephardic. I ask what the proportion is now. "Nothing changes," Tzadik says. The others just shrug; they don't know, aren't sure.

Talk turns to how they are sick of doing subservient work—driving tourists around, working long hours at construction sites, manning their families' grocery stores. These are their work options, given at birth, so they claim. "Because we're from Arab countries, we're excluded from the rich life," Joseph says bitterly.

"It's not just the university, but the best army units reject us, too," Tzadik adds. That Shuki and his friends each do a full month of reserve duty in the army every year, yet are never given plum assignments is something I see must be maddening. I'm also touched by how, beneath their macho bravado, they fear for each other, worry about each other's kids—all of whom are, or soon may be, stationed near Lebanon's dangerous border.

For a few minutes I'm distracted by the crowds that have been pouring into the streets since the weekly end-of-*Shabbat* siren sounded for a full minute, a while ago. Pedestrians walk past our table, peer into shop windows, fill the other cafes. Sounds from musicians nearby crisscross around us. It always astounds me how life billows onto these streets in a collective awakening after the hushed quiet of *Shabbat*. I never get used to this shift from complete silence to full animation in one hour.

When I focus back to our table, the conversation has already reverted to the "Arabs." I now see this derogatory talk as a way these men try to bolster their self-esteem. In a country that excludes them from the meritocracy, they get lifted by berating those lower down in status: Israeli Arabs and then the Arabs from the territories—the lowest of the low. Their epithets and slurs are too exaggerated to take seriously, especially as they're now laughing again. Since their families all lived in Arab lands, they must feel *some* connection to Arab cultures, I muse. But, if so, it's well hidden.

I think of asking my Ashkenazi friends about this prejudice toward Arab Jews, a thought that, of course, proves their point: that Israelis of European descent are considered better informed about everything, even about them, the Sephardim. Whatever is or isn't true, hearing them talk so crudely about Arabs, I realize how much racist banter is permissible here. There are boisterous slurs against the religious, as I heard from the moment I arrived at that apartment-hotel. There is bigotry against these Sephardim; dismissals against us who are secular. Racism in Israel is far more open and contentious than in America; of the many American imports that arrive here daily, politically correct attitudes are not among them, I think. Joseph, the most sour of the men, stares at me, then says knowingly, "It's written in the Torah. One Jewish fingernail is worth more than a hundred Arab lives." This comment pushes me over the edge. Shuki picks up my mood, saying, "Careful, guys, we're sitting with a woman who thinks the Arabs might mean well." Yet he knows that I'm ignorant and green and I know it, too.

As they order more hummus and tahini, I make a last stab at appealing to reason, which, as I'm learning, is not central to most conversations here. "We see how Jews are divided, right?" I say.

"You bet," one replies, dipping pita bread into olive oil.

"So why do you imagine that Arabs are all alike?" I have their attention momentarily and so rush to talk about a book I've just read by Israeli columnist Danny Rubinstein. "In *The People of Nowhere*," I say, "he describes the attachment of the '48 generation of Palestinians to their land, what's now our land. He shows how horribly other Arab nations treat them and . . ." Here Tzadik interrupts me. "Read all you want. They're all the same. They hate us. And we hate them."

I walk home thinking that these guys are the backbone and the energy of this country. They love Israel. They're kind and loyal, dynamic and smart. But mention the word "Arab" and they become madmen.

•   •   •

One summer-like day in late November, I'm eating lunch in a large restaurant with Sandy Schwartz. I've told her I've yet to meet a Palestinian. "No one does, not from the territories," she says, adding that there *are* Israeli Arabs (those who stayed here in 1948 and are Israeli citizens) who are easier to get to know. Some run restaurants in "safe" towns. One is called Abu Ghosh. It's fifteen minutes west of Jerusalem, and that's where we are today. This village has proven safe for Jews; the atmosphere is welcoming. We're chatting with friends Sandy has bumped into when I notice two well-dressed Arab businessmen at the next table. They've placed British-Arabic newspapers and leather computer cases right beneath me, and are talking in accented English about their software company. "Whatever else we say, admit it, these Israelis are damned good at business," one says.

"But for them, there's no business like *Shoah* business." They chuckle. I'm speechless.

Driving home through a misty twilight, Sandy concentrates on the road, as I try to imagine what creates such attitudes. I've sensed that we Jews often abuse the legacy of the incomprehensible violence done against us in the past. Whether cynically, manipulatively or out of gaping wounds, our constant litany of persecutions, the way we drumbeat old traumas, does alienate many who could be our allies. Harping on history, as if we're the only ethnic group with a lock on suffering, creates rage in others and disallows us from celebrating our current blessings, which are considerable.

In my Pardes classes, I begin to understand what fuels the collective Israeli psyche, how our history of oppression lives on here as the foundation of the generic Israeli character. As Levi Lauer has remarked, in Israel there's a phobia against *any* passivity. He underscores that the slogans "Never again" and "No more lambs to the slaughter" are credos that run deep in this country's veins, not only in relation to our perceived or real enemies, but as notions that inform interactions among ourselves as well. This helps explain the wild, confrontational dramas I often see when out on the streets: fierce arguments over parking spaces, caustic fury over divvying up a restaurant bill, or the typical Israeli refusal to comply with traffic regulations and other laws. I begin to glimpse that to be an Israeli is to be fixed on never getting caught, even momentarily, in a posture of weakness or apparent defeat. That fear operates in work, in love, even in passing encounters. To be fooled is to risk falling into that most dreaded Israeli category, a *freir* (one who can be taken). Americans are seen as missing those antennae, as sitting ducks. Is this why I often feel that to say I'm an American is to be a potential victim of a con? That's another mystery I had better figure out before I am one.

•   •   •

After months of lively interest in this new world of meanings, one morning it ends. It's early December when wet skies and freezing winds assault Jerusalem. After the unending summer I'm not prepared for the intensity of these winter storms. But then, how could anyone have anticipated a winter of such extremes, what will become the worst in Jerusalem's recorded history? Six months of continuous sunlight give way. We wake each morning to downpours so fierce and hail so large that when it pounds at our windows it sounds as if we're being hit by Intifada stones. Next comes torrential rain, then unprecedented snowstorms. Usually, there's no snow at all in Jerusalem. But now, whenever the sun seems about to break through the coverlet of clouds, another round of hail, sleet, rain or snow pours down. And with a ferocity that seems biblical in its proportions, that obscures all light.

I've never experienced weather so unrelentingly miserable, not even in Boston. Six to eight feet of snow close the city down, on and off, during December, January, and into February. There's little central heating, and since snow is so rare, there are no official preparations for coping with it—no snow tires or snow plows; no way to drain the water that floods many homes; no emergency crews to deal with the electrical blackouts that zap one neighborhood after another. For weeks at a time, driving—even walking—is dangerous. Children's classes and adult work are often canceled. This collective confinement does not create a mood of cozy intimacy, as it well might elsewhere, but suggests that we've all been put under some mythological curse.

I'm determined to keep getting out, fearing a decline into winter's torpor. But all attempts at normal life are doomed. I walk five steps outside, bundled up and full of bravado, sure I'll get to a meeting. Within seconds, I turn back to our apartment. The winter's isolation cuts the girls and me off from our fragile connections, gives us too much time to contemplate the downside of this move. Even visits from Daphie, Shimon and Tal, from Sandy Schwartz and her two daughters, from Shuki and friends—all of whom drop over frequently—don't help. Though I usually love winter for its permission to read and write, I now watch in despair as my feelings about living in Israel shift from certainty that I belong here into certainty that I do not. I'm homesick for my friends and work, and maybe most of all for an English-speaking world.

Jackie and Eliza briefly revel in the snow, sled on the dazzling white hills of Jerusalem under tree branches bowed under thick layers of ice. But soon they, too, turn grouchy and feel lethargic. They *hate* Hebrew and can't learn it. (I, too, can still barely decipher a word.) They complain about *Shabbat* and the Jewish holidays, which they find *sooo* boring. They begin a campaign begging me to leave Israel. I'm tempted. "Why are we here?" Eliza cries. The truth is that I don't remember.

Jackie is terrified of our landlords, the Patchorniks, who drop by often, concerned about how we're acclimating. They're eager to help us, but as soon as they knock at the front door, Jackie dashes to the bathroom and locks herself inside. She believes that she's going to land in a Jewish hell—a horrid thought for a practicing Christian—because she thinks we've mixed up the meat with the milk dishes in this Orthodox, kosher home. I laugh at her fears and try to tease her out of them. But I fail and then am forced to make lame excuses about her whereabouts to our landlords. Secretly, I identify with Jackie's primitive fears. I, too, have a constant sensation that something I'm doing or thinking is breaking one of the 613 Jewish laws of conduct.

It's embarrassing. Time after time, this kind elderly couple express worry about how Jackie could possibly be safe outside in "this wicked weather." I know they suspect she's out having some illicit love affair. Yet I know she's so nearby that she can overhear us. I keep my promise and don't give her secret away. In a way that seems more polite anyway. How would our landlords feel if they knew Jackie was terrified of their religious practices?

But Jackie is miserable and Eliza wants to go home, and they whittle away at me. I feel under house arrest with the horrid weather and the two strong-willed girls—and we're not even settled into our own home. An Orthodox woman, an artist I met last June named Abigail whom I talk to on the phone regularly, is sure my current confusion and confinement is less about the weather, more about getting through the first year of *aliyah*. "This is initiation time. This is *your* initiation," she says. "*Something* always throws a curve to anyone who moves here. Panic to leave Israel is commonplace. That's what you must overcome."

"But how?"

She suggests I talk with her *rebbe* (rabbi), a spiritual teacher in the Old City. He has helped many *olim* and knows how to handle the pain of an immigrant's dislocation. She gives me his phone number and I call him. A woman takes my name and number and says he'll get back to me soon. I flop onto my couch, sunk in anomie. Will the *rebbe* really get my message? Return my call? I hope so. I hope I won't give up. All I know, sitting under this latest round of gray skies and pounding hail, is that I can't seem to cope.

CHAPTER FIVE

Initiation

The *rebbe* calls back within minutes and we talk. He sounds mystically at-tuned, almost psychic. He tells me a lot about myself that feels true. He says he's certain that I do belong in Israel, that my biggest mistake was in trying penetrate Judaism by studying Torah at Pardes, a yeshiva he disdains. He says that if I come to study with him, I'll receive transmissions from ancient prophets and a direct inspiration from him *chik-chak* (quickly). His parting words are, "Not to worry. You'll feel stronger in no time. You'll regain the spiritual ground that Jerusalem requires." A few mornings later I'm trekking up the narrow path from Yemin Moshe to his Old City home.

I wait in a small downstairs room. The *rebbe* bellows out that he'll soon be with me. In half an hour he finishes a spiritual consultation upstairs in his study. An old man, skeletal, slowly descends the stairs, then fumbles with his winter gear. I'm called to come upstairs.

He looks nothing like the man I imagined. This *rebbe* is unkempt, has a huge pot belly, smokes nonstop, with eyes that dart about. I find it hard to be-lieve that this is the man who so elevated me over the phone. He's dressed in black and his unusually white skin seems pallid. His nose is running (though he doesn't seem to notice). Each time one of his many kids dashes in, he can't set limits or negotiate with them, but becomes, within seconds, rabidly impa-tient. Parenting is hard, as I well know, but he seems unusually short-fused. Where is his wife? I wonder. Why isn't someone from his community pitching in with child care while he works?

I'm trying to follow his convoluted lecture. He's quoting Maimonides and the Ramban and other ancient interpreters of the Talmud. Sensing that I'm glazing over in confusion, he simplifies his talk, turning it into a one-note re-frain, "Torah." And again: "Torah." The thermometer takes its usual 3 P.M. dive, as do my hopes for a Talmudic healing. But now neither of us can ignore the sounds of bedlam, the shrieking that's growing louder below us. With a shrug of his shoulders, the *rebbe* excuses himself, leaving me to study this week's Torah *parsha* (chapter). He's typed it out in English and instructed me to read it first aloud and then silently while he's gone. I'm not to try to understand the words, but to allow them to wash over me and begin mending my spirit. After that, I'm to move to his chair, close my eyes and do deep breathing. He has assured me that I'll be uplifted by ancient transmissions, though he warns that there's much I won't understand.

As he races down the stairs, he calls out over his shoulder to remember to sit in his chair. That's critical. But when I move to the *rebbe*'s side of the desk, I can't quite keep my eyes closed. I steal a look around at rubber bands, chewing gum and cigarettes broken in half on his desktop, a view not visible from the other side. I remind myself that I'm not here to learn *about* him, but *from* him. I force my eyes shut and breathe deeply, a posture I manage to hold for an hour, as the aroma of cooked chicken floats up to me.

When the *rebbe* returns, it's clear he's exhausted from dealing with his children. I tell him that I feel numb and hungry. He smiles. "You're too impatient. It can take years to find a relation to the text. But I guarantee, Torah study with me will change your life." (What about that *chik-chak* over the phone? What about "You'll feel stronger in no time"?) The psychologist in me listens, dubious, wondering how this worn-out man can recharge me. "Kids are tough," he says, as we begin to reverse roles. He tells me that his wife's parents are sick, in need of her help, and that the woman slated for child care has a cold, "as usual." He's been left in charge of his children; he admits to feeling "trapped." I nod, agreeing that children who are cooped up can be especially demanding. I add that I can't imagine handling six kids under the age of ten.

"Neither can I," he quips as he sees me out.

As he suggested, I head to the Western (Wailing) Wall to pray and to place letters to God in the stone's crevices. I touch them, repositioning myself five or six times. But no matter what I do or where I stand, nothing about this sacred stone wall stirs me. If anything, this sight adds to my sense of bleakness.

I decide to pursue a more familiar form of healing—psychotherapy. By the first week of January, I have the names of two therapists.

First I meet with a sabra woman psychoanalyst. Her tiny office in Rehavia seems set up to ensure intimacy. I settle into my chair and tell her that I've just recently moved here, have a young daughter, an older foster child, am feeling disoriented both by this move and this winter weather. I add that I'm here to talk about my current confusions, my desire to leave Israel.

After six sentences she stops me cold, saying, "I'll do the talking today," sounding harsh and impatient, adding, "I get the picture." She proceeds to tell me that she can read me like a book, that I'm arrogant and expect the world on a platter, "just like every other American I've analyzed." After a few more direct insults, I ask, "But on what basis do you say such things? And if you're right, how can such instant criticism, such a harsh manner, possibly be therapeutic?"

My question, fresh ammunition, proves her point. "Don't you see? You come to me for help. Now you want to tell me how to do my job! Isn't that your life in a nutshell?" "Absolutely not," I say, as we terminate our session. I reel out onto the streets, into a world of snowdrifts.

My next appointment is with a male therapist in the suburb of Mevasseret, usually a short drive from Jerusalem. These days it's a dangerous haul down the icy Tel Aviv highway. Ever-inventive Shuki has mastered how to navigate winter roads. He's bought snow tires and other accoutrements few others have bothered to find, and he offers me a ride. On the way down, he's confused. "Let me get this straight," he says. "You're about to pay a complete stranger to hear what you've already told me?" I laugh. In a way that's true. We see each other often and have begun talking openly about whatever comes into our minds. When we hit a few bumps, we keep our cool by staying inside our conversation, which lately seems as much like psychoanalysis as friendship. In his white Toyota taxi, we've both noticed that distant memories rise up as we drive.

When we reach Mevasseret, Shuki removes a bundle of newspapers from under his seat, while I enter the doctor's basement office. This therapist is nondescript, in late middle age. He tells me that he's had three cancellations due to driving conditions, offering me a double session: two full hours. I go out to check with Shuki. He says it's okay with him, but to holler if the guy's a weirdo. I laugh, assuring him I'll be fine.

By contrast with the Rehavia analyst, this man seems at least generically therapeutic. He's a hard read, but at least he listens, takes copious notes, and soon I'm deep in the labyrinth of what brought me to Israel. I describe my current discomforts. He nods for me to continue. Before I know why, I'm reliving my parents' deaths, detailing the long labor of each one's sickness, making the connection between my love for my father and my sudden move to his beloved Israel. But after what seems a long time, I can't ignore the unusually lopsided rhythm to this session. I've talked a great deal, shared more intimate matters than I'd intended—for well over an hour. This man hasn't volunteered a single grunt. So I ask him, "What do you think?"

Very slowly, he puts his yellow notepad on a table and gazes at me with an anguish I mistake for empathy. He sighs several times and his face shows a pained expression. And then, slowly and with an intensity that unnerves me, he launches into a feverish recollection of a troubled love affair he suffered during his college days. He describes the woman who hurt him as being very like me—her looks, her voice, her history. (I'm forty-six; he's in his late sixties!) He details their ugly breakup, sharing sexual details that have no place in anyone's session except his own.

Abruptly, he stands up, as if his past is too overwhelming to bear, and announces that his counter-transference (the therapist's personal reaction to a patient) is "sky high"; there's no way that he can work with me. We're both standing. He gives me an odd, teary look, motioning me to the exit. It's when we're standing at the foot of his newly constructed circular staircase that I surprise myself by bursting into tears. Soon I'm wracked by rare, impossible-to-control sobs. After all, I've just relived my parents' deaths, the depth of my responsibility to Eliza and Jackie, my love and fear and ambivalent relationship to Israel. And all the while this man was zoned out in *his* distant past. Why did I spill my guts without checking him out more carefully? I'm still gasping the last of my dry sobs when he announces coldly: "You'll never find happiness in Israel. You're far too trusting."

I'm trudging out to Shuki's waiting car, thinking that this therapist didn't have the faintest notion, not to mention ethical obligation, of placing his own life in parentheses long enough to listen and respond to a patient.

As we head back toward Jerusalem, I repeat for Shuki the therapist's parting words: "Those sabras will eat you for breakfast and then lick their chops." This phrase sends the two of us into peals of laughter. Just as we're convulsed by these weird words, the car begins skidding on a layer of fresh ice that's covering the highway with a dangerous film; it swivels 180 degrees around and we grab each other's hands to keep calm. We don't let go even after we pull off the main road to stop for coffee.

Holding hands makes us both shy, yet we seem equally eager to touch each other, to break out of this winter's ennui. Our hands continue exploring each other's until soon we're both aroused. Within a week we become lovers. Both of us admit that we believe this will only be a short fling, and might well ruin our friendship to boot. But, to our surprise, after six months of friendship, our touch is far more affecting than we'd imagined. Soon, we're madly in love.

At the same time, spring is arriving. By mid-March the streets are alive. Everyone greets each other jovially, all of us are thrilled to leave our winter hibernation behind. Now the atmosphere is one of near-ecstasy under the sun's dependable light. Bright day follows bright day as Shuki and I begin to merge, to look alike, to trade identities. As if by the magic of love's contagion we both undergo radical changes. Shuki's gold bracelet and wing-tipped shoes are replaced by casual Birkenstocks. I'm growing younger. Passing us on Ben Yehuda, Sandy exclaims that we look like characters in a Hollywood love story. After so many months of camaraderie, clear boundaries and fixed roles, this mutual chemistry astounds us both. I've never felt closer to anyone. Nor has he. Our intimacy alters everything—adds a luster to people we meet, to the land, the stones, the sky, whatever we look at together. We notice that our happiness is cheering up Eliza and Jackie. They seem to have emerged from this hard winter feeling lighthearted. I attribute their mood to *our* loving energy, but I then discover that we're not the only lovers in this household. Eliza has become inseparable from a girlfriend two years older than she, Gracie, Sandy Schwartz's youngest daughter. Jackie, also glowing, confesses over breakfast one morning that she's in love, too.

"Who is he?" I ask, amazed.

"Also a cabdriver!" she laughs. Except, as she tells me, hers is an Arab Christian, which is "perfect," she adds, since she's Christian, too.

Jackie, Eliza and I seem suddenly like college roommates. We blast love songs over our tape deck, dancing around the house for hours. One night, after drinking a glass of wine, I tell Shuki about Jackie's involvement despite an intuition that this is not a good idea. Immediately, he confirms my worst fears by jumping up and asking for the man's name. I tell him that I didn't ask and don't know. I add that I can trust Jackie; she's wise and self-protective, always takes good care of herself. Shuki insists on investigating her new friend. I can't stop him. He and Jackie, who've grown closer since he moved in with us, head outside onto our front steps for a "private" talk. Soon, phone calls are made. I overhear him talking fast in heated Hebrew.

I'm glad he's taking the girls on, being protective, but his involvement seems more controlling than loving. Shuki goes outside and an hour later he returns from "a meeting" with Jackie's guy in a nearby parking lot. As he walks inside we study his face. He announces that Yussef is a good guy, a very good guy. Jackie grins. I relax. But their relationship must end, he says. An Arab, however nice, even an Israeli Arab, cannot be privy to any details of our household. I argue that he doesn't even come into the house (though I don't know why; that seems rude). I argue that they're not sleeping together.

Jackie races to her room, slamming her door. Finally allowed in, I find her sitting on the floor, crying hysterically. She cannot believe that Shuki has the nerve to interfere in her relationship. I'm equally appalled. But he's adamant that an Arab can bring problems to us, something, he insists, neither of us can possibly understand. Jackie and I have been reading each other's minds and moods for many years. Our looks now say: Maybe we'll pay him no attention on this matter.

I endure a week of Jackie's sulking and then we manage to regroup into a loving family. I strongly suspect that Jackie is still seeing Yussef and I'm glad. I have no interest in stopping her. To keep her secret, I keep Shuki busy. We're trying to find a permanent apartment and soon we do. It's nearby, across from the Laromme Hotel on Jabotinsky Street with a two-year lease. It's owned— extremely unusual in Jewish Jerusalem—by a very rich Arab landlord named Mr. Khouri.

By mid-May it's high summer. The June elections are approaching. With pressure from the Americans as a major factor (Bush and Baker have carried out their threat and withheld funds from Israel after Shamir did not curtail settlement building) the political pendulum swings. The Likud conservatives are dislodged. Labor's Yitzhak Rabin is elected prime minister. For many complicated reasons, he has no choice but to appoint his old nemesis, Shimon Peres, as foreign minister. In addition, twelve Knesset members are elected from the Meretz (Peace and Justice) party, an astounding number, propitious for peace. Even Shuki and his Likud friends, for reasons he does not yet make clear to me, change allegiances, voting for Labor or Meretz.

Along with the new leadership, there's a political euphoria in the air, a feeling that real change may be under way. This is mirrored by events in Washington, where the peace talks were moved months ago. Unlike Shamir, Rabin is at home in Washington (as Israel's ambassador to the U.S., he lived there for years). It's a long shot, but he may adapt to changing circumstances, especially with Peres, a committed dove on the Palestinian issue, at his side.

It's August 1992, exactly a year since we moved here from the U.S. I'm sitting in the kitchen of our new apartment on the fourth floor of 4 Jabotinsky Street when I'm startled by a loud banging at my door. I rush to open it and find standing in the hallway an Israeli building contractor along with his Palestinian partner. They're lost and ask to use my phone. I'm relieved that Shuki isn't home; I couldn't be hospitable if he were. I invite them in.

Having mastered the minor art of making great Turkish coffee, I invite these two men, who seem to be the best of friends, to sit and have a cup after they make their call. Soon, as is so often true in Israel, work takes second place to socializing. After talking about their business for half an hour, I ask them whether they believe, after Rabin's election and with the ongoing Washington talks, if peace is possible.

Nearly in unison, they both say cheerfully, "Never!"

Why is the Palestinian Arab as adamant as the Israeli Jew? Does his world, too, distrust dialogue and refuse hope? Do Palestinians in the territories demonize "us" as readily as Israeli Jews demonize "them"? After they leave, I think about how I've yet to meet an Arab from the territories. The truth is, I haven't had a single conversation with one Palestinian all year, except with this man, just met.

I've been crossing streets to avoid "them," warned often that a gardener in kaffiyeh might be a terrorist, that cars with blue license plates (signifying Arabs from the territories) might hold bombs. When I do peer into a car driving through Jerusalem, it's usually packed with eight or ten stern-faced passengers. On the streets, I haven't found one Arab face that expresses anything positive. I see tight grimaces and cold faces, and have come to expect all "Arabs" to look menacing.

One recent afternoon, in Liberty Bell Park, just as Eliza and Tal were getting the hang of speed skating and shouting excitedly for me to watch, I realized that we were surrounded by Arab teenagers. Instinctively (and brusquely) I yanked the two confused girls away. I, who initially came here for a cross-cultural peace conference, haven't witnessed, not even on the evening news, one live dialogue between a Palestinian and an Israeli. Now that I feel somewhat familiar with Israel, I'm getting tired of hearing about Arabs without knowing any; I'm worn down from being infected with the certainty that "they" are all violent. The editor in New York queries me again. He wants to know if I'll *ever* be ready to write about life and politics here. If so, he now suggests that I capture what's going on "on the ground," using direct scenarios that show rather than tell what life here is really about.

In order to do what he's asked, I'd have to suspend my scary stereotypes and dare to cross the Green Line. I'd have to enter the Palestinian world. How? Though I carry a press pass, I have no idea where to begin such an expedition. Yet my need to test the waters is growing stronger. It's not only that I want to write; I'm also dying of curiosity.

A few weeks go by when one morning at Eliza's bus stop, I spot a new friend, Sara—a lively, well-known Israeli journalist. She's had me over for coffee a few times; she lives just down the block. Our daughters are in the same school, which is how we met at the bus stop. I ask her advice. She says that she knows a Palestinian who takes foreign journalists to visit the West Bank. As promised, she calls back later that day. His name is Hakam, but she can't find his phone number. She'll call again as soon as she locates it.

Waiting for Sara to fish Hakam's number out from somewhere in her kitchen drawers, I cast about for another possible route into the West Bank. And then, as so often happens in Jerusalem, a wish turns to reality, in no time flat.

Part II
Among the Palestinians

Most journalism textbooks will advise you that if you want to get the most objective journalist possible for the Middle East, find a Gentile from Wyoming who has never met an Arab or Jew in his life. To that I say, nonsense. Objectivity should not be synonymous with ignorance.

. . . I can't possibly write a fair story, an insightful story, an honest story unless I get close enough to my subjects to understand what makes them tick. I can't possibly write a fair story about Israelis or Palestinians unless I become knowledgeable about their history, and also get close enough to them as individuals so that I am almost inside their heads, looking at the world as they do. Because without that kind of deep understanding—understanding that borders on sympathy—I can't possibly be fair.

—*Thomas L. Friedman,*
"From Beirut to Jerusalem to Washington,"
in The Writing Life

CHAPTER SIX

Crossing Over the Green Line

The High Holy Days, my second in Israel, have ended. The sun overhead is strong in Jerusalem's mild autumn as I drive to Salah el-Din Street in East Jerusalem. It's six minutes away, yet a neighborhood I'd never have visited if my Arab landlord hadn't insisted that I come in person to sign my lease.

Mr. Khouri's office is congested. Arab women and children sit cramped together on long wooden benches. In each corner of the room, men squat in small groups, smoking and talking, their heads bent together as if they're negotiating secret business deals. Others, elegantly attired, arrive and wait patiently on the few available chairs. Why are so many disparate people crowding into a landlord's office? I squeeze onto a bench and strike up a conversation with a man sitting next to me.

In excellent English, he introduces himself as a journalist named Hakam. Could this be Sara's friend? His eyes light up at the mention of her name. Yes, they're good friends, he smiles. He displays the easy familiarity I associate with Israelis. "Why so crowded in here?" I ask him, as we stare at the door; people are still pushing through, into the room. Wording his response carefully, Hakam says that Mr. Khouri wears many hats; he's a lawyer and in other ways is a powerful man on this side of the city. I picture him as some kind of godfather, a don figure.

I ask Hakam if he's the man who takes foreign correspondents on tours of the West Bank. Yes, he does, often. I barrage him with questions about Palestinian life for a half hour until Mr. Khouri's secretary calls me to go inside. As she does, Hakam hands me his card, suggesting that he or one of his assistants can take me anywhere into Gaza, the West Bank or East Jerusalem. Then I'll see for myself what Palestinian life is like, he says. He can set up interviews with any of his people—whether members of the intellectual elite, people living in refugee camps or Intifada street fighters (*shabab*). "We'll keep you safe," he assures me.

Back in West Jerusalem, I don't mention the plan to "cross over" to anyone except Sara, the only person I know who passes the Green Line regularly. My guess is that all my friends would try to dissuade me. But this expedition might give me something to write about. Even more important, I've begun to see Israel as a stage set that's half darkened and I long to see into that darkness.

While waiting for Hakam to return my call, I try to envision what awaits me, but I can't. I call Sara, who's dashing out on assignment to Gaza. She assures me that Hakam will keep me safe, adding that I'm in for an adventure, "like Alice going through the looking glass." Yet, I begin to worry. What am I getting myself into? Why am I doing this? Increasingly on edge, I wonder if there isn't a very good reason no one I know voluntarily enters the Palestinian world. Sara calls back to say she forgot to tell me that I must rent a cellular phone and carry it with me at all times. I must call her every few hours. It's critical, she says, for someone to know my exact whereabouts. These are routine precautions, she ends breezily, having just stoked my worst fears.

A week later Hakam picks me up, then drops me off at an office building in East Jerusalem. All he's told me is that I'm scheduled to interview an important man named Riad Maliki. I stand on the sidewalk watching Hakam and his white Honda disappear down a busy commercial street. He leans out an open window and shouts that he'll pick me up "in about an hour."

Inside a dilapidated building, I climb three flights, careful to step over broken or missing stairs, noticing the Arabic graffiti that covers every inch of the cement walls. Maliki's office door is opened by a woman in her mid-twenties. She gives her name as Rula, then curtly lets me in. With thick blonde curls, a wide face and her elegant pants suit, she fits none of my images of an Arab. Hardly looking at me, she says, in clipped tones, that I'm to wait; Mr. Maliki is running late. Then she bends back over her paperwork at a desk. After minutes, I ask who Riad Maliki is, adding that Hakam was too rushed to give me details. Surprised at my ignorance, she says he's the leader of the PFLP. We're quiet as I ponder this confusing political acronym. "And the PFLP is . . . ?" I ask. Rula studies me for the first time. No doubt she's wondering what I'm doing here if I'm so uninformed. "The Popular Front for the Liberation of Palestine," she says distinctly. She describes the group as "obstructionist," as one that works against the Madrid peace, and returns to her work. Her silence leaves me alone with my thoughts, which already center on how to get out of here.

If our telegraphic small talk is strained, what will be gained by talking to a zealot against peace? Over loudspeakers, I hear the wail of the Arabic muezzin calls to prayers, keening sounds that underscore that I'm in an all-Arab environment.

To distract myself, I study the walls. Next to huge pictures of Jerusalem's Old City are yellowing photographs of Arabic warriors from the turn of the century. Each man sits proudly astride a horse, shrouded in military garb. Stifling my impulse to run from this room, I cross and uncross my legs. Neither Rula nor I say a word.

Finally, needing to dispel the tension, I tell her that this is my first visit to East Jerusalem, that I feel unnerved by the sounds of Islamic prayers blasting outside, and that . . . I'm Jewish and so maybe interviewing her boss, who espouses violence and is against peace, is not such a great idea. Before she has time to answer me, I whisper that I'm feeling dizzy. Could she call me a cab?

"Think how I feel whenever I go to a cafe on Ben Yehuda Street!" Rula exclaims. "I don't look Palestinian, but the minute a Jewish waiter overhears me or my friends speaking Arabic, he signals the Jewish soldiers to move closer. Those soldiers with guns pointed God-knows-where? Drunk on beer? You'll admit, that's creepy."

"It's not what I see," I reply honestly. "I've never even noticed the soldiers drinking beer. I see them as ensuring safety. It's *here* that I feel threatened."

Rula moves her chair close to mine. She brings me a glass of water, then takes my hand. As we talk, we discover that both of us have recently moved to the Mideast. Though she was born in Ramallah, her father worked in public health in Washington, D.C., for the last decade. She, along with her family, have just returned home a month ago. She found this secretarial job only last week. As we trade fears about the precise sounds or sights that spark our anxieties, we begin to laugh. However free of ethnic identity each of us feels abroad, back here we're instantly stripped of any cosmopolitan gloss. In my Jerusalem and in hers, we're thrown into primitive tribal tensions. My fears are dissipating until I hear Maliki's footsteps. My body becomes rigid again.

"Don't be afraid," Rula says, putting her hand on my shoulder. "He's against the peace process, for sure, but he's not against peace. You'll see," she whispers as Maliki walks in. He's wearing a tweed jacket and horn-rimmed glasses. He nods for me to follow him into his office; Rula throws me a wink.

After honest talk with Rula, Maliki's wall of Arab iconography already seems less menacing. Maybe he will, too. We sit down at his large desk. He excuses himself as he fumbles through a stack of papers. As I watch him, I see how much he resembles the New Left radical men I knew well in the sixties, with their Marxist logic and all-consuming political obsessions. Maliki looks up and, in perfect English, gives a talk he could probably deliver in his sleep. He wants me to grasp his group's "bottom line"—that until UN resolutions concerning Israel (242 and 338) are implemented, until Israel retreats to its pre-'67 borders, it's suicidal for Palestinians to talk of making peace.

"Peace?" he declares. "The way things are going, the West Bank will soon be in 'pieces.' "

Since honesty worked with Rula, I try to get beneath Maliki's recitation. He soon softens, describing the death threats proliferating not only against him, but also against his wife and children. What's most frightening (his face knots up) is that he has no idea if these leaflets are being written and spread by Israelis or by a rival faction of Palestinians. He lifts up a paper written in Arabic, which he says is full of disinformation about him. Yet, so many copies are being circulated that he's frightened, especially at night. "And I don't know who's setting me up," he repeats.

We discover that we both went to college in Manhattan. Trading memories of Sunday ennui in the vast city, of going to movies or museums, we agree that wandering about in that freedom can easily turn into "lack of purpose," as he mutters, or "dark alienation," as I say. We laugh at how alike were our bouts of disconnection.

Maliki muses, "Look, here we're all part of meaningful struggles. I desperately wish we didn't have to be violent towards each other. But I'm glad you reminded me of New York. I wouldn't trade [he waves the Arabic paper] all these death threats for that free-floating anomie." We talk for an hour. We hardly become allies or see the world through the same lens, but we do meet beneath the political rhetoric. For me, this is a first—breaking through caricature into a shared human moment with a Palestinian leader. For years after this morning, whenever I read in the *Jerusalem Post* about Riad Maliki's "dangerous" politics, I picture a man walking around Manhattan, starved for community, and I smile.

As Rula and I shake hands goodbye, we're equally "green" about the current "situation," the waning Intifada. We could not know, this October morning, how often and in what altered circumstances our paths will cross in the coming years.

• • •

A few weeks later, on the first rainy afternoon in early November, Hakam sends a Palestinian journalist named Manal to accompany me on a trip to Nablus, the largest (and reputedly dirtiest) city in the northern West Bank, the city farthest from Jerusalem. Manal is a beauty. She's casually dressed, with wild black hair, and has an amazingly infectious smile. Driving a Petra (Arab rental) car we set off to interview a newspaper editor who was just released from fifteen years in Israeli prisons.

After parking near his downtown office, I step into a city known to be unusually dangerous to Jews from Israel or abroad. As we walk through the crowded Casbah toward our appointment, Manal chatters lightheartedly to anyone in our path, while I glimpse around at a city that's dark and grim.

I'm shocked by my reaction. I seem to have forgotten my experience with Rula and Maliki in East Jerusalem. Here on Nablus's bustling, shabby streets, I am overtaken by terror again, stronger than before. I'm too frightened to look around. I stare at the sidewalk, counting cracks to calm myself, even though my head, like Manal's, is draped in a kaffiyeh (the black-and-white-checkered scarf emblematic of Arab "solidarity"). I'm irrationally certain that at any moment someone will throw rocks my way or stab me. At last we arrive at the editor's office building, indistinguishable from the others that line the drab street.

We climb six flights, then walk into his waiting room, where fifteen Palestinian boys and men are gathered. All wear black jackets. I glance at them quickly, then gaze down at the floor. They look exactly like those furious kids I see every night on Israeli TV news—the stone-throwers.

Manal whispers, "It's okay. We're fine. Trust me." But I don't; I begin to actively resent that she persists in seeing only what's positive. I wish I was traveling with someone more realistic about the dangers here. Still immobilized by fear, I study the mud-tracked cement floor. Finally, I brave another glance around the room and see that the Arab boys and men, with their kaffiyehs thrown around their necks, are all staring at me. I sense that I've walked into a trap.

At last, the famous editor emerges. In my nervous state I leap up into an awkward pirouette (more stares) as my kaffiyeh, this most revered Palestinian symbol, falls to the floor. Before I realize it, I've stomped on it with my muddy boots. As I reach down to reclaim my lifeline in this Arab world, fifteen sets of eyes follow my movements. I grab the sullied scarf and look up, praying that my face conveys the abject apology this transgression demands. As I do, the entire group of men and boys bursts into laughter. They've been told I'm Jewish. That's why they're here: to meet a Jewish journalist.

The editor sits down in his own waiting room. Some of the boys are still doubled over in laughter. Others assure me they're eager to meet a Jew, especially one who's willing to listen to stories of their life under the occupation. Hakam has relayed that I'm "okay," one says. The editor talks bitterly of his life in prison, but is not hostile to me. He seems to regard me as someone who might broadcast his story. Soon everyone is talking. At first, they seem more eager to hear about life in New York than to talk about Nablus. They press me for details about colleges, asking which ones are best, which give the most generous scholarships.

When the conversation turns to their lives, it's full of *their* fears: of hearing Hebrew, of Israeli soldiers, of Jews. Since their laughter has shown an understanding of my predicament, they've relaxed me. I listen as each takes a turn describing the way occupation imprisons them. Hearing details of how every aspect of their lives is dominated by Israelis, I realize that my ever-present images of the Holocaust (fed in my childhood, by the racial slurs here and through a lifetime of books and movies) had led me to mistake Nablus for a Nazi war zone, where any Jew is in mortal danger. That I'm sitting with Palestinians so at variance with this fantasy is a relief. These men and boys seem to actively want to overcome the belief that all Jews are against them. Though I feel safe, it's hard to believe this group is representative of what goes on outside this room. Maybe I'm lucky today. Or maybe this friendliness *is* an attempt to dupe me.

Safely home, I call Hakam. I say that I need more preparation for my visits, that I want to know precisely what I'm walking into when he sends me out. And I don't want him telling people ahead of time that I'm Jewish. I end by accusing him of not protecting me adequately as he promised.

He responds cheerfully that I'm in luck. On my next outing I will be accompanied by Achmed Mashall, his most trusted assistant, who has just returned to work with him. The next thing I know Achmed himself is on the phone. He tells me that he grew up in the Shu'afat refugee camp in East Jerusalem and has just arrived home after five years in Vienna. There, he studied and worked as a civil engineer. I like his soft, lilting voice; the sophisticated language he uses. I'm especially heartened when he says that since we both missed the wildest days of the Intifada, ours will be a mutual adventure. He hands the phone back to Hakam, who tells me that if we can trust each other, Achmed will be my guide from now on.

Our first direct meeting is at the elegant American Colony Hotel in East Jerusalem. Achmed, in person, is reassuring. He's thirty-three but seems older, and exudes a quiet integrity. He's direct, soft-spoken, and seems to have modeled himself on his good mother, whom he drives me to visit, in the camp nearby, within an hour. After several days touring together, I feel completely safe putting my life in his hands. A good thing, this, since on a day in late November he drives me and another American Jew, Roger, a sociologist from Chicago, for a day-long visit to his cousin, Mohammed, who lives at the Deheishe refugee camp. It's situated past Bethlehem, south of Jerusalem, a mere twelve minutes' travel time from my home. We pull to a stop next to a barbed-wire fence on the main road. Mohammed is standing outside, waiting for us. He hugs Achmed tightly, shakes our hands, and then we all step gingerly inside the camp. We follow Mohammed down a garbage-strewn alleyway, careful not to cut ourselves on sharp rocks or twisted wires that rise from the muddy, uneven ground. Though it's a sunny morning, this place is dreary, as if shrouded in perpetual twilight.

Deheishe, so close to my home, is a truly alien world. The road we traverse is made of sand and stones, and has open sewers. We enter Mohammed's family room, which looks more like a chicken coop than a living space. Roger and I sit down on wooden milk cartons as Mohammed calls his family to join us. His home seems cagelike not only because of its small size, but also because one wall is knitted from wire strippings, which gives no protection from today's bitterly cold winds. Roger and I trade looks that say, *Oy vay,* are we up for this?

A young girl brings hot tea in glass cups, which we grab to warm our icy hands, and we all begin to talk. What at first looked purely gruesome and harsh begins to recede as we listen to Mohammed. He describes his years in and out of prison. His manner is severe, yet concentrated. During the first outbreak of the Intifada, he tells us, he was young, apolitical, just married. He was taking his bride to visit his older brother in Jordan when he was rounded up by Israeli soldiers in a group detainment. Those first months in prison have formed what he's become. "Prison was the university for the Intifada," he says. "Thirty of us were arrested together that first time. Just grabbed off the street. You see, the Israelis aren't certain who's a terrorist or who has maybe heard something, or knows someone who has heard something. So everyone is arrested. After lockup, you endure twenty-five days of terrifying torture. First we were exposed to unbearable heat, then extreme cold, and all the while our heads were draped under thick black hoods which blinded us during Israeli interrogations."

" 'Interrogation?' " He is repeating my question. "That means physical beatings, genital shocks. Soon, everyone goes delirious." He looks straight at me. "It's an experience you both can't believe you're living through, yet one you will never forget. In your madness you don't even know what you're saying. But by the time you get out of jail, if you weren't politically active in the first place, you are now. You know that Israeli domination is real, that you have to study this situation and fight for your people."

Roger and I are transported by Mohammed's calm clarity. As he speaks, his experience is etched into some essential part of me. Soon we're moving around the camp. By our third hour at Deheishe, we are glad to move on from this terrible, almost unbelievable story. A lively group of fifteen men gathers around us (the women are said to be "at market"). Together, we move from house to house. Some rooms are less grim than Mohammed's, decorated with calendars tacked onto their walls that show Swiss mountain scenes. At each home, we're given tours of the enlarged photographs of the family's dead "martyrs" (boys killed in the Intifada)—shrines adorned with thick black velvet sashes. We're shown windows shot through with old bullet holes. The adults are solemn as they show us signs of the toll the Intifada has taken, especially when standing beside altars honoring dead sons or brothers. Friendly children run in and out, excited by our presence.

In each room, we drink cups of sweet tea proffered with an urgency that is impossible to refuse. The tea is too sweet, but the cups warm our hands. Soon, we're all leaning forward in a conversation. The men are telling us that the Intifada, which began in 1987, has gone through distinct stages, and has even laid the groundwork for the current peace talks. "By 1990, we accepted that we must be open to talking with Israelis," one says. "If they aren't our cousins, at least they're our neighbors."

All the men are between twenty-four and forty. Each fits the physical stereotype of an Arab terrorist—black jackets, dark skin and thin bodies. What is it that so surprises me about these men? Their subtlety or their intelligence? Their easy bantering? Or how polite they are, not only to us but to each other? More than anything else, it's the communal feeling among them that surprises me. I'm thinking that I have to write about this.

By now, Roger and I are relaxed. We have entered and are sitting in one of the "upscale" homes, arguing about last June's Israeli elections. Each Palestinian is certain that Rabin is not interested in peace, that Israelis vote only with their pocketbooks. I argue that Rabin is different from Shamir, that many Israelis want real policy change, that there's reason for hope. As I say these words, there's a banging at the door. Conversation ceases. Four Israeli soldiers rush in, hands placed on their guns.

They storm around the room as we sit mutely. None of these soldiers seem like nephews, my best friends' kids or the neighbor's sons. They do not resemble the soldiers who casually walk around Jerusalem by day or loll about in groups on Ben Yehuda or King David Street every night. These four are tight-lipped and gruff. They arouse sheer terror—moving fast, emptying every closet, toppling the single bookcase in the room. They interrogate each of the men in Arabic. Now finished, they ask in English to see Roger's and my passports, which they study under a dim light. They return them with a look of suspicion. After confiscating the only book on the coffee table and flinging a mattress onto the floor, they're about to leave, but not before taking one last cold look at every face in the room. The sequence proves Mohammed's point:

that the form "Jewish" takes in this place and time is, for the Palestinians, demonic and abusive—exactly what we Jews do not believe ourselves to be.

"What have we turned into—the Germans?" Roger hisses under his breath, a comment that, in the context of this room, is an association that's possible for any Jew. When the soldiers left, they issued a stern warning that they'd be back soon. My heart is still racing when one soldier does return. He rechecks Roger's passport. As he walks toward me, I tell him I'm a journalist. I try to convey that I'm Jewish, just in case they're planning to blow up this place. But how do I let him know that I'm Jewish without words, words that would enrage my new acquaintances? As the soldier again slams out the warped door, I realize that who we are is utterly irrelevant to him. I'm shaking: Why were they so rough? Perhaps they were desperate to find a terrorist operating somewhere in this camp. Maybe they had a tip that a Deheishe resident was building a bomb? It's possible that their attitude was warranted. But whatever their reasons, I tremble for half an hour while the men try to calm me. It's clear that they're accustomed to these intrusions.

By December, I've become an old hand at visiting Palestinians. Following my talk with Riad Maliki, with the editor and boys in Nablus, and the men at Deheishe, I've interviewed Hanan Ashwari (who's just hired Rula as her assistant!) in Ramallah and visited well-known intellectuals in East Jerusalem. I've sat for long hours with elderly, melancholy refugees in camps as they fold and unfold faded handkerchiefs that hold decrepit keys they claim are to their original homes in Jaffa, Haifa and Jerusalem. Daily, I've tasted the varieties of Palestinian consciousness: sweetness, depression, generosity, cunning, frustration, along with the more predictable black hate that fills some hearts. When the hate doesn't numb me, I begin to glimpse several reasons for it.

I'm stunned when my Israeli friends dismiss my reports. Shuki doesn't even let me finish a sentence. Daphie and Shimon shake their heads, as if they can't fathom how I've allowed myself to be duped so easily. Virtually everyone I know refuses to believe that Palestinians are not necessarily the furious, taunting kids televised nightly. They insist I'm getting a "cleaned-up" tour, not being shown "real" Arabs, the violent ones who terrorize our soldiers. My impressions and anecdotes are scoffed at.

"You don't understand the Arabs," my neighbor Moshe Ben-Ami, a veteran of many Israeli wars, barks at me.

"Of course I don't. I don't pretend to. I'm just trying to tell you about my day," I answer. But he's already pointing to the morning's daily paper *Yediot Ahronot* (Israel's version of the *New York Post*). His hands shake as he unfurls a color photo that covers three quarters of the front page. "You see that picture?" I nod. It shows one Arab shooting another at close range in Gaza. The murdered man's head is blowing off backward, accentuated by bright red ink which gives the killing a grisly, sensational, in-your-face quality. "That's the Arab mentality!" Ben-Ami shouts, shaking his head. "They kill each other. How can they make peace with us?"

His adult sons circle around us to shout at me about the latest political crime against us Jews. Are they trying to convince or to protect me? I wonder. They're describing a violent faction of Palestinians, a new group called the Hamas. They've just kidnaped and then mutilated an Israeli border guard, Sergeant Nissim Toledano, who has become the latest Israeli victim and the newest rallying point for Israeli rage in this round of spiraling violence. Toledano's death cements the mistrust that is central to life here. The murder in Gaza and the fate of the border guard define most Israelis' views of the Palestinians. I have been meeting many other people who live in the territories. I suggest that one murder or kidnaping doesn't represent an entire population of two million. My neighbors turn from jokes about Arabs to jokes about me.

"You know," I say, "whether or not you admit it, that there's a huge difference between media images and direct dialogue. You know that because you become furious when news of Israel is skewed, when we're given unfair, bad press."

My arguments are futile. Everyone seems resolutely deaf. For a while I persist. I describe self-disclosure as liberating; I reiterate that listening to Palestinians and being heard isn't that hard. "Many are friendly, hospitable, even astute."

"You shouldn't be anywhere near the territories" is the rejoinder. "You think you're safe, but you're not." "They're crazy." And, most often: "You're just so naive."

My Israeli friends seem to want to view our Arab neighbors as uniform, a stance they can hold only from a distance where it's easy to maintain certainties. I've been keeping copious notes of my days in the West Bank, beginning with (and largely because of) Mohammed, whom I trust, and whose truthfulness was confirmed that day in Deheishe when Israeli soldiers broke into the room.

Yet often I'm afraid—far more than I admit to my friends. I know they'd use my fears as proof for their views. It's only to Sara that I talk freely and at length. She acts fearless, going daily into Gaza or the West Bank. Yet she, too, has many bad moments and, especially when caught in a cross fire, admits that she's often terrified.

The morning of December 4, 1992, I'm back on the road to Nablus with Achmed and Roger. Today we're not in an Arab rental car, but in my small blue Renault, with yellow license plates, signifying that we're Israeli Jews. Achmed is at the wheel, and we follow his instructions to slowly navigate the winding rural roads that connect Jerusalem to Nablus. He tells us to hang our arms out the window, to remove sunglasses that are associated with high-level Israeli army officers and, most important, to leave our right blinker on at all times. These signs show solidarity with the Intifada and are essential when driving a "Jewish" car into the territories. We've spread two kaffiyehs across the front dashboard and placed an Arabic sign (I can never remember which side goes up) across our back window. Even with these props, I feel vulnerable and am searching the roadside for signs of trouble.

Today, Israeli families will be welcomed by Palestinian strangers into their homes. A large contingent from both sides will meet face-to-face for the first time. Achmed describes this as central to the dialogue method. Roger is familiar with the work of these dialogue groups. He says that even though those involved are a tiny minority, they're fiercely committed to spreading their work, to encouraging more people on both sides to talk to each other.

"In between two tragedies," he says, "they're trying to create a space." This phrase sounds lovely and so I write it down on my pad. Nablus is only an hour-plus drive, but it's a trip into another world of meanings. We're now surrounded only by cars with blue (Arab) license plates. It's well known that the obstacles to peace come from extremists on both sides, and that Nablus is home to many of them. A Jew driving deep into the territories is pried loose from all safe moorings. Yet because so much propaganda here is passed off as information no one can distinguish what's truly dangerous from what's not. Given the possibilities, I have decided the risk is worthwhile. Or so I try to convince myself as we arrive at Al-Najah University, a campus on a hill in Nablus.

The parking lot is empty. We pull in and walk into the meeting hall, where huge crowds are expected, only to be greeted by the news that the buses and TV crews never left Jerusalem. The three of us sit down in the near-empty auditorium surrounded by fifteen Palestinian organizers; each is shaking with emotion. One man says, "We can't believe no one showed up." Another adds, "Do you realize some of us have worked eighty hours a week since July on this peace conference? We selected those families most hurt by the occupation and the Intifada, ones who've suffered deaths or losses, both Jewish and Arab."

"So much work. All down the drain," says Sami Kilani, a middle-aged man who introduces himself as a member of the Palestinian peace delegation to Washington.

"What happened?" I ask. The organizers take turns explaining that Israel's civil administration, which monitors Nablus, called off the event last night, at the last possible moment. "They said it was unsafe for any Jew to travel into Nablus without military escort today. That is an idea we totally reject. The whole concept of this Dialogue Day was to show Israelis, and the whole world, that even in Nablus it's one hundred percent safe for Israelis to visit without military 'protection.' But the Israeli authorities countered that because a Palestinian boy blew himself up yesterday in a refugee camp nearby while concocting a bomb, it's too dangerous for the group to come. As though one man represents our huge community."

Hearing the word "bomb," I become suspicious again. "Why did you want to talk to these Israelis?" I ask another man. "We want to put an end to the mistrust between us," says Samir Yaish, a slim, handsome man who turns out to be a professor of literature and a poet. "We need to show them our hopes, aspirations and humanity. And we need to see theirs. We want to live in a just peace. That means doing everything possible to break the ice between our two populations. Now, both sides live in hatred. We're sure we can cut through that wall, but only by listening to each other directly. That's what we've been doing regularly these last few years with the Israeli facilitators, our good friends. It's lethal to hear each other only through media distortions or from our so-called political leaders."

Samir invites us to his house. We see his dining room table is elegantly set for visitors. The handwoven tablecloth with matching linen napkins is a poignant sight. The Yaish house fills up with disappointed Nablus families, who have also prepared food in anticipation of hosting their Israeli guests. I learn that these Palestinians, most of whom have served long jail terms, are now as pro-dialogue as they were once rabidly pro-violence. Achmed leans toward me. "This is like a bad dream. You make a beautiful vision, and then it gets smashed. Today's event was as important as Madrid."

I look around the room at all these smiling faces and I know that some were active terrorists in the 1960s and 1970s. I'm introduced to two women, Mariam and Rawda. Mariam is thin and missing several front teeth; Rawda, heavyset, is cheerful. In fact, both women are radiant. I soon learn that they've spent eight and ten years, respectively, locked in Israeli prisons. I don't ask them why, though I wonder. They seem less affected by this cancellation than the men. As the Yaish house fills up with more Palestinians, each expresses gratitude that we came, saying politely (always politely) how disappointed they are that this long-planned meeting was canceled. "We're so glad you came," Rawda repeats, beaming at Roger and me. I'm glad, too, especially when, within an hour, four Israeli organizers arrive from Jerusalem.

Soon we're all sitting around Samir and Netiz Yaish's table. I become aware

of the strong friendships between the Palestinian leaders and their Israeli counterparts, most of whom, I'm surprised to learn, are observant Jews. This is my
first encounter with any Israeli Rapprochement organizers. One of them, Judith Green, who is sitting to my right, begins quietly telling me about herself
and her group. Thin and serious, she is a trained archaeologist. She tells me
that she made *aliyah* twenty years ago and then she points out Veronica Cohen, an unusually outgoing woman with a buoyant face and a sunny smile. Judith says that Veronica, the only child of two Holocaust survivors, is an
activist, too. She adds that Veronica is a musician and a professor who, like
herself, is Orthodox, except, as Judith points out, Veronica always keeps her
head covered. We look over to see her in a large red hat, engaged in an animated conversation with several of the Palestinians.

Two other organizers, Alison Ha'oz and Hillel Bardin, seem deflated. Each
is wearing a Rapprochement T-shirt stamped with their slogan—in Hebrew,
Arabic and English—"We Want a Just Peace. Between Israel and Palestine.
Each Free and Secure." Hillel is slender and seems to be in his mid-fifties; Alison's age is harder to gauge. Both seem terribly upset by today's cancellation.
Hillel gives the group a pep talk, tries to cheer up the Palestinians and, in the
process, cheers himself. He explains in what ways there has been progress,
then suggests concrete reasons for hope.

As ornate desserts are served, I find myself wishing that those Israeli newcomers on the bus had found a way to get up here to Nablus. Later, as we head
home, Roger says, "Imagine if we had been on those buses this morning and
were told by the Israeli authorities that the territories were in upheaval, that it
was too risky for us to come today. How would we have felt?" "Grateful," we
acknowledge, "and protected," one of us says, realizing that the most menacing images of Arabs would have been reinforced had we stayed behind. We feel
lucky.

In Jerusalem, we learn that Rabin has just taken action in response to the
killing of Sergeant Toledano. He's rounded up 415 "Hamas leaders" and deported them with no notice. Their plight fills the international news in an
episode known as "The Expulsion of the Hamas 415." Rabin's action seems
counterproductive. Rather than dividing Palestinians into their separate factions, the expulsions bring them into a rare unity and create worldwide sympathy for their cause.

A few days later I drive with Manal (Achmed is visiting friends in Vienna)
the few miles to Bethlehem, a "stone's throw" from Jerusalem. We park, then
wander up and down curving hills trying to locate the address we were given.
As usual, Manal stops and chats with kids of all ages until we finally make our

way to the home of a woman whom Hakam has identified as the wife of one of the Hamas deportees.

All I can see are her glaring eyes, stonily fixed on me. Though Manal tries to work her charms on this woman (whose head is wound tight in a clean white scarf), she doesn't budge, not physically nor emotionally. Ever-seductive Manal cannot get her to relax. There's been a glitch. This woman wasn't notified that we were coming. As a result, she's wary, treating me as if I'm an Israeli spy. Without her willingness to relax, her fears become contagious. Try as I do, I cannot let down my guard, but become increasingly stiff. My rigidity only fuels this woman's worst fears. The more she stares harshly at me, the more anxious I become, and vice versa. Finally, she tears off a piece of paper from an envelope on her table and hands it to Manal, instructing her in Arabic that I must write down the name of the newspaper I'm working for.

I've contracted to do an article on the deportations for a magazine with a Hebrew name. But in this setting, I'm not about to write a single Hebrew word (I've told every other Palestinian I've interviewed that I'm Jewish). Self-disclosure is out of the question in this room. I pluck the words "The American Wing." I then write them down, as officially as possible, and say these words aloud a few times in hopes of conveying, not Jewish; I am definitely not Jewish.

The wife nods. Now I can ask questions. But I find it hard to muster creative inquiries in this strained atmosphere. Through Manal, I ask cursorily about her husband, his activism, her feelings toward his work and especially about his sudden forced departure. She states proudly that he's a militant working to destroy "that Zionist entity."

Driving home, Manal and I settle into an easy, post-interview analysis. Both of us wonder aloud why this past hour felt as endless as it was uninformative. I say I understand why even peace-loving Israelis feel hopeless about the Hamas. Manal replies, "You have your extremists; we have ours. Shouldn't we each handle our own?"

I find it impossible to hold onto the Palestinian and Israeli viewpoints at the same time. It's like trying to see both a vase and a face simultaneously in a Gestalt double image. Lying in bed, I'm glad to be home, seduced into letting the whole mess recede, to return to being Jewish in a Jewish world. I can, after all, leave "the Palestinian problem" to the army, the media, the Israeli government. Many Jews here believe that the Palestinians' problems are of their own making. They reason that since Israel holds all the cards and is the dominant power, it can do as it wants—that it's up to the Palestinians to make the necessary compromises, to learn to respect Israeli power. Of course, I could argue the exact opposite—that power necessitates largesse. But I don't. Because in Jewish Jerusalem, the occupation is invisible.

Though Arabs are everywhere on the streets—as gardeners, construction workers, cleaning women—in the year and a half since I've moved here, I've seen no ethnic clashes. There's less generalized fear and anxiety on these streets than in any other big city I know (New York, Boston, London). Children walk unescorted to school, to ballet classes or grocery stores. Seven-year-olds navigate buses alone. Kidnapings, danger, murders: virtually none.

It's a week since the deportation crisis began as I watch CNN. There, to my surprise, the expelled Hamas leaders revert to one-dimensional stick figures in my mind. I see their beards and makeshift tents, and hear them spouting angry anti-Israel rhetoric; they seem simply enemies of our state. The mainstream media don't help any of us to hold onto complexity. In between our two cultures' tragic pasts, members on both sides, as Roger has said, are valiantly trying to create a space in between, an opening for dialogue. But this does not appear on television.

Through the eyes of the media, the Palestinian narrative evaporates for me, while the Israeli plight grows more vivid. With Achmed out of the country, without access to his soft voice and quiet pain, I fall under the Israeli spell and forget why these expulsions are morally wrong. That they're strategically dangerous remains clear, though not to most around me.

In polls, 91 percent of Israelis are confident that Palestinian rage will blow over and that Israel will be safer for these deportations. On the streets, in restaurants, on buses and in cafes, I hear Israelis of every political stripe, class and age group say that these expulsions will further peace and security. The horror that this act has aroused among Palestinians—rage, fear, more solidarity and no doubt more terrorists—is lost on most Israelis. That Palestinians are hardening their hearts in reaction to the deportations, ever more certain that Israel is *only* brutal and *always* unfair, is also ignored.

Achmed calls. He's just returned from Vienna. "Tomorrow is an important day," he says. "You must come. This, you can't miss." So, on a clear January morning, we drive up and down mountain roads toward the Palestinian campus of Bir Zeit, a university located north of Jerusalem with an activist student population. We pull into the parking lot along with five or six thousand Palestinian students and professors. Soon, they flood the halls to hear a speech from Dr. Haidar Abdel Shafi. He's the grandfatherly physician from Gaza, widely revered among his people, who was head of the Palestinian peace delegation in Madrid. His talk focuses on the necessity for Palestinian unity against Israel.

Achmed translates as Dr. Shafi urges all Palestinians to reject the peace talks, begun in Madrid, now moved to Washington, D.C., taking place in intermittent rounds. His voice rises as he contends that the Israelis have yielded nothing, *absolutely nothing* after fifteen months, and suggests that Palestinians join together in a boycott. "The Israelis are intransigent," he says. "They refuse to understand our people's situation. So I tell you, *I implore you,* to reject this rotten process, at least until our men, stranded cruelly between our homeland and Lebanon, are returned."

These sentiments, greeted by jeers of agreement from all around me, are the last words that Achmed translates. Uncharacteristically, he disappears into the packed crowd. I look, but can't see him. I realize how cool he's been to me all day. Usually we hug warmly, then talk easily, sharing details of our personal lives before we even broach politics. But today he hardly spoke at all, gave no hug, not even a smile. He was remote the entire ride up here. Only once he mumbled something about how defeated the deportations make him feel.

Without our usual trust, without even being able to spot him among the Arabs who crush and overflow the halls of Bir Zeit, I find the crowd purely menacing. Then I remember that this is the campus where an American professor was murdered a few months ago. The details escape me. Was he Jewish? I can't recall. Shoved about by students who are trying to get closer to the loudspeakers, I finally glimpse Achmed. Taking notes on the talk, he's facing away from me.

I sit in a corner and open my notebook. Since I don't understand Arabic, I begin taking notes on my mood. As the shouts and jeers escalate, I become too frightened to look up. Without Achmed by my side, all those Israeli stories of Arab violence whistle through my mind.

Hostage-taking occurs here. I haven't followed Sara's advice; I haven't rented a cell phone. I didn't call her. No one knows where I am today. As I keep writing, I picture being pulled away and flung into a waiting van. Maybe it's Achmed who's plotted something sinister, I think. It's impossible to stem this sudden flood of suspicion. The sweetness of dialogue in Nablus, that day of mutual mirroring I've extolled, is fading fast. When I force myself to look around me, I find the Arabs as frightening as when I first moved to Israel. No one is smiling. I imagine a subtext afloat in these crowded halls: Kill a Jew. Then I imagine that my Jewishness is written all over my face. As the loudspeakers continue to amplify Dr. Shafi's Arabic speech, a loud siren of fear envelops me. I am glued to the floor, writing in my journal, checking my watch, longing to get out of here. I can't recall why I've been attracted to hanging out on this borderland where Jewish history, what I embody today, meets Arab history, as embodied by this crowd. I catch another glimpse of Achmed. He still doesn't check on or look around for me. He hasn't given one reassuring glance in over an hour—most unlike him. Instead, I begin checking *him* out; my mind is working overtime. Why was he so intent on bringing me here today? Why did he pitch this speech as so important and then stop translating it? And mostly, what do I really know about him?

In the jostling crowd, someone accidentally brushes against him and the sheets of thin white stationery he's been writing on float toward the floor. I scramble to help him retrieve his notes. And there, on one sheet of paper, written in English—all else is in Arabic—are the words "An American Jew."

My head is spinning as I hand him back the pages. Why would he write these words? To whom else could this phrase possibly refer? Is this the note he's about to pass to waiting terrorists ready to drag me into their van with blue license plates?

Finally Achmed comes for me and we find his car and drive away from Bir Zeit. With only a few stones thrown at us, we're back in East Jerusalem, where we go to an underground cafe, order a meal and begin talking for hours.

We two are now living out the essential paradox between our peoples. We can move against this war only by moving toward trust and friendship, by keeping the channels of communication open across ethnicity. Yet, any incipient trust that's "merely personal" is vulnerable to being crushed by powerful collective forces. Things improve over dinner that includes a great Arabic dessert. But mistrust lingers as well. I haven't recovered from seeing that note. I keep trying to ask him about it, but have no idea how to word my question. What can I possibly say?

Instead, we talk of plans for the coming days. Achmed wants to return to Nablus tomorrow, to begin touring Gaza on Friday. He'll set up meetings with members of the peace delegation. If we have time—he's thinking out loud—we can visit the spot where the Intifada began in Gaza. He has close relatives there. I'm so thrilled to be alive and away from Bir Zeit that whatever he suggests sounds plausible and I nod in agreement. But the next morning I awake knowing that I'm in no shape to reenter the West Bank. Overnight, there were shootings at Israeli cars in Nablus. Achmed keeps calling, switching ideas about which rental car is safest for us to drive. Finally I tell him that I can't go anywhere today and quickly hang up the phone.

CHAPTER SEVEN

Shifting Landscapes:
Four Days in May

In the aftermath of the deportation crisis, the streets are flooded with fear. The Palestinians support their leaders' refusal to return to the Washington peace talks. In Gaza and the West Bank, children are being killed by Israeli soldiers daily. In March, thirteen Israelis are murdered by Palestinian extremists as a "reprisal." This violence creates the new round of self-fulfilling prophecies, though both sides have much to lose by losing the Madrid-Washington talks.

And then the fortuitous occurs: Rabin relents and allows Faisal Husseini, a Palestinian from East Jerusalem, into the official peace delegation; Arafat, in Tunis, then agrees to continue with the Washington rounds. Rabin makes another goodwill gesture: Thirty Palestinian exiles, all deported twenty-four years ago for membership in the PLO, are allowed back home. Relatively speaking, these are small moves, yet they symbolize a political thaw.

I study the May 2 front-page photos in all the Israeli newspapers. Each shows joyous reunions between the first fifteen long-exiled with their families and friends. Here's evidence of a new cycle of generosity being set into motion. Though the territories have been closed for weeks because of the murdered Israelis, on Monday, May 3, I head down to Jericho with my press pass, along with Hakam and Achmed, who has laughed at my scary version of his note. We're going to witness the last returnees.

For those of us who went on peace and civil rights demonstrations in America in the sixties, the crowd here may seem modest. But for the three to five thousand Palestinians traveling into Jericho from all over the West Bank—cramming into buses, vans, cars and taxis, free to wave Palestinian flags and carry enlarged photos of Arafat on posters—today represents the end of a hopeless era, the beginning of a better one. "You have to understand," Achmed says, "for the last twenty years, carrying a small flag or a miniature photo of

Arafat hidden in a back pocket could cost anyone seven years in prison. *This* is new." He gazes around in wonder, seeing how this gesture from the Israelis has shifted the emotional tenor.

Unlike Achmed, Hakam remains dubious. The intellectuals in the crowd are most skeptical, are less the leaders than the led, for the jubilation of the "ordinary" people is propelling the rest of us into seductive rejoicing. Hakam keeps shaking his head. "It's a con," he says. "These returnees. Who are they? Not vigorous or young. Is there one Nelson Mandela among them?" he asks. "This is just safe symbolism for the Israelis." Even if he's right, it's impossible to ignore the energy of the celebrants around us; impossible, for me, to distance from this collective hope. Euphoria encircles us as we pull into Jericho, as close as we can get to the Allenby Bridge, over which the final fifteen returnees will soon arrive.

A Japanese journalist and I sit in the town square, miniature tape recorders in hand. We try to interview Dr. Nazim Al Jubeh, a member of the peace delegation. The chanting around us is so thunderous that we're forced to move from bench to bench merely to hear him. He leans forward to explain that the outpouring of optimism today *is* warranted, even if ordinary Palestinians don't understand the intricacies in Washington. Dr. Jubeh believes his people rightly intuit that progress is being made, that real peace is to begin. There will be a Palestinian state, he's sure, and sure that the days of Shamir's stalling are gone forever.

Yes, he agrees, these returnees are not, in themselves, powerful. But this gesture is, especially with the Americans pushing Arab countries toward a Marshall Plan for the occupied territories, encouraging an influx of funds for new life in the "autonomous zones." The Palestinian families getting reunited will quiet the Hamas, Dr. Jubeh says, for extremists also react to every gesture—for or against—their people. That Palestinians are being given respect by Israel is a fact that isn't lost on his constituents.

Other journalists join us as we watch many hundreds more converge, congesting the rural roads, adding volume to the chanting and singing. All are waving flags with abandon. Just when the town feels saturated, more arrive. Dr. Jubeh departs to go to a meeting. After he leaves, the Japanese journalist speaks quietly about World War II, of the depth of hatred the Japanese felt toward Americans. He reflects how in his lifetime, "we in Japan went from total enmity to active emulation of Americans."

According to the press wires, the returnees are due at 2 P.M. Already it's three. The exiled are sure to arrive at any minute. We can't go directly to the Allenby Bridge (minutes to our south), but Jericho is so tightly packed that we're instructed to drive north into an old refugee camp ("a real bad one," Hakam remarks), what's now an abandoned field, the size of a large stadium.

The Israeli Defense Forces (IDF) aren't swarming around this road or the field either. They've withdrawn to survey the crowds from nearby rooftops. The few who are visible direct traffic. This shift in the usual power arrangements is so sudden that it's surreal. I listen as Hakam, whose Hebrew is perfect, argues with an Israeli soldier over where we will park. In seconds, the two are screaming at fever pitch, exactly like equals. Finally, it's Hakam, the Palestinian, who wins; we park where he wants. The Israeli soldiers must be under strict orders.

But what do these soldiers, who are trained to be on razor-edge alert around any large group of Arabs, think? What do they observe as they scan these crowds and see hugging and chatting; men and women sharing water, Coca-Cola, cigarettes?

Mariam, one of the first women I met in Nablus, comes and hugs me, then grabs my arm. Smiling her luminous, toothless grin, she urges me to meet Shahab Shaheen, one of the first returnees, a woman who was bused over the Allenby Bridge four days ago, plucked, with little warning, from her long exile in Amman. In a far corner of this field, Shahab stands perfectly erect, as if surrounded by invisible Plexiglas. Quietly composed, she's observing the crowd. I move beside her, but sense that she doesn't want to speak. Mariam is prodding me to "talk to her; interview her." Then she leaves as I sneak sideways glances at this returnee. We stand mutely together, facing the jubilant crowd. I glimpse her starched black blazer, generous brown hair sprayed perfectly in place, a thin line of purple eyeliner expertly applied. This elegance gives Shahab a stern profile, in contrast to the majority here who are wearing torn clothes and shabby, if any, shoes. Finally I work up the courage to ask her how she feels. Her response is to take my hand and hold it, remaining silent. I watch her study this generation of Intifada kids she's never met. I soon see tears falling down her cheek. I'll later learn her story and all that was going on for her today. For now, we continue squeezing hands while gazing at the raucous landscape.

•　•　•

"Good word, 'sweetness,'" Robert says in response to my offhand observation about the Palestinians. He is a TV anchorman, a household face. Though we've never met, we wander off to talk in private. It's after 4 P.M. Most of the other journalists, photographers, cameramen and writers have moved outside the field and are sitting on rocks along the main dirt road. They're scanning for the bus, expected hours ago. Robert, also Jewish, also American, covered the

Lebanon War, was once stationed in Cairo and also reported from Northern Ireland before coming to Tel Aviv.

"Off the record," he mumbles, "I'd love to be out of here." During the Lebanon War he was fully disabused about Israel as a "light unto nations," he says. "I saw our own people as thugs, as base in their motives as any other thugs." He is bitter and weary. "This might be the year of the breakthrough. But my heart isn't in this place anymore."

His viewpoint is not unusual for those journalists who grew up in Zionist households, and believed in an idealized Israel, which then became tarnished here. A tough-looking type in uniform pushes roughly between us as if to prove Robert's point—that some Israelis are interested only in a show of power. Busily locking up a small wire gate, he's making an empty gesture. The fence nearby is trampled down. Locked or open, no one is going to use this gate. Robert gives him a horrified look. He says, "Why is that idiot busy working at a completely useless task?"

No one else pays him any attention until our potbellied captain, bedecked with medals, shouts in Hebrew for everyone to back off. We move toward the road backward, staring at him and his tight, angry face. We agree that he's the portrait of the worst Israeli attitude. Robert mutters, "I grew up thinking Israel was redemption, but this is degradation. If you see Zionism as tribalism, eventually you have to say to yourself, Maybe creating a Jewish state was not a good idea." I am reeling from these harsh words but luckily I do not have to respond because an Arab Israeli Knesset member, Ahmed Tibi, is approaching us. Elated to spot Robert, he enthuses, "I just returned from Washington, spoke with the higher-ups; the Americans are pushing things along. Peace is coming." This is a popular phrase today.

Under the strain of all these strong opinions and the long wait, I become aware of the heat. Achmed takes a long look at us fanning ourselves on rocks that dot the dirt road. He disappears and reappears carrying bottled water and grape soda which are passed around. Everyone has grown irritable in the heat. Even Manal's lively optimism is gone. She who remained cheerful during the dark days of the deportations says, "Where the hell are they?" She's speaking for us all, inhabiting a mood that contrasts with those still dancing inside the field.

It's four-thirty. Perhaps our relation to time is self-indulgent, I think, watching those who have collectively done so many years in prison, who've waited decades for such a day. What's a few hours, more or less, for them?

And now we see, arriving by foot down the main road, not the bus with the returning Palestinians, but a small group of extremist Jewish settlers. Marching directly toward us, they're carrying huge posters with the word "Kach" written on them (the name of a far-right militia group). As they come closer we see that they're carrying yellow helium balloons, hand-printed with thick black Stars of David. They let these fly. The crowd sees impending danger.

The eight Jewish fanatics position themselves a few feet from us as those in the field surge, as if with one body, toward the road, shouting, "Settlers!" while Hakam sarcastically mutters, "Perfect." We see the long barrels of the settlers' rifles pointing up. Round after round of shots reverberate as bullets burst toward the sky.

The crowd rushes at the settlers. I dash the other way, trying to get as far as possible from this hair-raising confrontation. Racing into the parking lot, I feel weak in my legs; my heart is beating hard. Hakam's hand is soon on my elbow. "Hell, we can't miss this," he says, pulling me back.

Only a few feet from the Kach settlers, journalists are talking among themselves: "Who allowed this?" "The army had to know they were coming!" "Why are settlers free to wander here?" they're asking, while the IDF, so peripheral all afternoon, begin swooping down the main road in bulky military tanks and trucks. They stop in front of us, blocking our view of the settlers. Behind us, the Palestinians have formed into battalions; each line moves toward the road. The Israeli soldiers climb onto their tanks and trucks, trying to separate the two groups. "This could be a massacre," an Israeli says.

"Not with the international press here," Hakam answers, straining for a view of the settlers. "The IDF can't afford a conflagration, even if they provoked it."

The soldiers talk to the settlers and within minutes Kach posters are seen drifting down the road, visible under a bright blue sky. Immediately, the Palestinians return to the field, to their singing and chanting. But the Israeli soldiers on top of their huge green tanks stay put. Not one budges. Each keeps a rifle, Uzi or shotgun pointed directly into the Palestinian crowd, as if the commotion arose there rather than instigated by the settlers. To my amazement, the soldiers remain in place for the next hour. And still, the bus with the returnees is nowhere in sight. "It makes me furious," a native Israeli writer, a child of Auschwitz survivors, says vehemently. "The Israelis do this on purpose. Why else do they keep the exiled for so many hours? Why else point guns at these people? It's a pure show of power. Look at them," she adds in disgust. They *have* killed the innocence of this day. Most of the press now believe that the delay, the settlers and the IDF guns are meant to create conditions for a riot. Too stunned to think at all, I'm holding Achmed's arm and shaking.

"It *could* have been a massacre," Robert says.

"Someone is doing a good job of disciplining these crowds," Manal observes.

"I told you, it's a con. And Israelis can't even pull off an empty gesture with finesse," Hakam retorts while most of the journalists check their watches. The arrival was scheduled for 2 P.M.; it's after six. "They just couldn't allow them in on time. Israelis have to distort anything they give, to show who's boss around here. We know the Allenby Bridge is only ten minutes away." An Israeli photographer says, "We won't get good photographs during a glaring sunset or after dark." I see those in the field are refusing to be distracted by Israeli machinations.

Finally, in the distance we spot the yellow bus. It's crawling down the road. It chugs into the parking lot at 6:45. By now, I'm infected with the prevailing view and am thinking, "They chose 6:45 because they knew the sun would blind us and ruin the photographs."

The Israeli soldiers have returned to nearby rooftops; the crowd is rushing to greet the returnees. The rest of us are captivated by aging men and women stepping haltingly down the steep bus steps. They are well groomed and weak, shielding the sun from their eyes as they scout for a familiar face.

"Who's this one?" "Who's that?" journalists shout to organizers, notepads open. The Palestinians shrug. "They were deported when I was a young child," Samir Yaish, the poet from Nablus, says wistfully. Only the youngest among us continue bellowing a welcome to the dazed exiles who are struggling to find friends or family. As soon as a loved one is found, there are kisses, tears, fierce emotions. We are all included. I am literally caught up in two long, tangled kaffiyehs. Two old men weep as they embrace each other, accidentally hugging me as well. I feel their tears on my hair, the strong grip of their arms encircling me.

• • •

Early the next morning I open the *Jerusalem Post* and read a feature story which says, "No Jewish patriot watching photographs of Arafat floating through Jericho's streets yesterday could feel anything but revulsion at what's being unleashed in the name of peace." I read this sentence over, wondering what planet I inhabit or what set of assumptions this right-wing paper labors under. I call Information and find a listing for another *Post* writer, Jon Immanuel, a friend of Sara's. He's recently been assigned to cover Palestinian affairs. I reach him and say that I've followed his coverage and would love to talk to him. We make a date to meet for breakfast in an hour. Waiting in West Jerusalem's YMCA's cafe, I remember how often he's credited, by Israelis and Palestinians alike, for giving fair, factual accounts.

We're meeting for the first time, but after only several minutes I feel an emotion more suitable to sitting with a cousin. Jon is good-looking and straightforward. Originally from England, he made *aliyah* twenty years ago with his wife, Anna, a writer from New Jersey. They have four sabra kids. Though we connect easily, once we turn to politics we discover differences. Whereas I tend toward impressionistic, intuitive reactions, Jon is meticulous and focused on specific details. He seems to define levelheaded. *He's* certainly not under any illusions about Palestinian "sweetness." He says that he pins all hopes for a resolution on a "political settlement." Until one is signed, if ever (he sighs), he believes that Israel acts from fair motives.

"Our security is paramount," he says. Referring to human rights, he adds, "It's in the nature of occupation that you lose them." I ask if dominating the Palestinians doesn't lead to excesses of Israeli violence. He responds carefully, "But don't you see? We always have to show them that their stones will not work. We must be sure *never* to legitimize *any* violence against us. Even the 'open fire' policy in the territories, what the Supreme Court has made legal, along with 'minimum torture,' has a just rationale. The Palestinians must learn that they will *never* win anything with brutality."

I ask about the long delay yesterday. He gives the Israeli viewpoint, which he shares: that it's critical for Israelis to let Palestinians know that under no circumstances will they be lax. That's why each Palestinian returning yesterday, without exception, had to be checked over carefully. "Those men and women were searched and scrutinized with a fine-toothed comb. How else can we know who's carrying weapons? Human rights! That's pittance when you think about terrorism," he says.

He, too, was surprised at the high energy of yesterday's crowds. "For them the word 'return,' which in Arabic is *auder,* is analogous to *aliyah* for us," Jon says. "It's the most charged word in the Palestinian lexicon. That's why there was such euphoria." He pauses, adding, "Sometimes I think it's lucky most Israelis and Palestinians don't understand each other's most charged symbols. In the best-case scenario, such misunderstandings can be exploited so that each side will give concessions neither realizes are so impactful."

I tell Jon that one prominent journalist has said he's fallen into a mild version of Stockholm syndrome—of identifying with the enemy.

Jon shrugs. He's in no danger of mixed loyalties. "I expect human rights abuses," he states matter-of-factly. "I certainly don't tear my hair out over them. By and large, I've yet to see an Israeli soldier act with undue brutality. I've seen Israelis acting disrespectful, with arrogance, humiliating the Palestinians. But outright violence? No, that I haven't seen."

I wonder if believing is seeing in this part of the world, rather than the other way around. Other Israeli journalist friends have described plenty of direct, gratuitous Israeli brutality.

"You think I'm cold-blooded?" Jon asks, concerned.

"I don't know what to think," I say, "except that many disagree with you." Two days ago one Israeli journalist who's been covering Gaza for two years described in excruciating detail seeing Israeli troops pick off Palestinians through a magnified sniper lens, while in no danger themselves—not a rock was thrown their way. He watched five soldiers standing on a rooftop and laughing, as they shot and wounded fourteen Gazan kids "in only half an hour." I tell Jon this man said such incidents are underreported or censored since they don't conform to Israel's official rationale.

He listens attentively, as if processing what I say. I wonder if I've been too much under the sway of the Palestinian view lately. Jon checks his watch and asks if I'm free to travel with him to Bethlehem and Ramallah this afternoon. He has a story to write.

I ask which Palestinian is his escort. Jon looks at me blankly. "None," he says, "I always travel alone." I tell him I'm used to being accompanied by Achmed or others who have extended clan connections, which gives me protection. I'm not at all sure that an unescorted trip is wise. Yet, despite my wariness, by 1 P.M., the two of us are tooling around the winding back roads that connect Bethlehem to Ramallah, a stretch about which Jon will file his report.

For now, this back road is the only way for Palestinians to travel. Since the recent closure, roadblocks on the main highway are heavily manned, deterring most Palestinians from taking that route. They've resorted to this road, one that Jon has never seen. As we drive, he tells me how closures are intended to create complete division of Palestinians in the territories from Jewish and Arab Israelis, who've lived inside Israel proper since 1948. Closures always create terrible economic hardships for Palestinians, he says, but this one, curiously, has been welcomed by both sides: Israelis feel less paranoia on their streets, Jon says, while Palestinians view this tight separation as a tangible sign that Rabin recognizes two "lands."

We talk of this as Jon swerves around magnificent curving roads that lie between mountain ranges. This region is so undeveloped that the views look biblical. We follow a trail that twists through tiny villages. We pass old Arab men on donkeys, then mosques and occasional churches. Jon's car has yellow (Israeli) license plates; we have no kaffiyeh, rosary beads or Arabic signs to adorn his car. For me, this is a first. We're obviously Israelis, yet we're completely without safeguards. My inclination to panic is exacerbated by Jon's running commentary. He details which Jews were murdered where in this area, pointing out exact spots, giving dates. I'm busy calculating our chances, spinning out worst-possible scenarios.

Yet whenever we stop to ask for directions, even though Jon's Arabic is comically hesitant and makes those we talk to laugh, each Palestinian is glad to give us accurate information. We don't encounter a harsh look during our three-hour drive. On the contrary, each pedestrian, shop owner or driver is helpful, for the mountain cliffs on each side of this narrow road are frightening to everyone who is driving here. We all take extreme caution not to veer too close to each other or to either side of the road. We wave and give a thumbs-up sign when anyone makes it through the dangerous cuts of road, those filled with boulders or with the steepest drop-offs. The need for constant vigilance gives this drive a communal, adventurous quality. Politics are the last thing on anyone's mind as we focus intently on the twisting road.

Jon is on a deadline. By five tonight, he has to submit an article about this road. I'm making notes for him, trying to respond to his precise questions: How long since we passed that last little town? What was its name? Were there one or two shops there? Did you see a makeshift mosque? As I respond with pure guesses, I'm thinking that though official Israeli policy says nothing about two states, anyone doubting that there are two distinct geographical entities here would find this drive edifying. I also see that, unlike most of Israel, this region in the West Bank has long naked stretches, with no visible housing, no farms. We pass view after view of untrammeled land that has a wildly untamed quality.

To our mutual surprise, after an hour's arduous ride, we come upon a section that's being modernized. Churning cement trucks are widening the road. This labor, we're told, has been under way since the territories were closed. Jon dictates to me that some Israeli officials must be readying for a deal; building roads for Palestinians is virtually never done, he says. I see we've discovered something here, but what it means I can't be sure. Once we reach the end in Ramallah, we turn around.

As we approach Jerusalem, I ask Jon: "Why do you do this, and why alone? Today was gorgeous; it was aesthetic; we've had an adventure. But let's face it: You aren't safe in a car with yellow plates. You never know who's going to jump out of these bushes or run after you from a mountain path." "Sometimes," Jon responds thoughtfully, "after spending a few hours in this world, *especially* alone, I feel as if I've passed through a looking glass. Then, I return to Israel and see our world with new eyes."

We aren't so far apart on this score, I think, mentioning that I'm going to tour Gaza with Hakam on May 14. Neither Jon nor I have gone to Gaza yet; I suggest he join us. Hakam is known for his street savvy, I tell him. There's sure to be a story. "Great," he says, as I rush to call Hakam. I look forward to sitting with two men who hold utterly opposing views. I'll learn a lot by seeing Gaza through the eyes of the pragmatic Palestinian who knows Israel well and with the realistic Israeli who's beginning to know the territories. If I see that everyone here has blind spots and biases, then, as a relative newcomer, I certainly haven't achieved anything close to a balanced viewpoint myself.

Initially Hakam says, "No problem; Jon's welcome." But an hour later he calls back to say he has changed his mind. Jon can visit Gaza alone, but he's worried about his reputation and my safety if we travel with someone connected to the *Jerusalem Post*. I argue that Jon's okay, that he has nothing to do with the paper's right-wing editorials, but Hakam is adamant. Finally he agrees to talk to Jon directly by phone.

An hour later Hakam calls back to say he has relented. Jon has agreed to his ground rules: that any Palestinian who kills a soldier or a settler will not be described as "a freedom fighter" (the Palestinian vernacular), but as a "gunman" or "warrior," never as a "terrorist." That term, they've agreed, will apply only to Palestinians who kill Israeli civilians. From this negotiation, I learn that Palestinians view Israeli soldiers not as defending their country but as terrorists who commit acts of brutality against *them*. The term "terrorist" is, I see, highly charged: what it means, to whom it applies. Language is an ever-present source of friction here, central to the publicity battle, central to each culture's identity.

Headlines in the Israeli press two days before our Gazan expedition warn of the dangers to any Israeli or Jew who enters Gaza, a warning which pointedly includes journalists, a first. After a flurry of phone calls this new edict is traced to have most likely come from Israel's Civil Administration, not, as the papers suggested, from the Hamas or the Islamic Jihad. It's believed that increasing violence between Israeli soldiers and Palestinian stone-throwers is something Israeli officials don't want seen or described. But many wonder, is this the whole truth? Maybe the recent murder of Ian Feinberg, a lawyer from Tel Aviv, is a sign that the rules of the game have changed—that any Jew, journalist or not, is not welcome.

Feinberg, a man in his forties, worked for Palestinian civil rights. He crossed the physical and cultural divide daily, trying to help those in Gaza unable to afford good lawyers. He gave his services for free. A week ago gunmen entered his office and shot him. Though his Palestinian co-workers risked their lives trying to shield him, he was killed instantly. The question raging among journalists is whether his death signifies the beginning of a more dangerous Gazan era. Is the Palestinian world, so long dependent upon and welcoming to the press, saying, "We don't want you here, not even Jews who help us"? It's impossible to interpret the shifting rules, but Ian Feinberg's dead body is on every Jewish journalist's mind.

• • •

In Israel, people who hold opposing political views don't usually share the same bed. Shuki and I have been living together for over a year, and have begun struggling not only with our pronounced personal differences, but also with our conflicting views of Palestinians. In many ways, he reminds me of my father, who never allowed us, his kids, to wear loden coats or permit a single German product to enter our home. He once refused to let his sister park her Volkswagen in our driveway.

Long ago I realized that Shuki views anything Arab the way my dad saw all things German. I've tried to stay sensitive to his reality; I understand how hard it is for him to hear me on the phone having cheery conversations with people named Achmed, Hakam, Mariam, Samir, Rawda and Rula (whose calls are precious; she's now become Ashwari's most trusted aide, and is at the center of the political action these days).

Near the beginning of our love affair, Shuki underwent a remarkable reversal. After voting Likud all his life, he not only voted for Rabin, but he and his son, Yoni, actively worked for the Knesset Meretz members (a party to the left of Labor) in last June's elections. His radical shift in affiliation happened after he left our apartment early one morning to ask his favorite army commander, a retired general he served under during the Yom Kippur War, for a favor for Yoni. During their long conversation Shuki learned that this officer, once a hawk, was now a dove because he detested the way Israel acts in the territories. So impressed was Shuki with his officer's conversion experience—a phenomenon not uncommon among retired military personnel—that he, too, came to see the Palestinian issue with fresh eyes, had a change of heart similar to the old man's.

Shuki returned home pro-Meretz. It was too sudden and unearned a shift in view to last. But for months afterward we were in rare agreement about the need for coexistence. Soon after his political conversion, we sat in an outdoor cafe next to Jerusalem's Cinémathèque, looking over at the Judean hills nearby, seeing the Arab town of Silwan. For once we were able to talk about the terrible house demolitions going on over there. We discussed the ongoing removal of Palestinians from their homes and agreed it was provocative and morally wrong. I remember the look on Shuki's face that day: He winced as if he'd long known that Israelis are unnecessarily violent toward those who were dispossessed of much of their land long ago. It was a mellow, loving moment between us, even as it was also wrenching. As if an agony was floating in the air from Silwan to our table, we both felt the terrible suffering taking place in that village. We held hands for hours. When dusk fell, through the shadows of Silwan, we knew its people's pain.

That day Shuki was convinced that the time was ripe to trade land for peace. He became so energized that he organized taxi drivers and tour guides to vote against Likud. But this interlude was short-lived. Based on a few moments of conversation with someone else, he reverted to distrusting Arabs, and again refused to listen to anything about my daily encounters, often storming out of the room when an Arab caller was on the line. Yet, his son, Yoni, is in the army now. Shuki knows, from taking tourists around, that though Israel may control the territories, we don't belong there and can't safely travel into them.

Today is a good example of the inconveniences of occupation. We have to take the long road to Tiberias instead of the short, direct route. If we drove directly we'd be risking our lives. By the time we arrive up north, it feels as if we've driven from New York to Chicago via New Orleans. During this seemingly endless ride, we've been focusing on our relationship, trying to name where we are, where we're heading. This conversation requires delicacy. We seem to have six relationships going on simultaneously. We need to call on our healthiest energies to examine our growing mistrust.

I suspect that Shuki wants me to choose between journalism and him. He half believes I'm disloyal to Israel and is also upset that I pay too much attention to Eliza, refusing to serve his needs as I once did. Though he can be subtle when he feels psychologically safe, this talk is full of emotional land mines. At first, he's in his right-wing mode, baiting me with tired slogans, "The best Arab is a dead Arab," one of several slurs he utters as we drive through shifting landscapes. I've no interest in rising to his bait; I love this man. I want to work things out with him.

As we enter the Galilee in northern Israel, I suddenly feel far away from all our problems in Jerusalem. It's as if we've left politics and our own power struggles behind. Driving into the Lake Kinneret district, I feel a rush of compassion for the Israeli plight. I see how the physiognomy of the Holy Land inevitably gives rise to Jewish paranoia. I stare up at the Golan Heights, see how near we are to Syria and Lebanon. I study their mountains towering above us and shudder. We park the car, get out and stretch, then walk arm in arm into the vacation town of Tiberias. We amble past cafes that dot this placid lake-shore and see many Israelis trying to simply enjoy this *Shabbat*. Shuki and I watch an elderly couple attempting to spoon hot soup into their mouths with shaking hands. We meet young families just back from a day of boating; others are heading off on fishing trips.

Shuki keeps bumping into old acquaintances. As they speak in Hebrew, I stand to the side. They greet each other with hugs and back pats, not unlike what I've observed among Palestinian men. Shuki enjoys high-spirited reunions with old buddies as I gaze about at this landscape. And as I do, my heart opens as it once did toward my own wounded family. After years of psychoanalysis, what I was finally left with was a simple, poignant love for my parents, our fallibilities and our eternal bond. Just so, I suddenly see that these people in Tiberias are *my* people, that viewing Israel from the Palestinians' point of view has been as rigorous as a personal psychoanalysis, equally painful. Hearing and seeing what we inflict on others has been pulling me away from my primal identity as a Jew. Only here and now, after a long hiatus, do I feel at home.

I muse that we Jews are deeply maimed. If we're untrusting, it's for the best of reasons. With war after war, living so close to despotic neighbors, how can *we* be expected to trust? So often the Palestinians use a favored phrase: "Israeli intransigence." But today in Tiberias, I know that such intransigence has been, sadly, earned. Israeli aggression doesn't spring solely from our tortured history—a history the Palestinians seem unwilling to imagine—but also from this geography.

Shuki, who often claims he can read me ten miles away, does that today. While he appears to be fully engaged with old pals, he tunes in to me, picking up my mood: my love for him, the pain of our differences. Like many Israelis, he's as vigilant about American liberal distortions as he is wary of Arabs. As soon as he remembers that I'm not some stereotypical pro-Palestinian lefty, he comes over to hug me as his demeanor lightens. We sit close together ready to share a meal. We fantasize about growing old together as we watch the elderly couple finish their meal and hold onto each other as they leave the cafe arm in arm.

We, too, are holding hands (is there anything as deliciously silky as our fingers entwined?). Shuki's face lights up as he begins to tell me, again, about the week Anwar Sadat arrived in Jerusalem. He's beaming while describing the joy Sadat elicited among all Israelis, saying that this gesture of recognition gave everyone he knows a huge dose of hope. Like all Israelis I've talked with, Shuki knows, despite his wearying rhetoric, how constricting is the warrior posture he and all Israelis are forced to inhabit. He's deeply exhausted from the constant need to be on alert for the next war, especially as his only son, Yoni, may well be fighting it. As he regales me with details of Sadat's visit, I see our main difference is that he's still waiting for Sadat while, rightly or not, I believe Israel now has the power to offer the gesture of largesse. Though I don't say so, I think Israel is wrong to place each act of our own aggression into the rubric of security.

Israelis are far less obsessed with "the situation" than are the weakened Palestinians. Yet we have as much to gain from peace as they do. Shuki, like everyone here, knows that we're sitting on a time bomb from which Israel's massive weaponry can't free us.

Without talking our relationship to death, it's springing back to life today. During these hours of harmony by this mountainous lakeside, our love is like subtle music passing back and forth between us. We head back to Jerusalem, driving through the Israeli Christian Arab town of Nazareth. Happy with each other, we revive our old magnetism and draw other customers in a bakery—Jewish and Arab Israelis, Christian tourists and a Muslim chef—into a lively, communal conversation. Friendly vacationers of every persuasion from far-flung regions begin intermingling with laughter.

Everyone comments on how tasty we find these sweet desserts. As they do, I experience another premonition of peace. Like the day in Jericho two weeks ago, I feel that I'm glimpsing life after a political settlement, tasting a time that will be richer for our cultural differences. Maybe such images of coexistence are pure fantasy or result only from my personal joy. Yet, as we sit in the small Nazareth Arab bakery shop, a multicultural, porous Mideast seems as real and as sweet as the cakes we devour. It's as if we're inside the future, inhabiting a Middle East with permeable boundaries—unquestionably the most interesting place on the globe.

•   •   •

Today I go to Gaza. I wake early, dress in a long, draping skirt and a borrowed shawl, am busy searching for a blouse with full-length sleeves, all necessary for an appearance of modesty in Islamic Gaza, when the phone rings. It's Jon. He's just gotten an important assignment to cover the Palestinian peace delegates who are arriving in Jerusalem this morning. He can't join us in Gaza. He doesn't sound sorry, but begins to lecture me. He wants me to reconsider taking this trip. Detailing the risks, he says that Hakam has a prearranged day planned; people expect a reporter from the *Jerusalem Post*. "What if they mistake *you* for *me*? Don't you see that any Gazan nut who wants to harm us has already been alerted, knows the schedule?" He goes on to say that if I insist on going, he strongly recommends that I scramble Hakam's timetable. If I get shot, he adds, I'll look like a bloody fool.

I laugh and say that the last thing on my mind is how I will appear in my obituary—an obsession that strikes me as singularly Israeli. I feel sad that I won't see Gaza through both Jon and Hakam's eyes, as planned. More disappointed than apprehensive, I drive down to the Erez Checkpoint, surprised that it's only an hour's ride from Jerusalem.

Hakam hardly recognizes me at Yad Mordechai, the gas station that is the final stopover in Israel before entering Gaza. As soon as we drive off, we're in another world—mile after mile of sandy roads littered with garbage and filled with kids hanging about in torn underwear. Donkeys loiter near cement walls awash with spray-painted, colorful graffiti. I don't see Gaza as dangerous but as monotonous. Despite Hakam's statistics ("Gaza is one of the most densely populated spots on earth; over a million people live inside a space that's only thirty miles long, three and a half to five miles wide") this place just seems flat and endless to me. As Hakam drives, I read aloud from today's newspaper: "There were forty-seven casualties and two deaths in Gaza yesterday." "Oh God," I say. Hakam shrugs.

After more miles of sand and slums, we finally arrive at the mental health clinic, our first scheduled visit. It's a large, rambling white house situated right along the seacoast with Mediterranean views and abundant flowers blooming all around it. This is the only clinic where Gazan kids—the stressed and the traumatized—can come for psychological help. Those seen here are too neurotic to function, as director-psychiatrist Dr. Eyad Sarraj begins telling us, after hugging Hakam and ushering the two of us into a comfortably large, air-conditioned room that is his office. Most can't get through an hour, not to mention a day, without disabling panic attacks, Dr. Sarraj says. The majority seen here are children with insomnia, terrifying nightmares and phobias of all sorts, but his clinicians also see some adults—primarily ex-prisoners who've endured torture. These are the most disturbed among Gaza's population.

Despite his arduous work, Dr. Sarraj seems unusually well balanced. He's not exactly relaxed, but stays focused while describing the day the Intifada broke out, one that began with a car accident and grew into a war when he happened to be visiting London with his wife and four children. Immediately he left his family in England so that his children could study and live in a sane society and returned to Gaza, his home since 1948—he had no choice. The more he talks, the more this doctor strikes me as a man on a mission, dedicated to his people. Speaking of his clients' emotional lives more than of politics, we focus on the moods that permeate this war zone.

This psychiatrist holds an intricate vision, unusual in both the Palestinian and Israeli Middle East. Talking with him, I realize how many of us, myself included, latch onto the drama-of-the-moment while omitting a focus on psychological complexity. Dr. Sarraj and I agree that Israelis and Palestinians are maddeningly uninterested in seeing into their own blind spots. Particularly wearying, we also agree, is how each side projects its own dark shadows, then blames the other, refusing responsibility for any pain inflicted. As I listen to him, I see that I've become too attached to superficial, news-driven talk.

Though he is Palestinian to the bone, Dr. Sarraj's talk is neither rote nor predictable. He says: "The problem here is between two victims. We're trying to learn from you Jews, especially from the older generation, those who didn't or couldn't deal with a whole range of emotions after the Holocaust. Many who denied or buried their grief and rage turned those emotions against us." He pauses, then admits, "There's an identical impulse among the Palestinians. I see plenty of paranoia. As a people, we too are in grave danger, not only from Israeli domination but from inside ourselves as well. Many who I treat are projecting their aggressions outward. I watch Israelis harm us; of course they also harm themselves. I fear the same will be true, eventually, for Gazans."

Dr. Sarraj's perspective brings me back to a style of talking so common in my professional circle in the U.S. He's a welcome breath of fresh air for me, but Hakam is restless. He wants to switch off this "heavy stuff" as he says, and, his leg fidgeting, he begins gossiping in Arabic with Dr. Sarraj, who looks at me as if to say, What can I do? Within minutes, I nudge Hakam's arm and ask if he can find us some coffee.

"Here at the clinic," Dr. Sarraj says, winking at my small act of manipulation, "we try to get our kids to express everything in words. I hope some of them will stay healthy and not rigidify into denial or become one-dimensional in their outlook, hell-bent on violence." As he's speaking we hear Hakam, meeting old friends out in the hallway. He's chatting and laughing, which frees me to listen to Dr. Sarraj's analysis.

He says that he welcomes foreign Jewish visitors, especially psychologists, for we are the ones who can witness directly the immense brutality going on here and also perceive the deeper problems under the surface of war. He believes that it's also good for Gazans to meet foreign Jews who aren't soldiers, aren't brutal. He searches his desk and then offers me a pamphlet announcing an upcoming conference for Arab and Jewish psychologists from Europe and America. He says that such events are unusually successful, that those who attend are "more open-minded" than anyone living here.

"You foreigners are freer than we are; you haven't memorized each litany of hatred, or lived through each round of killings," he says. I look at him, thinking that he's heaven-sent to his people. His perspective is nuanced yet solid; he's able to be analytic but isn't cold; he's emotionally accessible yet in no way ingratiating. I tell him that I marvel that he can work in relative calm despite the anger of many around him—both Israelis *and* Palestinians—with their addictions to violence. In an ideal world, he says with true melancholy, he'd try to lead his people in a Gandhian nonviolent resistance. He'd much prefer burning identity cards, cleaning the streets and beaches, or creating experimental poetry and theater to counter the occupation. But he must be realistic, and these ideals are not. Leaning forward in his chair, he tells me that the stone-throwing Intifada gives many young Gazans great self-esteem. He asks if I find it ironic that those who refuse to participate in the violence, whether by force from parents or from fear, are at higher risk for breakdown. The ones who sit out the fighting are most rejected and ostracized by their peers, most vulnerable to being used by the Israelis as "informers." The kids who throw stones and burn tires are the ones seen as heroes. Dr. Sarraj shakes his head, half smiling. "The entire situation is pure paradox, yes?" he asks.

Long ago he realized that he can't dictate his people's choices, so he tries to underscore optimism, even as he must accept that *this is war.* He counsels everyone to resist all impulse to kill Israeli civilians, even though the *shabab* (street fighters) argue that *their* civilians are continually under fire. They have a point, he concedes.

Our talk turns to the murder of Ian Feinberg. For Dr. Sarraj, this is an example of his own people's violence, what he considers "inexcusably stupid, unforgivably immoral." And here he stops talking and shakes his head, as if overwhelmed by sadness. When he composes himself, he tells me that he knew Feinberg well. After the "senseless" murder he created discussion groups. He's sorry to report that they raised no one's consciousness. His clients argued that they must fight for their lives, that Israelis refuse to see the stone-throwers as reacting to oppression; they believe there are no "good" Jews. Such talk makes his job as "frustrating as it is important," he laments.

The doctor is hot on his next topic—Rabin as a war criminal—when his voice begins to feel far away. I've felt intensely engaged, but somehow missed the moment when the whole weight of this aged conflict began to invade me. I'm unable to remain logical and only wish that Jon were here. Distancing myself from the doctor's angry words, I'm remembering Jon's: "Of course it's ugly. Occupation is war." Yet, denial has never been my strong point and I wonder (once again) if I'm being duped.

Sensing that I'm growing weary, the doctor finds Hakam and sends the two of us to a room to watch psychotherapy sessions through a one-way mirror. The children we see aren't playing to us. Their side of the wall is darkened; they don't even know we're here. Again and again, I hear them discuss or act out their fears of "Jews" (in none of the sessions is the word "Israeli" used). After a few hours I regress to my own childhood, to my obsession with Nazis, for these children live with a comparable terror of us Jews. I watch a therapy session with an eight-year-old boy who seems much older. He says that he's worried, that he can't sleep. When he does, he often sleepwalks.

Asked what he fears, the boy says it's "the nightmares." "They're all the same. I have to get up and shut the window, but I can't. I can't move."

"Why do you need to close your window?" the therapist asks gently.

"Because I'm scared the Jews are coming. They have big guns; they want to hurt my family." The therapist leads the child to talk of the night Israeli soldiers came to his house. The boy tells of waking up and seeing soldiers marching around and carrying his two-year-old brother, screaming, from their shared bed. In a low-keyed voice, the therapist suggests reenacting that night. The boy does, first as the scowling soldier, then as his little brother—crying hysterically. The therapist leans down to console him. He says that his brother was back in bed within minutes. Wasn't he? The boy nods. The counselor underscores that the "Jews" didn't hurt him. "Okay," the boy agrees, "but they took my dad away. To prison. I worry every day and especially at night. That they'll kill him," he says in a cadence that sounds like a thirteen-year-old's, not the voice of a boy of eight. The therapist, kindly and supportive, doesn't whitewash the pain: "You've seen too much for a child your age," he says. "That night was terribly frightening. But you are not in charge of the household. Your uncle and aunt are, along with your mom. Your dad may be home soon. There are good lawyers trying hard to get him free. . . . Tell me, do you feel better when you sleep in bed with your family?" the therapist asks.

For the first time, this child seems childlike. He cries, then bends his head into his hands, ashamed. "I don't want to sleep with my family. Well, I do, sometimes. But if I wet the bed, that makes more trouble for everyone."

The two go on to discuss practical solutions to his fears, loneliness, nightmares, bed-wetting, sleepwalking.

"Well, these are things we'll work on here," the therapist soothingly responds, "and then you'll feel more in control." The boy nods. Whether he believes his life will be better or not is hard to gauge. While I'm transported by this session (translated word by word for me by a female Palestinian therapist who's fluent in English), Hakam is bored. He yawns. He doesn't realize that this Gazan world he knows so well is new (and fascinating) to me. Nor does he know how much these sessions evoke flashbacks of my own work as a psychologist and of my childhood terrors.

At 3 P.M., Hakam says irritably that it's time to leave the clinic. Back in his car, he shuts off his radio as we wend our way out of Gaza. Though I'm sitting next to him, I'm inside my own world, thinking of the ambiguities, the thousand shades of gray that exist in Gaza; how there are more than two sides to every aspect of this miserable situation.

Yet logic doesn't help. This day in Gaza has left me torn apart inside. I begin to understand why so many Jewish reporters, intellectuals and concerned citizens don't come here to see for themselves what's going on. It's not only fear of physical danger that's daunting but the emotional dislocation such a visit evokes. I know that many Jews, hearing those therapy sessions or seeing what the adults here endure, would feel much as I do: Dr. Sarraj, his clients, the therapists I have just met, all leave me in a state of exhaustion, one weighted with personal guilt. For I didn't convey to the Gazans anything about Jewish fears. Now I'm feeling traitorous for staying silent. I'm too weak to absorb or analyze what I've seen today. It is hard to see the accurate proportions. Crisscrossing identifications collide inside me. If I believe everything I've heard, I'll have to believe that Israel created this situation single-handedly, which we did not.

My silence annoys Hakam, who turns the radio on, switching stations. Finding nothing of interest, he shuts it off, saying, "Shit, I won't put my life on hold because of this madness." I'm twisting inside, unable to hold onto the Israeli rationale and the Palestinian narrative at the same time. Yet, who can?

Hakam is humming while I'm fending off an asthma attack, one of my body's reactions to stress. How could I have known that the doctor and his staff's words would wound me far more than any fanatic's? Lining up on one's own side of the ethnic divide, no matter how blindly, now strikes me as understandable—it allows for inner stability, ongoing certainty.

Seeing my exhaustion, Hakam says, "You don't have to solve this situation. You're not that grandiose, are you?" he jokes, as we pull up to my building in Jerusalem. It's as if we've been in Gaza not for a day, but for weeks. I climb the stairs up to my fourth-floor apartment, longing for a bath and hugs with Eliza and Jackie. To my surprise I find Shuki is already home. He's pacing our living room along with his friend Tzadik and two women from my writing group. As I walk in, they're all moving in anxious circles. Immediately after I open the door, each runs to me. "Two Jews and two Arabs have just been murdered in Gaza," someone screeches. "We didn't know if it was you."

We turn on the TV. A breaking story says the murders were a reaction to four men, two from each side, who were trying to smuggle cheap vegetables out of Gaza. The gunmen acted to make sure that no one benefits financially from the current closure, the reporter says. We hear that an eighteen-month-old baby and an eleven-year-old boy were killed an hour ago. The killings must have taken place minutes after Hakam and I drove off.

Everyone turns on me. "We told you not to go. See what could have happened?"

CHAPTER EIGHT

Today Is Not like Yesterday

Your knots are in my soul.

—Old rabbinic saying

Summer arrives, as usual, in May. In June, Shuki and I take Eliza, Jackie and his son, Yoni, on a long trip to the States—in place of a honeymoon, as we tell them. We haven't married yet, but that's in the cards. On a Sunday in late August, I'm the only one who needs to get back to Israel to work. I leave our blended family in Niagara Falls and head to New York City to catch an El Al flight.

At JFK Airport, I barely have time to grab the Sunday *Times*. Without glancing at it, I settle into my seat. Only after liftoff do I pick up the front page. There I see in bold headlines: "SECRET OSLO MEETINGS YIELD ISRAELI-PALESTINIAN ACCORDS." I read that after months of secret meetings, "mutual recognition" between the Palestine Liberation Organization and the Israeli government is about to become the law of the land. My spirits soar along with the plane, especially as I suddenly recall that today's date, August 29, is the date of Theodor Herzl's first Zionist Congress held in 1897. Maybe, just maybe, the same date in the year 1993 will also go down in history.

These accords mean that we will soon see a torrent of legal documents, meetings and public ceremonies signifying the beginning of a real peace accord, after fifty years of warring, terrorism and hostility. That's being dismantled from the very top echelons.

Those of us who've followed every twist and turn of the peace process have been hanging on information from the *wrong* channel! We've followed every thirdhand source, every dour sound bite from the snail-paced meetings in Washington, not knowing of a secret channel up in Norway. The *Times* describes this accord as the fruit of many meetings, carried out in complete privacy. These covert encounters between highest-level officials on both sides have been going on *for nearly a year* in a remote country villa, without leaks to the press or grandstanding for the public. This has culminated in what the headlines refer to as the Oslo Accords, which includes the Declaration of Principles, or DOP, to be signed shortly.

In Israel, I find this news even more amazing. What was abstract on the plane feels more immediate and more real here on the ground. In the early dawn, I grab a cab and drive up the mountain to Jerusalem. At this hour the ride is especially beautiful. The thought of the peace pact today adds a bright sheen to everything we pass, to stones and shrubs, to the red-roofed houses, to each flowering garden.

Once home, I'm alone in our apartment, too excited to sit still. I drop my bags, open the glass doors, stepping out onto the terrace. As I do, the rose-hued sky turns yellowish blue. I gaze down at the blossoming flowers in *Gana Palmach* (Liberty Bell Park), then across to the Judean desert mountains, to minarets and citadels in the distance. Everything looks more vivid than usual. Even the ever-cheerful sparrows sound more musical, chirping, "Tirey, Tirey," as if to say, Look! Look!

By 7 A.M., I'm on the phone. Everyone in the press and peace communities confirms that this *is* real news, is *the* watershed event. I'm told that virtually no one knew anything about Oslo—that the secret channel was kept fully secret, in itself almost as much a feat as the agreement. Among those who knew nothing, I learn, are the Washington peace delegates (both the Israeli and the Palestinian teams), every high official not directly involved, all Arab heads of state. Even President Bill Clinton and Secretary of State Warren Christopher were informed *after* the fact—only days ago.

All around Jerusalem, everyone is poring over the Oslo Accords, whose Declaration of Principles outlines how and when the Palestinians will take control over their own lives. This will begin with Israeli troop withdrawals (or redeployment, as the papers call them) in most of Gaza and all of Jericho. This is Oslo's first phase (the so-called Gaza and Jericho First), where the Israelis will withdraw on December 13, two and a half months from today. Then gradually, over the next few years, "autonomy" is to spread to every major and minor Palestinian city and town in the West Bank. The Jewish settlements are to stay, though they are not to be expanded. How they'll be protected or by whom isn't clear. What *is* certain is that Israeli troops will guard the borders, accompanied by Palestinian police. There's a timetable, specific dates, a concrete plan. Even the most heated and contested issues—"the right of return" for diaspora Palestinians; the question of who controls which section of Jerusalem—are included, if only as items to be negotiated in "final status" talks in May 1999.

Everyone I speak to is in a state of disbelief. All are glad that the Oslo Accords will not be an overnight upheaval, but call for a slow transition. This gradated autonomy will give time for the necessary rearrangements on the ground—readying military maneuvers and building psychological trust. Both need careful orchestration, especially the latter. Trust is absent among the majority in each population, and between those leaders who didn't attend the Norway meetings. The peace many have worked toward, dreamed about, believed in, mistrusted, wanted in one form or feared in another is now, overnight, public policy. Amazing!

Israel, the West Bank and Gaza are already flooded with journalists, writers, TV crews and photographers who are flying in, on plane after plane from all over the globe. By ten o'clock, when I enter the American Colony Hotel's courtyard in East Jerusalem, the place where journalists usually congregate, I see a huge contingent checking in. The summer air is filled with expectation, even from the most jaded among us, the "been there, done that" crowd. Despite all the flaws in the document, nitpicking, even from those who openly dislike the agreement, can't disrupt the infectious mood—an emotional elevation that is spreading all around this courtyard.

Every conversation is high-pitched with exhilaration. There's a continuous ringing of cellular phones and beepers. Reporters trying to scope out or predict what's ahead are greeted by laughter. Political prophecy is futile in the Mideast. "Who'd have predicted *this?*" one Argentinean feature writer asks. He's right.

I see Achmed. He's looking for me and is thinner and more elegant than two months ago; I see he's gotten a European haircut, is wearing tailored clothes. We give each other a bear hug, then sit at a small white table whose shiny surface reflects the blazing noon sun. At first we just gape at each other. Soon Achmed pulls a photo from his wallet, one taken last May in Jericho when the long-exiled returned. Someone had mentioned then that we were beginning to look alike. We study the photograph, which shows the two of us standing on Jericho's main dirt road with the metal fence as our backdrop. We're smiling, our heads bent toward each other. In that moment we *do* look uncannily similar, nearly indistinguishable, which makes us smile as we sip fresh orange juice, then drink Turkish coffee.

"You know, I've been thinking all morning that this peace process has been a rebirth for each of us. Even before this accord," he says. It's true. We've come to share similar fascinations and identical hopes while traveling together so often. Such a coincidence of minds is rare even between close Palestinian and Jewish friends.

This courtyard is a perfect place to savor the news. We've met here many times amidst these rounded arches and lemon and orange trees under colorful Arab tapestries hanging from balconies above. "Let's freeze this moment," Achmed says. Then he tells me how *he* reads the situation. Though he lives only blocks away (with his family in East Jerusalem's Shu'afat camp), Achmed spent the last three weeks in Gaza. He was working with Italian filmmakers, helping them find locations and people to interview and translating Arabic into Italian. That's where he was when the news broke. He's talked to many Gazans since yesterday, has just this hour returned to Jerusalem. I lean across the table, eager to hear what's being said down there.

He warns me not to get too excited; Gazans are wary of the accord. As always, they suspect and fear Israeli tricks. They're also worried about what Arafat's return will mean on the ground. The Intifada generation prides itself on being the leaders in the two-state struggle, taking credit for worldwide recognition for their cause. And for attracting the attention that's led to this breakthrough. Now they fear Arafat and his cronies' return from exile in Tunis. Will they arbitrarily dismiss or oust the local *shabab* (street fighters) from power? This thought worries many because the men closest to Arafat are known for corruption, greed and autocratic ways. Some in Gaza are already predicting a dictatorship.

Though everything he says is true, even realistic doubts are impossible to sustain today. In this courtyard filling with more TV crews, print journalists and historians, an excitement is spreading from table to table. A tangible compromise has been agreed to by Rabin *and* Arafat. This is huge.

Within an hour Achmed and I are driving to Jericho on desert roads that curve through huge sand mountains. We want to hear how people in that tropical town are reacting to the news of "Jericho and Gaza First." We pass a group of Jewish settlers who are holding a protest in a synagogue on the outskirts of Jericho. I see a placard written in Hebrew which shows Rabin's face wearing Arafat's trademark kaffiyeh. We hear people chanting a single Hebrew word over and over, which Achmed translates as "traitor." Whizzing past them, we hear "traitor" echoing from the distance. Achmed shrugs. "They're fighting this peace," he says. "It means a dismantling of their world." It's true. Overnight these people seem marginalized, powerless to halt the momentum toward coexistence.

Just outside Jericho, TV crews are pulling up outside a small, pink stucco house. We park behind them; other cars follow us. Once inside, we're told that this is where Arafat will soon move. Film crews and photographers crowd inside. Five proud Palestinian women take us all on a tour. Then each woman stands erect, holds onto a broom or a mop, posing for photographs. One woman stoops over a bed as if she's turning down the sheets where "Arafat and Suha [his wife] will soon be sleeping." An elderly woman, her eyes aglow, pretends to clean an already spotless kitchen. The photographers flash away, but we see this show as pure guesswork and drive to Jericho's town square, hoping to find Achmed's close buddy, Izhaq Shawa.

Shawa owns a grocery store, situated at the intersection of Jericho's two main streets, surrounded by palm trees, close to the town's square. We find him inside, sitting amidst a chaos of milk and stationery, tuna fish and pens, grape sodas and paper clips. The disorder on his shelves contrasts with the determined look on his face and the clarity of his voice. The three of us sit close together on high stools. Achmed hugs his old school friend warmly, then says to me, "Izhaq is the pulse of this town." Nodding my way, he says to Shawa, "*She,* you can completely trust." We smile at each other. Despite the rising heat and flies buzzing around us, we begin chatting while fanning ourselves with pages ripped from my notebook. Our conversation continues even when others congregate around us, offering their opinions in long untranslated speeches or begging for food and toiletries on credit. Items are plucked so rapidly from the shelves that Shawa barely has time to assent, which he invariably does. Since the latest closure, the Palestinian economy has again shriveled, he explains, speaking in English for my benefit. "We have bad food shortages; many people can't afford to feed their families. But, you see, that's unimportant." Moving closer, while motioning new customers away, he says in a hoarse voice: "Listen to me. I saw Rabin on our satellite TV a few days ago. He was talking to reporters in Gaza. The scene lasted, at most, five seconds. A reporter asked him, 'Will you withdraw troops from here?' and I heard him whisper, 'Definitely.' Then another asked, 'And Jericho?' I heard him say, 'Very soon.'

"Nobody else heard these words. But at that moment *I* knew something new and strange was happening. I felt it in my bones. Images filled my dreams. My brothers, friends and customers all teased me. Yet I was not dreaming. That interview replayed in my mind and I told everyone, 'Believe me, the occupation is about to end.' They laughed, called me crazy, but they began buying more newspapers. Even those who can't read." He stands to give a customer aspirin and juice, then sits and continues, "An old Bedouin lady— she comes in here every day. The others joke with her, 'But Bedouins don't even read papers.' Yet she was determined. She said that her sons and daughters were reading aloud to her and insisted that I save her a paper every day. You see, it was in the air. And now we hear the news."

Izhaq Shawa—lean, short, intense—is approaching forty. Though he is educated as a civil engineer, this small store is his main source of income. He's smart, if not above a bit of self-promotion. "See, look around. Everyone comes to *me*. You wonder why? Because I felt this change before this news. Now listen," he says, waving away more customers. "This morning a family came knocking at my door. A couple, four kids. Early, before 8 A.M. They spoke in English, said they were American tourists who just heard the news and wanted to visit a Palestinian family. My wife made them a beautiful breakfast: eggs, pancakes, salad, pita bread. We all sat in our kitchen, eating and talking for hours, even after our kids and theirs ran out to play in our backyard. We adults kept talking and talking. That's why my shop was closed all morning."

Achmed and I exchange looks—what's his point?

"As they were leaving, I said out loud, right in front of all the children: 'Now you listen to me. We know you aren't Americans. You are Israelis; you are our neighbors who we've never met before.' Right away, they look nervous. So I say, 'Don't ever hide your identity from us. You must be honest. It's good you want to get to know us. For we will live together.' Everyone laughed and laughed. They thought they'd deceived us. So I repeat, sternly: 'Don't lie to us. There is no need. We are ready to forget the past and to make friends with you.' Once they knew *we* knew who they were, they tell us where they live, what they do for work, how they feel when coming here. In that moment, the whole atmosphere turned giddy. No one could stop laughing. I tell you: *In three hours of laughing and talking together, seven years of the Intifada disappeared.* They drove off waving, promised to come back. My wife called out: 'Remember to tell your people they are welcome. We are ready to be your friends.' "

Shawa's face beams. He's happy with this story. I ask if he really trusts this Oslo plan. "I trust, but I warn," he responds, his face tightening. "If there's deception . . . If this is Gaza and Jericho *only*, not Gaza and Jericho *first*, that will mean *hell*. You see, we always worry Israelis are tricking us. But this time, maybe not. We try to believe."

I ask if Intifada violence will recur (though Jericho was never especially violent) if and when his people don't get their freedom just as they imagine it. He doesn't answer directly. "We are ready to live side by side with Israelis," he repeats. "We Palestinians, we keep our word. We don't cheat or deceive. Our security is theirs now, and their business is ours. Believe me, eighty percent in Jericho want this Oslo Accord to succeed. Those who don't agree—they will have a voice too."

He answers my next question: "The Hamas? Oh, they will come around." Shawa laughs, "They will be the first to shave their beards and line up to build discos, drop all fanatic talk." He passes a pound of coffee to a customer, says, "You have to understand. Under occupation everyone postures. Each is a big shot, a great warrior. But with change on the ground, mark my words, no violence will come from us." He pauses, leaning over my pad. "Write this down. Write my words: 'If this is a trick, I, Izhaq Shawa, will join the Hamas myself.' "

He tells how he'll measure deception, for he knows this accord won't be implemented overnight. "We measure by the end of the second or third year of autonomy. [I see he's read the official document more carefully than I have.] By then, the large cities of the West Bank will be liberated. This will happen. We will show the Israelis that their fears are unfounded. Our people will pass their trial. But in the third and fourth years, there's the danger. By then *all eyes will be on Jerusalem; all issues will be coming home to Jerusalem.* If they won't negotiate on that, Palestinian hearts will harden. Doubt and pessimism will overtake us again. Yes"—he's frowning—"East Jerusalem is our big worry. Until then, I predict the Hamas will join in creating our state."

Shawa has his share of bravado, but is no fool. He must know that the anger of his people, who've been dominated by the Israelis, isn't going to disappear overnight. Despite his high spirits, I'm sure he, like all of us, has doubts about how the accords will translate into reality. But his excitement at meeting ordinary Israeli Jews is sincere. Latching onto hope, not dwelling on past wrongs, is common among most Palestinians I meet. After they recite their predictable litany of blame, the list of Israeli wrongs, what's interesting to hear is their longing, not for revenge, but for peace, for a better life.

However paranoid their ideology, Palestinians in the territories welcome visiting Jews and are acutely alert to signs of Jewish decency. Again and again, I've seen them study us, less interested in our words than in our attitudes—a test that, when passed, gives them a reason to hope. Because the great majority have political acumen; they know that Jews who want a fair settlement are critical for *their* future.

• • •

Two days later I have lunch with Judith Green, the Rapprochement facilitator I first met up in Nablus. We're sitting at an outdoor table on Ben Yehuda Street that's half shaded by a wobbly, striped umbrella. We order hummus and eggs, but are so engrossed that we lose our appetite for food. Judith describes how she sees the peace accord: as "a dialogue group writ large," similar to the work she and other Rapprochement facilitators do every week, bringing Israelis and Palestinians together, often for the first time. It's a method of conflict resolution often derided as sentimental or scorned as meaningless, "even by those on the left," she says. What she's heard about the Oslo meetings is that they used many of the same dialogue techniques. Particularly fascinating is news that comes to her via a Norwegian academic who attended the Beit Sahur and Nablus dialogue groups last year, supposedly to gather material for his doctoral dissertation. He just called to say what he couldn't tell her at the time: that while he was going to her meetings, he was working as an advisor to the Norwegians. That they used what he learned in dialogue to set the best possible stage in Oslo.

This man told Judith that "Oslo" was no political science coup but arose from human recognitions between top-level Palestinian and Israeli officials. These men repeatedly traveled up to Norway, using aliases, putting their lives into their hosts' hands. Some knew each other already; many had never met before.

But how did trust arise? I ask. She tells me what she knows: The meetings were held in an elegant, isolated country house; the hosts were shrewd enough to anticipate the likely barriers. They set a stage that was full of homey props—a fireplace, great food, commodious rooms, quiet isolation. Her Norwegian friend faxed her today, saying that, like beginners in dialogue, nothing positive emerged at first. There were screaming matches and threats to leave. Only after many months did their masks drop. In the end, the mood, so emotionally alive, included riotous laughing as well as copious crying.

Judith reflects that that's the only way sworn enemies become devoted colleagues—through intensely personal rapport. And that *is* what happened. "My friend says that the wall of ethnic solidarity was broken, that new affinities formed—friendships based less on race than on character or a shared vision."

Judith tells me about another coup scored by the Rapprochement movement. It happened the week before the announcement, after a year of failed attempts: She and other leaders finally secured permits for the Nablus-Jerusalem members to meet—first in one city, then in the other—an event whose timing led to much publicity, which would never have occurred without the peace accord. Three weeks ago busloads of Israelis finally made the long-postponed trip to Nablus. Over a hundred Israeli families were traveling, most clearly terrified, to the northern West Bank. These Israelis were bracing for the worst. When they got off at the Casbah in Nablus, some were shaking in fear. What they found were Palestinian crowds lining the streets to greet them, giving warm handshakes, smiling and gracious, as is their custom.

"The contrast between the 'terrorists' the Israelis imagined and the loving responses received was so powerful, it verged on comical," she says. "I watched each Israeli move from fear to surprise. Within hours there was exultation. It was worth the year-long wait just to see their faces." I picture the scene. I know how fear can fuel the elation she describes.

"Then it was the Palestinians' turn," Judith says. "If possible, they dreaded the excursion to West Jerusalem even more than the Israelis had feared Nablus. Picture this: Busloads of Palestinians, all recruited by word of mouth, arriving in Jerusalem, terrified. A hundred and thirty adults kept up a brave front for their kids, but the tension was thick.

"At a bus stop near Abu Tor, the Palestinians debarked, open-mouthed. They were astonished at what was awaiting them—excitement, generosity and, mostly, warmth. Even before they dispersed into twenty Israeli homes for lunch, they began to relax. After lunch, the entire group of Israelis and Palestinians, as planned, joined in a peace march. Walking en masse toward a meeting house in Talpiot, we kept attracting more people. Our crowd grew to over five hundred. The Israeli police had to stop traffic for us. Can you imagine what the Israelis passing by were thinking? They just stared. Our cheerful procession must have seemed like a scene out of Fellini: a bizarre contingent of smiling Palestinians and Israelis stopping traffic and holding banners proclaiming 'Two States Side by Side.' "

She says the day was particularly charged because Israeli police were escorting the Palestinians. "That's what most astounded our guests from Nablus," she exclaims. "I walked alongside a family who couldn't believe that our soldiers were joining hands to protect *their* right to demonstrate. They were shocked to see uniformed 'enemies' supporting them! It's so contrary to their usual images of Israeli soldiers.

"This event gave them fresh insight into how many Israelis do believe in peace," she relates. We haven't touched our food, so delicious and nourishing is her story. "Here's the irony," Judith continues. "Although there was no plan to use this event for publicity, television crews from all over the world did cover it. As you know, nothing newsworthy happens at the tail end of August. It was a photographer's dream: large groups of Palestinians and Jewish Israelis singing, laughing and marching at the center of West Jerusalem. At the time we had no clue that these photos and films would become famous. But because this march was the best visual image of what the Oslo Accords meant, they did. You see, when the news broke the next morning, our Jerusalem march was plastered over front pages of newspapers and magazines—in Europe, South America, North America, everywhere. The television footage was used too. With no photographers or TV crews up in Oslo, these images best illustrated what may develop."

Always soft-spoken and modest about her role in dialogue work, Judith can't contain her enthusiasm today. "Can you imagine? Palestinians rushing to get back home before the Israeli curfew, arriving in Nablus at 11 P.M., only to wake and see themselves on every news outlet?"

Checking her watch, Judith reminds me that tonight is our biweekly meeting in Beit Sahur, the town just beyond Bethlehem. To my surprise, I instantly sink into . . . fear, heart-pounding fear. It's fine to celebrate cross-cultural pacts in abstraction, but I'd completely forgotten that I'm due to travel into the West Bank tonight. After a month abroad, and only a few days back in Jerusalem, I'm afraid to go there.

I know this fear is unwarranted, but rational thought doesn't help. As I struggle with myself, I realize that most Jewish activists and journalists I know repeatedly slide down this mysterious slope away from known reality into anticipatory dread. I've visited the Palestinian world often, but now I worry about the new Palestinian entity being so close to Israel, so near to West Jerusalem. *Well, where exactly did I think the Palestinian autonomy would be located?* I'm amazed at how quickly old fears and one-dimensional stereotypes resurface. Do we have to travel daily to the other side just to cleanse ourselves of macabre fantasies and implacable notions?

Judith is one of a handful of Israelis who never miss a week in the West Bank, who will go anywhere in the territories to plan and attend meetings, without thinking twice. She's never out of touch with her Palestinian friends and co-workers. So my wild fear surprises her. She's dismayed that I need her assurances and wishes that, by now, I'd "know" we aren't heading into danger. She remains patient, though that takes obvious effort. She asks calmly, in a tone that betrays annoyance, "Why can't you remember what you've lived through? You never feel this way when you're actually talking with Palestinians. Why *do* you forget so easily?"

I don't really understand and say so. All I know is that I've been away for a few weeks, and from the moment I stepped off the plane I was drawn into blind allegiance with Israel, picking up Israeli phobias instantly. Fear of "them" seems so ancient and unrelenting; I find it hard to hold onto personal memories. Judith is puzzled.

"Look," I say, "I don't pretend that this anxiety makes sense. But my experience may explain why so few Israeli, American and foreign Jews join dialogue and why most refuse to go near the West Bank. I can't explain it. I just went to Jericho, but I've lost an organic sense of Palestinian generosity. Yet, when visiting America, I talked and wrote about dialogue; I embodied enthusiasm. . . ."

"Well, we've all been brainwashed," Judith responds. "Everyone here has been subjected to a profound miseducation. We all see others through a distorting lens."

Despite her calm manner and reasonable words, my fear doesn't abate. As with any terror, my mind germinates a thousand reasons why *tonight* is sure to be different—more dangerous. "Judith, think about it," I say. "Isn't this night the perfect one for the extremists to go on a spree—whether theirs (the Hamas) or ours (the settlers)? Why wouldn't they come out in droves now? Isn't this *the* time for fanatics to act?"

"You say that before *every* meeting." Judith laughs. "The only thing *I* fear is that Arafat will change his mind and won't sign those papers."

We're paying our lunch bill, standing out on Ben Yehuda Street, now filled with late-afternoon crowds. "You must be kidding," she adds. "You've been to what? Thirty, forty meetings?" Seeing that I'm not kidding at all, she switches her approach and says, "How you feel is not so unusual. . . . Maybe this little anecdote will help . . . maybe not. Last week I was in Nablus for a committee meeting. As always, Veronica was wearing a head scarf, her husband his *kippah*. No doubt we were the only Jews wandering around the city, and we looked, for all the world, like settlers. We went from door to door, offering peace posters and T-shirts, with slogans written in Hebrew, Arabic and English. Remember, this was in Nablus, supposedly a Hamas stronghold, where only forty percent favor this peace accord. Yet not a single person refused a T-shirt. No one even smirked at us as we randomly rang doorbells. We didn't encounter one unfriendly face. You know how Palestinians are: first smiling, then insisting we come in—to talk, drink tea, engage in long conversations."

While walking up Ben Yehuda, Judith muses, "We didn't have a single bad moment that entire afternoon. By evening, we were lost. But ambling about far into the night, we found nothing but smiles and helpful guides around us."

I place a hand on her arm and thank her for giving me back my instinct to trust.

At 5:45, the bus picks us up in Jerusalem and heads toward the Rapprochement Center in Beit Sahur. It's a fifteen-minute ride on steep, winding roads. The sun is setting, dispersing its rosy light over the land, like a prolonged whisper of hope. I can't stop looking at the beauty. If I had to die, what better place and for what better reason than this?

On the bus are faces both familiar and new. An elderly Holocaust survivor, active in dialogue since its inception, is near me. Next to him sits an earnest, young Jewish intellectual who's visiting from Europe. Behind them, others exclaim at the lovely landscape, especially two fresh-faced kids, introduced as having just moved here from Argentina. Most of the others, men and women, are middle-aged, observant Jews wearing *kippot* and head scarves. A few are casually dressed. A rabbi sitting to my left remarks that the spirit inside our bus mirrors the beauty outside our open windows. As he talks, I notice that I feel no fear at all. In truth, I'm never happier than during these expeditions.

Tonight, in the Beit Sahur meeting room, there are forty-five Palestinians, spanning all ages, awaiting us. Many have been meeting with Israelis for years, even during the long Intifada. As I look at these faces, the idea that this peace process is sudden vanishes. As soon as we walk into the room, I see that the newly born mutual recognition agreement, the one that's filling every headline, has long been operative here, forged through regular, direct encounters. Despite contradictory readings of history, the subtext of these talks favors shelving past differences. We've learned that only by putting our contrary histories aside can we create a safer future for both peoples. It's a lesson that has to be relearned often, as each meeting brings newcomers into the process.

Sitting in a large circle of wooden chairs in the main meeting room, we begin the hard work of talking together with respectful honesty. Veronica Cohen and Ghassan Andoni are chairing tonight's meeting. After laughing and small talk, Veronica repeats for the newcomers our two basic rules: no interruptions and polite, but honest talk.

Then, as is our custom, we go around as each of us introduces him- or herself by name, town and profession. One woman says that she's a German Jew, was a judge in her home country and has recently moved to Israel, where she's working as a guide at Yad Vashem, the Israeli Holocaust memorial. A Palestinian man asks her what would happen if the Palestinians began erecting their own version of Yad Vashem.

"What are you really asking?" Veronica interrupts.

"That I believe such a monument would be lethal for our people. We don't need shrines to remind us of our suffering or our sad history. Isn't that the last thing we need? That's not for now. Not for a long time to come. Look at yourselves." He sweeps a hand toward the Jewish Israeli dialogue members. "You built your state based on remembering. And have you ever been at peace? Now we have a chance to build *our* state, at last. I'm saying that we can learn from your mistakes. We will try to forget rather than 'always remember' what was done to us. If we take that motto, we'll have better relations among ourselves, and with you, our neighbors—" He pauses. "Whether we like you or not," he adds, to chuckles all around.

Immediately, an elderly, stooped Israeli I've not met before, who well may be a Holocaust survivor, argues that there's no parallel between our Holocaust and any aspect of Palestinian history; that however hard it's been for those in the territories and for the generation displaced from their homes in 1948, "You've suffered *nothing,* I repeat *nothing,* comparable to our disasters." I see a look of bemused patience suffusing the faces of the Rapprochement facilitators. Clearly, they've been over this turf many times and seem to have long ago realized that comparing past sufferings leads nowhere. They gently move the discussion.

Next, the breaking news of the Oslo Accords, takes center stage. "We don't like this business of a trial period; we certainly don't fully trust it," says Elias Rishmawi, the local pharmacist. "But we must show Israelis that we can create our own entity without internal strife or risk to Israeli lives. I believe we will pass this test. I'm cautious about this agreement, but in nearly equal measure, I'm hopeful, too."

Another Palestinian jumps in. "Can we deliver?" he asks. "Are our people ready? I can't say with certainty. What I say to you, my Palestinian sisters and brothers, is lament all you want. Cry for all we've lost. You can blame the occupation and the Zionists for many past injustices, for distortions of and violence to our lives. But I tell you, my friends, if four months from now we aren't in control of a democratic Gaza and Jericho, we can blame only ourselves."

A Palestinian old-timer vehemently disagrees: "Have you lost all balance? Four months to clean up Gaza? Arafat hasn't even arrived yet; who knows what he'll bring? We're better off not blaming anyone. But given the choice, I would not recommend blaming our own people—not for a long time."

Judith interjects quietly, "This is going to be a hard time for you. Have no illusions about that. So far this change is only written on official papers. Soon this new peace process will create all kinds of unexpected problems. It may splinter your solidarity. It's not going to be as easy as when you were naturally united. But remember there's also new hope."

Now, a teenaged Palestinian, new to the group, raises his hand. Veronica nods at him and he says, "Going back to the lady at the beginning. What *is* Yad Vashem?" Amidst an outburst of friendly laughter, he gets his explanation, which is followed by an Israeli woman, in her mid-thirties, known as an original thinker. With slow deliberation, she says, "Those I know best say the Oslo timetable is too slow and too vague. But I say to them and to you: slow and vague are what's best. 'Slow and vague' will give us time to make this agreement solid. We each have serious work ahead in educating our own people. We Israelis need to work with the settlers [she rolls her eyes]. That's not going to be any picnic [laughter]. And you Palestinians have to work with *your* extremists—the Hamas, the Islamic Jihad. We both need time to create a consensus away from violence. So let's not be impatient. 'Not enough' and 'Not fast enough' may be the real blessings. We have to cover a lot of ground in order to get the majority on both sides to join us."

Near the end of the two hours, Veronica says sadly (someone always does), "There's never enough time." Everyone nods. It's true. These meetings fly by so fast, and, for me, always without a boring moment. Fighting tears, I add: "I haven't felt this emotional since Nelson Mandela was let out of prison. Since August 29, I've felt that we may soon all step out of our collective jail." Others in the room tear up *and* beam at each other.

Less than two weeks later, it's predawn and I'm on a line in Washington, along with many journalists, lower-echelon diplomats and Mideast players. We're waiting to enter a side gate that leads to the White House's south lawn. It's September 13, 1993. Within two hours, three hundred of us are sitting in a semicircle of chairs—Israelis, Americans, Palestinian dignitaries. Many who are here live in the States; others have just arrived from the Mideast, jet-lagged but excited.

As this historic ceremony between Arafat and Rabin unfolds, we're passing tissues around, crying in disbelief at the handshake we witness. High emotion flows throughout the crowds during the public speeches. Rabin is eloquent. Shimon Peres utters his memorable line, "You don't leap over a chasm in two steps." Immediately after the speeches, the leaders sign papers, committing both cultures to mutual recognition. With the formalities over, a freewheeling lawn party gets under way. Everyone needs to circulate and talk. The spirit is so inclusive that even at the highest levels no one pulls rank. It's as though if you're here, you're important. That's what makes intimate talk with any and everyone possible. I wander about the lawn, have a long talk with Elie Wiesel, the writer and Holocaust survivor, a chat with President Clinton's advisor George Stephanopoulos and then with an assortment of senators. But the exchange that means most to me is with Thomas Friedman. I tell him how much his work has meant to me, how his descriptions of the Mideast kept me good company when I arrived there, and continue to be the foundation for all that I've learned since. Like everyone else I encounter, Friedman is incredibly gracious, as though my words have only added to the joy of the occasion.

This spirit isn't distilled for the major TV stations; but then neither are the schisms growing among us as afternoon turns to early evening. The first tensions I pick up are at a party inside a large tent set up near the White House. It's filled with Jewish American philanthropists, many of whom detest Arafat. It's only hours after the ceremony when Rabin addresses this high-profile crowd, which includes leaders of the mainstream Jewish organizations. I watch this pearly, elegant group as they listen. It's obvious that the Israeli leaders know their audience well, for their tone changes markedly when speaking here. The unbridled optimism of their morning talks is more muted as they speak directly to this assembly's widespread suspicion of Arab intentions.

Responding to the ambivalence that is present here, Rabin states: "We Jews were once seen as intellectually disciplined but weak in self-defense. Then we were seen as champions of winning wars but inept at creating peace. Now is the time for us to be strong in peace making, even though we dislike our partners, and, of course, as you can well imagine, we will never loosen our vigilance with *them*. We will make sure, every single step of the way, that the Arabs keep their word—down to the most minute details. Trust us, we will make sure they prove what they say. They'll be watched like hawks."

After this cocktail hour I go with friends to a party in a hotel basement, where the tensions are of another kind. On a back stairwell, I literally bump into the Palestinian Washington delegation. They look ashen, and are walking slowly downstairs, as if resistant to enter the party room below. I talk to Faisal Husseini, the leader. Though we don't know each other personally, I'm drawn to him, as I am to the other Palestinians, whom I do know. They've all traveled a long way for this occasion, but there's a hesitancy and discomfort that's visible in their faces and body language. Hanan Ashwari, whom I've interviewed several times, tells me that they knew nothing about the Oslo process. Husseini, whose manner is polite, almost shy, attempts to hide what he's feeling, but he looks uneasy. The press has announced how much these Palestinians have gained, but that's not what I am seeing. To me, they seem to be simply bearing up, as if conscious that they have much to lose and have great pressures upon them. Clearly, they have their collective hands full, not just with creating the future, but with the immediate ordeal of navigating tonight's emotional shoals.

I come down to earth. Back in Israel and in the territories there must be conflicts within everyone, an awareness of how much work is ahead in order to translate today's public ceremony into grounds for peace. Each must be watching the worldwide news with a mixture of joy, shock and anxiety. The American Jews I talk with strike me as a world apart. Even those who are active in peace work seem to miss the shadows that threaten this bright occasion.

Not that I'm in any position to judge anyone. I, too, am riding the excitement. Yet I am becoming dimly aware that most Arabs I've met today, whether from Syria, Egypt, Saudi Arabia or Jordan, are, like most of the Palestinians, ambivalent. A Syrian doctor now working in Chicago says in passing, "Just remember. None of this means anything without Syria. It's [President Hafez al-]

Assad who can make or break this deal. He's the one we have to watch now."
He's right, but few of today's celebrants seem able to focus on anything but
Rabin and Arafat and that reluctant, ropily extended handshake.

Flying back to the Mideast, I focus on those discordant moments I witnessed in Washington. And I see that, for all the essential drama of the handshake, it will be Beit Sahur's Rapprochement room that is most critical to a
living, livable peace. Because on-the-ground meetings across ethnic lines will
constitute the true recognitions-in-action.

As I watch clouds pass beneath my plane's window, I'm envisioning a Diaspora Peace Corps—Jews and Palestinians from abroad who will travel to the
Mideast, willing to visit each other's homes. Although almost everyone on this
plane is fast asleep, I'm wide awake, daydreaming of how ever-wary Jews and
ever-weary Palestinians, who think they already understand each other, finally
meet. What momentous occasions those will be, I muse.

I open my notebook and begin writing: "The psyche is hungry for meaning.
And what meaning is as charged as being accurately mirrored by an ancient
enemy? What can compare to seeing and then being seen by strangers who
turn out to be so unlike our long-held images?"

I lean back, pleased with these rhythms, when my reverie is interrupted by a
vivid flashback—of Faisal Husseini's inscrutably sad face. This memory breaks
apart my rosy visions. So I turn the page and write: "Find out how the Palestinians in the Mideast felt while watching the Handshake."

Part III
After the Handshake

Take a look at this stage. The King of Jordan, the President of Egypt, Chairman Arafat, and us, the Prime Minister and the Foreign Minister of Israel . . . The sight before you at this moment was impossible, was unthinkable, just two years ago. Only poets dreamed of it; and, to our great pain, soldiers and civilians went to their deaths to make this moment possible. Here we stand before you, men whom fate and history have sent on a mission of peace: to end, once and for all, one hundred years of bloodshed.

—Yitzhak Rabin in Washington, September 13, 1993

You don't leap over a chasm in two steps.

—Shimon Peres, Washington, "The Handshake"

CHAPTER NINE

Scenes from an Uneasy Peace

I drop in to visit my next-door neighbors, Moshe and Ruth Ben-Ami. They're a devoted couple (and wonderful neighbors) in their late seventies. Since the Handshake, I've avoided them. Moshe has told me only too clearly what he thinks of the Arabs. Before Oslo, we could, at least obliquely, joke about our opposing political views. But I doubt this ease will continue and I don't relish what awaits me across our common hallway.

Ruth greets me warmly, her face creasing into her usual, all-encompassing smile. She motions for me to come in, come in already. Two steps inside, I catch sight of Moshe, an Israeli-born war veteran and engineering magnate, macho to the core. He's slumped deep into his brown leather chair, gazing out his wall-to-wall living room windows.

When I walk over to him he looks up and spots the name "Shimon Peres" on a government press release that I'm carrying. This sight unleashes his pent-up fury. He stands up and shouts, "Shimon Peres! He's killing us! You know nothing! You have no idea what Arabs do!" He walks agitatedly back and forth, railing against "this crazy process," yelling about which Arabs tried to kill him where, how he showed them "who's boss around here. And now they're getting the Jerusalem–Tel Aviv highway!" With this said, he slumps back into his chair, shaking his leonine head back and forth, back and forth. He can't relax, but keeps swiveling his body to find a comfortable position. "They're handing over the Jerusalem–Tel Aviv highway," he repeats quietly. "Don't speak to me of Shimon Peres. He's killing us."

His voice drops to a whisper, his eyes are clamped shut, and he's wheezing. Fearing that he'll have another heart attack, Ruth and I say: "No, not Tel Aviv; Gaza."

"Gaza now. Tel Aviv next. You know nothing," he mutters.

Ruth, married to him for fifty years, whispers to me, "He's been fighting the

Arabs since he was seventeen," as if to say, You have to understand. I do understand.

"They want a smaller country, and for that they want us to celebrate," Moshe whispers hoarsely. "Our own government is stealing land from us. Do they think we're blind? Does your Mr. Peres think we don't understand? It's *you* who don't understand. You give an Arab a finger, he takes a hand." He pauses. "No one loves a Jew. Who helped us during the Holocaust? You answer that. No, *I'll* answer. Not a single bloody country, that's who. You know what they want from us? Our money, period. Name one country whose doors opened to Jews when we were being murdered like cockroaches."

Ruth and I agree that's true, so true. No country let us Jews in. None tried to stop Auschwitz. No one bombed those train tracks.

"You see, she thinks *just* like you," Ruth says. Moshe's eyes remain shut. He's a man deep in grief. Now Ruth and I are monitoring his breathing, trying to encourage him to relax. Ruth puts Israeli folk music on the tape deck. Moshe remains stiff with fury in his chair. Standing right above him, she repeats softly, "Moshe, she agrees with you," gesturing to me to change the subject.

We talk about his sons, his new Dead Sea project. But it's mission impossible. "Not Tel Aviv, Gaza," I hear Ruth repeating as I leave, late for an appointment to interview Achmed's uncle, who's waiting for me in the tiny village of Arram, outside Ramallah.

Forty minutes later I'm sitting with Mahmoud Kouri in his crowded apartment. A rotund man in his late fifties, he once owned a packaging plant in Ramallah, lost his factory and now works part-time with the United Nations. He looks miserable on his threadbare couch. "Oslo!" he mutters. "Let me tell you what we got. One percent of our land. This is something to wave flags about? Quote me here. Write this down. Now we have occupation *and* Arafat to worry about—not one, but two bullies. Mark my words. They'll work together and strangle us." (This fear of "institutional collaboration" between Arafat and Rabin is becoming an epidemic among Palestinians.)

Kouri motions for me to move closer. He wants me to catch his every word. "Arafat will wave his money. The Palestinians will fight and kill over it. He'll become Rabin's henchman and those two will end up dividing our people. Things will only get worse for the ordinary among us. Trust me, the worst is yet to come." All I'm thinking is how much he resembles Moshe Ben-Ami. Though their words give voice to contrary fears, their emotional states are identical—fury, betrayal and, most of all, dread for what's to come.

Another week. It's *Shabbat*. Jackie and Eliza are with Daphie and Tal, their second home. Shuki is, what's the norm these days, out, to where I'm never certain. I'm with a group of Israeli journalists, enjoying dinner on a candlelit terrace in Moshav Beit Zayit, ten minutes south of Jerusalem. This is where Sara and her kids have recently moved. We're watching the lights of Jerusalem blink on above us, like a bright umbrella. Sara shouts out from the kitchen. We run inside and hear the news flash: Two Israeli teenagers have just been found, hacked to death in a popular hiking area, the Wadi Kelt, near Jericho.

The geography of Israel has its own rules, which are not obvious to those abroad. Wadi Kelt is not across the Green Line, where the settlements provoke frequent attacks, but in Israel proper. It's a desert terrain attracting all types of Israelis for *Shabbat* picnics, family outings or student field trips. That it's so close to Jericho, where Palestinians are due to take control on December 13, makes these killings especially ominous. The Israeli teens could have been any of our kids; their murders speak to every Israeli's fears about security. Silently, we all head back outside.

Each guest now recalls aloud when he or she last hiked in the Wadi Kelt. They describe the seductions of that magnificent stretch of desert: its birds, flowering cactus plants and light-filled vistas. We all shudder. "I shouldn't go to Jericho tomorrow," I say, remembering my plan to drive past Wadi Kelt with a Palestinian I've never met—a man Hakam has said will give me interesting insights into current Palestinian reality. As if with one voice, the Israeli journalists turn on me: "Of course, you go. You never let violence win."

And so early the next morning I arrive at East Jerusalem's American Colony Hotel and watch as a very tall man lumbers my way. He carries his body awkwardly, like a coat that doesn't quite fit. Yet the moment Adnan starts talking his appearance shifts from awkward to robustly confident. We begin driving and almost immediately I realize that he's gifted with a lucky brain. His mind churns excitably and is far-ranging. Every subject he touches grows vivid, a talent that's pleasurably contagious. In no time we're trading perspectives on a dizzying number of topics, so engaged that we forget to stop and place flowers where the murders occurred.

Adnan is half my age and has spent most of his life in Amman, Jordan. Despite such differences, we click. His mental agility lifts us into a conversation that resembles jazz; we're riffing together, laughing, interrupting each other and then allowing each other long solo speeches. Both of us have tracked the minutiae of the peace process and in addition, we discover common interests in literature and psychology. After half an hour of checking each other out—a test we both pass—I feel comfortable enough to ask how he and his friends felt watching the Handshake.

"The truth or the sanitized version?" he asks. Answering himself, he says, "Contrary to the 'euphoria' and 'cautious hope' reported in the news, that handshake brought us all down emotionally. For us intellectuals and for ordinary people as well, seeing Rabin and Arafat on that stage made us sick." As he says this, we hit a bump in the road and we both almost hit the roof of his car. We buckle into our seat belts and he continues. "What was it like, watching them in Washington? . . . It was like watching Hamlet jump into a clown costume at the grand finale of that play—turning our great epic for emancipation into a mockery, a badly written farce. Watching Arafat play the joker at the White House gave every Palestinian a grim sense that our myth is over, that we'll forever be trapped inside the wrong play, one lacking any internal coherence."

"But why?"

"Why? We want high tragedy, not the twilight zone. Everyone had this same horrible, sinking sensation: 'This is how it ends. . . . The world applauds while we cry.' " So this is what Faisal Husseini and the others from the Palestinian delegation were feeling on September 13, I think. And then, in response to Adnan's mention of Shakespeare, I remember something. As he drives, with his long fingers gripping his steering wheel, I rummage through my backpack.

I flip through the *Newsweek* I'm carrying, then read aloud what Amos Oz wrote the day after September 13, in an essay that begins with the obvious: That the Israeli-Palestinian conflict is a tragic clash between "right and right," that both sides have legitimate claims to this land. "We do not want a Shakespearean conclusion with poetic justice hovering over a stage littered with dead bodies," he writes, but rather "we wish for a typical Chekhovian finale, where the players are disillusioned and worried, but *alive*. . . . Israelis and Palestinians never again have to get past the terrible emotional obstacle of shaking hands for the first time. That cognitive barrier has . . . broken down."

Has Adnan read this or is it pure coincidence that both he and Oz refer to Shakespeare? I'm wondering about this as his fingers loosen on the wheel. "Yes," he replies softly, "Oz is right. You see, Israelis personify a Western mindset. They're drawn to gradations, to gradual developments. But we Palestinians have an Eastern consciousness, are attracted to great dramas. Maybe we're hooked on the tragic elements in life."

Caught in traffic, Adnan repeats: "Oz is absolutely right. We can avoid Shakespeare's lifeless bodies if we can accept Chekhov, accept our sorrows and so end this bloody play of ours." He seems relieved after saying this and becomes lively again. He describes the days *after* the Handshake, remembering how his people's mood did lift. "Little by little everyone saw the positive side of what occurred, began to welcome the worldwide acknowledgment, the new, public affirmation that Palestinians are a people with rights to a part of this land. Whatever our feelings, we started gearing up for hard work," he says. "We helped build Israel. We helped build Arab countries. We can build our own state. Hell, I won't pretend that our strong point is organization. But if no one reneges, cuts us off financially or humiliates us, we'll work hard to succeed."

After dropping a letter in his parents' mailbox in Ramallah, we swing around and head toward Jericho on the road that winds through desert mountains. Adnan tells me about his father's abrupt exile to Jordan the year he, Adnan, turned seven. Before his departure, his father was a beloved pediatrician in the Nablus area. When notified of his deportation, he was first enraged, then in shock. His father loved and served his community here, treating any child who needed medical care, often for free. As a result, he won more than respect, he elicited love. But after he arrived in Jordan, although he was professionally successful, earning more money than ever before, he fell into an inconsolable despair. This morose and remote man was the only father whom Adnan knew. "All these years he remained morbidly homesick for his land, his people, his clan. Recently, he was allowed to return home. And I watched his lifelong depression disappear overnight. A miracle," Adnan says as we drive into Jericho.

To our mutual surprise, this sleepy town has had an overnight upheaval. Instead of sinking under the usual tropical torpor, Jericho is alive with crowds today. The main street is so packed with buses, cars and foreign tourists that it takes us twenty minutes to find a place to park, a task usually accomplished in minutes.

Out on the main street hawkers are selling Palestinian and Israeli flags, T-shirts with logos praising coexistence in English, Hebrew and Arabic. These tourist items are being grabbed up by eager customers. Inside a crowded restaurant we find a table in a quiet corner and order lunch. Soon, the owner is standing above us. His pockets are overflowing with shekels which he shoves back inside, while asking distractedly how we like our meal. He's so busy surveying the crowd in glee that he's hardly looking at or listening to us. "So many!" he exclaims, glad for the windfall, this long-awaited economic boom.

Adnan and I wink at each other. The promise of a better economy may be driving the peace process and increasing Jericho's business, but that's not what attracts us. We're more interested in the psychological riches accompanying peace. Even the hackneyed, long-improbable "breakfast in Damascus, lunch in Jerusalem, dinner in Amman" isn't what moves us. We imagine Israeli and Palestinian soldiers sharing coffee while guarding the Allenby Bridge together, doctors and teachers, economists, ecologists and businesspeople from our two cultures, finally meeting, as two democratic states gradually unite into one force field.

Carried away, we envision the coming generations when the clan warmth, emotional depth and poetry of the East join with the rationalism, industriousness and technological sophistication of the West. Over hummus and tabbouleh, we agree that our two peoples already share more than is commonly acknowledged. Palestinians and Israelis are intensely loyal to family. Adnan says, "Our peoples are like the Italians. We know there are bastards in the family, but we take care of each other. We don't distance or psychoanalyze our blood relations." He pauses. "Family bonds are more tenuous in the States?" he asks.

"Fractured, dissipating, alienated . . . for sure," I respond. "Sometimes America seems to have devolved into a culture of ambitious orphans." He nods sagely as we agree that Israeli Jews and Palestinian Arabs share many other traits, such as an ingenuity for navigating life under oppression. Both our peoples have been forced into agility; both have developed street savvy to circumvent physical, psychological and economic constrictions. We both know how to outmaneuver those in power, though, we agree, laughing, that Palestinians are far too patient and Israelis often too impatient.

Adnan and I look around this tinsel-laden cafeteria. We see rows of tourists—German, French and Swedish Christians—eating in long rows at rectangular tables. The Palestinian entrepreneurs at the next table drink saki, toasting the coming boon. Adnan and I are getting high, too—on ideas. We're discussing Martin Buber. Using Buber's vernacular, Adnan says that what is needed to make this peace a reality is to turn "I-It relations" into "I-Thou recognitions." He recites passages from Buber by heart, as we look into each other's eyes, sure that all we dream about will unfold *"l'hat, l'hat; adoui, adoui"* (slowly, slowly). Once the Oslo Accords become official policy, we imagine Israelis will stop viewing Palestinians as terrorists or cheap labor; most Palestinians will begin seeing Israelis as partners and not bullying occupiers. And so the two of us, having settled the Israeli-Palestinian conflict, drive back to Jerusalem, at peace with each other and the world.

●   ●   ●

Three weeks later, on a sun-drenched Jerusalem morning in November, I'm on my way to Nablus for a short planning session between Israeli and Palestinian

Rapprochement facilitators. We're meeting to clarify which issues will be covered in a new dialogue series beginning this afternoon. As a result of the Oslo Accords, the freewheeling conversations we've been having are now going to evolve into more structured sessions, with pre-planned topics. Today's meeting will bring together lawyers from each side for the first time. We'll discuss issues relevant to the eventual formation of a Palestinian state. At 10 A.M., we arrive at Sami Kilani's light and airy Nablus apartment. While the facilitators review details for the afternoon session, I step out onto the terrace, meditating on the special mood that crossing cultures evokes, one I felt most recently with Adnan. I'm wondering why, even when there is lingering mistrust, there is so much pleasure in traversing boundaries. This spirit of joy is a well-kept secret, I think; and, anyway, I don't understand the reasons for such happiness. What are the origins of this pulse of pleasure, this chemistry that arises between us, who are supposed enemies?

The Nablus morning sun is tempered by a breeze. I lean over the terrace to look at the beds of multicolored flowers, the saplings swaying in the yard below. Well-being rises up in me as I gaze at the towering Nablus mountains in the distance. Leaning over this thin fence, I think of Theodor Herzl's famous terrace photo. Samir Yaish, who by now seems an old friend, soon joins me on the terrace, sharing my pleasure in the beauty of the scene. With his bright eyes and his long black beard, it's now that I see how much *he* resembles Herzl.

I remember the day we met. It was during my first visit to Nablus, in December 1992. At the time I knew few Palestinians and I kept staring at his handsome face, thin body and smart clothes, unable to match what I was seeing with my preconceptions of what an Arab must look like. I half wondered if he was an outside infiltrator, some sort of spy. Telling him now of my thoughts, I make him laugh. A poet and a professor of literature, Samir does cut an unusually glamorous figure *and* he's Palestinian to the core—his family has lived in Nablus for nine generations. But what I value most about him are his unique perceptions. I know he'll have something interesting to say about these dialogues.

"Pleasure," he muses when I ask. "Try this on. See if it's true for you. . . . Sometimes I feel I know my own people almost too well. When talking to any of my people, each slips into one or another category easily, and usually within minutes. Do you feel that? As if you know your people almost too well?" I nod as he continues: "I think the most exciting love affairs are those fueled by mystery. Without it, even passion can turn claustrophobic, grow dull. Do you agree?" I nod again. "And I think something of that same excitement touches our friendships with one another. Speaking for myself, when I meet new Palestinians, there's camaraderie or compassion, but no mystery. Yet, when I meet

Jews and Israelis informally, I'm truly curious, fascinated. There's so much I don't know. That curiosity is the joy, the pleasure."

Samir looks inside the room and an expression of fondness floods his face. He's savoring warm feelings about his Israeli friends who are gathered around a dining room table talking animatedly with the Palestinian organizers. "I couldn't dream up one of them," he says. "However could I imagine a Judith, a Veronica, a Hillel?" Through his eyes I see each as wondrous. And then, everyone inside suddenly leaps up. They shout out to us to hurry, that we're late. We all pile into a caravan of cars and drive uphill to another Palestinian home where, inside an elegantly furnished, oversized living room, more than sixty Israelis and Palestinians are assembled, palpably uncomfortable with one another. The Israelis, in Nablus for the first time, don't know what to do with themselves. Some sit stiffly, feigning aloofness. Others, eyes downcast, chat quietly among themselves. One Israeli lawyer, who's worked for years for Palestinian civil rights, looks as though he's having a full-blown panic attack.

As soon as we enter, the dialogue leaders express apologies for our lateness. Rawda and Samir, Veronica and Hillel all begin sparring good-naturedly with each other in an attempt to convey ease. As our hosts serve sweet tea and cookies, the facilitators suggest we go around and introduce ourselves by name, town and profession. Soon we are listening to each other and forget to be nervous.

The subject today is what constitutes a democracy, what conditions will best protect civil and human rights in the nascent Palestinian autonomy. The first speaker is Eliyahu Abrams, an Israeli civil rights attorney who works for a well-known human rights group. Eliyahu seems nondescript. He's of medium height, has sandy brown hair and eyes. But as he speaks, his intensity and humility change him from bland to vivid as he attracts an attentive audience.

Eliyahu admits he's nervous. He apologizes for reading from a prepared paper. Yet once he begins talking, he makes eye contact with everyone in the room and never refers to his script. He points out the necessity for Palestinian lawyers to build an independent judiciary; this is the best hope for their evolving state to move toward a democracy. He describes the legal structures Israel created to protect free speech and a free press, even the rights of religious minorities.

After twenty minutes Eliyahu says, "I have to admit to being a pessimist for a very long time. My parents survived the Holocaust, yet their ordeal lives in me. Growing up in Israel, I felt lucky, that is, until I saw what we 'survivors' do to you, to your people. That's when I lost heart. The more I represented Palestinians in Israeli courts, the more I felt that our human spirit is too flawed, too corrupt, too uncaring; that the legal structures we had created to protect ourselves were used to victimize you." He looks around the room. "Only at this very minute," he says, "while I look into your faces, you who've collectively spent lifetimes in Israeli prisons [he looks at Rawda and Mohammed, who've done ten and thirteen years in jail, respectively], do I start to feel hope again. You're so open and trusting, so willing to listen to us who represent a country that's oppressed you." He pauses, holding back tears. "If *you* can keep your hearts open, maybe it's time for me to practice optimism."

Many of the Palestinian lawyers, half of whom are women, are visibly moved. But soon they recover themselves and begin to voice their concerns. One is worried about Arafat's dictatorial style. Another questions the wisdom of modeling laws based on Israel's. "If your state doesn't protect Israeli Arabs, doesn't even pretend to protect those living in the territories, how will we Palestinians do any better? How can we be more just, given our weak position, with no infrastructure and with so much internal disarray?"

A Palestinian woman with long black hair and dark eyes says that she is dubious, fearing what lies ahead. If Israel, with all its laws, is so violent, can Palestinians in chronic poverty and disarray really get organized? It may be impossible to do half as well.

Eliyahu responds that the Palestinian legal community needs to remember that if and when Arafat threatens to rule as a dictator, there are ways to combat that. "Arafat can't live forever," one aging Palestinian lawyer sighs, as talk turns to the benefits of having a constitution, which Israel itself does not. Such a document can guard civil rights and due process for all Palestinians. The lawyers are talking with urgency, creating a mood that spreads all around the room.

The meeting continues for hours. Everyone in the room participates as all reserve disappears. During a brief break my eyes meet those of Shahab Shaheen, whom I haven't seen since the day I went to Jericho to witness the return of the PLO exiles. She still looks as if she is dressed by Bergdorf Goodman. She surprises me by giving me a warm hug, saying: "I'll never forget you. You were one of the first I met after returning from Jordan. I see you and remember that day in Jericho when I was too overwhelmed with happiness to speak."

While the lawyers continue discussing the finer points of constitutional democracy, I catch Samir's eye and realize that our talk this morning was missing a key element about pleasure in dialogue. The joy filling this room goes beyond curiosity; it seems an ethical signal that we're working toward right action. I see the brightening faces around me as a response of the soul.

As the meeting draws to a close, Jon Immanuel, whom I've invited, says, in his concise way, "Think about it. Israel is the only country in history with the chance to give birth to two states in one lifetime."

• • •

November moves into December with the predictable and sudden spasms of icy rain. After six arid months under an unremitting sun, the desert mountains are drenched. This is how winter always begins in Jerusalem, yet this year's weather mimics the general consciousness, a chilly and widespread retreat into pessimism. It's become a dispirited time, especially as the rejectionists on both sides cleverly provoke each other.

In early December, as the thirteenth approaches, the day when troop withdrawals from Jericho are due, two settlers are killed in the West Bank by Palestinians. It's unclear if these killers are from the Hamas or not. But immediately, some settlers retaliate. They burn Palestinian schools and cars and shoot at pedestrians. If these settlers were Palestinians, they'd be killed or imprisoned in a millisecond by the Israelis. They are not. This Israeli government, eager to build a consensus for the Oslo Accords, curries favor with these rampaging fanatics. Everyone knows who the Jewish culprits are, but even the few who are arrested are back on the streets within days. Some journalists and writers compare such settler attacks to a Jewish-led pogrom.

At one of the biweekly Beit Sahur dialogue meetings that occurs around this time I express my discouragement over the outbreaks of hostility. Will our two sides ever act in good faith toward one another, ever be able to trust? Veronica Cohen looks at my sad face. Then she looks around the room and sees that my mood is mirrored by the others. In her warm, lilting voice, she begins telling us about a nine-year-old Israeli boy named Addy. Addy's family, she says, was preparing to host a group from Nablus late in August, just before the news of Oslo broke. Addy overheard his parents planning the luncheon menu for Palestinian guests and he announced that if a single Arab arrived in his house, he'd run away from home and "never come back." He repeatedly pulled at his mother's dress, demanding she call "those Arabs" and cancel the meal because "Arabs are bad." His parents tried, without success, to reason with him.

When the Palestinian family arrived, Addy didn't (to his parents' immense relief) act aggressively. He crawled behind a large armchair. Everyone ignored him as best they could and the two families began having a wonderful time. After a while they watched Addy peer out from behind his fortress. He was staring at Jamal, a boy his own age from Nablus who was quietly playing with a deck of cards. When he thought no one was looking, Addy inched his way from behind the chair toward the Palestinian boy. At first, he just studied him, while the adults tried not to smile, pretending to pay him no attention. Soon Addy slid over to sit beside Jamal. He quickly handed Jamal a piece of candy before scurrying back behind his chair.

The following week when Addy's parents set out to Nablus for a peace picnic, they assumed they'd leave Addy behind. But now he insisted on coming. Immediately upon arriving in Nablus, he found Jamal and ran off with him and his friends. He had such a good time that his parents had to yank him away at the end of the day. Veronica finishes: "Now each time his family drives into the territories, Addy urges them to stop whenever he sees Palestinian kids, even those who look wild or unsavory to his folks. The boy runs off before they can assess his safety. He thinks all Palestinian kids are like Jamal, fun to play with."

We all laugh, realizing that this nine-year-old shows us the two sides of ourselves—the part that is frightened and wants to continue to hide behind our respective "chairs," and the part that, having met "the enemy," becomes *too* enchanted, unable to differentiate who is trustworthy and who isn't. Inside each of us, optimism and pessimism seesaw. Whatever constitutes "realism" hasn't yet been scripted into this adventure that's been thrust upon us all.

CHAPTER TEN

Tomorrow and Tomorrow:
Winter Vignettes

Tomorrow, December 13, is the day when we are supposed to see the first tangible signs of the peace process in motion. Once again, journalists are converging. But tonight, at the last possible moment, Rabin has announced that Israeli troops will *not* leave Jericho as planned. The reasons given are hazy. The prime minister says only that "no date is sacred," a line that will become a too-familiar refrain, but one that's shocking tonight.

On the morning of the thirteenth, I head for Jericho anyway, with a Palestinian woman named Suher Ismael, a filmmaker. She goes her own way as I head for Izhaq Shawa's grocery store. I remember how tuned in Shawa is to every micro-movement of hope, and I'm worried about how he's bearing up after news of this delay. As I walk into his store, he shows me today's *Al Quds* (the largest Arabic paper), where the front page features the story of the stalled peace. Then he shouts, "This could have been written twenty years ago!" I see that he's despondent. "It's always the same story," he hollers. "Don't talk to me of peace today—talk of war."

For months, he tells me, he's been encouraging neighbors, cousins, friends and customers to keep their spirits up. Since he predicted the Oslo breakthrough, they all credit him with the ability to read between the lines of the news, to catch those deeper currents underlying surface stories. Now he feels like a fool. After Rabin's announcement last night, neither he nor his wife could sleep, he tells me, and then he sinks into sadness. "I've been barking at journalists all day," he admits.

It's true that Jericho seems to have ten journalists for each Palestinian. Instead of showing their disappointment to the press, most express rage.

"But we feel terrible, too," I say.

"I see you do," he says. "Well, do *you* see hope?"

"In the long run, yes," I say honestly. I know Shawa wants to feel hope and I sense that he's still searching for seeds of it.

"Look," he says, "maybe the Israelis have their reasons. What really bothers me is that even if Rabin had to call off the troop withdrawals, he could give us symbolic signs of kindness, give us something . . . anything." We look out his open door to see, directly across the street, a large contingent of Israeli soldiers. They were doubtless sent here in case riots break out. We watch as they set up tents on a small hill. "Did they have to *intensify* occupation on the very day it was to be dismantled?" Shawa asks. The soldiers we're studying don't look at all amiable. Probably, they're angry that they had to come and work overtime.

"My mind is at war with my heart," Shawa says. "My mind believes that the Israelis are not ever going to trust or recognize us. But my heart is stubborn. It says, Okay, maybe in ten days. . . ." I watch him resisting the anti-Israeli sentiments that are rising in him. He says he feels very "nervous," that he's suffering from a mild version of what all extremists feel—that the Israelis can never be trusted.

I know that the Israelis have parallel fears. Most believe that the Palestinians aren't well enough organized to take control of Jericho. It's even possible that Arafat asked for this delay. We know so little of what's going on inside the closed negotiations, and that ignorance amplifies a mutual paranoia. But despite the symmetries of hate and demonizing, today's stall highlights the extreme asymmetry of power. For we Jews in Israel enjoy a full range of freedoms in a thriving democracy, while the Palestinians have mere existence and dashed hopes.

"When you really want anything to happen, you can make it happen," Shawa says. "There are a hundred solutions, a hundred ways to compromise and feed hope, if the Israelis wanted to. If they really knew how much Palestinians need signs of change, they'd do something." I nod in agreement. "I'm sorry to tell you," he continues, "but I believe Israel wants to humiliate and laugh at us. Their actions today say, You people are only good for dreams. We'll throw you a dream, and then we'll step on it."

Then, as if he's forgotten I'm Jewish, he adds, "Well, maybe the Jews only know trouble and war. Look at their history. Why so much trouble for centuries wherever they go?"

I know his statement arises from pain. I don't hear his bitter words as an echo of the irrational anti-Semitism of Europe, Russia or elsewhere in the world—that disease which, like Elvis-sightings, can flourish independent of any reality. Shawa's comment springs directly from the present context: seeing Jews camped outside his store, seeing their guns and troops multiplying, in contrast to the promised departure. Yet sitting in the intense heat, I sense this distinction is one that's lost on most Israelis and American Jews. Although

Shawa is against "Jews," as are many throughout the territories today, there's nothing abstract about his racist comment. And, for me, what is particularly poignant about Shawa and those he typifies—intelligent, hardworking family men—is that two months ago he was thrilled to share a generous breakfast with his Israeli guests. Moreover, he's often said he wants a Palestinian society "just like Israel." Like many Palestinians, Shawa watches Israeli TV and sees the Knesset in action; he understands democracy. That he admires much about Israel, and actively fears any Palestinian entity that's molded on the governments of dictatorial Arab countries—regimes he despises—puts him in a quandary. Not surprisingly, he responds by retreating into distrust of Israeli intentions, expending what's left of his energy in rage against Jews.

I leave Shawa's grocery heavy-hearted and go to meet Suher. We find each other easily and are soon walking together down the darkening streets toward my car. A storm is fast approaching, one that looks like a hurricane. The sky is turning from dark gray to black, and the winds are picking up speed. We agree to rush back up to Jerusalem, when a Palestinian friend of hers, Khalid, sees us passing by and invites us to wait out the storm in the small shop where he's standing.

Once inside, I realize this shop is the makeshift Reuters TV office. It is crowded with Palestinians and Israelis, five of each, speaking an animated mix of Hebrew and Arabic, sprinkled with an occasional English phrase. They're so enmeshed that I can barely distinguish who's Palestinian and who's Israeli.

Some in the room are in a frenzy, rushing to finish today's TV tape, called "December 13th in Jericho." Others have completed their part of the work and have collapsed in exhaustion. But the entire group shares that wild giddiness of a joint endeavor under deadline pressure.

I become fascinated by two women working in a corner who are busy re-editing the final tape. In the first scene, Palestinians are lining a side street in Jericho, shouting in Arabic, "Rabin is a terrorist; we are not terrorists." Then there's a cut to a settler speaking from a nearby synagogue, shouting, "Send the mass murderer Arafat to hell. Then we'll live with the local Arabs in peace."

Apparently, it's difficult to synchronize the words with the visual images, so in the next hour I hear these same phrases repeated some twenty-six times. The editors keep playing and then replaying this tiny news segment. Here in this room is a group that works so closely with one another that *they* are the future (what the dialogue groups have only dreamed of). These journalists are paying no attention to the old script on Arab-Israeli relations. But up on the TV monitor, the constant cut, replay, cut, replay mirrors the tensions in the world around us: Jew, Arab, hate, terror, mistrust, murder. I'm sitting in a maelstrom of consciousness so far beyond these brute simplicities of venom and fear, while up on the screen is what people the world over will watch on tonight's news. The atmosphere in this room will remain a secret, which is ironic because the people who are distilling the imagery from today's events have fully transcended it. Mutual recognitions tonight are unfolding only behind these cameras, not in front of them.

• • •

This delay in Jericho has a ripple effect. A few weeks later I visit Hamdi Faraj. We're in his chaotic, paper-strewn office in Bethlehem. A thirty-something freelance journalist, he has no interest in giving me a sanitized tour of the West Bank. His aim is not to ensure my safety, but to live this day to the fullest, however it unfolds. I can read this attitude in his animated hand gestures and excitable manner. He's a man wired for wild energy. We're talking politics, about the "delay" in troop withdrawals. "I don't really understand what's going on," I say.

"If *you* don't, if *I* don't, how can the ordinary Palestinian understand?" he says.

Just then, we hear shouting from beneath his office window. A volley of gunshots is ringing out right below us. Ruella, Hamdi's sister, shrieks, "Army!" as I race behind them down circular stairs. Halfway up this slanted road, kids are throwing the heaviest stones they can heft. We continue to hear gunshots from a few feet away; the soldiers must be right around the corner. Instantly, the streets are deluged with Palestinians, as if this outbreak of fighting is essentially festive. Everyone cascades uphill toward the action in an air of excitement. I stand frozen in front of Hamdi's office.

Minutes later Hamdi and I are driving away in his car, on our way to the El Khader refugee camp. I show him my cardboard camera, the kind you throw away once you've completed shooting the film. He's never seen anything like this. Soon he pulls into a gas station to take a better look. There, out of the blue, we're surrounded by men in black T-shirts and black jeans, carrying huge machine guns and blocking our way. Hamdi grabs my camera and sticks it outside his window, aiming it aggressively at them. The sight of this camera drives these guys into a frenzy. They turn on us, pointing their guns' barrels, which are so long that they reach almost inside the car. One rifle is an inch from Hamdi's head.

My heart is pounding. In the suddenness of this confrontation, a numbing panic fills me, along with the words "This is *it*." For this is the kind of confrontation that's daily described in the newspapers, what usually ends in death, followed by conflicting stories about who initiated the combat. I don't know whether these gunmen are a rival Palestinian faction or are settlers. I only know that they aren't Israeli soldiers, and they aren't kidding around. To my amazement, Hamdi persists in furiously clicking away, taking their pictures, even with guns poised at his temple. Then he starts shouting in Arabic; the guys scream back at him, apparently ready to shoot.

I grab his arm, beg him to put down the camera and to stop provoking these men. Pushing my hand away, Hamdi keeps shouting, now in English, while his whole body is shaking, "This area isn't closed!" he's screaming. "I can shoot any photograph I want!" I wonder if he's crazy, for it's clear that these frenzied gunmen aren't about to be deterred by a mere technicality. Now they're shouting in Hebrew, which convinces me that they're settlers on the loose, looking for Palestinian victims, a certainty that pushes me over the top.

Five or six Israeli soldiers drive up and approach our car. They order us not to move. I don't know whether to jump out or to stay put. I am tempted to yell, I'm Jewish. On immediate second thought, I shout, "I'm a journalist, an American." A young soldier leans into my car window. "I hate guns," I scream, which gives everyone pause. I look into this soldier's young face and see that his expression matches my words. He's about nineteen. He seems in way over his head with this ugliness.

Hamdi is stalled in his rage. The soldiers withdraw and are talking among themselves in a tight circle. Clearly unhappy about my role in this cease-fire, Hamdi slumps back in his seat. "I only stopped because of you," he says between gritted teeth. The men in black disperse as suddenly as they appeared. The soldiers wave us away.

"We could have been killed," I say as we drive off. Hamdi shrugs. He's furious that my panic and screaming interrupted the fight. "They had no right. You have to show them you know your rights," he insists. These men in black were, I later learn, members of the Shin Bet, the secret Israeli military force, whose anonymity is critical for them to slip into the Palestinians' world. Hamdi's camera was a weapon that could have blown their cover. Later, savvy journalists tell me that his show of power certainly could have provoked them to violence, that it's good I was so vocal.

We drive into the El Khader refugee camp. I've never been here before, but it's much like Deheishe, where Achmed had taken me to visit his cousin. Most of the housing consists of cement, cagelike rooms, with a scattering of somewhat more substantial homes. Walls are graffiti-strewn, the alleyways filled with garbage. The resident men and boys loiter, sneering at the Israeli soldiers who patrol the camp. These soldiers are a constant presence, stalking the alleyways or pointing their guns downward from the rooftops where many stand guard.

I step cautiously into Suher Ismael's room. She's been waiting for me, along with her mother-in-law, aunt, sisters and several children. We flop down on the futons that line the floor. Suher is ready to show me a videotape she's participated in filming. It consists of the work of three Palestinian film students, Suher among them, who have been putting together video journals of their daily lives dating back to the Gulf war. This project includes three companion pieces, filmed by Israeli settlers and an Israeli artist living in Tel Aviv. All six are recording their everyday lives and surroundings. As I sit on the floor, Suher's family gives me cursory nods.

Suher pops the ninety-minute tape into her VCR. The scenes capture Palestinian lives—families, friends and daily routines—that highlight personal sensibilities. Suher tells me that each filmmaker was given the freedom to choose whatever he or she wanted to emphasize in their lives. One Palestinian has focused on the Rafah and Jabaliya camps in Gaza. Another's footage is of life in Nablus. Suher's film takes place in El Khader, a small village near here, where she lived before she married.

I'm inside the film *and* inside this room, sitting amidst the simmering rage of this Palestinian family who've had more than the usual share of deaths (Suher's father and her brother) and deportations (her husband's three brothers). The refugee camp setting intensifies the horrors I see on the screen. My primary emotion is not compassion but revulsion at the violence—physical and psychological—that I am watching on the screen. One segment shows well-executed scenes of masked Palestinians on the run, battling soldiers, joining rallies where hatred for occupation and Israel is laced with wild grief over men and children who've been killed.

Suher's segment focuses on portraits of peasant women performing their never-ending physical labors: feeding chickens, cutting grapes, arranging tables for family meals. Their faces are hard and miserable. Each speaks to the camera, telling stories of sons deported or murdered. Then comes a piece where Suher interviews her own mother about the death of her brother Jabor. Jabor had gone outside to help a wounded friend on the road three years ago, where he was accidentally shot in the chest near their home. He was twenty-one. In every frame, Suher's mother is depressed. Her face doesn't brighten, even at her only daughter's huge wedding party. Toward the end of this footage, she sits at her kitchen table, her head bent, clutched in her hands. What we see of her face is ashen and cold.

She lifts her face, looks directly into the camera. "Why are we born? Life is so miserable. Jabor was my life; he's gone. Why am I still here?" she asks, as her three younger children from her second marriage listen. "There's nothing to live for," she says as her twelve-year-old son looks over at her, clearly hurt.

Suher turns her camera to interview this young half brother. Her lens zooms into a close-up of his pre-adolescent face. He is describing the day his older brother, Jabor, was shot. Pointing out his window, he says that the death occurred right there, right outside. His lips tremble. He's trying to hold back tears. Suher's film ends as he breaks into sobs.

The focus switches to the Nablus-made segment, which begins with men sitting on a floor inside a house, talking of violence, acting fierce, showing off with warrior rhetoric. Through the window curtains we can glimpse the Israeli soldiers who are shadowing the Palestinians, whether on the street or from neighboring rooftops. These Israeli soldiers both contain and enrage the film's protagonists. One especially horrid scene shows a group of adults initiating a boy of five into becoming a fighter. They give him a large stick and then show him how to attack an Israeli soldier, which he practices by running wildly up against a steel door, slamming into it with his small body. His family shouts encouragement, praising his prowess.

Each of these filmmakers gives me a window onto Palestinian rage, suffering and what's left of their decimated social structure. And in some way that I don't quite understand—I know only that this result is inevitable—each filmmaker has stoked the fires of hatred. As soon as the tape is over, the elder women turn on me with hostile questions, which Suher translates. "Why are you Americans always coming here? You come here year after year, yet you do nothing. Why don't you help us? Why come if you never help us?" Their anger is directed at me right now. Although it doesn't feel personal, they're more right than they could know, I think, as images of my parents' and grandparents' wholly uncritical support for Israel—our family religion—come to my mind. I don't answer these matriarchs. I can't. I turn my attention to the children in the room—five of them—who are all emotionally tuned into us adults in ways American kids I know rarely are. Like children I've met in Gaza, they seem lit by an odd radiance, and are nothing like children their age I've lived with in other poor areas around the globe: Jamaica, Guatemala, Harlem. They're old before their time. The women continue barking at me in Arabic, as I pick up three-year-old Anna. Her warm body, her wide, responsive eyes make her seem like the softest, most wonderful creature in the world. The imprint of her sweet plumpness stays with me for days.

Driving back toward Jerusalem, I try to re-create the sequences of this scary day. As if it happened long ago, I remember the wild confrontation in Bethlehem between Hamdi and the Shin Bet, the anger in El Khader, the killing and misery shown in those films. In each instance, I had a front-row seat on the choreography of war, on the magnetism of the fight that has a life of its own. What I saw today is that inside the compulsion to posture, to meet violence with violence, no one is victim or victor, oppressed or oppressor. Inside the dance of hate, every participant colludes to keep the hostility moving at a white heat.

• • •

Exhausted, I take a few days off. On the last morning I go for a swim with my Israeli-born friend Yehuda, a bohemian painter. As we're drying off, I remember that I've promised to return a book to a Spanish journalist who's staying at the American Colony. We get into my car to drive toward East Jerusalem. I'm surprised to notice Yehuda growing nervous, obviously on edge. I know he's sympathetic to Palestinians; often he talks of his close Palestinian friend, also a painter. Yet now he's fidgeting so much that he's distracting me at the wheel. "What's up?" I ask.

He confesses that he's avoided East Jerusalem since he fought here in '67. As we drive into the hotel's parking lot, Yehuda recounts the battle he fought on this very spot. How did I not anticipate that this short trip would be wrenching for him? I come here almost daily to enjoy the camaraderie of Palestinian, Israeli and foreign journalists, many of whom have working relationships dating back years. Usually, I feel elated inside this sophisticated and aesthetic ambiance, relishing the absence of primitive tribal tensions. (In any single conversation at this hotel, people slip in and out of Hebrew, Arabic, French, Spanish and English.) I've forgotten the charged ambivalence with which any Israeli can view anything Arab, the hostilities so dominant in the world outside this small oasis. It's clear that what for journalists is a space of creative conversations is for Yehuda the site of deathly flashbacks.

We enter into the indoor garden cafe, passing through scents of mimosa and lemon leaves, a sweetened air. I sit down, but Yehuda stands erect, surveying the bountiful, graceful Arab tapestries lining these walls. This mélange of carefully chosen artwork clearly does not enthrall him. Colleagues and acquaintances wave my way but he glowers. I sense that we should hightail it out of here (and fast), but Yehuda now insists that we sit and eat, even though he's growing more, not less, tense. When my favorite waiter, Mahmoud, takes our orders, Yehuda's face tightens. He cross-examines him about our food's ingredients, as if this hardworking man might just be planning to poison us. After this interrogation Yehuda swings around in his seat to survey our company. His glares create ripples of suspicious anxiety. Just when I'm sure it can't get much worse, it does. He begins to loudly criticize the grapefruit juice and the hummus, and then sneers at Mahmoud while he clears our dishes, accusing him of shortchanging us, which he has not.

A few Palestinian journalists come by to say hello. I hold my breath. Sure enough, Yehuda launches into the '67 war, telling where he fought and which Arabs he killed while he was a paratrooper. Mouths drop open. Within minutes, the ten or fifteen others in the room turn away, more than glad to leave us to ourselves.

Scowling, Yehuda leans forward. Sure that I've missed the "downside" of every breezy interaction, he begins decoding the "conniving manipulations" he's certain I've willfully ignored. By the time we leave, he's no longer imagining the icy hostility he single-handedly has created.

On our drive home we're quiet. Though I feel a measure of sympathy for my Israeli friend, I primarily feel like an idiot for having brought Yehuda with me.

• • •

By early February, Hebron is the hot spot on the West Bank, the place where settlers and Palestinians are having it out almost daily. It's a quiet morning, with no settlers about. After fifteen minutes of sitting and drinking soda outside a small Palestinian shop under a light rain, a group of photographers I've been traveling with notices an old Orthodox Jew with a long white beard, covered in a tallis (a Jewish prayer shawl). He's walking down the main street alone—a sight so rare in this city that he looks like an apparition.

Walking purposefully into the Palestinian shop, he speaks in English to two old Arabs who are drinking coffee in the corner. Immediately, they're on alert. But speaking slowly, in a high-pitched voice, the old Jew introduces himself with courtesy. "I'm Dr. Leitwaller," he says, adding, "and I've come to meet with your Sheikh Ja'abari. Can you get me to his house right away?" The Palestinians look shocked.

"Sheikh Ja'abari," the shopkeeper whispers to the press, "is from the oldest family in Hebron. They've ruled this city for centuries."

"I'm a professor of mathematics at Hebrew Union College in Ontario," the man says. "I've come here to make peace. That's why I must see the sheikh." Everyone is stunned. Before the photographers can make any snap judgments, he announces, "I do know how to make peace; that's why I'm here. I'm going to start a college for you Arabs, a special one. I'll teach you mathematics, science, how to use computers, and you will also learn Jewish history so this terrible fighting will come to a halt. There's no need for this war. Take me to your sheikh."

"A crackpot," one photographer whispers to another. The old Jew doesn't realize how dangerous and volatile the situation in Hebron is. Yet since it's nearly impossible to get photographs of aging Palestinians and Jews in any conversation, within minutes six photographers are aiming their cameras at this scene.

Only one Israeli photographer refuses to join in. "This has to be staged," he says. The old Arab is looking at the old Jew with awe: The name Ja'abari elicits immediate respect.

These photographers may know the man is a nut, but the Arabs are welcoming, all smiles. They crowd around him in friendly curiosity. The six photographers keep shooting. Within minutes, crowds pour out of shops and homes to the main street to witness this remarkable event.

"Our gods are the same," Dr. Leitwaller declaims. "We don't need violence." Since it's a godsend for these photographers to get a shot of a Jew in religious garb eliciting smiles from Arabs, they're pushing against each other, each trying to get the best angle.

Now the streets are filled with Palestinians. What started out as four in one small shop swells to fifteen, then forty, until it's packed to overflowing while another hundred or so fill the length of the marketplace. The doctor and the aging Arab he first buttonholed move out onto the street. It's obvious that this elderly Jew is getting nervous, that he didn't expect this attention, these large crowds. Neither did the IDF soldiers who, in English, begin shouting that everyone must clear the streets—all must step aside.

"This could be a flashpoint," one photographer says. Yet the Palestinians from Hebron remain quietly curious. There's no anger. It's only the doctor who is getting frantic, shouting, "I have an appointment with Sheikh Ja'abari; I don't want soldiers; I don't want guns; I'm a man of peace!"

As an army jeep pulls down the road, the old man slips into a vegetable stand, startling three old Arabs wearing kaffiyehs. Immediately the soldiers take their rifles and try to clear the area.

"Don't touch me; I'll speak to your commander," the doctor screams, as soldiers elbow onto either side of him. The Palestinians are still running into the street to see what's going on. The photographers are still angling for shots. "I'm an old man," Dr. Leitwaller shouts. "My heart is not too good. I can't run so fast anymore." Suddenly he stops and lies down perfectly still on the ground. The photographers stoop to lie beside him, still shooting their film continuously.

The doctor leaps up and runs. He stops; he runs; he stops. The crowd follows. Obviously he's in way over his head with the commotion he's caused, especially as everyone in this section of town is meticulously miming his quirky, staccato rhythms, back and forth in this Hebron market. He grows increasingly frenetic; each time he runs, the crowds part for him, so that he can dart into one, then another Palestinian shop, dodging the IDF.

An army jeep's siren is wailing and coming closer. The Jew turns to an Arab, saying, "I must pray for peace on Arab fruit. There, I'll take that orange. Sorry," he shrugs, "no money." The Arab hands him the orange, over which the Jew davens slowly, while reciting a short Hebrew meditation. He's obviously crazy, but he has somehow connected with the Arabs. Every face here is lit up.

Over loudspeakers, the soldiers in the nearby jeep bark out in English: "Enough. Come with us. Right now." This command sets the packed marketplace on edge. One photographer says to another, "A *meshuggeneh.*"

A Palestinian standing nearby asks, "What's that?"

"*Majoon,*" the photographer says, translating "nut" into Arabic.

The Palestinian takes offense: "You only say he's crazy because he wants peace."

Animated discussions are now breaking out between photographers and Palestinians.

"He's come for peace; why does the army want to take him away?" one asks.

"Because they're afraid you'll put a knife in his back," an Israeli photographer answers forthrightly.

"But we don't knife peace lovers; he's safe with us," the Palestinian retorts.

Another Palestinian, a teenager who speaks perfect English, asks, "What's with this guy?"

The Israeli answers, "He says he wants to make peace."

In a tone of voice so quintessentially Jewish I have to wonder where he learned his English, the Palestinian boy responds, "He wants to make peace and the Israelis want to take him away. Isn't that *typical?*"

The soldiers are getting fed up. They keep trying but fail to grab the old man, who nimbly pulls away to evade them. Once free, he again drops to the ground, then just as suddenly runs a few feet, wrapping his arms with his tefillin, praying aloud again. Some photographers burst out laughing.

The Palestinians catch the mood and start bellowing laughter too.

Now a tough commando Israeli soldier succeeds in pushing close to the old man. The crowd looks on in wide-eyed amazement. They have never seen an Israeli soldier hassle any Jew.

The doctor is now yelling at the officer, "Let me go!" while saying in Hebrew, *"Koom shev"* (Rise, sit) as if he's in a synagogue.

"We're doing this for your own good," the officer says. "We're only trying to protect you."

"Only my wife cares about me," Dr. Leitwaller snaps. "You want to use me, but you don't care about me," he says. *"Koom shev; Koom shev."*

The soldiers turn deadly serious, as the Palestinians disperse into shops or run down side streets, racing to get out of the way. And now we see making their way down a hillside from the settlements, a gun-toting group. These settlers—Orthodox Americans wearing *kippot*, L. L. Bean shoes and jeans—are accompanied by Rabbi Moshe Levinger, the chief rabbi in the Hebron settler community. He's well known for his extremist views and his ability to ignite settler rage. Levinger approaches the old man, as if to protect one of his own. But Dr. Leitwaller wails, "No. No. No. No. No guns. No rabbis. No settlers. Go away with your guns," humiliating this Jewish leader in front of astounded Palestinians.

This scene has become too much for the soldiers; they will put up with no more of it. They grab the Jewish peacenik, and the last we see of him, he's lying in the back of their open jeep. His pants have accidentally been yanked down in the fracas; his naked legs are splayed helplessly, the final view that the crowd gets, as he's driven away, shouting, "I don't want soldiers! I want to talk to the sheikh!"

CHAPTER ELEVEN

After the Massacre

On February 25, 1994, a settler doctor named Baruch Goldstein walked into a basement Hebron mosque through a synagogue upstairs and opened fire with his automatic army rifle. Within minutes he killed twenty-nine Muslims as they were bent over in morning prayers and then was killed himself. This act horrified most Israelis. Prime Minister Rabin expressed his revulsion in strong language, condemning the settler fanatics as a blight upon Judaism. Yet the 450 Jewish settlers living in downtown Hebron weren't required to move out and join the thousands of Jews living nearby in the Hebron settlement called Kiryat Arba. Neither of these two Jewish Hebron groups dissociated itself from Goldstein's act, or expressed contrition for it. They are free all this month to wander around, to dance in celebration of Goldstein and Purim. In contrast, the 130,000 Palestinians living here and throughout Hebron's suburbs are under house arrest, given only a few hours every few days to go out to market. Today, March 26, the closure and house arrests are officially lifted. The town is finally open for journalists to visit.

I'm phoning around to find a trustworthy Arab taxi driver to begin my journey into the West Bank. After a month of terrible hostilities, of guns and stone-throwing battles between the Palestinian street fighters and the Israeli soldiers, it would be unwise to travel any other way.

Sara, imperturbable as ever, sits at her breakfast table as I make my calls. I tell her I'm worried about this trip, that I'm more than worried. The Hebrew word *Tikkun* is printed across my press card. "It's fine," Sara says calmly. "Pronounce it 'ty-COON' and say it's a human rights magazine."

"Tycoon," I say, "a human rights magazine for the very wealthy," and we both laugh nervously. These days, no one enters the West Bank without inner hysteria or acute anxiety.

By 9 A.M., I'm sitting in the back of Yassir's taxi (he's the brother of a Palestinian woman I know well). I'm surveying the hillsides we traverse, back roads taken to circumvent Israeli checkpoints. For unknown reasons, Hebron has again just been declared a "closed military zone." Yassir is a good choice. He navigates well the steep dirt roads that spiral up the mountain toward the city. We pass farms with olive, grape and plum orchards; the land is dotted with flocks of goat and sheep. As the miles go by, I watch animals clambering among flowering trees and blossoming vines.

We're giving a ride to Bashir, a slim boy of twenty-three who was caught in East Jerusalem for the last three days and couldn't get by the checkpoints to go home to Hebron. He couldn't get through to his family on the phone. He's sure they're worried about him. I am eager to meet and interview them. When we arrive at his house, his father, mother, six brothers and sisters (ranging in age from twelve to twenty-five) and assorted neighbors all rush to greet and hug him.

"What did you think?" I ask as we sit in the living room of their immaculate home, situated above the Ibrahim Mosque. "When we didn't hear from him, we thought the worst," they answer, still hugging Bashir. Some are crying; others hold him close.

Hassan, his twenty-one-year-old brother, fluent in English, translates for the others. "We thought he was taken by soldiers, shot or imprisoned. Our fears were terrible. We knew that no one from Israel would inform us if anything happened."

Yassir, the driver, leaves to visit his mother. This house fills with neighbors who talk about the day of the massacre, how the town woke to the sounds of screams and cries for help over the mosque's loudspeaker. One neighbor tells me that her husband ran to the hospital to give blood, as did many others. She points to the unfinished cement building visible on an adjacent hillside. "Seven who went to donate blood were murdered by Israeli soldiers, right outside that hospital, shot, one by one, in the head," she says, speaking through Hassan. Fighting tears, she adds that her husband was among them, killed by a gunshot to his head. I haven't read or heard about this second massacre, but all present tell me it happened. Later I hear the Israeli version: that soldiers converged on the hospital and shot into the crowd when the kids ferociously stoned them.

Hassan continues to translate. "Everyone ran toward the hospital because it lacks even the most basic supplies: no cotton, not even water. Our first need was to get medical supplies and to donate blood. But the soldiers refused to allow Daoud, our taxi driver, to carry the wounded to the hospital. They repeatedly stopped his car, forbidding him to drive even though he was carrying the dying in his backseat. Daoud went through the police barricades despite the threats; he was screaming, 'Kill me if you want to, but I won't stop. Are you crazy? These people are seriously injured.'

"Israeli television showed a live interview with Daoud," Hassan explains. "They do that. They show some real news just to keep the impression that they are fair, which is totally false." Hassan's wiry frame comes alive with this story; his hands are busy gesticulating. "The curfew began immediately, but no one kept to it. Everyone threw stones and rocks. Even when the soldiers shouted in Arabic over loudspeakers that we must stay inside, no one did. After the killings at the hospital, they stopped shooting at us. They saw we were determined to help our neighbors, to bury our dead."

As I listen to Hassan I think that if you had to guess his age, you'd subtract five years. As for his nationality, you'd say Irish or English. (Everyone in this family, except for the father, is light-skinned with auburn hair, blue eyes, and thin, delicate features.) Hassan radiates intelligence. His credibility seems unimpeachable, especially in the context of this family which, as I quickly learn, isn't given to histrionics. They're willing to talk, though we don't get to the heart of the matter for several hours, by which time no one wants the conversation to stop. I gradually realize that my unanticipated presence is a catalyst for this outpouring of grief, this catharsis, for as they tell their story, their collective depression begins to lift.

They explain that in the immediate aftermath of the massacre, everyone, except for those living right next to the mosque, slipped outdoors or dug tunnels from their houses in order to secretly visit neighbors. At any opportunity, they threw stones at Israeli soldiers.

They tell me (the silent nod vigorously) that the dead are now "between God's hands," that those who survived are envious, "because everyone here wishes to die. As a martyr you go right to heaven. To die in the midst of early-morning Ramadan prayers is the best, most powerful death." This religiously inspired death instinct is hard for me to fathom; I say so. Gradually it becomes understandable to me. The hopelessness here gives rise to a yearning for death, which is given meaning when poured into a religious frame. "All of us want to leave this life," Hassan says, giving vivid details of their grim Hebron existence. This family, which under any other circumstances would be regarded as lucky—middle class, intellectually gifted—is living in an underworld. Hassan's father has to work two jobs to earn a living wage; he has opened an electronics shop to supplement the meager $100 a month he makes teaching science at the local elementary school. Kids duck into his shop to avoid the settlers and the army, which, they tell me, chase after them with guns. They shoot into the air, taunt Palestinians whenever they pass through the downtown shopping district. The soldiers and settlers are said to be in cahoots, harassing the town's people in the shops or on the main street. Images of the Ku Klux Klan come to my mind as they describe Rabbi Moshe Levinger and his followers, though "Mafia" is the term Hassan uses.

"Why do you think they hate you so much?" I ask.

The group responds, almost in unison, heads bobbing in agreement: "Zionist mentality. The Zionists want to take all of our land, want us to leave or give up. It's not only land; it's religion as well; Jews against Islamics." As for peace, even those in the room who once felt hope have lost it. This does not seem like rhetoric, though I sense that with tangible shifts on the ground, their hopelessness might lift. But how they'll ever think of Jews as other than vicious or racist is hard to imagine; their hatred seems airtight.

I ask how they feel about the many Israelis who fight for *their* human rights, who sent food and money after the killings. They scoff, shaking their heads. Hassan says, "All Jews are on only their own side. We don't want their money. We don't want their food. We want *our* freedom." What they've seen since the Handshake, and especially since the massacre, is an unrelentingly punitive Israeli attitude. This has convinced them that there's no Israeli aim toward peace. "Understand this," Hassan says, "we have *no hope* for the future. We *fear* the future."

He leans forward. "*Three* years ago we needed permission to go to Jaffa or Tel Aviv. *Two* years ago we needed papers to go to East Jerusalem. *One* year ago we needed permits to get to Nablus. *Now* we need permits to leave our home or to go into our own market, in Hebron. Next year we'll need papers to leave our own bedrooms. It *only* gets worse and worse."

After catching his breath, he continues, "You ask me about human rights. I tell you, there are *no* human rights, not *here*. The victim is us and us and us. Every family has trouble: no work, no study, no money, no food. But most of all, most important: no freedom. Hear this. The soldiers came here, right here, in the middle of one night. They were supposedly checking for guns or for terrorists. They woke every one of us, forced us all to stand outside in the rain and, of course, found nothing. Yet, they left without a single wave or smile, not even an apology. They never show a sign that we're human."

Sulei, a sister, pulls me aside and says she is studying psychology at Hebron University. She implores me to come talk to the women there. "You see, the women and girls have the hardest lives. We're the most confined, the most defeated," she explains. "The boys can go and throw stones. But we girls aren't allowed to express ourselves. We have no outlet." (This fits exactly what the Gazan psychiatrist Dr. Eyad Sarraj told me a year ago, that those who are active, even in the most violent ways, feel more self-esteem and win more respect from their peers, staying mentally more robust.) What began hours ago as an interview has become a condolence call. They obviously feel the strong chord of emotion that is resonating between us. Hassan's mother wants me to stay for dinner.

"I write in my journal every day," Sulei says. I tell her about the free writing groups popular in the States, how women write their hearts out, then read aloud together. "Exactly what we do in Hebron," she says. "We write together when we don't have housework to do." I tell her that I hope she keeps writing. "It's very important," I say, as she holds my hand in hers, crying.

Yassir returns for me. After a long goodbye with this family, he drives me up and down the back streets of Hebron before heading to Jerusalem. Though it's still daylight, we see no signs of life, no cars on the roads, no faces peering through the windows of the many apartment buildings. No children play outside on bikes or swings. Even though the curfew has finally lifted, the city seems ghostly, as if everyone is already dead.

This day, which began in blissful spring weather, with soft breezes and a blossoming throughout this land, has turned ugly. The sky is as dark and ominous as my mood. Yassir and I wend our way past checkpoints. "Look up there," he says after a few minutes, pointing up to a hill dotted with sheep and goats, the one we traversed this morning, while circumventing checkpoints. We see a bright red fire outlined against the darkened sky. A tire is ablaze, maybe the very one we saw earlier today in the middle of what seemed an innocuous dirt road. Against a curtain of red fire, we now see five or six soldiers. They're silhouetted in black and are running with machine guns pointed at invisible targets.

So caught up am I in the contagious Hebron sadness that I'm startled to find we're back inside the Green Line, in a world of vitality, where people take for granted simple things like walking to visit friends, sitting in sidewalk cafes, sending their children outside to play.

Back in my own car after Yassir drops me off, I pull into a gas station near my home. Immediately, I'm surrounded by guys cheerfully asking me about the Arabic sign in my window. What kind of journalist am I? Where from? Where have I been today? Their questions sound so casual, so cavalier, as though I've just come back from a tourist jaunt.

I look about the street. Most of the people walking about here don't really know (or want to know) about what goes on in their name every day, only a short ride from here. As I drive the final mile home, I'm stopped by a teen wearing a *kippah*. He's passing out Hebrew bumper stickers which say, "All

Israel is Hebron," in preparation for a settler rally in Kiryat Arba, the settlement on the hilltop above Hebron, scheduled for tomorrow.

"No way," I reply.

"Hag sameach" (Happy holiday), he says breezily, moving cheerfully on to the next car.

I will be back in Hebron to cover that rally, not join it. Very early the next morning, I'm inside an Israel Radio van, along with five Israeli correspondents and one TV cameraman, on our way to the other Hebron: Kiryat Arba. The ostensible reason for today's solidarity march is the sixty-fifth anniversary of the time Jews were killed in a 1929 massacre in Hebron. But the real agenda is to show the strength of settler opposition to the peace process, their support for right-wing rabbis who have issued injunctions to resist Israeli soldiers if they try to move the 450 settlers out of downtown Hebron. Thousands of Jewish settlers live in the huge apartment complex of Kiryat Arba (separated from the small enclave of Jews living downtown), along with many soldiers, sent there to "protect" them. This modern hilltop housing development comes replete with a gym, a large library, a shopping mall, several synagogues, many playgrounds and banks. I see a large Co-op City complex that could be anywhere in America.

I discover, as I stroll the perimeters, that Kiryat Arba has a thick border of green tents where the Israeli soldiers camp out. Security guards, high-wire gates and cattle fences complete the separation of Jews here from Palestinians below. We seven, the first to arrive today, soon hear screaming. We rush toward the sounds to find a group of settlers setting up a chant: "Doctor Goldstein! There is no one like you in the whole world." A few feet away we hear the more popular slogan, "We are all Baruch Goldstein!" From this hilltop, surrounded by these chants and screams, I see the marchers, who number in the many thousands, climbing toward us, toward the baseball field where I'm standing. Their parade will culminate in a rally here. The marchers hoist huge banners announcing "Hebron from the Past Until Forever" and "Hebron, City of Our Fathers."

I move among the crowds, talking to anyone who's willing. On the edge of one cliff I stand with a man who refuses to give me his name. We manage to keep talking for half an hour, during which he allows only that he lives in a settlement outside Jericho. He explains patiently that the "Arabs are a cancer. You don't coexist with cancer. Right? You cut it out of your body. Isn't that right?"

"But what's a realistic scenario?" I ask.

"Nothing in Jewish history is realistic," he responds. "Zionism wasn't realistic, and here we are. The Bible predicts just what I predict: that the Arabs will get up and leave."

I'm invited to join Aaron Hadump, the main spokesperson for settlers from "Judea and Samaria," the term the settlers use when speaking of the West Bank. He is seated inside a dark purple Mercedes. With effort, he leans over to open the passenger car door, motioning me to sit inside, all without breaking the conversation he's conducting on his car phone. The minute he hangs up, it rings again. He's so busy organizing the day ahead, he hardly looks at or talks to me as we sit side by side in the "office" he's made in his car.

We see thousands and thousands climbing the hill, coming toward us. Most are wearing large buttons proclaiming solidarity with Hebron's settlers. Most wear *kippot*. Some are dressed in black; a few wear secular garb. All are waving Israeli flags, marching in loose formations; virtually every man is carrying a gun—small guns in pocket holsters or rifles slung over their shoulders.

"But what of the peace process?" I ask Hadump.

"This *is* the peace process," he says, gesturing with his hand toward the crowd. Then his cell phone rings again, and I decide to leave.

Soon, ten thousand plus are swarming about a huge baseball field. Likud party leaders Bibi Netanyahu and Ariel Sharon, as well as assorted "Greater Israel" rabbis, begin addressing the crowd over loudspeakers from a wooden podium built for today's event. In between each talk, music blares. I hear "Waiting for the Messiah," a love song to God, written to a rock-'n'-roll beat. I wander about. One group holds high a sign: "The People Who Dr. Goldstein Killed Were Sick; He Gave Them the Right Medicine." Tiny black hearts are drawn all around the edges.

On the crowded field, groups are picnicking. By noon, blankets cover the hilltop as those who have eaten lie back, their guns resting beside them. Organizers are passing out pamphlets denouncing Peres and Rabin as Nazis. Meanwhile, in a Hebrew that sounds increasingly harsh, or maybe simply angrier than usual, one after another speaker spits out the name "Rabin" and then "Peres" to jeers, boos and hissing from the crowds. Other names are barked, also to intensified hoots: Amos Oz, Shulamit Aloni, Yossi Beilin, Yossi Sarid.

I begin to understand that this rally is mounted more in protest against Rabin's government and the peace process than against the Arab population. Each person I manage to converse with, not an easy feat, makes light of the Arabs. "We know how to handle them," they say dismissively. Their energy is focused on fighting current Israeli policy that's been initiated by "our SS leaders." In the twenty-odd interviews I conduct, whether with groups of Habad Moroccans who carry "their messiah" Rabbi Menachem Schneerson's photograph, or the black-hatted ultra-Orthodox, or the middle-aged settlers passing rifles to their teenagers, the words spoken are the same. "Nobody will admit it, but we love Goldstein," most say. Or, "Rabin will fall and all Judea and Samaria will be ours." Others repeat: "This Nazi regime will never be free of us." This is the most mean-spirited crowd I've ever encountered.

Until finally, a welcome sight. I see an attractive man, without a gun, who has an expressive, friendly face. He actually smiles at me. Cheerfully, he then invites me to join his family for lunch. Soon, I'm sitting next to him on a picnic blanket; he introduces himself, "Doron Mori here." Ascertaining that I'm Jewish, he insists I taste his potato latkes. "Better than your *safta's* [grandma's]?" he asks good-naturedly. "Almost," I reply, glad for an apolitical exchange. I sit and eat and try to understand Mori's views.

He says that he is originally from Morocco and now lives in a settlement near Tel Aviv. He warms to the tale of his conversion to religious life: "I was once confused," he begins. "I thought about Israel from the left-wing point of view for years, yet I was never personally happy. I went from cafe to cafe, from one unhappy love affair to the next. And then, thanks to my beloved *rebbe* [he playfully pats the knee of the man sitting next to him], I finally found true Judaism. Since then, my whole life has changed; since I found God, everything makes sense."

Mori's dark eyes gleam. A rhapsodic look rises into his face. "What is life if we don't make sense of ourselves and our situation?" he asks. "Listen, I'm no fanatic. I learn only from what my life teaches. When I was associated with the left, I was running after women, but none of my relationships lasted. After my good *rebbe* assured me that by living a religious Jewish life, I'd find the right woman, guess what? I did. After my very first *Shabbat* observance, I met my wife. It sounds incredible, but is the truth. So I made a pact with God, that I will follow Jewish law to the letter as long as He makes my life richer, more satisfying. It's worked. I wouldn't lie to you about something this serious. I swear on the Bible, miracles keep happening."

Mori beams at his *rebbe*. Almost whispering, he says to me, "I feel sorry for the secular left-wing Jews. They will never have our strength because we have one hundred percent commitment to Torah. All that they have, as I know from my own life, are discos, coffee shops, passing love affairs. That's why they have no time to care about Israel as we do. They're self-involved. That's why they are willing to give up our land. But we are strong. We can fight for the real Israel, the Greater Israel."

Glad to at least hear someone speaking from his heart, I ask Mori about the Hebron massacre. "About Goldstein at first I was very confused," he says, as his eyes cloud and his face darkens. "Since I know that the Arabs will leave of their own volition, I don't endorse outright killings—that is, until I learned more of what Goldstein lived through, praying above that mosque. It's then that I became certain that he was following Jewish law, as everyone here knows, though I doubt they'd say so directly. You see, what he did was a necessity. The Israeli papers don't report the truth, that the Arabs in the mosque were not coming just to pray, but to kill. They would announce in Arabic, not 'Come to prayer,' but 'Kill all Jews.' When I learned this, I realized that Goldstein did, bravely, what the army refused to accomplish. If you study Judaism as I do, you learn that there's a Jewish law that's higher than any Israeli law. Did you know that? That the law says if someone is going to kill a Jew, you must kill first?"

"Those Muslims bent in prayer were killers?" I ask.

"Oh yes, this is common knowledge now. Every one of their muezzin prayers was coded. There are many ways to say, 'Kill Jews.' They didn't think we would understand. But Goldstein did understand. So he had no choice; he followed Jewish law. He killed them first. It was self-defense. They were planning to kill us and he knew it. So, imagine! He sacrificed his own life for the Greater Israel. That's why he's our martyr. He did what no one else had the guts to do. The army wouldn't do their job. They didn't shoot those Muslims. My honest opinion? Goldstein heard the voice of God and heeded God's wisdom."

Mori looks at me, possibly for the first time during this oration. As he catches the wave of revulsion that crosses my face, he says, "Come now. Don't react so emotionally. Just look at the facts. Since September 13, when Rabin shook the murderer Arafat's hand in front of the whole world, what has happened? I can tell you precisely. I follow politics carefully. Thirty-three innocent Jews have been killed by Arabs since that day, only six months ago. You will see, if you haven't yet, how this government is too easy on Arabs. That's why we are setting up an alternative government that will preserve essential Jewish values."

Leaving Mori, I move slowly down mountain stairs in search of Baruch Goldstein's grave. The only grave situated at the end of Meir Kahane Park, a quarter mile below the baseball field, it's easy to spot. The tomb has been encased in gray cement so that no one can remove or desecrate it. Roped barricades surround the site, but don't stop crowds of worshipers from lining up and slipping underneath. Once close to his tomb, his many followers hug, kiss and cry over it, placing small stones on top, in keeping with Jewish custom.

Off to the side, on a small patch of lawn, Hasidim are dancing and singing,

"Goldstein, our Messiah, our Messiah." Those on line repeat this chant, or add, "Our martyr, our holy man."

During the next two hours I watch hundreds take their turn, bending over to kiss this tombstone. Woman after woman prostrates herself by lying full bodied on this cement slab. Entire families line up to have their pictures taken. One hefty settler, an Uzi slung over his shoulder, squints at his family through the lens of a red Instamatic camera. "Lower," he shouts to his wife. "Get down. Closer. I gotta get Goldstein and the kids all together."

I study one woman lying across the cement slab. She sits up suddenly to spit sunflower shells, crudely but carefully, aiming to miss the beloved stone. An American journalist takes notes nearby. The woman stares at him, then starts cursing: "What are you writing? He's dead. You're alive. That's a crime." She spits shells toward him, some of which land on, and so desecrate, Goldstein's remains. "See what you made me do," she shouts as the reporter keeps writing. I can almost read his mind, "This woman is a great find for my story." Another Israeli journalist is shooting away with her camera, oblivious to an oddly garbed man who's emerging from the crowd. He's wearing a bright orange sweater over his head (whether as a shield from the sun or as a *kippah*, it's impossible to know). He's carrying an ice cream cone that drips chocolate "tears" onto the grave. Suddenly he swerves and tries to attack her. Screaming obscenities, he succeeds for a few seconds in prying her camera from her shoulder. She grabs it back.

Rula Halawani, a Palestinian photographer standing next to me, says that she's come today ready to say she's Turkish, if anyone asks. "But if that's how they treat an Israeli, God only knows what they'd do to me," she whispers, adding, "Even the Hamas would not treat a Jewish journalist this way."

Just then, a man arrives, upstaging the others. He's loudly hawking rental rights to "Goldstein's tallis." He calls out, "Six shekels for use of his prayer shawl."

"How do we know it's his?" a woman shouts.

"Don't ask such questions," the potbellied merchant retorts. A young settler moves closer and carefully begins inspecting the goods. The crowd watches attentively. He touches the material, inspects it, puts on his glasses, muses and then declares with authority, "Not Goldstein's. Goldstein had thinner stripes."

I wander back to the radio van. Exhausted and depressed, I collapse in the back, figuring that we'll soon be out of here.

No such luck. Just as we were the first to arrive this morning, we're the last to leave tonight. It's after 7 P.M. and dark as we head down the roads that connect Kiryat Arba with downtown Hebron. We're following and are indistinguishable from the last caravan of settler cars. The only sound in our van is the gravelly voice of Prime Minister Yitzhak Rabin. He's giving a speech carried live over the radio. His voice sounds tired and tense, as we all are. Periodically, his talk is interrupted by loud bursts of sound. It's the static that arises when the radio loses connection, but it seems like gunshots, an ominous noise to hear as we drive through Hebron behind the settlers.

After what feels like forever, I turn to an Israeli radio reporter named Alon. "Are we safe yet?" I ask. He shakes his head and makes a sucking sound through his teeth. It's then I see the road sign: 22 kilometers (about fourteen miles) to Jerusalem. We all remain on edge, in silence, until finally we arrive back inside Jerusalem. "It's like another planet," Alon says, as we climb out of the van. "The West Bank is like another planet," he repeats.

The next morning I discover that my own horror is shared by many foreign Jewish journalists. Over the phone, several describe what they felt on the fields of Kiryat Arba. Robert says, "For me, this rally was another view of how the settler version of Judaism takes a three-thousand-year-old religion, throws out two thousand years of ethical development, turning post-enlightenment Judaism into barbarism." He adds, "Let's hope that they're on the road to their own destruction." Another American Jewish journalist remarks, "Standing near Goldstein's grave, I realized that a monster has been created. Looking at the settler Jews I saw their ideology as ugly but strong. I was shocked to realize that we can't dismiss them. They're a powerful force."

A third journalist friend is forlorn. "I grew up with a yeshiva education. But on the fields of Kiryat Arba, I saw my Judaism being raped."

•   •   •

I'm sorely tempted to skip today's meeting in Nablus, the second to take place between Israeli and Palestinian lawyers in the West Bank, the first since the Hebron massacre. I sit, morose and fearful, under a blazing noon sun near the Damascus Gate of the Old City. I'm watching donkeys stroll by, then Arabs in kaffiyehs and Christian Orthodox clergy in black robes, as I try to talk myself into going.

"The birth of a second democracy in the Middle East"—a phrase so alive in November—seems dead in the sands today. By chance, as I lean against the stones of the Old City walls, cherubic Tzadik, an old friend of Shuki's and a favorite friend of mine, strolls by. I ask him if he thinks it's safe to go to Nablus. Tzadik, a tour guide and cabdriver, has good radar about what's safe and what's not. "You'll be fine," he says, "and you should go." This, from a man who votes Likud and whose son was recently stabbed by terrorists who attacked the boy's high school. Though he distrusts Arabs, he supports the work of dialogue. Most of all, he seems sorry to see me so downcast. He takes my hand and lifts me to my feet. I'm dizzy from the heat, the steaming sunlight, the stress. With his encouragement, I force myself to meet the others at our *sherut* (Arab taxi). Each Israeli waiting here wears a wide cap and carries water bottles. Nobody looks happy about this trip.

The courage of those who came to the last meeting gave us a sense of living on the cutting edge, creating a revolution of meanings for Israelis and Palestinians. The courage required today is of a different sort. The spiraling violence in Hebron has frightened everyone. The Israeli civil rights lawyers, most of whom are going to Nablus for the first time, are, with the exception of Eliyahu Abrams, trembling as our ride gets under way.

Only too soon, our van approaches the place where we'll meet—a huge auditorium at Al-Najah University, a far cry from the warm and welcoming atmosphere of the home where we last had a meeting. As the Palestinian lawyers follow us into the room, I see that each is wearing a suit and tie, carrying a briefcase and bringing an atmosphere that's tense.

Present today is an almost all new cast of characters. Very few from the November meeting are here. The Palestinians are, to a man, icy. They emanate a hostility toward the Israeli lawyers that was entirely absent last time. These West Bank lawyers seem ready to take offense at the very notion that Israelis can help them. Who do they think they are, these "enemies"? What right do they have to lecture us about democracy? This spirit does little to relax the Israelis. First, they've had to overcome their fears about going to the West Bank. Now these eight men and one woman, all of whom do pro bono human rights work for Palestinians, rightly feel that their work is being dismissed. They stiffen with resentment at the perceptions afloat in this drab room. It's a wonder no one has stalked out yet. Somehow, each Israeli manages, with a fair amount of thrashing about in his or her seat, to listen to the Palestinians' lectures on the evils of occupation, as if they had created or supported the worst Israeli abuses, instead of dedicating themselves to correcting them.

Tamar Peleg, a lawyer who is considered by many the Israeli equivalent of Helen Suzman, the South African lawyer who worked to dismantle apartheid, is here among the forty of us. I've heard from many about her work in the territories, how she rarely refuses a case but goes to Gaza and the West Bank daily. There, in courts that are not fair, she mounts passionate defenses for each of her many clients. I watch her checking out the enmity filling this room. And then, seemingly calm, having sized up the obvious, she says nothing.

Each Palestinian lawyer derides Israel's judicial system and claims that his own law degree and insight into the underpinnings of democracy surpass the wisdom of the visiting Israelis. One man leans across the table and says, "I don't approve of this meeting. I have no idea why you men and you, young lady, came today. Do we need you? I don't believe so."

Veronica and I roll our eyes at each other and almost laugh. I pass her a note. "Why do we always have to begin at square one?" I scrawl. She writes back, "Because that's how we *do* begin." One seriously puffed-up Palestinian says, "With all due respect to our Israeli colleagues, may I ask what you have accomplished for us in all these years of injustice that your country has perpetrated against ours?"

We few non-lawyers sit quietly, trying to work the room with smiles and eye contact, our meager attempts to raise the level of discourse, to express through our presence how important such meetings can be. We're trying to generate the respect that's lacking among these protagonists, appalled by the posturing. Still, we've been to this movie before. We know the script is written from mistrust and fear, well earned.

Some of the Israelis start arguing, which only heightens the enmity. Two hours pass in this fashion. I'm about to call the day a dud, when the emotional meltdown, that vital thaw that always surprises us, begins. An elderly Palestinian judge, long retired, who's seated next to Eliyahu Abrams, speaks up.

Dr. Malik seems to be in his mid-eighties. He's a slight man, with thin white hair and an angular, intelligent face. Once he begins speaking, it's obvious that, however frail his body, his mind is still enviably clear. He interrupts the younger Palestinian lawyers, reprimands them for their inhospitality and arrogance, reminds us why we are all here. "We carry dark images of the occupation as we come to this meeting," he begins softly, looking directly at the Israeli lawyers. Everyone at the brown plastic table around which we sit leans forward. "Every day, after Oslo, after so much publicity about peace, every single day I see violations of both human and civil rights. Every day we witness killings of children. I am twice as old as any of you in this room, and I want you to know about our relation to Jews in the old days."

Scanning the table to confirm that he has everyone's attention, he proceeds: "Do you know that before 1948 I used to go to sleep in Jewish homes, as the Jews did in ours. My own father died peacefully in the arms of a great Jewish doctor, Dr. Gal. He had tears in his eyes; he loved my father. Our families were bonded more closely than you can imagine. What I want you young people to know [we are mostly in our forties and fifties!] is that, as Arab Muslims, the great majority of us are not, absolutely not, fanatical. We respect Judaism. I respect Judaism. The Koran doesn't distinguish between Mohammed and Moses. Islam did not arise to abolish your religion, or any religion.

"You know, you must know, that we Palestinians are the Jews of the Arab world. Like you, we have been discriminated against. Like you, we've been scattered around the earth, then persecuted in most places we settle. Like you, we have professors in the highest places. We, too, can be found in the great universities in Europe, in the States, at Harvard. But your Israeli judiciary erred when they acquiesced and let us be deported. A great Jewish judge, a great friend of mine, was named Haim Cohen. He once told me: 'We should not justify deportation, not we Jews of all people.' And yet we Palestinians *were* deported, even as I fought with every ounce of my legal wisdom to prevent it.

"Haim Cohen took my point of view. But his voice wasn't strong enough to convince the others. I lived through the British Mandate, through the Jordanian occupation and now this Israeli occupation. Tell me, tell me, my young friends, where I am biased or nearsighted when I say to you: What is happening now cannot be believed. They shoot boys in the head! Why? Why not in the leg? Why are these administrative detentions allowed? Why do the Israelis hold our people for six months, or longer, without charges, without any trial?"

He pauses to catch his breath. After this burst of passion, he seems exceedingly fragile. Veronica leaves the room and returns with a glass of water for him. Everyone is hanging on his next words, worried he'll give way, faint or grow mute. But Dr. Malik's mind is stronger than his body. He drinks the glass of water and takes his time to regain his voice.

"I was in my own home last week and I heard a loud knocking at my door," he says. "I opened to see soldiers. They rush in, see me sitting in a wheelchair; see that I'm an old man. Yet one walks over and barks at me: 'Wipe off that graffiti near your house! Right now!' They point out my window to a wall down the road. 'We will give you one hour before we arrest you.' That's exactly what this soldier said.

"I say to him, to all of them: 'Go away. Right this minute. I am an old man. What can you be thinking? I will do no such thing.' " The judge now drinks more water. "Yes, we need to work together to get rid of this bloody occupation. We are lovers of peace. We want peace. We say so not because of Arafat, and not through Arafat, but as the people who live here. We want peace, but what kind of peace?"

Now Eliyahu, sitting next to him, catches the spirit that Dr. Malik has brought into our midst. He masterfully sums up the meeting, as if it's been a necessary starting place. Eliyahu highlights only the positive. In doing so, he casts a spell over the group. Turning to each Palestinian lawyer, he calls them by name, concedes that the attitude they brought into the room was understandable, then captures their arguments, selecting his words so that each feels affirmed. He insists that since there's much collaborative work lying ahead, lawyers on both sides must continue to meet with each other. "I believe there will be many areas where we'll be fighting together in the future—for compensation or transferring our judiciary powers into your hands, for things we can't predict as each society goes through its transformations." Through today's turmoil, Eliyahu has been able to keep his eye on the prize—the goal of building two democracies, side by side. His gift for language and the respect he has expressed pay off. For everyone in the room admits that we are in this together and can divorce only at our peril.

Now, just as the meeting is about to end, do all the Palestinian fears—of Arafat and his "people"—gush forth. "Of course, we're afraid," one after another confesses. Everyone wants to make up for the emotions concealed, the time wasted, and begins revealing every possible hidden thought. The Palestinian lawyers are talking two at a time, with tears in their eyes, clearly wanting the Israelis not to leave. Their practical concerns about "institutional collaboration," along with much else that's been on their minds, keeps pouring out

When we have to leave Nablus to return to Jerusalem, Tamar Peleg says, "Next time, why don't we take a specific aspect of the legal system and try and work it through together?"—her first words of the day.

CHAPTER TWELVE

Double Vision:
Gaza in My Mind

Six weeks later, on May 10, I get a midnight call from Sara to get to Gaza. Now, on a hot sunny morning, I'm here, along with dozens of members of the press, to witness what may be the beginning of the end of the Intifada and the occupation. Earlier this morning, at 3 A.M., while Palestinians and journalists were asleep, Israeli troops departed after twenty-seven years. They carted away telecommunications systems, barbed wire, trucks, jeeps, computers, prison and office supplies, tents and cots, the vast infrastructure that sustained the occupation. Everything was hauled down the dusty Gazan streets as aging PLO fighters from Jordan and Egypt arrived to replace the Israeli soldiers. These men, the new Palestinian police force, are everywhere. They're wearing green army uniforms, curiously similar to the Israelis', except for their rounded berets.

Are we moving toward real autonomy and peace here in Gaza, the West Bank and ultimately Jerusalem? Can the Palestinians replace the infrastructure the Israelis removed? Will the new Palestinian police transform themselves from revolutionaries into civil servants? For many of us here, these questions form a muffled counterpoint to the raucous cheering and earsplitting gunshots around us.

But whether or not this peace can be sustained, what I see today under the grilling Gazan sun in Dir el-Balah, close to the site where the Intifada began seven years ago, is a cultural landscape that's changed completely. As the morning brightens, we catch the wide smiles and thumbs-up gestures from the last of the departing soldiers. Their body language and exaggerated winks signal that they're as happy to be leaving Gaza as the Palestinians are clearly euphoric to be free of them.

I watch journalists trying to conduct interviews in the growing heat, but they're drowned out by loud hand-clapping crowds who keep giving a wild welcome to their new police. Guns are everywhere. Palestinian boys and men shoot upward toward the sky, a salutation to the PLO fighters. Tears run down the faces of some of the men. Stepping into the scene, I ask one fighter, wearing a crisp, new police uniform, his age. Choked with tears, he answers: "I'm only three days old."

Eight boys swagger toward me, kicking up dust. Each holds a long gun as he shoots questions at me: "Where you from?" each asks. Then they jeer: "American. American. America makes all our problems." Surrounded by children with loaded guns, I'm far more uneasy than celebratory.

Soon I stroll toward friends, wondering if other journalists, especially those who are Jewish, also feel on edge or estranged. Gazans have a legacy of hating Jews. For the first time in decades, we're the only ones in sight. I move anxiously through the commotion until I catch up with my friend Robert. As we exchange looks, I see I'm not alone in my discomfort. I ask what he picks up beneath this pandemonium. We're talking softly. "How do I feel?" he repeats. "Disoriented; muddled; dislocated. This is history, but I'm numb. The mood here isn't like on September 13. Today it's only superficially euphoric. There's a strong undercurrent of rage. Maybe it's my sleep deprivation or this god-awful heat, but I see a pure sullenness in these kids.

"There's so much bad faith on both sides, and that's been reflected in the way the negotiations have been stumbling along these past nine months." I, too, feel the distrust surrounding us as a mirror of the deal-making that's occurred since the Handshake. There's a lingering doubt, a niggardly spirit evident in all the negotiations which, as I say to Robert, seems completely different from the tempo of Oslo. Robert pauses. As he does, hundreds of kids surge past us, kicking up sand and stones. After they've gone, we move to a quiet rock and wearily sit down.

Robert says, "There's been no real preparation, no implementation, no 'mutual recognitions'; not even the beginnings of an infrastructure put into place. The Palestinians well know that anything they get is on sufferance. They rightly believe the Israelis departed mainly because it was inconvenient to keep on fighting." As he talks we hear cheering, shouting and a cannonade of gun blasts. All have escalated since early this morning.

Robert is pensive. "Look, people here know they're about to move from a liberation struggle into the tedium of administrative nitty-gritty. Along with their new freedoms, they face immense challenges. I wonder, who's going to take out the garbage after the revolution when no one did before?"

Jon Immanuel joins us. "I think it's good that the Gazans aren't wildly enthusiastic," he says, evenhandedly as ever. "That's realistic. They're glad and they're not glad. That's sensible. Too much euphoria leads to disappointment, which will only lead us back to war. This is exactly the right mood," he adds, as he looks around.

A day later I'm talking with Sara over coffee in Jerusalem, telling her about the negativity we felt in the air, the undercurrent of hostility, the sense of anxiety about the future. She knows Gaza "like the back of my hand," as she often says. It's true. She's gone there regularly for years, lived there this entire past week. "It's amazing," she says. "I've been covering Gaza for so long, but I never saw the people of Gaza happy. Now everyone there is smiling. Yesterday I walked to the ocean and saw, for the first time, thousands of Gazans swimming in the Mediterranean. Others were barbecuing on the edge of the beach with their kids, playing along the seashore, one that's always seemed desolate, even ominous. If the women weren't trailing their long dresses and veils into the water, I might have mistaken Gaza for Tel Aviv! It's suddenly so relaxed. New coffee shops are springing up every day. Music, theater groups and poetry readings fill the streets late into the night."

She shakes her head. "You and your TV friends missed the moment. You missed the elation," she says, annoyed.

"Listen. There's a tiny park. It's not what anyone else would call a park, just a patch of yellowish grass with six trees, four flowers, a swing. The *shabab* [street fighters] kept it closed all through the Intifada to protect it. Now, hundreds of Gazans dress up in their finery, lining up respectfully to see a place that doesn't even qualify as a playground! Honestly, you'd never stop to notice it anywhere else in the world. But for them, it's symbolic of freedom, of ownership and rights to their own land. The Gazans grow ecstatic over a patch of land that, to us, looks dreary. Go back. Open your eyes."

Sara is more experienced and more attuned to the collective psyche than most journalists. She rarely misses the detail that's lost upon others, those who don't work as hard as she does. I listen to her and trust that I did miss something important. Within hours, though my throat constricts at the thought, I return to Gaza. I don't look forward to the dust, heat or guns.

I drive down to the Erez Checkpoint, where I hop a cab to the Jabaliya refugee camp to visit my closest Gazan friend, Mohammed Dawas, a Palestinian journalist I met over a year ago. Since then, we've spent several long afternoons together. He has conveyed how he experiences Gaza as a giant prison. Mohammed was born and raised here; typically his face is immobile, expressing an air of perpetual defeat.

Today, as I enter his quarters in this teeming camp, I see a man so blissfully ebullient that his appearance is transformed. "Come in; welcome," he says animatedly before I even have a chance to sit. As he prepares coffee, I listen. He announces proudly: "I was the first Gazan to see the returning Palestinian troops." He beams at me. "You see, I couldn't sleep, so I waited up and watched our men arriving from Rafah. What I saw were not *signs* of freedom, but *real* freedom. Can you imagine, elderly fighters from abroad, all seven thousand, who will soon bring their families? Twenty thousand of our people returning? *That's* important."

"What's the biggest change?" I ask, sitting down at his kitchen table.

"Most amazing is the walking after dark. For the first time in seven years, we're free of curfew, aren't locked inside every night at 9 P.M. For so many years, walking after dark meant darting home as fast as possible. We were, all of us, afraid. But now! Now we are walking all night until 3 or 4 A.M. We bring our children along. There's no fear; we are all completely relaxed. We look around and still can't believe there are no Israeli troops, that they're gone. Do you realize what this means? Can you imagine? For the first time in my life I feel at ease in my own neighborhood. Is that possible for you to imagine?" He gets up to talk to one of his children.

"Before the Israelis left," he says, sitting down, "we were in prison here. Some say it's still a prison because we're cut off from the West Bank and East Jerusalem. But, believe me, strolling around at night or standing on our own rooftops without soldiers to worry about, we are not thinking prison. We are thinking freedom. We are thinking celebration. Of course, in a few weeks everyone will look around, needing work, money, waiting for our country's life to begin. Will this exuberance wind down? Without a doubt. But right now, being free to walk anywhere at night." He pauses. "I don't have the words. You can't imagine. . . ."

All I noticed at first, I confess, were guns. "There are so many and they're in the hands of such young, angry kids. That's why I almost didn't come to visit today."

"In truth," Mohammed responds, "I don't like these guns either. We hear them going off all the time, every hour. I'll be as happy as you when the police take over, taking security into their own hands. I wish for a victory without guns. But what can we do? There's a generation of kids for whom holding a gun is a symbol of power. Remember, they grew up seeing the Israelis with guns which gave *them* power."

Mohammed changes the subject. "What I resent is the press. They always say, 'Gaza is hell.' Well, for us, Gaza is our land, the land we need to build. Every night the Hamas and the PLO meet in joint councils. Both factions agree that no more Palestinian blood must be shed, that we must work together. And you should know, my friend, that killing Israelis is not condoned either. Our extremists are no fools. They know, whether they like it or not, that the time for violence against Israelis has passed; this is the time for organizing and building our country. Think about it. We Palestinians built Kuwait, Abu Dhabi, Saudi Arabia, Jordan. We built Israel. So why do the media say we can't build our own country? We must. We will."

Our talk turns to Arafat and to the many Palestinians who worry about his return, who fear that he'll be unable to make the transition from revolutionary to statesman. Mohammed says, "Look, I cannot speak without emotion about Arafat. I was born in 1960. As soon as I opened my eyes, I saw posters of his face on every wall. Yes, he's made many mistakes, we all know that. But he remains a hero. Like many people here, I long for his arrival. It cannot come soon enough for us. But don't you see? For once, we're not living in the future; we are enjoying the moment. The journalists think about what's to come, while we are breathing the free air, beginning to acclimate to a life without fear."

Mohammed's wife brings us a tray of tea and crackers. They exchange smiles before she returns to their children, who are playing quietly in the back room. "Many times," he continues, "I'd leave my dear wife and my beautiful children in the morning, not sure that I'd be alive to see them that night. I lived with fear, in dread of the Israeli guns everywhere. Many times I thought I was going to die. Did I ever tell you? Once I got caught between the *shabab* and the IDF. A live tear gas canister landed directly on my foot. I passed out, was rushed to the hospital, certain I was going to die. This will not happen now. And, my friend, that's as far as my mind can travel today."

As Mohammed walks me out of his house, he spots two men right outside his door and whispers to me that they belong to the Hamas. I freeze as he introduces us, but the two slim men both smile. Surprising myself, I ask casually, "What do you think of all this?"

"We were not for this peace," one says, "but who can deny it's wonderful to be here right now?"

Driving home, I remember an incident Sara has told me about. Two years ago, five months pregnant, she was on assignment to interview Islamic Jihad fanatics. She was rushing to finish her work, needing to get to Tel Aviv for a sonogram. She arrived with an escort in Jenin, at the time a wild West Bank village. Against the Palestinian driver's strong advice, she went off alone with six militants to get their stories and pictures. They drove her into a remote forest. Though she feared the worst, they politely offered her tea, serving her with impeccable manners while masked with ski caps and shrouded in kaffiyehs, with only their eyes visible. Of course, they saw she was pregnant. When they learned that she had to get to the hospital in Tel Aviv, they rushed the session, talking and posing quickly, holding their guns erect, then urging her to hurry so she could find out about her baby.

"Get to doctor. Baby is best," one masked man said, escorting her back onto a main road.

As she drove toward Tel Aviv, she heard a radio bulletin. Israeli soldiers had just discovered a secret location where members of the violent Jihad organization were hiding. The report said that Israeli soldiers had ambushed and killed six extremists. Though she felt it was irrational, Sara listened fearfully, hoping the dead men didn't include those she had just left. And she found herself sighing in relief when descriptions of those who were murdered didn't match.

• • •

In Jerusalem a few nights later, we few journalists who are not in Gaza wait outside Rabin's office for him and U.S. Secretary of State Warren Christopher to emerge. The light in Israel this time of day and this time of the year seems clearer and more redolent of hope than light anywhere else. As I walk to this press conference, I am surrounded by the fragrance of roses blossoming in the parks and lawns around the Supreme Court, the Knesset, Rabin's office. There's a slight evening breeze.

Soon we see Christopher, Rabin and Peres walking toward us. I've heard moderate, educated Palestinians call Rabin a war criminal, and having witnessed what some have lived through, I've had moments of understanding their viewpoint. Yet standing fifteen feet from our prime minister, I see him as enormously changed. His work these past two years has awakened a greatness, given him a moral stature that few, even on the left here in Israel, possess.

Rabin may be no visionary. For years he was certainly no dove. Yet, at this moment of ever closer negotiations between Israel and Syria, of final troop withdrawals in Gaza and Jericho, I listen to his speech in praise of "not ruling over another people, not denying others what we ourselves have achieved," and I see him with new eyes. Rabin has worked hard. There's something in his persistence, his contradictions, his past firmness and current courage that moves me to tears.

As he speaks to the fifteen journalists, his first subject is Syria. The tone is hopeful. Then he turns to Arafat's speech (for "a jihad for Jerusalem," secretly taped in a South African mosque) and his tone becomes rightfully forceful. Rabin says that Arafat's speech violates the peace agreement. He warns that such wild words can throw the future of the West Bank into jeopardy. He wants clarification from the chairman. For a brief moment, I relive the rage and fear that speech evoked in almost everyone I know, at least on this side of the Green Line.

But then, unbidden, another vision rises and hovers about me in this fading sunlight, in this summer season of politics and roses—that we are, in our own Middle Eastern way, creating conditions for peace. No one knows for sure what lies ahead, but we have left Gaza and Jericho and we are legally committed to leaving much of the rest of the West Bank.

The sense of Jewish renewal in Israel, however fragile, is passing through each of us. As I watch Rabin, I see that, against great odds and terribly late, after unnecessary deaths on both sides, work has begun. Israelis and Palestinians are moving forward into an unknown, unknowable future. Despite everything that's unfair or ambiguous, for the first moment all month, I gaze at Rabin and feel a surge of pure hope.

I've never defined myself primarily by politics, wherever I live. Like most of us, I'm too self-centered, or just merely human, to think of others' suffering when pleasure comes my way. Yet somehow in Israel, the Palestinian plight has lived inside me as an affliction, a refutation, almost, of the uniquely Israeli talent for joyous abandon.

For years, I've felt cursed with double vision. I'll sit at a party in Tel Aviv and start to imagine what the people in Nablus are, or aren't, doing. I'm sipping wine at an outdoor cafe on Ben Yehuda late at night in "our" Jerusalem, overcome by images of the eerily quiet streets in "their" Jerusalem. The joy in one society always, sooner or later, rises up to contrast with the suffering nearby, inflicted by our troops in the Jewish name. My love for living here in Israel has been dogged and at times marred by the specter of what I know about the West Bank and Gaza.

No matter how lopsided or unfair many find Oslo and the Declaration of Principles, no matter how many issues have yet to be addressed or redressed, autonomy has begun. That my few friends in Gaza, along with many who would never be my friends, are walking in freedom, at their own pace and in their own place, liberates me to enjoy this night. However prematurely, there are no hovering shadows.

CHAPTER THIRTEEN

Waiting for Arafat

After every war
someone has to tidy up.
Things won't pick
themselves up, after all. . . .
Someone has to shove
the rubble to the roadsides
so the carts loaded with corpses
can get by.
Someone has to trudge
through sludge and ashes,
through the sofa springs,
the shards of glass,
the bloody rags. . . .
No sound bites, no photo opportunities
and it takes years.
All the cameras have gone
to other wars. . . .
Someone, broom in hand,
still remembers how it was.
Someone else listens, nodding
his unshattered head. . . .
Those who knew
what this was all about
must make way for those
who know little.
And less than that.
And at last nothing less than nothing.

—Wislawa Szymborska, "The End and the Beginning"

Arafat is said to be slowly preparing to enter Gaza in August, at the earliest. But on June 30, with a single day's notice, he's en route.

It's early afternoon as I drive into Gaza, searching to find the address where Hakam has booked me a room for four nights, at the Barazi home. He's told me that Mrs. Elena Barazi owns the oldest, most beautiful house in the neighborhood of El Ramal in Gaza City. Driving through the streets, looking at the graffiti-laced walls, the broken shards of glass lying everywhere, inhaling the stench of uncollected garbage, I find it difficult to believe there could be anything beautiful in this place. But when I find the house, I see he's right; it has a wraparound terrace and high decorative glass windows, an anomaly in the slum Gaza has become. Hakam has said that her long-deceased husband was born into a prominent Gazan family at the turn of the century and that for decades this was home to their large brood. Now that her children are grown, Mrs. Barazi ordinarily lives by herself, alone with her memories. But this, the eve of Arafat's return after twenty-seven years in exile, is no ordinary night.

Overwhelmed by heat, dust and crowds, I begin to relax only when Mrs. Barazi's daughter-in-law, Leila, opens their ornate front door. We warm to each other instantly with a flash of recognition passing between us. We look alike, both in our late forties, both with long, dark hair, not dissimilar faces, a comparable friendliness.

After showing me my mattress, one of four set down on a bedroom floor, she offers me tea as I look around at this grand house with high-domed ceilings, oversized windows and spacious rooms; it stands as an eloquent reminder of a lost world. Padding behind Leila into her mother-in-law's all-white kitchen, I imagine her as being as strong as her muscular shoulders suggest. Yet once we sit at the table, I see that, along with a sharp intelligence, there's a chronic anxiety etched onto Leila's face. Conversing in female shorthand, we don't pause, even when a slew of foreign journalists arrive. They drop bags, computers and camera gear on the floor, then immediately begin a loud debate about Arafat's return. They're talking so loudly that Leila and I have to move rooms away to keep hearing each other.

She tells me that her husband, Suhar, once owned a thriving gas station, but it was closed down by the Israeli authorities because he couldn't control the Intifada kids. They'd circle Israeli army trucks as they fueled up, jeer at them and throw rocks. "How could *he* control them when the Israelis couldn't?" Leila asks. She says that she and Suhar live in an apartment only a few blocks away. After an agonizing debate they've agreed to open this, her mother-in-law's home, to paying guests. Despite Suhar's family's status and Leila's own privilege (they're both from the Palestinian upper class), they haven't been able to live through the Egyptian and Israeli occupations and then seven years of the Intifada without falling upon hard times. Because they need the money badly, they've decided to trick Suhar's strong-willed mother, telling her that we who are arriving are his old college friends.

Deceiving her mother-in-law is not going to be easy, Leila says. They've told a lie that's likely going to be impossible to pull off, especially as these journalists think this is a hostel, as Hakam has told us. As we talk, we hear the others arguing politics, audible even from rooms away.

"Believe me," she sighs, "*nothing* is worth upsetting my mother-in-law. But nothing." She pauses. "I never imagined the Israelis would leave before she died."

"You mean you have your own occupation under this roof?" I ask, eliciting laughter. "Oh, we do. Most definitely. Our own little occupation," she repeats, as I see that the dominant drama in this decaying mansion is less Arafat's arrival than the ruse to keep aged Mrs. Barazi in the dark that her home is being rented out to strangers. I learn that Leila and Suhar have worked hard to sustain the old lady's illusion that she's still living in the elegant ambiance of the Arabian upper class, circa 1925. If we journalists let on that we're crashing for pay, we'll not only infuriate her, but also break her heart, Leila tells me.

Just as she does, Suhar walks wearily inside, with his mother trailing behind him. He's tall, dignified and reserved. Though he has a handsome face and thick salted white hair, I see the strain on his face, the tension in his shoulders.

He bends over to Leila. These two exchange looks that suggest their battle is already lost. I get up to join them. We three urge elderly Mrs. Barazi into her kitchen for dinner, leaving the journalists to serve themselves in her large dining room.

I sit down next to this frail, aristocratic woman, who seems to have leapt straight out of a Tennessee Williams play. Proudly showing off her hands and perfectly polished nails, she sweeps them through her thinning but carefully sprayed white hair, asking me, "Would you believe eighty-nine?" Then she begins interrogating me.

Suhar and I improvise memories of our college days in Michigan. But she's barely listening. Her eyes dart about, trying to register what's amiss. Despite her fragility, she clearly has a will of steel. Within minutes, she abruptly stands up and quickly strides out of her kitchen "to see what my son's other friends are up to." We race after her, but she's scurried so fast that by the time we catch up, she's standing and scrutinizing the ten journalists. They're slouched over couches and chairs, drinking beer that's forbidden in Islamic Gaza. All the tables have been rearranged to accommodate the piles of media paraphernalia that are heaped on top of them. Mrs. Barazi stares, her eyes registering that something is wrong. Just as she's about to discover what, Suhar urgently pulls at her sleeve, encouraging her to come with him on another "errand" that will give her more "healthy fresh air."

By 3 A.M., I'm sitting alone in the Barazi living room, listening to Arabic prayers flowing in through the high arched windows from a mosque next door. The sounds are full-bodied and resonant. Then, one lone voice rises and falls operatically, filling the room with a meditative feeling as I ponder the strange theater piece I've entered.

Early the next morning, more foreign journalists pile in, along with Imnan, a poet from Ramallah who was sent by Hakam to translate for me. Wearing jeans and T-shirts, the two of us hightail it away from the growing tension in the Barazi household, stepping out into the sauna heat of a humid morning. A mile down the main road, we find a cavernous building that's being used as the new "Palestine Press Headquarters."

Inside, we're surrounded by hundreds of disgruntled journalists who are squeezed together along low benches. No special consideration is offered to the famous, the renowned writers or well-known TV anchormen and women among us. All are waiting for their press passes, as they must do every day because, for no discernible reason, the Palestinians issue fresh cards regularly. This forces the press corps, including high-profile journalists and photographers on tight deadlines, to wait long hours to be recertified. Since the new cards look no different from the last ones, this waste of time infuriates everyone. Most in this room are used to deferential treatment, to limousines and easy access to kings and prime ministers. Here in Gaza, they have no choice but to submit to the Palestinian press officers' wacky regulations.

The men in charge, all new to power, stand around a coffee-stained table piled high with papers, scissors, cellophane tape and safety pins. They slump over it, overwhelmed by frustration, as if stumped about how to sort out photos and names. Then, remembering who they've just become, each one puffs up, bellowing out the name of a journalist who's now allowed to come forward.

"What is this, Ellis Island?" Clyde Haberman, the bureau chief of the *New York Times,* asks. I laugh. Since I'm not on a tight deadline, I have the leisure to find the small details of the new "autonomy" intriguing, to cast this as a study in what sudden power does to anyone, a subject that strikes me as crucial to Arafat's return. While everyone around me is cursing, I'm fascinated by the chaos.

When my new card is finally ready, the men in charge call me up in excitement, are so in need of affirmation that in response to my wide smile, one actually hugs me. Together we paste together the exact materials needed to create a "valid" card. And soon, with bulky green official passes pinned to our shirts, Imnan and I are free to wander outside.

We move toward the outdoor stage where Arafat will soon appear. Security guards stop us to check our small bags. New to this common routine, they take a long time examining dental floss, cigarettes and keys. Still worried that they haven't been thorough, one man, as if hitting pay dirt, points at Imnan's baseball cap. "Well, what's under there?" he asks, frowning.

"My head," she laughs.

The July heat so saturates the air that soon we both find mere breathing laborious. Despite the fact that we've just put in hours getting our press passes, we decide to cover this story from the Barazis' living room, where we can watch Arafat on TV. In that cool room, we rationalize, we'll be able to catch both his speech and the Gazan reaction to his return. Once back at the Barazis', we discover we're not the only ones who have made this decision. Most of the other journalists from last night are still here, gathered around a small TV they've set up in the kitchen.

Imnan and I join the Barazi family in the living room, where they have tuned into Israel's Channel 2, the only station covering today's events, the only channel available in Israel, Gaza and the West Bank. Anchormen announce the schedule, telling viewers what they can expect during this "historic moment," a phrase invoked repeatedly. Unfortunately, no one in this room that's filling up with Palestinian neighbors knows any Hebrew. Which means that even this singularly Palestinian event seems to them to be dominated by the Israelis.

"I don't know why I never learned it," Suhar says quietly. "Maybe it's a psychological barrier. I speak French, German and English, yet I could never retain even the rudiments of Hebrew. But how much would it have cost them to let Palestinians in on this event by running Arabic subtitles?" he asks. Coverage switches to a helicopter view of Arafat's white car as it crawls along a dirt road, moving from Rafah, Egypt, into Gaza. We see a few donkeys ambling toward his motorcade in the sweltering heat but there are no crowds.

The Barazis' living room fills up with more Gazans. Though their emotions are high, they keep them in check. By contrast, the deadline-driven journalists are emitting a buzz from the next room as they try to catch details from their transistor radio and their small TV, set up along with laptops, modems and all the high-technology of news gathering.

At last, two blocks from where we sit, Arafat arrives. He steps onto the stage. We lean forward. "This is the critical moment," Leila says. She means the moment when someone might try to assassinate him. Arafat's demeanor is surprisingly childlike. At first he says nothing as he raises his hands and cheerfully throws small white objects that sail out into the crowds. Three, four, eight times, he repeats this motion. Before the neighbors set me straight, I wonder if he's throwing paper airplanes at his people. I'm told that they're white carnations.

Then, as Arafat begins his speech, Leila, Suhar, Imnan and assorted neighbors translate. "In the name of God, I salute all our prisoners," they repeat. "My brothers, while we are here together in Gaza, we must remember our martyrs." Everyone is perfectly still as Leila passes tissues around. Eyes well up with tears. I, too, am infected with emotion, by the simplicity of this scene. After twenty-seven years, the long, convoluted Palestinian struggle comes down to this; pure attentiveness engulfs us all. Until, within seconds, the television blanks out.

Leila leaps up in frustration. She pulls out, then replugs the electrical cord, while Suhar jiggles, and presses buttons on their remote control. Nothing! "But this never happens," Leila wails, as we switch to Egyptian and Jordanian channels, whose soccer games are also blacked out. "It's not the reception. It's your set," a neighbor observes. But I realize it's not the set either. The journalists' equipment has drained all the electrical juice from the house. Leila realizes this, too. She rolls her eyes, saying, "First, the Israelis give the news in Hebrew, which Palestinians can't understand. And now, in our own house, the Americans eradicate Arafat's speech." We cannot help smiling at each other at this irony. For most Palestinians believe that their narrative is always dominated, if not obliterated, by Israelis and Americans and that is what is happening here, in the most literal way. Suhar stands and walks, head bowed, in retreat toward his bedroom.

Under the pressure of their deadlines, the journalists in the kitchen remain oblivious, not only to the way they're rupturing the delicate fabric of Mrs. Barazi's life, but to the fact that they've just blacked out Arafat's long-awaited speech. Instead of apologizing, they shout for us to quiet down. "Get your radio," I yell to Leila, who emphatically shakes her head, while nodding toward her mother-in-law. We all look over at aged Mrs. Barazi. She's holding tight to the only radio they own, a tiny black transistor. Pressing it close to her ear, she sways to Arabic music. When she sees us watching her, she gives a sharp look that defies anyone even to think about asking for it.

Eventually, we improvise a system that assures sporadic coverage. First, I click the remote, while Leila unplugs and then replugs the cord. This guarantees us three minutes of Arafat's speech before the set blacks out again. Repeating this routine a few times, we get the gist of his speech.

"It's nice, he's back," Leila says, with a melancholy smile, half an hour later out on the front terrace. She's fluffing her long dark hair.

"Nice? It's nothing!" Suhar retorts, as if to himself. A wounded dignity rises in his voice and flushes his face. "We need substance, programs, real leaders," he says, an opinion I've heard from many here. Gazan crowds are filing down the street past this house, even though Arafat's speech hasn't yet ended. I hear some say it was too crowded, too hot, or that the public address system hadn't worked well. Though he is much loved and revered in Gaza, there are also many people, especially among intellectuals, who are skeptical about Arafat, who fear the dangers his leadership may unleash. On this late afternoon, when he has finally returned from long exile, he seems remote from the reality of the world he is inheriting. Following her husband with her eyes, Leila now looks more worried than hopeful.

"But it can't be worse than it has been," I say.

"Sometimes," she responds, "I get a feeling in here [she makes a fist near her gut] that something more terrible than Israeli occupation might occur."

• • •

West Bank Palestinians don't like visiting Gaza, even now that it's safer because Israeli troops have left. The sun is beginning to set as four East Jerusalem Palestinians and I weave in and out of the chaotic traffic, hoping to get to the Mediterranean before dark. No police are in sight, not even a traffic light. Eventually, we spot one lone cop gesticulating frantically, his futile attempt to direct traffic. Leaping from one side of the road to the other, he blows his whistle nonstop. But aged cars, whose metal underbellies sag close to the ground, ignore him. We park and walk along the beach's thick, brown sand. We're surrounded by heavyset women in white veils as they stroll with their children.

My Palestinian escorts seem ill at ease among these crowds as we sit to catch a blood-red sunset that's quickly slipping under the water's horizon. "Let me ask you a politically incorrect question," I begin, as we sit awkwardly on the dark sand. They look at me blankly, so I rephrase: "Does this scene feel weird to you guys?"

"Weird, ugly, horrible, disgusting," skinny, lively Ithab responds.

Mohammed, a Denzel Washington look-alike, interjects, "Gaza is closer to Egypt in every way. It's nothing like the West Bank. And compared to East Jerusalem? It's a totally different world." He's fingering his gold neck chain and jiggling an expensive watch as if unconsciously emphasizing the symbols of what he has that most Gazans do not. "There are too many guns here," he adds. "And no culture. Gazans aren't educated, like we are. They've known so much violence. Everyone says it's not dangerous anymore. But I wouldn't bet on it."

Half smiling, Ithab says, "We all agree, two hundred percent. The police should control these kids and take away their guns." It's turning dark as we get up and head back to the Barazis' home.

• • •

Early the next evening, the day before Arafat is scheduled to arrive in Jericho, Imnan and I pull into Jericho's tiny town square, an hour and a half from Gaza. The town square consists of a few yards of lawn dotted with palm trees. Three-story houses built side by side are nestled so close that people standing on adjacent terraces can touch each other. Standing out on one, I see the scene here resembles a small Caribbean outpost that's readying for a massive reggae concert. As the sky turns a musky mango, journalists drop by to chat in a small room Hakam has reserved. Soon, he and his assistants arrive with food, tape decks and radios. Someone plugs in an old fan, which we all watch with an interest bordering on lust; it slowly swivels its neck, circulating a thin current of very hot air.

We take turns out on the tiny balcony, gazing at the people partying below. I see dark-haired, slim Palestinian men and teenagers walking in groups or pairs, arms interlocked, engaged in conversation. Boys on bikes ride up and down, waving to anyone and everyone. Immediately below, I catch sight of Sara. She's chatting with friends from Spain, France and Italy—photographers and journalists who've spent decades covering the Mideast or meeting at other hot spots around the globe. They wave up to us before returning to their shoptalk. Despite ever-thickening crowds, the atmosphere remains agreeably relaxed, in clear contrast to Gaza's edgy intensity.

The heat doesn't subside even after nightfall, when the town is brightly lit by high-powered floodlights the TV crews have woven into the palm trees. We're all madly fanning ourselves. Imnan and I are too hot to talk as we examine the activities below. Twelve feet away, across this narrow street, TV journalists and their assistants scramble around rooftops, passing under huge TV equipment and satellite antennae. Palestinian flags, large and small, are draped everywhere. Some are dangling from heavy cords that stretch from the rooftops to the palm trees in the town square, which is dominated by a red helium balloon, shaped like a helicopter, advertising a local insurance company.

Despite the onrush of newcomers (Palestinians and journalists), there's an easygoing mood everywhere we look. These Palestinians well know that many of us, especially the visiting international press, are Jewish. Yet ethnic tensions are nonexistent. We're all in this together, waiting for Arafat. Except that the press corps are exhausted from working in the Gazan heat; some are complaining that this is a prefabricated "story," too pre-packaged to be interesting. They seem weary of the "historic moment" that's been protracted over three long days and nights. Jericho's residents are as avid to witness Arafat's arrival as the media are eager to have done with it.

At night, Imnan and I, along with several women journalists, try to get some sleep despite the still insufferable heat. Palestinian men and boys from the neighborhood move in and out of our tiny space looking for their friends as we toss on our cots in discomfort. Each of us has stripped down to skimpy T-shirt and short shorts. Yet there's no paranoia about strange men opening doors, no physical fear of harm. Long into the future, I'll conjure this night of easy trust, especially when I learn, over and over, how tenacious are the sinister stereotypes of Palestinian men.

We wake groggy to a hot, steamy dawn. At 8 A.M., we learn that, at the last possible moment, the site of Arafat's speech has been moved from the town square to a field three miles away. Is this about security? The TV crews, whose stations have blown hundreds of thousands of dollars waiting on the rooftops, are furiously reassembling complicated equipment, then hurrying to relocate. By 9 A.M., a group of us are sauntering down a long, dirt country road with nothing but flat fields visible. At well over 100 degrees, the air is stifling.

In the huge field where the chairman's helicopter is expected to land, high green bleachers are set up for the media. Behind the bleachers is a wire fence separating us from the Palestinians. Climbing the steps, I turn to see thousands from all over the West Bank ambling onto a field so vast that the estimated three thousand look more like three hundred. Everyone falls silent as an olive green Egyptian helicopter swoops toward us, soars, then flies low again, circling directly above until landing nearby, behind a clump of cypress trees.

Arafat emerges from the helicopter with a procession that includes Palestinian notables like Hanan Ashwari and Faisal Husseini. Um Jihad is here, the widow of Abu Jihad, Arafat's former right-hand man, who was killed by the Israelis in Lebanon. Also present is the hearty, ever cheerful Nabil Sha'ath, Arafat's newest and most vocal aide.

The chairman looks somber, tired and very small. He's surrounded by tall and burly security guards who strain to keep their guns high in the air while shuffling anxiously about him, moving as he moves. To my astonishment, when Arafat mounts the stage there's a burst of jeering and hissing from the crowd, the last response anyone has expected. As I turn, I realize these sounds are not in response to Arafat, but to *us,* the privileged press corps, positioned squarely in front of the stage and obscuring their view. They've come here to see Abu Amar, as Arafat is affectionately known, not the back of our heads or the clunky TV equipment. The hooting grows louder. Within minutes, the wire fence is trampled down as Palestinians rush toward the stage.

These West Bank citizens have rightly intuited what the press already well knows, that Arafat's security personnel are inept. They don't know how to call the shots, especially when the momentum grows, and right now, it's bedlam. Arafat is unable to speak while his people push onto the stage, encircling him. The security forces are holding hands, as if the delicate chain of their outstretched arms can deter a group hellbent on getting past them.

I see Arafat's face clearly. His lips are trembling; he looks vulnerable. Though conventional wisdom says that no one in Jericho will try to harm him, who knows for sure? All I know is that I must escape this human tornado, and within seconds I manage to duck under what's left of the fence and walk back down the road, the only person in sight until I arrive back in town.

In Jericho, I spot a Palestinian doctor I'd met the night before. He invites me to join him and his colleague, Dr. Jamal Abdullah, a short, squat and extremely somber-looking man in his late sixties. They're seated at a small outdoor table at one of the many cafes now lining Jericho's main street. As we sip our lemonades, trying to hear each other over the commotion, I ask Dr. Abdullah why he looks so grim. He lights a cigarette, bends his head close to mine and in a hoarse whisper tells his story: "Forty-seven years ago," he begins, "I was a young man working for the British Mandate in Jerusalem. At first I was only a clerk. But I was diligent and eventually became a trusted secretary, running their main office located in what's now the King David Hotel.

"In 1947, when the United Nations passed Resolution 181, the vote that divided Palestine into two states, one Jewish and one Arab, I was chosen to translate the official document from English into Arabic. I typed it out myself. Afterward, I tucked a copy under my shirt and smuggled it home in my underwear. I was afraid I'd get caught. But when I was searched, I was lucky and wasn't; the authorities didn't find those papers." He puts out his cigarette and lights another.

"As soon as I got home, into what's now the fashionable Jewish neighborhood of Talbieh, I called my friends to hurry over. We were the young intellectuals of that time. Eight or ten of us stayed up all night, studying every word in the documents, debating its merits line by line until we'd all memorized each fine point. By dawn, we were in full agreement, to a man: Our leaders should sign it; they must accept partition."

Dr. Abdullah's hands start shaking and he stops talking. He seems immersed in memories of that distant night. "Our superiors didn't agree with us. Not one of them saw the arrangement for our future the way we did. They were adamant, remained deaf to our entreaties, even though our arguments were strong, very strong. They wouldn't listen to us, though we were unanimous and sure of our position."

Dr. Abdullah sees my fascination, but he now seems worried about having told me so much. As that long ago event hangs between us, he stops, lights a cigarette and looks around at the crowds of thin young men drinking water and lemonade. When he speaks again, his voice is so soft that I have to put my ear close to his mouth to catch his words. "Now, it's forty-seven years later. And what do we get? Only what's left of Jericho and Gaza, for starters. After so many wrongheaded decisions from our leaders, so many, many mistakes that were made, we don't feel anything like those men are saying [he points up at the CNN, BBC, ABC and other crews gathered on a nearby roof]. No one likes this accord. But what can we do?" He shrugs, then shakes his head. As he does, I realize how often I've been jarred by the contrast between official and unofficial stories. I'll sit in Jerusalem, turn on CNN and get excited by something reporter Bill Delaney describes. But when I rush to that very spot, I'm often struck by how much the rosy spin leaves out. So much goes unreported. The undertow of sadness is what's usually missing.

"My generation is now old," Dr. Abdullah concludes. "It's the young who will have to create what we didn't." Studying the surrounding crowds, he doesn't seem optimistic. "It's a huge challenge. All I can think today is how different everything would have been if only they'd listened to us. . . ." Now he stops again, turning away. As I'm digesting this bite of living history, everyone at the cafe suddenly leaps up. The crowd from the stadium has started pouring into Jericho's already crowded town square. We all assume that the time for Arafat's entry into town is at hand. Both doctors seem excited. "I never met him face-to-face, you know," Dr. Abdullah says.

"I did, twice, in Cairo," his friend Dr. Bali says proudly, scanning the dirt road. "But that was twenty years ago."

The longing to see Arafat crosses class boundaries. Every Palestinian here in Jericho wants to get close to the president, to see, maybe to touch him in person. But despite weeks of anticipation, it's not to be. After the last of the crowd returns from the field, we hear the sirens of Arafat's caravan growing distant, not closer. Clearly, they're traveling in the opposite direction. Someone says they're heading toward a secret location, where they're planning to hold the first meeting of the Palestinian Authority Council on native ground.

My car is parked nearby, out on the main road. A young man named Nabil Suhan, a cousin of Hakam's, whom I met for the first time last night and who has the sweetest smile imaginable, locks eyes with me. Without a word, I throw him my car keys and we hop in, speeding away to where, we're not sure.

At each roadblock, novice security guards shout at us to stop, to turn back. I extend my bright purple Yasser Arafat press pass from my passenger window, while Nabil shouts in Arabic that we're part of the chairman's caravan, that they must help us, because if we lose Arafat, who's expecting us to follow him, we'll be in big trouble. Nabil keeps up this charade, smiling his magical grin as we are ushered through each security station and given exact directions. Every other car is turned away in a frenzy of hand motions and shouting. Finally we arrive at the new government office, a building we'd never have found on our own. We're told it was, until recently, a mental hospital. "Symbolic, or what?" Nabil jokes, as we speed into the parking lot.

We race on foot toward the front door of this isolated, rectangular building that's situated in the middle of a sandy plot of land. At the entrance we're swept into a crush of TV journalists who are pushing, shoving and yelling. Their protruding camera lenses and steel tripods are slammed against our knees and thighs. In fits and starts, Nabil and I manage to keep pressing forward until we amaze ourselves by being among the privileged few (only thirty) allowed into this building and up close to Arafat.

In a flood of flashing lights and rolling television film, Arafat begins swearing in his new cabinet, the first ministers of the Palestinian autonomy. Dressed in suits and ties, most of the twelve members line up, standing erect, waiting to take the oath of allegiance. Hanan Ashwari is not here, which leaves the widow of Abu Jihad as the only woman in the lineup. She has a chic silk kaffiyeh tossed elegantly around her neck. The anxious faces and rigid postures of these ministers speak to the tensions at the center of the new autonomy. Most of these surviving PLO officials, none of whom are young, look more than a little disoriented, not to say exhausted.

Arafat, standing four feet from my perch on a CNN ladder, looks determinedly serious but also as if in a trance. He's clearly intent on giving this ceremony the dignity it warrants. After each minister recites the long pledge of allegiance to the new autonomous entity, Arafat extends his arm for a formal handshake. But all formality crumbles because the exchanges between the chairman and his newly sworn ministers are so nakedly emotional—accompanied by tears, trembling and embraces. These ministers are among the last of Arafat's comrades, the lucky few who've made it alive to see this day. Many others have been killed or deserted him or were dismissed along the way.

Those here are at the end of one long road, the beginning of another equally arduous one. I can only guess at what ordeals they've endured, together or separately, to arrive into this moment, when the Palestinian future is being placed on their rounded, or in some cases noticeably stooped, shoulders.

I happen to be standing at a floor-to-ceiling glass window that faces a narrow corridor, one that Arafat and his ministers use to walk to their council meeting. First comes Arafat. He holds my eye for a second. I see he's aged considerably since the famous September 13 Handshake at the White House, less than a year ago. He seems neither the wily terrorist of yore nor the dignified statesman he needs to become to control the regions he has won from the Israelis.

Each Palestinian minister passes inches before me. Under the strain of sleep deprivation, constant travel, long weeks of work and unyielding media scrutiny, all, to my surprise, look fragile, even needy. Up close, these leaders, who are viewed as monsters by many Israelis and Americans, as saviors by some Palestinians, as sellouts by others (and who are uniformly ridiculed as bumbling and disorganized by the Western media), seem to be simply exhausted, middle-aged and middle-class leaders of a poor country. They are trying to hold on to some dignity, despite the immense strain, their internal power struggles and unthinkably hard work lying ahead.

Back at the town square, Nabil and I enter the largest coffee shop and order lemonades. We are feeling victorious after our successful chase. The thermometer in here registers 120 degrees. With no air-conditioning, we're close to hallucinating. Everyone in this large, crowded room looks dejected. At a neighboring booth, I see three men. One is sprawled over the tabletop, his face cradled in his crossed arms. A second man's head tilts back in his chair, at an awkward right angle to his body. The third is propped upright, betraying no emotion, either on his face or in his rigid posture.

Nabil and I ask if we can join them and pull over our chairs. We gently inquire what they're feeling. Surprisingly, a man from Jericho, named Said, offers a long political analysis that's completely upbeat, fully at odds with his appearance. "We've succeeded," he says lethargically. "The Intifada is over. We've won. Our people will build a great democratic state." Abdul Reshid, also from Jericho, slowly repositions his head and announces, unconvincingly, how happy and relaxed he feels.

"But then why do you all look so sad?" I ask. They're only tired, they assure us; they were up late last night. Yes, they are disappointed that Arafat didn't pass through the town square. But they are used to such feelings.

"To be a Palestinian is to be disappointed?" I venture.

"Oh, yes, you are so right," they agree, smiling for the first time.

Now the third man, a gap-toothed elder with a sun-darkened face and bright, alert eyes, interjects, in good English, that his name is Ahmoud Ajwar. "Let me tell you. This is the happiest day in my life," he says. He's believable. His eyes radiate happiness and his smile not only lights up his face but spreads joy all around our table. "I came from Hebron by private car. The buses were stopped by settlers throwing bottles or lying down across the road, but I made it through. Now I can go back and tell my people all that I've seen. I didn't see Arafat, but I was close to him. I saw our own police. With my own eyes, I saw the beginnings of our state, what will come to Hebron and Nablus and Ramallah too. The war is over. I will tell this to my friends, to my relatives, to my children. Then, they will feel the great blessings I do. I have lived to see all I ever wanted."

• • •

Across the street, Nabil Sha'ath holds a final press conference at the Hisham Hotel, where he details the decisions just made at the Palestinian Council. Arafat will move to Gaza immediately, as will he. Jericho, he tells us, is only symbolic, whereas Gaza, home to over a million residents, is the place where autonomy must begin. "Within a week," he promises.

"Precisely where will they live?" he's asked. "We're each looking for houses," Sha'ath replies, as the journalists press for details about his helicopter ride with Arafat. What was it like flying from Gaza this morning? What route did they take? How was the chairman's mood? "He was extremely emotional," Sha'ath says. "But what did Arafat say while flying over Tel Aviv and then over Jerusalem, getting an aerial view of Israel after all these years in exile?" a reporter asks.

"He didn't say a word; was more nostalgic and happier than I've ever seen him," Sha'ath responds, giving a perfectly blurry picture of the chairman's state of mind. "Tonight we're off to Cairo. Tomorrow we meet Rabin and Peres in Paris," he says cheerfully, ending the session, as journalists scramble to leave Jericho.

Driving back into Jerusalem at dusk, I gaze at the vitality, the prosperity and the beauty, all such a contrast to Gaza and Jericho. And suddenly I can't remember, despite years spent studying this situation, why so many Israelis are threatened by Palestinian autonomy. Why do the settlers hurl their bodies and throw scalding coffee at buses carrying Palestinians from the upper West Bank? Why have they spent an entire week burning tires or placing giant nails on the road to Jericho, trying to disrupt the flow of traffic?

Why, as I enter Jerusalem, do I see placards everywhere calling for the arrest of Arafat or the death of Rabin? Why do these posters show pictures of Rabin and Arafat in SS uniforms? Such signs of hatred miss entirely the depth of the collective Palestinian despair. They also miss the reality that, *with Israeli support,* most in Gaza and Jericho are ready to create a state modeled on (and to coexist with) Israel.

"I saw our peace," Mr. Ajwar has said. For now, that's what I'll choose to remember from these crazy, chaotic beginnings.

CHAPTER FOURTEEN

A Happy Interlude:
A Peace Accord

This summer, predicted by journalists to be boring, is turning out to be anything but. Not only has Arafat returned, but now, in mid-August, Israel's classical music station is interrupted for a news bulletin: King Hussein of Jordan and Prime Minister Rabin have just declared official peace between our two countries. Papers are to be signed in the Arava Desert tomorrow. As soon as I hear the news, I race to the American Colony Hotel, but I just miss the press bus to Eilat, the southernmost tip of Israel, where the ceremony is to be held. I manage to flag an Arab driver I know and soon am whizzing down to join the Israeli press corps, which has assembled at the regal, if garish, Princess Hotel.

A conference is in session. Uri Dromi, the Israeli press secretary, is detailing the next day's schedule. Afterward, several of us move to outdoor cafes, talking for hours all through the night until early dawn reveals our exquisite surroundings. Huge red rock mountains drop directly into the turquoise Red Sea. Yet it's already so hot that we're fanning ourselves madly with anything at hand: napkins, menus, paper torn from our pads.

At 8 A.M., we're bused to the tiny Eilat airport. Here, a larger bus will shuttle first us journalists, then the Israeli diplomats and finally the other major political players to the site of the peace event, in the middle of the vast desert. On our bus, most are quiet. Some half doze. One young woman snores loudly. Behind her, a heavyset man with three cameras draped around his neck is flopped across two seats, asleep. Only twelve minutes later, the bus stops and deposits us near a newly constructed arena, literally built overnight. As we exit, everyone gripes: Why do they have a ceremony at high noon? Why are Mideast events always staged to play to 7 P.M. news in the U.S., no matter what conditions are like here? Why have we been brought to this remote spot where we'll overheat, and feel dwarfed by the desert stretching out to the horizon in every direction?

Yet once we walk through the high white arches beneath a huge sign that announces "OPENING THE BORDERS" in three languages, we all wake up, realizing that we're about to witness something momentous. As the excitement builds, we get a second wind. Strangers chat with one another and exclaim in amazement at the speed of this unexpected peace. Wearing odd-shaped, wide-brimmed white caps that the medics have handed out, we're again fanning ourselves, while gulping bottled water.

Hillel Halkin—novelist, columnist, and translator of great Israeli novels—is sitting next to me in the freshly painted green bleachers where the press has been assigned. "This is our least painful peace," he says. Jay Bushinsky, of the *Chicago Sun-Times,* who has lived in Israel for decades, concurs. "Jordan and Israel are the two most Anglicized nations in the Mideast. We've been honorable enemies. Both of us have fought hard. With them we've had fewer human rights violations and less personal animosity than with other Arab countries."

I spot Akiva, a journalist friend from California, roaming on the field below and gawking up at Connie Chung of CBS. He waves to me to climb down and join him. As I step close to Chung, I see that she, like many of the famous TV anchors, is wearing clothes ill suited to this climate. Her red wool suit is unthinkable in this desert heat. Off camera, she holds a cigarette at an oblique angle, but the smoke somehow curls directly into Dan Rather's face. He sits stiffly beside her, reading. The highest-paid newscasters from afar are perched high on elevated swivel chairs.

Climbing back into the bleachers I watch as the dignitaries arrive. Each is ushered into a shaded tent that's roped off with velveteen cords. Then I study the Jordanian contingent. They're sitting together as far as possible from the Israelis, which, on this tiny spot, isn't very far. Between them are the Americans. They're mostly security personnel, the press corps and a few peace negotiators, including Secretary of State Warren Christopher. The Americans seem almost stiff in contrast to the excitable Israelis and Jordanians.

Finally, the ceremony begins. Rabin intones, "Three days ago this was a minefield, surrounded by sand and more sand. But today this desert is an opening. Just yesterday we installed telephone wires between Jordan and Israel. Soon it will seem as if this is the way it has always been. People say everything is moving too fast. But we who've had forty-six years of war, we cannot bear even one more day of hostility."

Some Shakespearean muse seems to be rising up through Rabin's speeches lately, "a reward for his courage," as I remark. "But don't forget, he has a heart of stone," someone comments wryly.

"Well, if true, then that's the beauty of it," I respond, as Crown Prince Hassan, the brother of the king, takes the microphone to plead against a "politics of despair" and then speaks of our common need for social justice. Finally, he surprises the Israelis by quoting from the Old Testament in Hebrew, "Where we have had a wilderness, we shall make a blossoming."

With the exception of Chris Hedges, an intrepid war correspondent for the *New York Times,* who has been sitting on the bleachers reading a novel throughout most of the ceremony, virtually everyone around me is riveted by each word and gesture below—as are those on the opposite bleachers—Jordanian soldiers, journalists and dignitaries. As Jews and Arabs, we are watching something tantamount to the end of a long-simmering family feud that involves us all.

Looking around, I see how much this ceremony *is* a family matter. Below us, parents and children of the war dead are converging to exchange gifts and handshakes. Soon, aging soldiers, the Israelis to a man in open-collared shirts and sandals, the Jordanians decked out in jackets and ties, move to meet in the center of the arena. They, too, are carrying presents for each other, and shake hands, hugging and crying. These encounters between former enemies are the physical enactment of those speeches we just heard.

I've seen how the towns of Eilat (Israel) and Aqaba (Jordan) are so close, they're almost kissing. Yet, for decades the respective residents could only gaze out at each other's activities, homes, boats, lights, cars and mountains, with no direct access to one another and no way to legally cross the two short miles of magnificent Red Sea. I think back to my first trip to Eilat, soon after I arrived to live here—how I saw that the Jordanian border runs the entire eastern flank of Israel, like a long zipper of fear. Back then, someone pointed out minefields, barbed wire and cutting-edge telescopes, all manned around the clock, for decades. I was shown places on Eilat's beaches where Jordanian terrorists had penetrated Israeli defenses by swimming across the Red Sea. Some were caught, their grenades defused before they had a chance to set them off. Others slipped through and did kill. Their victims were most often vacationing tourists. Though there's been relatively little violence at *this* border (unlike up north, near Lebanon), perpetual vigilance was a necessity until today.

The formalities end. Rabin announces that another service with President Clinton present will be held in October, two months away. Then he says that a road has just been opened between our two countries. Anyone with a passport is free to walk directly from Israel into Jordan and back. He adds, proudly, that construction was completed in the middle of this past night. Hillel and I exchange looks of amazement as we realize how much this sudden peace is not one of cold words, as with Egypt, but is grounded in the hot and sandy earth.

With the official events over, participants and witnesses surge onto the roped-off section of the desert. Everyone—journalists, diplomats and dignitaries—mills about, grinning widely, chatting, shaking hands or patting each other's backs. In the daunting heat, television crews circle the eminent, especially Abba Eban, a revered Israeli elder statesman, a diplomat who's long been a vocal proponent for peace. He's greeted by many, including Jordan's elegant water commissioner, Dr. Mansour Halladin, who strides toward Eban. "You, sir, have a special place in our hearts," he says.

The famous peace visionary is wobbling. Trying to get out of the sun, he's clearly dazed. "My doctor says to stick to the shade," Eban mumbles. Another journalist and I grab onto each of his arms, trying to help him move (slowly, shakily) to the safety of the tent. Another woman, noting his distress, runs to bring him more bottled water. Just as we're about to enter the tent, CNN cameramen close in on him. I'm trying to shoo the crew away, but Eban turns, removes his hat and talks briefly. We're now, more urgently, trying to move him into the coolness of the tent, fearing his imminent collapse. Inside, Chris Hedges approaches. The second that Abba Eban hears the words *New York Times,* he wakes from his febrile condition and becomes clarity itself. Elegant language rises through him as he cogently describes how inexorable is this momentum toward peace. He says that even Syria, despite Assad's long stall, has no option but to negotiate with Israel, too. Then he adds, "We will be wise never to forget that these breakthroughs could not have happened without Yasser Arafat. *We must show parallel devotion to the Jordanian and the Palestinian peace tracks.*"

Eban is alluding to the obvious: that making peace with Jordan is easier, more exciting and more trustworthy than the hard work of negotiating with Arafat over Gaza and the West Bank. He's stressing what's easy for many to forget—that these two processes are inextricably linked. As I listen to him, a spasm of sadness overcomes me, for I realize how much this leap into peace with the Jordanians must threaten the Palestinians, still languishing in the territories. Too often they're relegated to waiting and more waiting, unlike those under King Hussein's charismatic reign.

At 4 P.M., the buses arrive, and we're driven the few miles back to Eilat. From the windows, the site we've just left begins to look like any random Bedouin camp. Soon, the vast desert moonscape seems to swallow it up. It was the profound human event we witnessed that gave that tiny patch of land its mythic quality, I think, as I watch the tent flaps grow diminutive until they disappear completely. I turn to Hillel, who's again sitting beside me. He, too, grew up in New York but has lived in Israel for over twenty-five years. I ask him why this event felt so intensely emotional.

"Because we're all truly involved," he says. "In the United States it's rare for real intimacy to combine with politics. That's one reason I find America such a lonely place, maybe the loneliest place on this earth. If only I'd been born here."

"Born here!" I hear myself snapping. "You've spent practically your entire adult life in Israel, have raised sabra kids, while I was living in the wrong place all my life. I've had only three years here and my daughter seems irreversibly American. It's like I've been cheated out of my birthright."

Hillel looks hard at me for a long moment. "Oh, so you're one of *them*," he finally says.

"Them, *who?*"

He tells me matter-of-factly that one in a thousand secular American Jews falls madly in love with this place and can't leave. "And you can never guess who it will be."

I think how true his observation is, how unaccountably at home I feel here. I walk into the Moriah Hotel, which is serving as the journalists' headquarters in Eilat today. A group of us watch TV, where Rabin and King Hussein speak at a press conference in nearby Aqaba. They're smoking cigarettes together, jovially fielding questions, looking like the best of friends. I step outside to stroll along the Red Sea. Within minutes I catch sight of these two leaders. They're sailing in a yacht within clear view of Eilat's beach. King Hussein is steering his boat into and around Israeli waters, as if he is hosting his host.

I recall Rabin's words from the ceremony, "This will soon feel natural," he had said, as apparently it does to the vacationing Israelis who line the shore to witness this extraordinary scene. Taking a few minutes out from shuffleboard or swimming, they wave at the two men, a king and a prime minister, and then return, nonchalantly, to their holiday activities.

King Hussein's words also echo in my mind. Slowly, with deliberation, he had said, "The kind of peace I feel *with myself* on this day is something I have never experienced, not in all my many years." I gaze for a moment longer at the two warriors turned peacemakers who are moving across the mythical and literal Red Sea. Then I return to the quotidian, heading for an air-conditioned beach cafe and a tall glass of iced Turkish coffee.

CHAPTER FIFTEEN

Placed, and Misplaced

Later in the day, I run into Sara, who asks if I'll keep her company on the long drive back to Jerusalem. She's been assigned to the "press ship" that's following Rabin and Hussein in the yacht, but we can meet up once she's finished, she says. Glad for the prospect of time alone with her, I say, "Of course." Shortly after 9 P.M., we begin wending our way out of Eilat. We pass the Arava Desert and then traverse long country roads. After an hour we can see the outlines of huge desert mountains to our left, the shimmering Dead Sea on our right. This magical stretch of road is lit by a perfect half-moon. Sara, exhausted, is driving slowly, hugging the wheel with her long hair draped over it, almost to her waist. Mile after mile, no cars are visible. Both of us remark on how lovely it is to have this glistening, dramatic landscape entirely to ourselves.

Entranced by our exotic surroundings, we pull over to rest. The parking area overlooks the Dead Sea and we both feel simultaneously drunk with exhaustion and exhilarated by the beauty. We comment, almost in the same breath, on how much we love living here. Sara, born in Poland, moved here as a baby with her parents, who had survived the Holocaust because they were on Schindler's list. They settled in Haifa. After finishing her army duty, Sara began traveling and, although Israeli to the core, has been traveling, off and on, ever since. She spent years in Paris and in Africa, lived in Beirut for a while to cover the Lebanon War and attended journalism school in San Francisco. She remarks sleepily that she's so glad to be here now, raising her three children (two boys and one girl) as Israelis. It was the year she spent in the U.S., one she found incredibly isolating, that led her back home and convinced her to stay.

I tell her it's miraculous that I'm here at all, that three years ago, living in Boston, I didn't even know this world existed. Like her, I'm madly in love with this place. Sara nods as we study the shadows from mountains looming over us in this soft night, one we still have all to ourselves. Not a single car has passed by since we parked.

As we resume driving, we agree that no other place we have lived holds a candle to this one, and that part of what we love is the feeling of community. Our own relationship is typical. We met through our children: her daughter Michal and Eliza, who's now almost eight. Both of us remember the day, two years back, when Eliza and I flew into her apartment, excited to find English-speaking neighbors. We reminisce about how the kids hit it off instantly, as the two of us sat on her terrace and talked, how, by the end of that afternoon, we felt like old friends and have never been out of touch since. I thank her for the many gifts she's given me: entrée into the Government Press Office, introductions to Hakam and Palestinian journalists and to many from the Israeli and foreign press corps, none of whom I'd have met without her. I say that she opened a new career for me and I'm grateful. Then I add, "But *you* are the real gift," thinking that unquestionably she's my closest friend, the one with whom life makes the most sense, with whom anything we talk about inevitably becomes hilarious.

Sara, embarrassed by compliments, changes the subject to Eliza. She confesses that it's one reason she wanted to have this private talk. She doesn't quite know how to put this, but . . . she's worried about Eliza . . . Have I, too, noticed a huge change in her? . . . Before I can answer, she adds, "It's as if she's had a serious trauma; my oldest son used those very words."

A jolt of anxiety shoots through me. I'm now forced to confront my least favorite subject. Of course I'm worried about Eliza, I tell her. How can I not worry when I see my so ebullient child sinking into morbidity? I tell her how at bedtime Eliza talks about being bored all the time, asking me about death, if I think being dead is *sooo* boring too. Sara looks at me in dismay. I tell her to concentrate on the road, and I continue. "During the day Eliza's disconsolate too. Even ever-cheerful Jackie can't reach her. I don't know what's caused this upheaval. What has happened to my bright-eyed, lively, funny kid?"

"My guess is the school," I'm answering my own question, reminding Sara how in the *gan* (kindergarten), where the kids and teachers were all bilingual, Eliza thrived. She was a leader, considered the most "popular" kid in the class. It's only in the past two years, I muse, when thrown into all Hebrew-speaking classes, with teachers who also speak no English, that she's begun showing symptoms.

Sara counters that kids pick up a new language "like a sponge." Not this one, I assure her. "Eliza resists Hebrew like a rock, there's nothing spongelike in her relation to this language," I say. But Sara insists that Eliza is being stubborn, that she knows the language perfectly well and is refusing to speak it for her own reasons. "Maybe she's lobbying you to return to Cambridge," she suggests as I see that we're almost at my home.

"I once thought Eliza's phobia about this language was psychological, too. But, increasingly, I see that she simply doesn't get it. Not like a sponge, like a rock," I repeat, and, to prove my point, I describe an incident from this past June. I went to visit her class one day. There I found beautiful Eliza, braids to her waist, huge black eyes gazing at me from *under* her desk while the other kids were happily working. I leaned down and asked why she was hiding. She said, "Mom, I told you, it's *always* like this." Suddenly I got her reality, and was appalled at not having caught it earlier. Her teacher and I went out to the hallway where she talked *at* me in nonstop Hebrew, which I understand no better than Eliza. When I protested that I couldn't understand her, she kept chattering away, as if she didn't believe me. Having finally seen things from Eliza's point of view, I decided not to make her finish out the last weeks of the school year. That's when I hired Nurit, her *gan* teacher, to tutor her in Hebrew and English. Since then, with Daphie's help, I tell Sara, we've found a highly respected learning specialist who recently gave Eliza two full days of tests. "So we'll soon find out what's wrong, if anything," I say.

"What could it be?" Sara sounds worried.

"I'll know when I get those test results," I say. I put off testing her for far too long, I think to myself, partly because I was so immersed in work and my relationship with Shuki, but mostly because I was afraid of what I'd learn. Now, having unburdened myself, I feel better as we swing around the Old City, feeling the cool air pour through the car windows, moved as ever by the sight of Sultan's Pool, its ancient stones all lit up. These sights and sensations so relieve me that, however irrationally, I feel everything will work out. Sara pulls up to my home on Jabotinsky Street and thanks me for keeping her awake. Then as she's turning to drive to her home, she calls out her window, "Ring that tester tomorrow. Let me know right away."

Two days later, on a bright August morning, I drive with Daphie, now a full professor in charge of elementary school teachers, and Nurit, Eliza's tutor, to the office of the esteemed Dr. Feldenstern. We arrive at her home in the hilltop neighborhood of Beit Hakerem. Her office abuts her stone home; the room is painted dull gray and has only one window, an ambiance which gives me an ominous feeling. My friends tell me to lighten up, that everything will be fine. I study the children's drawings taped on the walls and see, in the center of the room, a large plastic table with eight chairs placed around it. This meeting is to include Eliza's principal, her teacher from school, two reading specialists and another psychologist. Taking our seats, we see Eliza's test materials spread around the table—drawings, math papers, a large graph that seems to assess her academic skills.

When everyone arrives, papers are passed around. Soon, they're all frowning.

"Let's get started," Dr. Feldenstern says forthrightly in English, "and no need to pull any punches." Then she turns to me and says without emotion, "Your daughter is severely dyslexic. She's almost eight but she hasn't a clue about reading in English. She can't decipher one vowel from another. Since you've read to her nightly and she's had English tutoring, this developmental delay isn't due to lack of exposure. This," she points at the graph, "shows she'll need remedial English just to learn the rudiments of her native language." She turns toward me, stone-faced. "You were right. She doesn't understand Hebrew, which is a major signifier for all dyslexics; they have trouble with the symbolism of language; foreign ones are contraindicated. You can forget about Hebrew until she's a teenager or in her twenties, if ever," she says matter-of-factly. I'm too shocked to say a word, but I am listening with unusual clarity.

The others begin discussing my daughter. Each addresses Dr. Feldenstern in Hebrew as Daphie and Nurit, who are both bilingual, take notes while taking turns patting me gently on the arm. The professionals, who've never met the famed doctor before, are pitching their opinions in obvious attempts to impress her.

When Daphie suggests they speak in English so I can understand them, everybody begins referring to me, when they remember me at all, as "the mother." One says, "And here, this drawing shows the child has trouble with sequence. I see organizational issues. Look at this: The girl was shown a simple house to replicate. Note that she missed the overall structure, focused on details, composing separate rooms but without a structure to link them." I see a perfectly beautiful series of detailed rooms, thinking it's likely that my so artistic daughter didn't want to re-create a dull house but preferred her own designs.

Galloping right along, Dr. Feldenstern announces, "The child's impaired auditory processing, her inability to read and lack of Hebrew, all go hand in hand." She pauses and looks sternly around the table, as if those assembled are the ones being tested. She continues, "The child needs a special school, one that's highly structured, with few students per class. Since we don't have such programs in English here, the mother must get her back to America right away.

The child speaks her own language fluently, but for her to commence reading and writing in her native tongue is going to be difficult. The long-term prognosis remains unclear."

The educators turn to the doctor, who addresses Daphie and Nurit in English. "The mother must find the right school. Fortunately, there are many fine ones for the learning disabled in the States." As I hear the phrase "learning disabled," I have the distinct impression that the table is elongating, that I myself have been swaddled in thick, deadening layers of bubble wrap. It's an Alice in Wonderland moment. Through the layers, I hear Daphie protest, "But this is the most creative kid I've ever met," as the others pore over their charts and drawings, offhandedly responding that her creativity is irrelevant.

The meeting continues. Each specialist is on a roll, giddy with the excitement of her own diagnostic brilliance. I've heard enough and slip out a back door. There I sit in the doctor's cheerful garden, surrounded by roses blossoming all around me. I spot a wooden bench, positioned under a weeping willow tree. In my altered state, it seems to beckon to me. I sit down and listen to the birds. My mind seesaws between Eliza's fate, the prescribed return to the United States, and my own. Panic-stricken, I think about having to leave Israel.

I calculate . . . it's mid-August . . . the "experts" say we have to leave immediately. I overhear them debating the merits of schools for dyslexics; comparing one in Boston to another in New York City . . . I start counting rosebushes, the number of birds flying into this yard. Then I study the edges of the willow tree's drooping, ropey branches, as if I've never seen such a marvel of nature.

When Daphie and Nurit eventually emerge, both seem unhinged. Daphie drives us to a cafe in the Tayelet, the huge stone park where we often take the kids to play, ride their bikes or enjoy hot chocolate. My mind is on ice; everything seems more dreamlike than a dream as I begin studying the table's smooth surface. I have the sensation that all this is happening to someone else.

Daphie and Nurit, who love Eliza, take turns exclaiming how gifted she is—in art, in imaginative play, in making friends. Daphie, who's been especially close to her, says defiantly, "I've always thought Eliza was smarter, more grounded and frankly more organized than the rest of us."

Nurit agrees that the diagnosis is a rough one and that Eliza's organizational issues were exaggerated at the meeting. But she adds that, unlike everyone else, she *has* been worried about her inability to absorb Hebrew. "These people don't know Eliza's strengths, but they do know what's wrong. Their attitude was horrid, even cruel. But they gave us important information today. Those tests were pretty conclusive for dyslexia. Frankly, I agree that she needs a specialized educational program. Think of it this way: Eliza's at the perfect age for remedial work." I hear Nurit, but manners fail and I say nothing. Nurit plows on, somehow aware that I am listening even though I can't respond. "I was her teacher. Trust me, they overstated her 'defects.' Of course you're upset, what parent wouldn't be? But I believe Eliza has all the 'markers' for reading issues. If you get her back to the States, and I have a friend who directs a great school outside Boston, you'll get her on a new path. She's extremely smart. She'll catch on fast; then you can come back to Israel. Maybe in just a year or two." Nurit's green-blue eyes light up. "If we call today, you'll get an interview in a few weeks, and you can enroll her by mid-September."

Only now do I begin to register the speed with which this move must happen. I'm immobilized and mute, not because my beloved daughter was described in negative, insensitive terms. I get the gist of her "condition." This "diagnosis," however harsh it sounds when described as a "disability," actually helps explain why such a bright kid never picked up this language. My mind registers that it could be a lot worse, that we're not talking about AIDS, tumors, a terminal disease. But my heart insists otherwise and says that for me nothing could be worse than having to leave Israel.

No, anything but that. Eliza can't be the only *aliyah* kid with this problem. I'll find those other parents. We can create a parallel school with a program of our own. Or I'll go back to that Anglican School I never should have left. I'm becoming proactive, moving into a problem-solving mode that wakes me from my stupor. Now ready to brainstorm with my friends, I look up at them and see that both are ashen and near tears. Clearly, they see a return to the States as the only solution. It's August, I calculate, awfully late to locate parents or to work with Israel's educational system. Academically, Eliza has already lost three years. I'm surprised to hear my own voice. "So, I have no choice but to go back to Boston again?" I ask.

Leave Israel? Live in the States again? I won't. I can't. Cambridge? The U.S.? "No way," I say out loud.

"Maybe it will only be for a year," Nurit suggests. Daphie agrees that once Eliza gets shored up with English basics in the States, I can come back and bring a tutor here. "Or she'll be accepted at the American School near Tel Aviv. They have a special program that goes all through high school."

We sit for another hour until we can't ignore the wind, blowing cold on this typical Jerusalem August night. We get up to leave. As we stand, I notice how heavy and tired I suddenly feel. I walk slowly to Daphie's car, and then somehow I'm home.

Jackie and Eliza and several friends are in the kitchen playing checkers.

Eliza looks perfectly happy. She waves at me before making her next move. The sheer normalcy of this scene makes the day's news all the more unreal. I tell the girls I've had a long afternoon and need to rest. I walk into my room, a room I love for its spaciousness, which allows it to do double duty as both study and bedroom. I love its curving shape, how the windows seem so close to the sky, how the light pours in, reflecting the moods of every season. I sit in my rocking chair, moving back and forth, as my thoughts shift between unrealistic schemes and realistic dread.

Everything about me is going to die, I think. This will all become memory.

As night falls, I close my curtains and go back to rocking, nearly hypnotized by the silky white curtains quivering in the night's strong winds. I remember the February evening when I finished hanging them, how they gave me a feeling of permanence. First thing each morning, I open them to see a panoramic view of Jerusalem. At night, when I close them, I'm comforted by the cozy feeling they give: the sense that I am no longer a wanderer in a foreign land, but am fully at home. I have never taken my good fortune for granted, I know, but have lived in gratitude. Now, I sit for a long time rocking in the chair until I hear the sound of Shuki's key in the door.

We lie on our bed. He listens to what I've learned today, listens well. He says, sad and wise: "Eliza comes first. We are the old donkeys. She's the one who counts." I nod. He says, "We've given each other so much. You don't know how much."

"Don't know?" I say, incredulous. "Whatever our problems, you've healed me. I can never tell *you* how much," and we begin reminiscing about our life together, focusing on our best times, naming the specific travels, movies and moments we cherish most. I tell Shuki that he's cured me of some unnameable sadness no one else could, how I hope he feels the same, even though I know he's been resentful of my growing absorption in a political process he doesn't believe in, and with my friends with whom he doesn't feel comfortable. He nods and says he's known for a long time that our love was stuck. It was not turning into the marriage we once believed inevitable.

We're holding hands when Shuki says, "I don't know why we couldn't bring our passion into the daylight, but we didn't. We never created an ordinary home life. I wasn't good to Eliza. You don't really like my friends, and your friends never accepted me. We couldn't have lasted, we both know that, don't we?" We aren't in recrimination mode. What we are is terribly sad. Even in our worst scenarios of the future, we expected to be there for each other if not as lovers, then as friends. Or, at the very least, as neighbors. Tears are falling from Shuki's dark brown eyes. Soon we stop talking and communicate without words, what we've always done best. Lying in bed, holding hands, I begin to feel numb again. He puts his hand gently over my forehead, a familiar gesture of affection that always calms me. And soon my churning mind does slow down. Soon, somehow, I fall asleep.

The next days are full of the hours that I'll regard as the worst of my life. The reality of leaving Israel has been thrown at me so suddenly and so unexpectedly. Can I really be yanked from my home, one so essential to my happiness? I'm paralyzed by disbelief. After losing my parents and then miraculously finding my rightful place on this earth, how can it be that I will have to face another great loss? How can a relatively small glitch in Eliza's otherwise healthy brain create such a rupture? I feel sure I won't ever recover if I leave.

And so I begin plotting how to stay, reaching out to everyone I know here in the hope that someone, somewhere, knows the answer to my problem. Various options surface briefly, and for days at a time I feel optimistic. I'm a fighter, I remind myself. Once I fully put my mind onto something, I'm usually lucky: the right ideas, people or circumstances are bound to materialize. I'll find a way to take care of Eliza *and* take care of myself, to stay in Israel.

• • •

I'm dreaming of a wide stretch of turquoise sea in Eilat. The color is intensely vivid, but as I look at it, the body of water begins to shrink. Afraid it will disappear completely, I spoon my hand to capture what's left. I'm holding a small turquoise gem in my hands as the dream dissolves and I wake in Cambridge on our third morning back. Lying in bed, I stare out my windows at the early September blanket of gray clouds. Then I gaze down at Eliza, who's crawled into my bed during the night and is still sleeping.

I study the contours of her face, the perfectly inverted V of her eyebrows, her long black eyelashes resting on her pudgy pink cheeks, this face that has changed little since infancy, when everyone agreed she was an unusually beautiful baby. A rush of love for her overcomes me. No one and nothing is as precious as this child, I think, slipping quietly out of bed to head downstairs to the kitchen to make coffee. I'm in shock, a state much worse, even, than the anticipatory dread of three weeks ago. Now I'm moving about in true melancholia, inside a wrenching ennui that invades me and coats everything I see. As I grind American coffee, this hollow gloom deepens. I sit, drink the coffee, stare down at the tan linoleum floor, then out the kitchen window at the yellowing maple leaves, the three-decker wooden house next door. I'm stranded. Where's the light? keeps replaying in my mind.

In Jerusalem, I was always surrounded by light. Even on gray winter days, my huge picture windows that seemed close to the sky gave a bright view of the Old City, the Judean hills, the Arab towns of the West Bank and West Jerusalem's only train station. Just a few weeks ago, surrounded by piled boxes of books, clothes, rugs and furniture, I watched the Middle Eastern light sweeping across the desert terrain. And I knew that being rightly placed is akin to great love or to God.

In Cambridge, I've returned to a world that shrinks my sense of self. In Israel, I felt abundant, overflowing; here I feel pinched, withered, almost nonexistent. How will I ever manage to accept this fate? I will because I must, I think, because it's Eliza's fate, too.

Eliza starts school. She flies into the house after her first day, her face aglow. I don't have to ask how her day went because she instantly announces: "Mom, I never went to any school where they make you feel right at home. This one is *really great.*" And then she gives me an unusually empathic hug. She may not read words yet, but she reads people; she reads me. She knows how much I miss Jerusalem. I hug her back and know that this move is right. But in the hours when she's in school, and then in the hours after she's asleep, that old New England bleakness invades me again.

"Get off it," an acquaintance breezily admonishes me as we bump pushcarts in Star Supermarket in Porter Square. I know she's voicing what all my other friends feel. However crudely, she's underscoring what I must do: I must turn the dial of my life to Cambridge again. But how I will manage that feat is hard to fathom. As of now, I'm moving in a fog, rotely doing my errands, longing, always, for my "other life."

Yet it also sometimes seems as if that other life is still happening. Moving about Cambridge, I'm also driving to Tel Aviv, up into the West Bank or inside Gaza. I'm flying to Petra, Jordan, or to Damascus, Syria, reporting on the latest developments, exploring both the Jewish and the Arab Mideast from my home in Jerusalem. Maybe the worst of it now is that, unlike grieving the death of someone loved, there's no language for my loss. Placed or misplaced, who talks of that in depth? Who dwells on *place* as primary? I now know what Sigmund Freud left out with his dictum that life centers on "work and love." I've had both in the States and in Israel, but what I've never achieved here, and not for lack of trying, is that feeling of belonging, of being part of a world rich in the meanings that accrue to the place we call home. That I'm the "one in a thousand" secular American Jews who needs to live in Israel and that my daughter is the one kid in a thousand who cannot, at least not now, live there is one strange denouement.

But then, I begin to console myself with these thoughts: For close to two millennia, Jews were filled with longing, lamentation and a passionate desire to return to Jerusalem. As long as I've been living in the Mideast, every Palestinian I've met has felt the same, has refused to consider the possibility of a Palestinian state without Al Quds (East Jerusalem) as its center. So I have to wonder if, despite my tenacious work, it wasn't just too easy to call Jerusalem *my* home. Maybe, like the mythic beloved, that most ineffable of cities can be reached only through long effort, constant prayer and this painful exile I now endure.

Part IV
Losing That Wild Earth

In the [United States] people start talking about "the Middle East peace process," and about how, say, Shamir is going to accept this plan and Arafat that plan. And all I can do is to sit back and say to myself, "Yes, but what about my grocer in Jerusalem? What will he accept?"

What about the wild earth? The first thing that happens to you when you come to Washington [back to the U.S.] is that you lose touch with that wild earth. And when you lose touch with the wild earth you are always going to be surprised by something, whether you are an official or a journalist or an author.

—*Thomas L. Friedman,*
"From Beirut to Jerusalem to Washington,"
in The Writing Life

Chapter Sixteen

My Mid-East Crisis

I become a replica of my grandparents decades ago—obsessed with news from Israel. I search for anything about the peace process, the Knesset, Gaza or the West Bank to pop up on radio (NPR) or TV (CNN). The thirty-second bites I do occasionally find add little to what I read in the *Boston Globe* or the *New York Times,* reports which, of course, lack what I miss most—the nuances, the languages, my friends, the views, the food!

My American friends exclaim over my lucky last-minute rental, a 1950s-style house on a cul-de-sac in the Episcopal Divinity School's housing complex. Identical to the six others on our block, it's a wood-frame house with peeling gray paint—wood as indigenous to Cambridge as stones are to Jerusalem. The bricks of the nearby buildings actually hurt my feelings. Try getting *that* across to anyone.

My heart sinks when neighbors describe what they're writing: Ph.D. dissertations and M.A. theses on medieval texts or New Testament themes. Walking into this quiet, deserted neighborhood at 10 P.M., I see through lighted windows that everyone is typing themselves back in time.

Within six months the household includes Eliza's and my friends Tal and her mom, Daphie, who has taken this sabbatical year to live with us in Cambridge. My hope is that this home will give Eliza security so that even without Jackie (who's back in Jamaica, leaving Eliza vulnerable to any loss), I'll be free to leave every few months to visit Israel. I set aside time and money for phoning and faxing Sara, Judith, Achmed, Samir Yaish, Jon and Anna Immanuel. I exchange a few calls with Shuki only to learn that after my hasty departure he reconciled with his ex-wife. That's the last move I'd have guessed he'd make, but then nothing is making much sense to me.

I go about rebuilding a skeletal work life, teaching classes on dreams and synchronicities, and doing a minimal amount of private psychotherapy. I keep aside enough free time to attend every symposium in or near Cambridge on the Israeli-Palestinian conflict. And when all else fails, as it usually does, I read novels and nonfiction about the Mideast—describing Israeli landscapes or Palestinian consciousness. But even reading seems completely different in Cambridge. It's nothing like reading in Jerusalem, where each page turned related to events and people I could see from my windows.

One late afternoon in October, after shopping for groceries, I'm at the wheel of my large green van daydreaming of my tiny blue Renault and the adventures I had in it. Stopped at a red light, the driver in front of me, whose body I've vacantly been staring at, suddenly captures my full attention. Something in the shape of his head strikes me as familiar. Within seconds, I'm convinced that this is Kanan Makiya, the Iraqi author of *Cruelty and Silence,* a book I've studied carefully and admire enormously. Controversial and beautifully written, it's a moving account of the people of Iraq, of what they've endured under the terrorizing reign of Saddam Hussein. It's also an indictment of Arab intellectuals who've maintained an almost unanimous silence in the face of such extreme cruelty.

I've never met Makiya; I saw him late one night on C-Span. He seemed one of the few speakers more passionate about righting the wrongs in his home country than about polishing his image before a Senate committee. In his book, he created realistic yet poetic human portraits, painting ordinary lives with great power. Speaking and writing so honestly took courage, for he surely knew that his words would exile him from the Arab cultural elite and might be exploited by Jewish chauvinists to boot (as indeed they were by A. M. Rosenthal in a *New York Times* op-ed article who used—misused—Makiya's work to argue that all Mideast troubles are due to dictatorial Arab regimes, fully distorting Makiya's point of view).

Aware that it's probably absurd to assume that the man in the car ahead of me is this admired author, I gun my motor anyway, the minute the light turns green and race after the white Fiat. This chase takes on a life of its own. As the small car swerves around Cambridge's side streets, I follow. The driver picks up speed, zigzagging onto empty back streets. I'm on his tail. Finally he realizes that he's not about to lose whatever nut is intent on this hot pursuit and he jerks to a halt. I brake directly behind him, certain that some stranger will emerge, rightfully furious.

But, head bowed and clearly expecting the worst, it is Makiya who exits slowly and hesitantly walks my way. I race to meet him more than halfway, spouting apologies. I quickly explain (to one very relieved man) that I have nothing to do with Iraqi intelligence, that I have followed him because I admire his work. "That's it?" he asks, rubbing his chin, still dubious. No, I admit, it's not just his writing (here a fresh streak of worry crosses over his face) but, I say breathlessly, that I've just returned from Jerusalem and am homesick, hungry to talk to someone else who's lived in and then was forced to leave the Mideast. To his great credit, instead of the tongue-lashing I deserve (this is a writer who had to protect his life, publishing under a pseudonym for years), Makiya gives me a wide smile. And on the spot, he invites me to his study to talk of cruelty and silence in Iraq, in Israel and in the territories.

A week later, at our second meeting, we are discussing Mideast discourse in America. Both Arabs and Jews living here are too abstract, lacking in subtlety, we say. Their ideas and arguments are not rooted in daily Mideast reality, in lives lived there, we also agree. I tell Kanan how miserable I am, continually mourning the world we've both had to leave. He's just read my reports from Jerusalem and kindly affirms them as akin to his ideas, encouraging me to keep writing. I say that I wrote well from Israel because I cared passionately about what was going on there, and then I mumble something about my writing days being over. Kanan vigorously shakes his head, suggesting that I can use this exile to find a sense of proportion that's impossible up close, in the heat of the Mideast. He advises me to try my hand at essays from afar or "even a memoir." I'll be freer to show American readers what we both believe is underreported here: the ethnic porousness in the Mideast, a racial cross-fertilization that takes place so visibly that no one over there finds it noteworthy.

Leaving Kanan's office, I notice a new energy, a bounce in my walk. Maybe he's right. Maybe my enforced distance from Mideast theatrics—the breakthroughs and breakdowns, the peace process and its discontents, all so compelling when in their midst—can be clarified from afar. Perhaps I'll uncover fresh insights from this distance. Have I really taken the space to reflect on what I saw in Israel? Is it possible to better convey from here the competing realities of Palestinians and Israelis?

Now, like my neighbors, I, too, am typing myself into the past. Under the sway of Kanan's suggestion that distance can confer clarity, I begin working on a series of op-ed pieces, aiming to achieve a new voice, one with professorial objectivity. But this venture soon backfires. My words sound as pale and abstract as the theorizing Kanan and I scorn. Instead of clarity I create confusion, especially for myself. This is the beginning of a cognitive breakdown not unlike the famed mid-life crisis, in which each hard-won point of view or achieved belief seems suddenly suspect. I begin to question, rather than affirm, all I once knew—a mental shift that will grow larger throughout the coming year.

• • •

It's a warm springlike morning in February and I'm on a ten-day visit to Israel—my first since I had to leave for the United States. Today, I'm traveling with Khalid, a friend from East Jerusalem, into the small village of El Khader, in the West Bank. It's the place where Suher Ismael, the Palestinian filmmaker, grew up and had filmed her wedding.

We join a group of Israelis and Palestinians who are converging on this rural valley in support of a "local" protest against a planned Israeli expansion for a Jewish settlement nearby. Strolling along the main dirt road that leads into the tiny town, Khalid and I receive a warm welcome. This crowd includes some we know. There are Rapprochement dialogue members, Peace Now activists and local Palestinian villagers, as well as intellectuals from both sides. Friends and strangers share water, soda, cigarettes, pretzels and hugs. In the growing heat, the crowds increase. Microphones are being set up. Just after one in the afternoon, political leaders begin to address the group, now numbering several hundred. An Israeli activist is followed by a prominent Palestinian leader, Saeb Erekat. They are then followed by others who are talking passionately in Hebrew or Arabic—both languages still nearly indecipherable to me. I'm lost in pleasure, gazing at this world I've lost. I feel filled, moved beyond desire.

In this state of physical bliss, I recall the words of a Palestinian poet who's written about *his* joy at seeing each olive or orange tree in his family's yard. Surrounded by the sights or sounds of "Palestine," he feels that he becomes not the land's cartographer, nor its poet, but its *lover*. How well I understand that passion for this place; I become transfixed by the views around me. A loud noise brings me back into the moment. I turn and see a stampede of kids and young men charging uphill, whooping war cries, jeering loudly. An American tells me that they've spontaneously decided to confront the Israeli soldiers stationed at a construction site just over the hill, though invisible from here. The Jewish settlers they'll encounter are doubtless armed, and all-too-ready to show these Palestinian boys just who's the boss here. Everyone else stays put, as if accepting this violence. I race to my car. Is this cowardice? Exhaustion? Or simply sanity?

As I begin to drive away, Khalid runs up and stops me, begging me to stay. "You're my ride," he says plaintively. I'm out of here, I tell him, "I can't stand this." I restart my motor and Khalid hops in. We move a few feet only to find that we're stuck on the traffic-clogged road. Within seconds, we're pelted with large stones.

Khalid jumps out, shouting at the stone-throwers in Arabic to stop. The teenagers swagger over, peer into my car and agree to stop only if I turn off my motor and stay put. "Do as they say," Khalid barks. "The *shabab* [street fighters] control all these roads; they're looking for settlers hiding in one of these cars," he explains.

Every car but ours is now under a barrage of stones, and soon we're also sitting in a cloud of tear gas as well, thanks to the canisters hurled at the angry mob by the Israeli soldiers, which further outrages the boys, who respond with more stones. Khalid jumps out again, screaming at them, "But don't you see that we here are all peace activists or your own villagers?" He's pointing at the wall-to-wall cars in front and behind us, all stamped with peace stickers. "Stay calm," he says to me as I see that for Khalid this is just another day in the life.

Half an hour later we're finally moving away from El Khader. Back in Jerusalem, I'm furious at having been put into danger by a bunch of reckless, hot-blooded kids, which is how I now view the *shabab*. I can hear echoes of those whoops and can picture them as they charged up that hill. I know that it's important to protest illegal land seizures and to show the Palestinians our support. But I've lost all taste for "right action" that includes violence. "I just want to enjoy living here for ten days," I say wistfully to Sara the following morning over coffee. "That's exactly what most Israelis feel every day," she says, chiding my self-indulgence.

On my last morning, a Tel Aviv commuter bus is blown up by a Palestinian suicide bomber during rush hour. Many Israelis are dead. I call home and extend my stay for another week so that I can attend funerals or sit by the TV and watch. Within days, two more bus explosions leave more Israelis dead and maimed in the towns of Beit Lid and Afula. Over a hundred Israelis have been murdered in the three weeks I am here. Just before I leave for Cambridge, I attend a funeral for one of Eliza's *kittah aleph* (first grade) classmates—an eight-year-old boy. He was killed while visiting his grandparents in Afula.

Sara gives me firsthand descriptions of the funerals for the Palestinian "victims" in Gaza, those who set off bombs and died with them. Most in Gaza believe these brave "martyrs to the cause" go straight to heaven if they die when killing Israelis. And, there, seventy-two virgins will await each one—with their legs open. In strict Islam, as practiced here, sex is prohibited outside marriage, one reason this afterlife fantasy is so seductive, especially to the youngsters who do most of the killings. Sara describes how virtually all Palestinians in Gaza were dancing and cheering about the Israelis killed; at nearly the same time, they were howling over their own dead boys. This reaction is incomprehensible to me. Had I once thought I understood these people?

For the first time in years, I don't care what the Palestinians are living through. I feel disgust at the descriptions and TV images of Gazans dancing over murdered Israelis. I'm sick of the convoluted logic that excuses Palestinian actions; I've no empathy, no desire to go to talk to anyone in the territories. All I can think is that the Palestinians haven't a clue about the Israeli psyche. Why do they refuse to accept that most Israelis are not trying to sadistically ruin their lives but simply trying to live their own? My certainty about the Oslo process is beginning to erode.

The night before I leave, Judith invites me to a birthday party in Beit Sahur, an event that brings more people to the Rapprochement Center than usual. There I spot Tzalli Rechef, the middle-aged and savvy lawyer, long a main force behind Peace Now. He's talking to Jad Isaac, a local resident often imprisoned for working on his botanical gardens in Beit Sahur, which the Israelis claim are not yet allowed because they are on disputed land. I approach them, and during a lull I ask Rechef, "Where do you get your emotional stamina?"

"Stamina?" he repeats the word dryly. "Long gone," he says. "I'm committed to this cause, but where the hell is the next generation?" I can't answer him because the truth is that the Palestinian plight has begun to live inside me in an altered way. This shift, set into motion while trying to write those op-ed pieces last fall, is hardening.

• • •

One March morning, shortly after my return to Cambridge, I'm sitting at my desk, missing Jerusalem—my habitual state—when I get a phone call from a man named Josh Brockman. He's a producer at PBS in New York, which next week will air a documentary called "In God's Bunker." Directed by an Israeli, Meir Peled, it focuses on the most extreme fundamentalist Jewish settlers living in downtown Hebron. Josh describes the film as "strong stuff." He tells me that he's phoning around, interviewing Jewish and Arab "intellectuals." Two from each side, he hopes, will, even on short notice, make a good "mix" for the panel discussion scheduled to follow the film.

I'm honest with Josh, pouring out my current confusions. I tell him that the killings and rage on both sides have left me numb, that my perceptions are shifting. I confess to having lost certainty, to seeing neither side as right or wrong but each as sullied, though there's no way that I can support the settlers, I assure him. He's a good listener, so I unburden myself. I talk of Israel's callousness toward the Palestinians, which creates so many unnecessary hardships in the daily lives of the most innocent, turning the already difficult Palestinian existence into a nightmare. I then describe how Palestinians cheered after the suicide bombers hit, and off I go on a riff about Palestinian addiction to hating Israelis and to seeing conspiracies everywhere. I tell him that I've begun to see their famous stoicism as a shield, a cop-out.

Josh hasn't been in Israel for years. I tell him the Palestinians could probably create their own state within a few years if they stopped putting all their energy into Israel-bashing. I say that everyone over there seems as rigid as they are despondent. I'm not ready to air such fragmented views publicly, though; my mind is far too scrambled. I don't know what I think.

Certain that I've just removed myself as a candidate, Josh surprises me by saying excitedly, "You're perfect. I don't want those with airtight views. I want moderates."

"But I'm *not* moderate." I laugh. "I'm someone who's lost all perspective."

"You're perfect," he says. We both laugh. "Of course, you can't say everything you've just told me on the air. But you don't sound as confused as you feel, or anyway no more confused than the situation itself." He pauses. "Maybe this discussion will help you." So he'll mail me a tape of the film. I'll watch it in preparation for the discussion next week in a New York studio. He says he doesn't yet know who else will participate, but there will be one other Jew along with two Palestinian intellectuals, and Bill Zimmerman, the program's moderator.

I watch "In God's Bunker" over and over on my VCR—six, eight times. It takes place in downtown Hebron, closely following the daily lives of five settler families. The hate is unrelenting. In scene after scene, we hear horrid racist epithets from adults and children alike, what's ordinary discourse among these extremists—who are, fortunately, only a tiny subculture. Each character shown is a strong and unique personality, subscribing to the same fanaticism. A siege mentality separates these settler famlies from most Israelis I've met. Their hatred for the Arabs is rancid and omnipresent. Their children could be mistaken for members of a Nazi-style youth group. As young as five they rotely, but with certainty, spout propaganda for Greater Israel, talking of Jewish superiority to Arabs or singing songs whose repetitive refrains contain such subtleties as "Kill all the Arabs" or "You Arabs all will die," songs they belt out on their school bus while looking down at Palestinians walking below. Strong stuff, indeed!

Occasionally, adult Palestinians are panned smiling sweetly into the camera. A few of their small children wave excitedly for half-minute scenes. That's all we see of Hebron's main population. Toward the film's end, we're shown settlers on rampages against Palestinians, carrying and using guns, openly supported by Israeli soldiers.

• • •

At La Guardia Airport, I'm picked up in a stretch limousine which is carrying the other Jewish panelist, Charles Leibman, a political science professor from Bar Ilan University in Israel, who is spending this semester teaching at NYU.

As we are driven the twenty minutes to the studio, Charles talks softly. Warm, self-effacing and easy to be with, as we arrive at the studio, Charles mentions, almost in a whisper, that I should know something: He doesn't want to shock me but he's pretty "left-wing." I might find him too "pro-Palestinian." I laugh at our shorthand. "Not to worry," I respond.

As we walk into the studio we meet our two Palestinian co-panelists. They are Naseer Aruri (a princely, articulate man, originally from Jerusalem, now a professor in Boston) and Najat Arafat (a highly educated, elegant woman born in Nablus, now a physics professor in Washington, D.C.). They are both acquaintances of mine. We shake hands warmly, as we three reminisce about where we last met—Najat and I at the Handshake; Naseer at a Mideast seminar he chaired in Boston. Within minutes we are, all four, enjoying an easy rapport, focusing on our shared desire for Mideast peace. We discover that we're all, more or less, on the same wavelength. As requested, we don't discuss the film.

During lunch our moderator, Bill Zimmerman, who is neither Jewish nor Arab, attempts to fire up ethnic divisions among us. We continue laughing together. The more Bill presses his agenda on us, the more we try to convince him that "moderate Jews and Palestinians" *do* work together and form close friendships. This idea seems to unnerve him. His agenda is to put on a lively, adversarial show. No matter how patiently we explain that allegiances in the Mideast aren't based solely on ethnicity, he can't seem to accept that we're not natural enemies.

When he takes his makeup break, his assistant confides that Bill arranged for us to get picked up in two separate limousines, though we all landed at La Guardia Airport within the same hour. She says he feared we'd have the fight he wants saved for the audience. When he returns to the room, Bill continues to try to orchestrate our enmity. But instead of goading us out of our camaraderie, he succeeds in creating the opposite. He gives up and leaves the room.

When Bill returns, it's to tell us that we're close to show time. Again, he attempts to intrude on our agreeable mood until we bond against him, the only one here not in the least passionate about the Mideast. One of us says, out of his earshot, "We'd clear up our problems in two days if we had a country of Bill Zimmermans next door." Then someone calls out, "Six minutes."

Najat grabs my hand, saying, "Let's get a little makeup on you." We squeeze into a tiny, drafty bathroom. She tries putting eyeliner on me but it smudges. We look in the mirror and see that I look like a battered woman, which convulses us with girlish giggles, because whatever this stuff is made of, nothing we try removes it. And so, still somewhat black-eyed, I follow her to the table. With "two minutes to airtime" we all give each other nervous smiles.

As soon as the camera begins rolling, each of us changes perceptibly, and in no time we are in serious disagreement about many issues the film addresses. At first we disagree about the tone of the film's narrator, but soon we're at more serious loggerheads, shriller and angrier with each other than any of us could have dreamed possible. Though we remain polite, the subtext is war.

Charles begins our discussion by referring to the extremism portrayed in the film. "Let's be clear. These people are not typical Israelis. They're more insane than even the other settlers. I don't say this in apology. I find their talk revolting and cannot begin to enter the hearts and minds of people with whom I feel absolutely no sympathy."

Bill Zimmerman asks me what I think of the film. I surprise myself. "Unfortunately in the Middle East, we could make ten or one hundred versions of this film—each one portraying a different extremist group. We could just as easily film groups in Gaza as they're initiated into their death cults. Sadly, these days, the fanatics on both sides are working almost hand in glove, while the middle, the fair-minded, are collapsing, folding up like a giant accordion. What this film shows is the extremism that is in the air everywhere so that what was once marginal—these very extremes—are now central."

Naseer shoots me a look that says, "I thought you were on our side." His response is a rebuttal. "This film is an accurate portrayal of the settlers of Hebron. What's missing is the larger context—that's my main criticism. . . . I disagree with Wendy; there is no symmetry between Jewish Israelis and us Palestinians. I disagree with Charles, too. These people *are* representatives of Israel." Charles and I stare at him and quickly he amends. "No, they're not representative of Israeli society, but they do represent the entire settler mentality. All settlers may not show such racist demeanor, but they do agree that our land is an area that's theirs to colonize. And, of course, the whole concept of settlements is promoted by each Israeli government, who could . . . should contain them. They're in occupied territory, as the UN recognizes."

Zimmerman nods to Najat. Is she the woman I was just laughing with in that bathroom? She's turned tight-faced and adversarial. With a furious glance at Charles and then at me, she says, "My first reaction was horror. This film does indeed depict the true nature of the settlers. It's horrible and shocking to see such hatred." Giving me an angry look, she says, "I disagree with her completely. I see no likeness on the Palestinian side; nothing like this hatred exists among our people."

We continue in this vein, livid with each other, each trying to convince viewers that the other side's terrorists and hate-mongers are worse than our own. Bill is relaxing. The mudslinging absent at our convivial lunch is going full blast now, as he had hoped. I see him smile as I turn to Naseer to say, "I'm in a curious position. Usually I argue your position to the Jewish right or middle wing. But as a Jewish witness to much in the Mideast, trying to see from the Palestinian point of view as much as possible, I'll say that after Baruch Goldstein committed that horrid massacre, Rabin spoke out strongly against him. Jewish groups all over the world raised money for hospitals and medical care for the Islamic wounded. I was in Hebron, paid condolence calls, as did many other Jews. I wish that you and all the intellectual, highly educated Palestinians would at least condemn the suicide bombers, these killers.

"After the last bus bomb, I called one of my best friends, Achmed. He's a Palestinian I've traveled with many times and in dangerous situations. We are usually united in our views. So I asked him to tell me, honestly, how he felt after the latest killings of Jews. He *was* honest. He said, 'For the first ten minutes I felt that the Israelis had gotten just what they deserve. Then for the rest of the day, I hated myself, couldn't believe how primitive my initial reaction was.' He admitted that Israelis do not get heartfelt responses to their losses from even the best among your people."

"Why would nineteen-year-olds blow themselves up?" Najat retorts. "We have to think about that and the answer is: the occupation, the root of all other problems." She turns to me. "By the way, we don't want your Jewish condolences; we want you to remove all your troops."

For what feels an eternity we go at each other. Attack. Counterattack. Attack. Counterattack. Each of us is magnetized by our most primitive ideas. Finally, Bill (who all of a sudden seems positively benign) is summing up. And then, our time is up. It's over. With the cameras off we're embarrassed, surprised that Bill got his way. But we're so unhappy with each other that we leave in separate Jewish and Arab cars—just as we arrived—only this time it's by choice. In the parking lot Najat throws me and Charles a bitter look. Naseer seems more vulnerable, seems sad.

Weeks later Josh Brockman sends me the tape. Watching it, I try to see how our two sides filled with derision so quickly. I see that, despite all we had in common, we four are, by birth and sensibility, living opposing narratives. What's minor for Jews leapt out as central for the Palestinians, and vice versa. I am puzzled by how we had shared such conviviality before airtime, and so little during and after our discussion. I watch the tape until eventually I see each view as accurate and inaccurate. I hear Charles and myself as sounding exactly like right-wing Jews. This doesn't help my Mid-east crisis, but compounds it. Is a TV camera like truth serum? Did we not know what we really thought until lit by those kleig lights?

Two months later, in early May, I'm sitting in on Herb Kelman's Mideast seminar at Harvard. Kelman, one of the oldest dialogue initiators, has brought Palestinians and Israelis together for decades. Today's speaker is Colette Avital, the Israeli consulate general to New York. She's as beautiful as she is poised; her sweep of perfect blond hair, her velvet skin and her clear sense of her role as diplomat make her words seductive, even though she appears more French than Israeli. Calm and soft-spoken, she begins to weave a narrative of the peace process that's lucid. She charms the twenty of us sitting in this small room. She talks for over an hour about the Syrian channel, the shifts in Israeli policy toward Palestinians and the results, thus far, from the Oslo Accords. I'm riveted.

But I can't help noticing that she seems to put an unduly rosy gloss over even the most troubled terrain, ignoring the land confiscations, the demoralization, the violence that's on the rise from both directions. The upcoming Palestinian elections and the expected infusion of European funds for six new industrial parks in the West Bank will solve most of the unrest, Ambassador Avital assures us. A turning point is right around the corner. We're on track despite the headlines that emphasize the negative.

This sounds plausible. I well know that a little goes a long way to raise Palestinian hopes, though I also know that nothing seemed remotely rosy on my visit two months ago. I sit taking notes, gratefully seduced by Avital's coherence. I become so immersed that the Oslo process sounds, once again, brilliantly workable. When her talk is over, Sarah Roy, a Jewish American who looks to be an Egyptian beauty (a woman reputed to be one of the world's experts on Gazan economy), presents her own, very different, view. The Palestinian economy is in dire straits, worse than ever, far worse than before the Oslo Accords; she offers statistics.

Colette Avital responds with equally calm aplomb. I watch as the dark wellgroomed beauty and the blond well-groomed beauty disagree with such élan, such soft tones and polite manners that this might be a mild conversation about the weather. I'm lulled into a strange calm by these women, a mood which persists until Hilda Silverman, a Jewish peace activist, who's working on a film called *Empathy After Auschwitz,* speaks up. Her voice is highpitched; her body trembles in anger. She cannot believe this conversation. She mentions all that the ambassador has omitted. She enumerates the escalating land confiscations, the Israeli government's coddling of "settler maniacs," the rapid expansion of the settlements. Her voice reaches a crescendo as she denounces Avital's rendition as dead wrong. She lists the continuous, provocative bullying of Palestinians everywhere, including in East Jerusalem: "Israel has never acted in the spirit or the laws set by the Oslo Accords," she says.

"Wrong," she repeats, going over each item again. *And* again: "Wrong."

She turns to me and says, "You were just there. Tell them. You saw all this with your own eyes. Go ahead. They don't have to believe me. I'm not alone with this view—far from it." Everyone in the room is waiting. "Go ahead. Tell them," Hilda repeats heatedly. Finally, in a weakened voice, I mumble, "But I have nothing to say." This is the truth. A blank has formed at the center of my mind; I find it impossible to switch gears or put this flood of disparate images into words.

"Bullshit," Hilda says. "You were in El Khader and you toured East Jerusalem, what, just a month ago?"

The room is quiet as I say, "I was there. But trust me, Hilda, if you were inside my mind right now, you'd know what I know. Which is nothing."

Minutes later, as Hilda gives me a look of anger and disappointment, the class disperses. Colette turns to me. "That's one *impassionata*," she says.

As night falls I leave the empty building and catch sight of Ambassador Avital's dark limousine wending its way through the nearly deserted Cambridge streets. That night I dream that I'm in Woodmere, Long Island, in my parents' home. I've been complicit in a murder, then a cover-up. Someone else has done the deed, but I've buried the corpse in the foundation of my parents' house. Though utterly evil, it's a job well done and we know we won't get caught. And then, inside the dream, strange things result from the killing: Eliza is no longer dyslexic; I no longer crave cigarettes. It's effortless. Each member of my family comes back to life, healthy and happy. My dreaming self knows we should all feel cursed, but this murderous deed and its cover-up heal us instead.

I wake on Saturday knowing that the murder is connected to the thoughts I'd blocked out while Colette Avital was talking, to the way I had colluded in murdering truth. All morning I taste the dream's mood of amoral joy. And then I file it away under My Mid-East Crisis. Thinking too much, that's my problem, I decide.

It's the outset of our second academic year in Cambridge and Eliza is thriving. She's making emotional and academic leaps impossible for her in the all-Hebrew schools of Jerusalem. One night as I read to her before sleep, she stops me, pointing to the lighted New England scene outside her bedroom window.

"I love American trees," she says.

"You don't miss the palms and apricots, all those lacy leaves in Jerusalem?" I ask.

"Miss them? I hate them," she says with that vehemence that defines children. She talks of the "boring" Hebrew holidays and how lucky she is to be back in America with Halloween, Thanksgiving and Valentine's Day. After she falls asleep, I realize that we two are living out a mirror image of the Israeli-Palestinian conflict. For they are two disparate peoples, with little love lost between them, forced to share one land. We two love each other fiercely, yet feel at home only in opposite lands. The appeal of this irony is short-lived. "I hate it here" pretty much sums up the truth of my reality, too.

Eliza not only loves living here, she *needs* to stay. Speaking and studying in English, she's blossoming, reverting to her old self-confident, outgoing, eager to learn, funny, wise self. Ever-mindful that this is her childhood and not mine, I know now what I didn't earlier: that we will be living in the States not for another year or two, but for the remainder of her childhood—a very long time. And I also know that I must stop living emotionally in Jerusalem.

One week later Yasser Arafat arrives to speak at Harvard. The excitement all around town energizes me and serves as a painful reminder of a time, now a dimming memory, when such excitement was my daily fare. Though I have a press pass, I choose to watch Arafat's speech on a special TV set up in a nearby coffee shop, one filled with Palestinians tonight. Those around me are all chatting in Arabic while waiting for Arafat to appear on the screen. When he does, the coffee shop becomes still. I feel the return of my real, fully engaged, most alive self.

Within mere minutes I'm adopted into three generations of a large Palestinian family who are now living outside Boston. When Arafat's speech is finished, they tell me they want to find a house where, they've been told, an event is scheduled to be held—a slide show for those interested in more discussion of the peace process. They badly want to attend this hard-to-find Quaker meeting, and, delighted to be among these people, I race around Cambridge until I locate the side street and the room where the meeting will soon begin. Quickly, I run back and busy myself with helping first the arthritic grandmother, then returning for the parents and their young Palestinian-American children. All told, this entails three trips back and forth to make sure that all interested Palestinians are escorted here.

This isn't altruism. This is visceral Mideast energy, a way of moving I'd nearly forgotten. How fully I've lost touch with that particular way that I can leap out of myself. Within an hour I'm sitting in a large room with a group of American Arabs and Quakers. The slides up on the screen show the suffering of the East Jerusalemites. A man talking at the podium underscores, with each scene shown, the way Israelis abuse power. Within a few minutes, everyone is spouting anti-Israel rhetoric. Enlarged photo slides dominate the room, accompanied by a running commentary about the evils of the occupation. I begin to feel angry. The Palestinian man, whose family I so enjoyed helping, leans close to me and gleefully whispers, "It's *so* good to have no Zionists here." I writhe in my seat, tempted to stand up and confront these speakers. They are talking so knowingly, so certainly, against Israel's occupation, but do they even try to see or convey the Israeli reality? I imagine giving a counter-narrative to this angry group, detailing all that they've left out about Israeli pain, Israeli fears, Israeli history.

Yet, I know how little logical arguments serve when a group embraces a common enemy. I see that everyone in this room is enjoying being righteous and feeling wronged.

I seesaw. One minute I feel honor-bound to speak out. The next—just as I'm about to stand and say, "You aren't seeing any of the subtleties; one-sided allegiance can't further understanding or peace work," I remember a slew of letters I received after one or another article, whether from Jewish zealots or others, the uninformed. One stands out. The writer asked, "Has this woman, your Mideast correspondent, ever met a terrorist she doesn't like?" At the time this sent me and the editors at the magazine into uproarious laughter. But actually, it was true: I had met very few Palestinians I didn't like. Unquestionably, I've met more than a few terrorists and so I've been exactly where this group is, have seen through their eyes, felt what they feel. And, more to the point, I too have been tempted into this kind of partisanship, weary of the energy required to hold more than one point of view in mind.

On my short walk home, I decide to stop obsessing. I've remained single-mindedly involved, even at this great distance. Now I vow to let my passion and fascination with Jerusalem recede, to turn away from my relentless focus on Israelis and Palestinians, on peace and war, on right and wrong, or as Amos Oz says repeatedly, on "right and right." The whole subject is too addictive for me. Since I can't live there, it's like falling in love with a married man, one I can never have. This crude image captures the source of my pain and reveals that my attachment to Jerusalem is serving nothing; is turning what's present too pale. Later this month, weeks after I begin to actively tune out Mideast news, I sign up to work in a soup kitchen. I begin visiting homeless shelters, keeping careful notes as I begin to get involved in an *American* subculture that's foreign to me. I must live where I live, I tell myself. And then, an event occurs that forever reverses my attempt to live outside the Israeli-Palestinian world.

CHAPTER SEVENTEEN

Rabin Is Dead

"One day there is life . . . and then, suddenly, it happens, there is death."

I'm in my Cambridge study, examining these words on the back jacket of Paul Auster's memoir, *The Invention of Solitude*. It's three-thirty on a Saturday afternoon, November 4, 1995. I'm flipping back and forth from the book's opening passage to this phrase on the cover, when the phone rings.

My friend Marge has just heard on the BBC news that, minutes ago, Rabin was shot. "They don't know if he'll live."

I'm alone in the house. My dog, Harry, is lying beside me, asleep on the floor. I start howling—guttural sounds so loud they seem to be coming from someone else. Harry looks up, then slinks under a chair as Marge keeps shouting, "Are you okay? Are you *okay?*"

On CNN, Yitzhak Rabin is not dead. And then he is.

The phone starts ringing. Calls are coming in from all over the country and from Israel just as Eliza, Daphie and Tal stroll in. I shout the news to them. They rush, screaming, into my room. We lie on my bed, gaping at the television in disbelief. Already Wolf Blitzer, the White House correspondent, is talking about the political fallout. He seems lifeless, giving details without feeling. I know that he lived in Jerusalem, worked for the *Jerusalem Post* for years. Yet he remains matter-of-fact, studiously devoid of emotion. Rabin is barely cold, yet the talk has already shifted to politics.

I've got to get to Israel, I think, no matter what. It's not the journalist in me who has to go, but the mourner. I need to pay respects directly to a man I've come to trust and admire.

I'd meant to get to the bank earlier. It's already 4:45 as I race to Harvard Square where students are milling about on a typical late Saturday afternoon. The contrast between my frenzied state and the casual ambiance brings to mind W. H. Auden's line: ". . . how everything turns away quite leisurely from the disaster." Then, as if blinking in neon: *Rabin Assassinated by a Jew* replays over and over. For me, the personal and the political have completely collapsed into each other.

Walking away from the bank to my car, I spot a well-groomed, middle-aged woman. She's dressed all in black and stands out from the college kids all around us.

"Are you Jewish?" I shout. "The prime minister of Israel was just assassinated . . . killed by a Jew," I say, staring at her. She stares back, dumbfounded—a complete stranger accosting her on this street. I feel her eyes on my back while racing to my car.

All El Al flights are booked. Only a Boston-to-Zurich Swissair flight with a connecting flight to Tel Aviv has one seat open; it's leaving in two hours. I pack as my daughter cries, "But, Mom, you promised not to work there anymore!" She looks panic-stricken. "Who will take care of me?" she asks.

"Daphie and Tal," I say. Then I lean over and whisper, "Eliza, I only hope that when you grow up you will care about something as much as I care about this." I add that I'll be gone for only two weeks.

I'm sure she can't understand my urgency, but as I dash for the door she hands me a note. "I love you, Mom," it says, below which she's drawn an amazingly accurate sketch of the two of us and Harry, the dog—all three figures dwarfed by a huge Israeli flag with equally huge teardrops dropping from it.

In Swissair's business-class lounge, everyone seems blasé. Only one Swiss man, a cosmopolitan, world-weary type, seems to be aware of what's just happened. He looks up from his newspaper and, rolling his eyes, he says, "What did you expect? It's the Middle East."

"Believe me, *this* we did not expect," I say.

The Swiss stewards are rigid down to the tiniest details—so opposite to the careless abandon that typifies an El Al flight. This isolation is not what I had in mind, not at all. It's then I realize that on El Al tonight there'd be something far worse: terrible undercurrents of hostility, the left and right schism; secular and religious Jews eyeing each other suspiciously. Rabbis, Haredim, diamond merchants and Internet moguls would not be of one mind about Rabin's murder. There'd be more overt friction among us Jews (American and Israeli) than is usual. Tonight anyone not in wild grief would seem highly suspect to me, I know, as our jet is jolted by turbulence. It ricochets and trembles, sinks and rises, all across the Atlantic until we finally land.

In the Zurich passenger lounge, CNN is showing Rabin's coffin being moved from Tel Aviv to Jerusalem. With three hours to wait for the flight to Tel Aviv, I stare at the solemn procession shown on the TV screen. Soon a family arrives and they sit down beside me. The mother, a sweet-looking, round-faced woman, is accompanied by her two gorgeous, well-dressed daughters, both in their twenties. "I'm an Israeli," she says. I take her hand. "Isn't this awful? By a Jew!" I say.

Her voice sounds strangely detached: "What can you do?" she responds.

"But a Jew killing a Jewish prime minister! Did you ever imagine?"

"I'm a *Palestinian* Israeli," she says. "From Nazareth. Or I was. Now I'm an American. We live in Los Angeles; the Israelis confiscated my passport. They only issued visas for us to come back for a few days. Wealthy Jews want to buy land I own ten miles outside Jerusalem." She seems soft and confused, claims that she's not involved with politics, though it's clear that politics have defined her life. "Should we sell?" this gentle woman with a pretty name, Wanda Valentine, asks.

"They're probably settlers," I say.

"Yes, Jews from the settlements working through Arab middlemen. They offered me $50,000. What can I do? All I care about is my daughters. I know it's bad, but I told them, 'Okay, for $60,000.' "

"I don't think you should sell Palestinian land," I say. Then softening, I add, "Though I understand about your daughters."

Now I'm seated next to a Jewish-American couple who are just returning from Israel. They've only heard the news here, in Zurich. "We were *this* far from him," the sixty-something, bleached blond woman is saying in a strong Brooklyn accent as her husband in the next seat is snoring loudly. She talks as if their proximity to Rabin is a trophy. Pointing to her husband she says, "He was on the dais at our conference on Diaspora Jewry last week, not *this* far. . . ." She holds her hands an inch apart. "What a trip!" she continues without missing a beat. "South Africa, Belgium, London, Israel—it's been a dream." Then, in a whisper, cocking her head toward her husband, she exclaims: "A fortune! He's made millions—is a philanthropist now, a big one. And the fuss! Everywhere we go. You can't imagine!" she says proudly as I watch Rabin's coffin making its slow procession up to Jerusalem.

In this lounge, men are chatting. Kids play with computer games. Couples nod off, waiting for connecting flights. Those going on to Tel Aviv are called to a shuttle bus which escorts us to a compound where our bags are carefully inspected. I'm with a large group of elderly German tourists. Nervous about Israel's unrest, I hear them say to each other, "Bad luck—going at such a time!"

Inside the tightly guarded luggage room, I spot one very old Jewish man. After staring eagerly into his distracted eyes, I see he's far away. He sits mute, as if frozen inside old tragedies from which he's never recovered.

On the flight to Tel Aviv, business class is full of journalists and others who look like politicians. An elegant Arab man walks up and down the aisles talking and joking nonstop for the entire four-hour flight. I vow never to forget this trim, middle-aged man with his well-cut suit, bright white teeth and chic Parisian haircut. I remember Woody Allen framing his film *Hannah and Her Sisters* as a novel with black-and-white chapter headings, each accompanied by Gershwin music. This little chapter, this tail-end flight from Zurich to Tel Aviv, this onset of a week of mourning, I name "The Arab businessman was far too cheerful."

But so too are the journalists. These newsmen and women from NBC in London exude that adrenaline excitement that defines the press corps whenever a hot story breaks. Drinks are being served; the chattering grows louder. Each jolt of the plane wakes me to jocular voices of the cameramen seated behind me. They're speaking in German. I hear French and English and I also hear, from across the aisle, laughter mixed with high-pitched, cheerful *Hebrew*. We must all have our own responses to shock, I think, trying to be kind, feeling miserable.

When we land at Ben-Gurion Airport, it's 7 P.M. Israeli time, Sunday night, November 5, less than twenty-four hours since the assassination. I grab my bag and computer off the revolving ramp and steer my cart past customs. Just as I'm about to exit the airport, I spot a small room with a TV on. Here is where the security and cleaning staff keep equipment and change in and out of their uniforms. I can't wheel my pushcart inside, so I stand at the doorway watching Israel's Channel 1. Haim Yavin is the anchorman, and in seconds I'm crying freely again, as are two thin Sephardic Israeli men and a heavyset woman sporting bright Israeli orange hair.

"Last hour on duty," one says in rudimentary English, better than my Hebrew. Even without language we're all connected by pain. They gesture for me to join them. Now all four of us are crying together, passing around tissues, as I see Yavin is also in shock. He's delivering the news with no attempt to mask his turmoil.

We see crowds screaming in Tel Aviv after last night's peace rally, a replay of the pandemonium. Then, we're shown Rabin's coffin arriving amid great fanfare, being placed outside the Knesset. Next come interviews with neighbors of the murderer, Yigal Amir, who live in the Tel Aviv suburb of Herzliya. Glad for company, I've no desire to leave this tiny room. But after half an hour, I force myself to head up to Jerusalem.

I walk into Yehuda's loft. There I find my painter friend standing dazed and distraught. I'm glad I came for my sake and for his as we hug solemnly, for longer than usual. He shows me the canvas he was working on when the news broke. It's made of driftwood and is a cubist rendition of the new Middle East. Israel is painted in a pastiche layer of green shades. Thick gold paint covers every region where peace has already been negotiated, a gold that spills lightly onto the West Bank and Gaza. Only Syria and Lebanon are completely vacant. Though heavily outlined in black, those are the only contiguous countries devoid of paint.

We two drive to Binyane-Ha-Uma, the massive building that becomes the international journalists' center during large events. The last time I was here was after the final peace treaty with Jordan was signed. I remember that October day of great hope. While Yehuda helps me update my press pass, I'm immersed in the past, recalling the collective euphoria, those hours when we raced back from the Arava to Jerusalem in time to greet Clinton, who was arriving for his first presidential visit just as a saturated blood-red sunset enveloped Jerusalem.

Uri Dromi, head of the Israeli press office, interrupts my reverie. I touch his arm and see his face is fragile. Right behind him, his assistant, Elisa Ben-Rafael, runs to me. I realize that it's been only three years since her husband, an Israeli diplomat, was killed in a Buenos Aires terror attack. She must be having horrid flashbacks. Near to us, five or six press aides are shouting for something Tom Brokaw has just requested.

Yehuda and I walk outside and head up to the Knesset. Soon, we're two among the huge throng. It's 2 A.M. Hundreds of thousands of Israelis are here in the middle of this soft, warm night. On the plane, I'd wondered, How does a country mourn? Now I see: Israelis in collective shock, sharing a silence that's astounding given the manic intensity they typically generate. In this hushed quiet, everyone moves slowly, staying in place. The crowds inch forward. There's no pushing, no stepping out of line, not one loud sound. Under an almost full moon, everyone is crying, but quietly. It's exactly what Channel 1 showed, yet so much more moving on the ground—*ba'aretz*—on this earth.

Youngsters of all ages, each in T-shirts and jeans, light candles while sitting in circles, singing softly. They lock arms, swaying back and forth. Their melodies are the only sounds reverberating in this unusually warm November night. It's as if the entire country, despite all we know to the contrary, is still one big pioneering kibbutz.

An old friend walks by. "I've been here since nine this morning," he says. "The guards just told me that one million have already passed Rabin's coffin."

"That's a fifth of Israel's population," Yehuda muses.

It's 4 A.M. The crowds remain patient, are silently grieving. For a change, there are no right-wing militants, none of their nasty heckling. How did we get so accustomed to those ubiquitous, mean-spirited protests? It's 5 A.M., then six. I see the soldiers guarding this site are also in tears. I gaze into their wet faces.

Finally we arrive at Rabin's coffin. It's brightly lit, encircled by hundreds of lighted candles, bouquets and handwritten letters, the farewell notes. As I approach the closed coffin, I'm drawn to gaze up at the sky. In the almost full moon, Rabin's face seems to be shining down from the lunar surface. I stare at his determined expression, his trademark half smile—both seem refracted up above. This impression, though weird, is strangely comforting.

Searching for our car, we climb, along with hundreds of others, over construction sites—mounds of dirt and sand lit only by moonlight. As if choreographed, we all move nimbly on this terrain. "Like astronauts," I say to Yehuda, who looks around and nods. We do all seem to be moving without gravity, without noise, without feeling, as if layers of padded grief are keeping all other sensations at bay.

I get into bed in Yehuda's guest loft just as dawn is rising. In this November heat wave, I hear the birds of Jerusalem, one of the most intimate sounds I know. Whenever I was in pain here, I was drawn to these unusually melodic creatures, little birds that hop about merrily. The birds, the birds are greeting this terrible day. I can't fall asleep so I return to Auster's *The Invention of Solitude*. Picking up where I left off, what seems a month ago, yesterday, I read again, "One day there is life . . . and then, suddenly, it happens, there is death."

I discover that Auster is attempting to penetrate the meaning of his Jewish father's death. It's a memoir full of chance discoveries, coincidences and internal synchronicities. He writes: "There has been a wound, and I realize now that it is very deep. . . . that if I am to understand anything, I must penetrate this image of darkness, must enter the absolute darkness of this earth."

The funeral—a mixture of pomp and frenzy, disbelief and soothing words—includes world leaders who sit in the heat alongside hand-picked ordinary citizens. President Clinton tells a funny anecdote about Rabin's antipathy to "dressing up" and then, head bowed, ends with *"Shalom, haver"* (Goodbye, friend), words that comfort and overnight become Israel's most popular sign, bumper sticker, new song.

After the burial, Leah Rabin speaks out. "I have more in common with some Arabs than with certain Jews." Her words fuse with images from the funeral itself: of King Hussein and Queen Noor weeping; Egyptian president Hosni Mubarak and his diplomatic corps standing in somber grief and then walking, for the first time, all around Jerusalem. Arafat and his wife, Suha, remain in Gaza (for security reasons) but are shown on TV, clearly shaken. Within days they make a condolence call to Leah Rabin in Tel Aviv, where Arafat removes his kaffiyeh (for the first time in anyone's memory) as he tightly grips the widow's hand. They're photographed sitting close together.

After the funeral, day and night, an extraordinary energy is let loose. Arab dignitaries from countries which, until recently, wouldn't allow the word "Israel" onto their broadcasts or in their newspapers wander around the King David Hotel's lobby or talk emotively to Israeli newscasters, as if it's perfectly natural to mingle with Israelis and Jews and other Americans in Jerusalem.

What's happened among these leaders holds a mirror to their peoples, showing what can happen for all of us. Rabin, "the quintessential Israeli," as everyone calls him, meant this much to his former enemies, was loved because "he was authentic," as is so often repeated. He's left a legacy unthinkable only a few years ago, a society no longer isolated from neighbors and from the world, no longer surrounded by enemies on all sides. Amazing.

The many powerful words and images that follow the funeral slip into the collective consciousness, which has been sliced open by the trauma. This tragic murder, as Leah Rabin notes, is ironically also a chance for new openings. The condolence call from Arafat and his wife, often replayed on Israeli TV, is powerful proof that Rabin has left a world transformed by his own transformation. The new unity across ethnic lines is based on friendships but, more important, on political affiliations that are in the process of re-forming. Now, the most powerful divisions are not those that pit Jew against Arab. Rather, the most obvious schism lies between those who are psychologically mobile (able and willing to take risks; open to a change of heart) and those who remain stonily fixed (gripped by a fundamentalist mindset), for whom land or enmity or fear of the stranger remains more important than life.

No one, of course, thinks that what now awaits us will be smooth sailing. But many Israelis are undergoing a palpable change. This is exemplified in interviews with men from a radical anti-peace kibbutz, a rarity, near the Golan. In the past, these men and women were frequently filmed declaring that they'd be moved from their homes "only in their coffins." Now they say, "Whatever the government decides, we agree. Life is more important than land. In the past we were being myopic, selfish." These who speak out have been thrust into a new narrative.

As have many in Tel Aviv, especially among the young. On interviews broadcast continuously on Israeli TV, I hear one teenager say, "I won't demonstrate with the far right again. I won't go near hate anymore." Another girl: "I was against this peace. But I was visiting the Kiryat Arba settlement in Hebron when the news broke." She's sobbing. "It was horrible to see people happy about this murder. Watching them, I realized that more deaths will occur if we don't stand together against violence. I went to King's Square, to the spot where Rabin was gunned down. I lit candles."

TV cameras move from house to house to house. A musician in Tel Aviv is seen lying on his bed, a large guitar placed across his chest. He sits up, with effort, and says, "Part of me died with Rabin. I didn't sleep all night. I was for peace, but I did nothing to help create it. Now peace work will be the center of my life."

The cameras swing to Rabin's official residence, just around the corner from where I'm sitting with friends in the Jerusalem neighborhood of Rehavia. We watch an outpouring of old and young, men and women. The "candle children" are sitting and singing in their by-now familiar circles. The newscaster says nothing, allowing the scene to speak for itself. My friends and I turn off the TV and walk into the exact scene we've just been viewing. One woman looks at me and I feel her tears. Someone walks away, leaving his sadness for another to embody.

"In the presence of extraordinary reality, consciousness takes the place of imagination," Auster writes.

Then, there are the others, those so crazed about Arabs that they'll kill their own prime minister and then blame *him,* for that's one motif at a right-wing rally four nights after Rabin's funeral, billed as "a night of soul searching." It's being held at Beit Agron's convention hall in downtown Jerusalem. Here they are—those who directly or tacitly sanctioned posters of Rabin in SS uniform, who held enlarged photos of him adorned with Arafat's odd-shaped kaffiyeh, his trademark Palestine headdress.

Here are the ones who demonstrated constantly, hurling invectives outside Rabin's apartment house in Tel Aviv each *Shabbat,* building tent cities across from his official residence in Jerusalem. Day and night, their rage was screechingly apparent and ever-present: in chants, on posters and bumper stickers, on banners flung from their apartment windows. Yet somehow none of us—not the academics, not the journalists, not anyone who studied the settlers and described the raging rhetoric of Likud rallies, not the filmmakers with documentaries of the armed Hebron settlers, not the Shin Bet, Israel's secret service, with their live footage of Yigal Amir stalking Rabin, armed—nobody took this open hatred literally enough. The Jews who branded Rabin a traitor, an enemy of the state, were heard but not attended to, noticed but not truly noted. So hooked were most of us on the myth of Jewish solidarity, on the notion of the Palestinians as the only hotheads of terrorism, that we missed the obvious:

that there are Jewish terrorists in our midst who, much like their Hamas counterparts, claim a direct line to God's will. This small percentage of Jews who talked of death and murder unfortunately still do.

The gathering at Beit Agron, this night of "soul-searching," is not that. The overflow crowds, too large for the auditorium, spread out into the hallways, where loudspeakers are hooked up, through which we can hear the voices of men lecturing inside. The speakers include not only those from the settlements but also many who live inside the Green Line, in Israel proper—men and women who, as we've now learned, have formed a silent fraternity composed of middle-class bank managers, lawyers, army officials, school administrators, all living "normal" lives while supporting extremists, including the now illegal Kach movement. In secret, these men and women have been giving arms, money and time to help run the settlers' pirate radio station Arutz 7, which broadcasts hate. (Their right to "free speech" is one of many fierce debates raging in Israel now.)

Making my way into the auditorium, I squeeze into a seat and listen to eight religious leaders seated on the stage. Each man takes his turn at the lectern. This is not soul-searching. All those lecturing agree that trading land for peace will lead only to disaster. (Are we not mired in disaster already?) The exception is Rabbi Yoel Bin-Nun, who's shouting, "Now is the time to see that *we* are complicit in this murder. Now is the time to look at ourselves, to admit that *we* created the environment for the assassination." The audience angrily shouts him down.

Leaving the assembly, I wander the hallways and soon begin talking to a man wearing a *kippah*. Multiple emotions (worry and sadness, agreement and disagreement) crisscross his exhausted face. Yet as we talk I see him searching for his "fix"—his fixed position on the assassination. For him, this involves a complicated labyrinth of ideas in which trading Jewish land for peace is treason, because Arabs must not live near nor on "our" land. Though this man is no stereotype (he's not *only* angry; his face doesn't display *only* hatred), he's working overtime to consolidate his position. We move outside to talk despite the cold winter rain that's been pelting down on Jerusalem since the hour Rabin's funeral ended.

Who is this confused-looking soul? What is he thinking? Finally, on condition that I don't know his name, he explains his reasoning. Then he surprises me by weeping. "I'm very sorry Rabin is dead," he says, shouting over the thunder. He seems to mean it, though he then adds, "But Rabin committed a crime. You know that. In your heart you do. He was one man. And then, without calling elections, without a consensus, he was another man. He changed his mind."

So that's the problem, I think sardonically, and don't try to reason with him.

I know that anything I say will redouble his efforts to keep his logic in place. I leave him standing in a fierce downpour and drive away from Beit Agron, meditating, as best I can, on the fundamentalist mindset. At first, I feel a rush of superiority in relation to the shouting rabbis with their angry faces or even this grieving Jerusalemite who, by my lights, is too rigid to understand that *all life is change*. But then, I begin to wonder if that fanatic also lives in me.

I don't have to search hard; I know that psychological space exists and I know where to find it, with surprising ease—the opinions I hold rigidly which no arguments can loosen, the attachments to ideas that no facts can refute. The only way I differ, and I think I do, is that at least sometimes, I can both inhabit *and* observe my own craziness—exactly what the fundamentalists seem incapable of doing.

Driving slowly through the Jerusalem storm, I see that these people may seem like caricatures, but they aren't all that different from the rest of us, with *our* passionate beliefs. A slew of insights are my reward for this tiny mental experiment. As I continue to drive, long obdurate puzzles about various friends and our children become clarified. It's elementary; we all have patches of rigid certainty, superstitions and distortions which we cling to as if our sanity depended on them. And if change does occur, it never arises from being angrily confronted. Where any of us are most rigid is also where we're most defensive, I know. But as my windshield wipers move frantically back and forth, back and forth, I wonder what this insight gives me. Do I have a single clue how to communicate with those who commit or condone the murder of the prime minister?

Exhausted, I return to Yehuda's late. He's asleep and I lie in my bed reading Auster. In this segment of his long story he uncovers facts about his grandfather's brother, a man who moved to Palestine, became an observant Jew, and eventually was mayor of Jerusalem. "The essence of what the rabbis have to teach is that if there is to be any justice at all, there must be justice for everyone. No one can be excluded, or else there is no such thing as justice." These words are comforting, yet how do they jell with what was so vocally expressed last night at Beit Agron? While pondering this, I fall, blessedly, asleep.

Each morning I wake in morbid disbelief. I can't accept that Rabin is dead. One midday, during this first week in Jerusalem, the week of shivah (mourning) I feel restless, so I drive aimlessly, thinking about many things before focusing on the Palestinians and wondering, for the first time, about *their* reactions. I loop toward Bethlehem's checkpoint and past it, to the town of Beit Sahur. I'm hoping to talk with local dialogue leaders. As expected, I find Ghassan and Elias, the local pharmacist, at the Rapprochement Center. They welcome me, and offer coffee and conversation. Once we're sitting comfortably, they tell me what's been happening in their part of this world. I hear that

Phase One of Oslo is proceeding, with Israeli troops moving out of the major cities of the West Bank ahead of schedule, instead of the usual stall. Just yesterday, I'm told, many soldiers were moved from Nablus with less fanfare and scrutiny than usual.

Since the murder, small mishaps in Jenin or the predictable scuffles in Ramallah aren't magnified into "riots" or "ambushes" in Israeli headlines. The Israelis, so encapsulated in their own sorrow, hardly notice that at this rate the West Bank may soon be increasingly under Palestinian rule. Together we see that, ironically, what Rabin was murdered for daring to implement is happening now at a quickened pace. "Two States for Two Peoples" (the Rapprochement slogan) is under way. I learn that there was no cheering over Rabin's death—not in Nablus, not in Ramallah or Jenin, not anywhere on the Palestinian street. Ordinary Palestinians have been sobered by Rabin's death out of fear, if not sadness, I'm told. Some of their leaders, including a few ex-terrorists, were truly saddened by this tragedy. Better than many Israelis or Palestinians, they know personally what undergoing a change of heart means. Many of them have had their own conversion experiences, the better to understand from the inside how Rabin-of-the-Intifada transformed into Rabin-of-the-Oslo-Accords.

I learn that several Nablus dialogue activists, my earliest Palestinian friends, had obtained passes to attend the peace rally, after which Rabin was murdered. Amid the singing and the speeches they heard the shots and felt the shock waves.

Though Rabin is no hero in Gaza or the West Bank, these Palestinians feel the pain that the great majority of Israelis are barely able to endure. They understand what Rabin meant for peace, and they wonder if his death will derail the process. In a Beit Sahur dialogue meeting, it's the Israelis who have to soothe and reassure Palestinians that in a democracy peace can't be killed through assassination (a fact that we will have to reassess and, for a time, recant). But, for now, theocracy versus democracy is a hot topic on both sides of the Green Line. From the depth of Islam and from the depth of Judaism, the pull to fundamentalism is fueled by a common fear of Westernization—every extremist's enemy. I find out that a few minutes before Yigal Amir raised his gun, he was watching a performance by hip, long-haired Israeli pop singer Avi Geffin. He's reputed to have muttered, "What's this society coming to? Who will sing next?"

•   •   •

Back in Cambridge after two weeks in Israel, I'm sitting at a low table facing a photo of Rabin which I've framed and set among lighted candles, surrounded with fresh flowers. The *Shalom Chaver* tapes that eulogize him in beautiful Hebrew music are playing in the background. I'm trying to bring back the spirit of shivah in Jerusalem.

I feel much as I did after each of my parents died. After each death it was as if the umbrella of my universe had been slit open, allowing bursts of icy wind to rush in—a cold current that lowered the temperature in the rest of my life. This coldness is what death leaves, especially the death of someone essential to the small world each of us holds dear: those figures, images and people who keep us intimate with life.

Rabin was part of my most essential cosmos because the peace process was my primary passion these past years and he was central to it. That's one reason I had such an overpowering response to his murder. Living and working in Israel, I was blessed to participate in all that he set in motion. I attended to the ups and downs of the process directly. As we who are parents tune in to our children, I felt shifts on the ground in an unmediated, intuitive way, saw how often the truth of a moment contrasted with the floating stereotypes. I've learned the hard way how much living in Jerusalem allowed me to know what isn't possible from afar. I miss that knowledge deeply.

As I stare blankly at the table in front of me, my eyes land on *The Invention of Solitude,* a book I've placed here as a reminder of the past two weeks in Israel, as I lived them. I pick it up and turn to the last page. I see that these words express what I need to do: to honor Rabin, to give meaning to what he set in motion, to keep alive my years in Jerusalem: I will write.

Auster paces in his room, overwhelmed by grief. He finds words too remote, is unable to write down what he knows, yet is committed to doing so. Writing will be my way too. Such a task seems as utterly necessary as it feels nearly impossible. I reread the last lines of his memoir. His words capture all I need to hear or say or write tonight: "It was. It will never be again. *Remember.*"

CHAPTER EIGHTEEN

Black Dreams and Blood-Red Streets: Israel Under Siege

On the grapes and oranges you gave me on a white plate: worry,
in the kitchen day worry, in the bedroom night worry
about a child getting killed; worry in the everyday gardens
of Jerusalem, on geraniums and roses from the time they bloom
in December, long as they live. In the desert wind
playing over the hair on a child's head and arms, worry.
In the morning you put on a soiled or clean shirt of worry
drink its tea. . . . I wish you the luxury of worrying about aging or money,
instead of a child getting killed,
that no mother or father should know the sorrow
that comes when there is nothing to worry about anymore.
                    —Stanley Moss, "A Guest in Jerusalem"

It's four months and one week since Rabin was killed. I'm counting the days on my calendar. I'm also listening to Miriam, my seatmate on this El Al plane, my first flight to Israel since the assassination.

"It's just like the Scud attacks," she says, referring to last week's suicide bus bombs. Two occurred on Jerusalem's number 18 bus, the third in Afula, the last in Tel Aviv, leaving many Israelis dead and all in shock.

"You never know where the next one will hit, you're just waiting," Miriam says. She pauses. "Everyone asks me, 'Why do you go home to Tel Aviv now? Why not stay in Chicago another month, as you planned?' They don't understand that when there's death or war in Israel, I need to be there." Miriam, a dead ringer for Leah Rabin, now talks of Prime Minister Peres. She raises her arms in despair. "He's all we've got. I'll vote for him in May. Even though he's put too much faith in Arafat, whose crackdown on the Palestinians is too little too late." I know what she means about getting back to Israel. I, too, wanted to hop the next plane after the fourth bomb went off in Tel Aviv, which happened on a Monday.

I was apartment-hunting in New York, in the midst of negotiating a rental, when the Jewish realtor mumbled, "Heard about the bus bomb in Israel?" What planet does he live on? I thought, amazed he was so slow to get the news; I'd just spent the day before, the second Sunday in a row, checking by phone with friends and their kids in Jerusalem. "Dizengoff," he continued, shaking his head. "In the heart of Tel Aviv."

"When?" I panicked.

"An hour ago," he said, motioning me to get back to negotiating with Sally, the owner of the building. Before the news about Tel Aviv, we were talking about bookshelves, rent, the times of garbage collection. I say to her, "My friends' kids hang out at Dizengoff Mall. Short of getting to Israel, I need CNN and a phone." Sally was sitting at her kitchen counter as I shifted into shock. She exclaimed cheerfully, "We love Jews here. Why don't they just get out of there? Give it up. Come to New York or Palm Beach."

I whispered, "Sally, let's keep that little thought to ourselves." She laughed, conceding, "I guess I don't know much about Israel. Giving up is so far out?"

This is a new angle, I thought, remembering yesterday when I was inundated with calls from Jewish acquaintances in Brookline and Newton, with more predictable reactions: "Decimate the West Bank." "Time to give up." And mostly: "Oslo was a total mistake." I kept saying, "A lot of decent people live there. We need to keep in touch with them, not decimate them." But what I was thinking about was Auster's words: "It will never be again. *Remember.*"

While waiting a week to make this trip, my initial urgency has given way to foreboding. In all my trips to Israel, this is the first time that I'm traveling in dread and fear. I feel fragile, picturing the horrors of war. In my section of the El Al jet, passengers pass around magazines, ferreting through the U.S. press for something, for anything, on the current, scary climate. Someone hands me an article by Israeli writer David Grossman in *Newsweek*. He says:

> *Fear masters everything: When you walk down the street you inspect all those who pass you with, as we say in Hebrew, seven eyes. Any one could be our murderer (and to your surprise you discover that in almost all of the familiar faces, you can discern some sort of sinister feature). . . . Should I stop for a drink at this stand, or wait until I reach the next one? . . . I find myself walking down a main street I have traversed since my boyhood . . . and my mind cuts that favorite landscape into little pieces. Everything is so fragile—the body, routine, family, the fabric of life.*

Yet Grossman doesn't shift visions:

Israelis are fired up demanding revenge and nullification of the entire peace process. . . . But even at this difficult hour Israel and moderate Palestinians must help each other in every possible way, because peace is the only promise for our grandchildren—I no longer believe it will be true for our children to live a life of security, normality, regularity, happiness.

On the next page, Sari Nusseibeh, a wise Palestinian teacher, echoes Grossman:

The best possible world for each society is in fact the best possible world for both. . . . Can an entire world be written off by isolated groups of fanatics? I consider this one of the darkest and most shameful periods in my history as a Palestinian and as a Muslim. . . . Such [violent] people do not understand pain, not even if it is inflicted on them, let alone if they inflict it on others. . . . Neither side will ever achieve the moral state of rest. . . . Neither side will feel complete or realized because each side will remain haunted by the other. . . . Hope exists . . . the challenge is stronger than ever . . . as in everything else, the interlocked Israeli and Palestinian societies are the most natural partners.

Up and down and across the aisles, we travelers hand around these articles the way visitors over the years have shared Frommer tour books. We read eagerly, as if we can possibly prepare ourselves psychologically to accurately anticipate what we're flying into.

On *Nightline* three nights back, Dave Marash, a veteran ABC journalist, hosted a revealing half-hour program while he was spending nine days covering the bus explosions. Crisscrossing from Israeli to Palestinian homes, Marash's camera crew showed sobbing Tel Aviv teenagers, bomb victims in hospitals, then entered Palestinian living rooms on the West Bank. Looking understandably exhausted, Marash showed compassion toward everyone he interviewed. Yet eventually he became most identified with Israeli pain, not because he was pro-Israel but because the Palestinians' reactions confounded him.

Those he interviewed weren't from the Hamas or its military arm, the Izz al-Qassam Brigade; they didn't openly support the suicide bombers. But they were a far cry from Sari Nusseibeh's levelheaded rationality. I share Marash's bafflement. Drinking tea among these gracious Palestinian people, he was confused because there was no straightforward grief among them, but rather zigzagging logic and uneven emotions. For example, one family's adult child was killed on the first Bus 18 explosion. They were sad, yet talked mainly about Israeli conspiracies (to blow themselves up?). This is what threw Marash off-center, leaving him speechless.

On the screen, he and his crew were then filming a pro-peace, anti-terror rally among Palestinians in the West Bank town of Kalkilya. His Arab-American translator was speaking for the several hundred people, mostly men and boys, who formed his backdrop. We saw them waving banners and shouting slogans. Suddenly, the translator turned from the camera and, in anger, burrowed through the crowds, jostling them while ignoring the ABC camera crews. Shouting in Arabic, he marked up their signs with his pen and scolded the leaders. What happened? The Palestinians had slipped from *anti-terror* to *anti-Israel* rhetoric. "Down with occupation," they'd begun to chant.

The translator tried to choreograph the crowd, yelling in English: "You're not *against Israel,* but *against Palestinian terror!* You're not *for* the suicide 'Engineer' Ayash [the mastermind of this terror], you're *against* him." This moment showed clearly the easy slippage from the "New Middle East" into the old.

What I saw was how terrorist attacks and counterattacks have thrown everyone back to square one. As the Hamas fractures and goes on bombing sprees, Israelis resort to reprisals (closure, house arrests, rounding up every possible suspect). The result is that Palestinian moderates on the street find rage magnetic. Like sleepwalkers, those under curfew move instantly back in time, while the Israelis blame all Arabs for a few men's crimes. "Not *against* occupation, *against* terror." The Intifada mindset is revived. The Israelis are in a murderous rage.

An hour off the plane and I'm waiting with my friend Shimon, Daphie's husband, on a long line at the motor vehicle bureau. It's on the third floor of a "mall" in downtown Jerusalem. I'm edgy, scrutinizing every face, truck, hauled box, random suitcase. These Jerusalem streets, usually jammed with cars and pedestrians at midday, are much quieter now. Shimon grew up on a northern kibbutz dodging bombs and carrying dead soldiers in his arms. Little seems to shake *him.* But I'm panicky and desperately want to get into Shimon's apartment, where I'm staying during this visit. "Home" is the only place where vigilance abates. I realize that the phrase "house arrest" has taken on a new meaning. The Palestinians are once again forced into theirs. We in Israel have the choice to go out, but for many it's a Sarajevo moment: bread or death.

I find the simplest decisions are no longer simple. Do I go to Mahane

Yehuda market or skip it? Should I drive to Tel Aviv or play it safe? Should I hurry and take my cappuccino to go? Such questions will subside, but right now a pandemic anxiety is forcing everyone I know into superstitious mind games. Yet, how can I come halfway around the world to stay inside? My body decides for me. Jet-lagged, I sleep for fifteen hours.

Late on the following afternoon, after watching, with friends, the highlights of an anti-terrorist summit on TV, one President Clinton has called in Egypt's Sharm el-Sheikh ("Charm those sheiks," someone jokes), I brave walking to the local cafe on busy Azza Street. Clinton is said to be en route from Egypt via Tel Aviv, is due to arrive at Jerusalem's Laromme Hotel within hours. Police are everywhere. This makes the streets feel safer. Yet, even in early evening, they're completely empty, quieter than on Yom Kippur. No cars are allowed on any roads. But I see no one walking around either. It's beyond surreal.

I chat with a soldier "from up north," a young man with an angelic face, not unlike many of the young Israelis in their army. He's smart, almost effete, the kind of kid you find lovable the minute you meet him because he's lacking in guile. He's also visibly depleted after daily fifteen-hour shifts.

We talk on the street corner, then enter the Cafe Moment together. "How do you know who to trust?" I ask.

"It's all in the eyes. The body doesn't lie," he answers.

"But now everyone's afraid," I say.

"The terror maniacs, their eyes are different. They're cold. Their bodies are rattled," he says. We sit down at the cafe counter and order coffee. The owner leans over to us, saying that his business has dropped by half this week, but he's sure it will return to normal, "after a full week without bombings." As we talk, a disheveled man enters. He's wearing a thin black jacket, and his eyes look shifty to me. He plops down two seats away from us. I study him while the soldier and the owner continue to talk. At very best, he looks unsavory. I nudge the soldier. "Did you check him out?" I ask.

"It's not polite to pick on everyone who looks strange," he answers softly. Without looking around, the soldier then says: "That one's drunk, in a bad way, but he's no killer."

"But you didn't even look," I say.

"I looked," he whispers, as the man orders two beers.

•   •   •

The following day the Israeli government goes ahead with its controversial plan—to destroy "The Engineer's" home. The engineer, Yahiya Ayash, the man behind the bombings, was killed two months ago by the very Israeli Shin

Bet officers who failed to protect Rabin. They did so with great technological fanfare, blowing him up through his portable cell phone in Gaza. This Israeli show of ingenuity (and retribution) is seen by Palestinians as reprehensible; they could have simply arrested him instead. And even moderate Israelis view this action as unfortunate, as twisted showmanship—more about machismo to compensate for not protecting Rabin than about removing a menace to Israel's security. The sophisticates on both sides well know this action was doomed, counterproductive. And in fact, Ayash's dramatic murder is the reason given for the recent bombing reprisals by Hamas. And now it's Israel's turn for another reprisal. It takes place in the tiny hamlet of Ramat, near Ramallah.

After endless delays, during which both the Palestinian and Israeli press corps endure hours of waiting on cold rocks in bone-chilling rain, the Ayash home is blown up. And with the exact amount of dynamite used in the last bombing in Tel Aviv. Not an eye for an eye, but a liter of TNT for a liter of TNT. While this is occurring, I attend a small press conference with Peres and Clinton. Peres's skin has a gray pallor; his eyes are swollen. Though his words are forceful, he looks ill. No one else at the press conference agrees. "He's just tired," friends who live here respond. But having been away from Israel since Rabin's murder, I'm certain that Peres has altered; he looks much older than he did last November.

As the two leaders speak and take questions, I watch Clinton. He must be exhausted, but he paces himself. Standing erect, he meditates with his head down, as if entering a beta zone. Journalists line up at a microphone with questions. Once one is asked, he stays quiet until the switch of his thought blinks on. Then he looks up, suddenly alert, responding clearly to all expected queries, especially ones about the upcoming Israeli elections. Clinton likes this repartee and his love for Israel encircles the mostly Jewish press—Israeli, foreign and White House corps—with warmth. He's behind Israel and Peres and the peace process 100 percent. A dim thought about the consequences of America's pro-Israel stance occurs, then flits away.

The action now moves to Rabin's grave site. A hot day was predicted, but it's cold, gray, raining on and off. There are only twenty of us here, mostly photographers and the American press corps. It takes over an hour to disassemble and check every camera, microphone and portable telephone, even though we've all passed through intensive security twice already this morning.

We wait. Finally, Clinton arrives with Leah Rabin. In front of the grave, she points out to him the new headstone, placed there a few weeks ago. Then she lays a bouquet of roses on top of her husband's resting place. Clinton takes a few stones that he's brought from the White House lawn from his pocket. Following Jewish tradition, he places them on Rabin's tombstone. Then he does his meditation routine again. His face flushes red. His eyes close as his mouth draws far down, forming a single sad line that reaches to the bottom of his chin. He takes Leah Rabin's hand as he tears up.

Seeing this, I also start to cry, a burst of feeling so in contrast to the edgy boredom of the last few hours; in contrast also to everyone around me. The professionals are shooting pictures. For them, this grave is by now familiar turf. I realize that I'm not only crying over Rabin's death, but equally for what may be the grave site for this attempt at peace.

Exactly as Clinton bows his head, the sky lightens. The rain stops and a slight glitter is reflected on Rabin's tomb. The light that weakly emerges from the darkened sky strikes me as a good metaphor for our collective consciousness. For no one knows who will win this upcoming election between Bibi Netanyahu and Shimon Peres. And beyond that, no one knows what's to become of the peace process, whoever wins. All around Israel, that play of dark and dim light fills the minds of many. No one knows where the next bomb will go off, or if Hamas will stop their killings. No one knows how we're to move forward after three weeks of chilling, wanton destruction.

There's a silent five-minute ceremony and then we all depart. Clinton heads for Tel Aviv. The press bus drops the rest of us off at a downtown Jerusalem street corner during rush hour. It's raining again. I can't remember where I parked my car and so I run toward a parking lot that, as luck would have it, turns out to be the Egged bus depot. Red and white buses are everywhere. "Keep away from buses," everyone warns. Lost, I run between them. With no one else around, I feel frenzied, while I also realize how ludicrous is the notion of complete security. The brutal truth is that we have no idea where it's safe, where it's not. I run up a hill and try to enter an official building, only to find a rope of metal chains dangling; it's locked from inside. I look down at the central bus station, at the main post office, at the rush hour crowds. Suddenly, I'm struck by the fact that the tens of millions of dollars Israel is spending on security devices is absurd. The only security is trust, and since Oslo we've never been further from achieving that.

I also notice how fears for my own safety dissipate, replaced by ordinary concerns, what's true for most Israelis. I'm busy thinking, Where's my car? Then, finding it, I'm busy getting to my next appointment on time. This is the way we live with terror, I realize: We don't think of it continuously. The mind simply can't hold immediate concerns and feed abstract terrors at the same time. It's still rush hour, and stuck in traffic, I listen to Clinton on the radio speaking from Tel Aviv. I get absorbed in his talk about the need to conquer fear and pursue peace.

Then he lavishes praise on Jewish Israelis, saying, "Overcoming persecution is the genius of the Jewish people." Growing rhapsodic, he adds that Israelis conquered the desert, made it bloom, and in Tel Aviv took a pile of sand and transformed it. I'm moved. But I'm also more awake, and now know what earlier I'd vaguely sensed: that Clinton is dangerously close to Chaim Weizmann's phrase: "This is a land without a people for a people without a land."

Clinton's support for Israel isn't evenhanded and will undoubtedly unhinge the Palestinians. (It does.) This speech from the American who is supposed to be an honest broker will make them irate. (It does.) If I were a Palestinian, I'd be furious, too, for we Jews are not the only victims here, though we're the most recent, and, right now, the most innocent. But, we are not the only ones with rightful claims to this land. Though I'm glad Clinton is consoling us, if anyone is ever to be truly safe in Israel, we need the Palestinians to have their own realistic hopes as well.

On Friday evening I arrive at the Greens' house for *Shabbat* dinner in the mixed Jerusalem neighborhood of Abu Tor, where they have lived for over a decade. I find Judith is quiet. Just back from Nablus after several other meetings in Beit Sahur this week, she's melancholy. Usually, we brim with ideas and trade lively information. Tonight, her silence says, Dialogue is not going well. She says she was too enervated to go to synagogue tonight. Soon, she adds, "Did you know it's been declared a crime for Israelis to visit the West Bank? That we have to send videotapes by courier, back and forth from Nablus to Jerusalem?" I don't ask how *she* got there, if she went before or after this new edict. I do ask, "But personal relations with your Palestinian friends are fine?" She nods. "Yes, they all called after the bombings," she answers. Then she reflects, "But what's purely personal here?" As she speaks, I realize I haven't spoken to a single Palestinian in months. In a strange way, I'm back to where I began in September 1991 when I moved to Jerusalem and knew only Jews.

Judith went to Wellesley with Hillary Clinton and met with her recently in Jerusalem. "Maybe we should write the Clintons about dialogue, not munitions," I suggest tepidly. Judith gives me a look that says, "Wake up. You're in last year's dream."

I step outside to the Greens' backyard. As always, I savor this wide view of the Judean hills in the distance, the sounds of Arabic prayers intermingling with Hebrew sounds. As always, the birds of Jerusalem sound more lively than birds elsewhere. How I love the scented air, these vistas opening beyond the fig, apricot and pomegranate trees in her yard. Again, I'm smitten with the way daylight gradually turns to twilight over this desert. But this evening, the beauty combines with images of death.

The next day, I relish the sun and the rest that floats from house to house on *Shabbat*. Even though the Hamas is threatening new attacks, I now feel safe. Jerusalem's streets are filled with people walking leisurely in the warmth. Everything seems normal after thirteen days and no bombings, even though Israel's most respected newspaper, *Ha'aretz,* just reported a foiled Hamas bomb at Ben-Gurion Airport, where I'll soon be heading. I'm calm now. Before leaving, I call to check in with Jon and Anna Immanuel. Anna, a jazz singer and writer, doesn't share my new feelings of ease. "This reminds me of the Warsaw Ghetto. My mother was a teenager in Poland then. She thought it was ridiculous to obey orders, to let fear infect her. She loved music and so she'd slip out of the ghetto to hear violin concertos at night. And now my teenager refuses all *my* injunctions, slips onto Bus 18 every morning, is driving me crazy." Jon, who still covers the West Bank for the *Jerusalem Post,* is more sanguine. "I'm out there every day," he says. "The majority I meet in the territories are strongly against terror attacks."

I pack up, as sad to leave for the States as I was scared when arriving here a week ago. What felt so dangerous from afar and during my first few days (and what still terrifies others) no longer frightens me. The tightest closure of Israeli-Palestinian borders in history has, despite the hardships created for the Palestinians, made Israel proper temporarily safer. It has also, of course, driven people back into primitive ethnic solidarity.

Driving to the airport, I am dispirited not only about leaving, but also about this setback. Coexistence and mutual recognition have everywhere been replaced by talk of fences, borders, separation. Not exactly what we "moderates" have been hoping for. Entering the terminal, I literally bump into Shuki. He's just dropped off a tourist. After two long years we look at each other. He quickly pulls me to him in a huge bear hug, one that seems as much a desire to hide his face as an expression of fondness. I feel the poignancy of what we had together, what we lost. He looks vulnerable, talking of our adventures, all those exotic, erotic travels. But before we reach full-blown nostalgia, Shuki's face shifts from longing into a glower, an expression I remember all too well. "I suppose you're going to tell me that the suicide bombers were just having a hard year?"

"You want to know what I really think? Those killers are basically good-hearted, are just in need of a little therapy," I say.

We burst out laughing. And then we share an honest, bittersweet hug.

"See you at the elections," he calls out as I head upstairs.

Part V
The World Is Upside Down

Yitzhak Rabin . . . stood on the White House lawn for the ceremony of signing the Oslo accord. For Rabin, it was the moment at which the countdown began that culminated in his assassination two years later. . . .

"Netanyahu is good for the Jews," the Chabadniks let it be known with posters and car stickers on the eve of the 1996 elections. The main thing that marked his three years in power was that religious and secular, Sephardim and Ashkenazim, moved poles apart from one another. . . . Netanyahu received . . . the used toy [he] called the State of Israel and he began turning it over and over, as though pondering what to do with it.

"The secular public are Hebrew-speaking *goys*," Brig. Gen. Ya'akov Amidror, the deputy head of Military Intelligence, pronounced as he straightened the knitted kippa on his brow.

"The leftists," Netanyahu whispered into the ear of the venerable kaballist Rabbi Kedouri, "have forgotten what it is to be Jews."

—*From "Here Comes the Millennium,"
Assaf Inbari in* Ha'aretz *magazine*

CHAPTER NINETEEN

Inside a Shipwreck:
Scenes from an Israeli Election

Five days before the Israeli elections scheduled for May 30, I'm once again on a plane from New York to Tel Aviv. On the small movie screen, a telegenic young Israeli woman is swirling silk scarves, performing a modern jazz routine. Her body undulates like a flag in the breeze; each movement is enhanced by computerized pyrotechnics. The backdrop is Masada, I see; this dancer symbolizes the "New Middle East."

The Israeli sitting next to me runs a software company. Like almost everyone on this plane, he's flying home to vote. He hums happily, fingering small computers and then tiny digital calculators. "Israelis have more fun," I say. He nods because, for him, it's true. He's going to Israel not only to vote for Oslo (and Peres) but equally for the influx of astro-dollars, the booming economy, Israel's growth in technology—what coalesces up on the screen—Masada in cyberspace.

In the mini-van from the airport, I'm with a family of Haredim, ultra-Orthodox Jews who've come to Israel for the unveiling of their mother's gravestone one year after her death. One of the daughters, Rachel, volunteers that she's nearing fifty. She wears a wig and an ankle-length skirt. Despite my secular garb, we fall into a lively conversation, discovering that we both made *aliyah* and then both had to leave Israel. She, too, much prefers Israel to life in New York. We talk of "the path not taken," of how our lives would have such different shapes had we been able to stay here.

No one in this van can vote, but this family is rooting for Bibi Netanyahu. "Peres is far too naive," Rachel says. "But many Palestinians are naive as well," I tell them, keeping a neutral voice. One man mumbles, "Let the Arabs stay naive." Then, echoing Bibi's motto, he adds, "That's good for the Jews."

At Daphie and Shimon's, I walk in just in time to catch the only televised debate between Peres and Netanyahu. At stake is Peres's bid to keep his lead and his office as prime minister. Throughout the hour-and-a-half debate, he's stiff and expressionless while the cameras lap up "Bibi's" winks and practiced hand gestures, products of his American media savvy. The contrast is so painful I can hardly watch because I sense defeat. The next day at Beit Agron, the journalist's center this week, assorted members of the international press arrive to listen to one, then another, representative of the many small Knesset parties who are giving their election pitch.

There's a peculiar quality to this democratic ritual as a cavalcade of marginal viewpoints are each put forward. We hear the Hadash Israeli-Arab Knesset member, Hashem Mahameed, whose constituents may vote *against* Bibi, not *for* Peres. In the recent Lebanon mini-war this past March, Peres ordered bombings and "accidentally" killed over a hundred civilian Palestinians in a refugee camp in Qana, Lebanon. The Arab Israelis, who were once in his pocket, have turned against him. Many don't plan to vote at all.

An Islamic Israeli from Nazareth speaks next, describing his party's platform: to work against Israel as a Jewish state. He describes his position matter-of-factly. The mostly Jewish journalists don't balk but keep taking notes. Then Yitzhak Meir, of the National Religious party, a man who seems good-natured, begins. He wins everyone's attention until he goes off on a long tangent no journalist in this room can follow. A reporter from Belgium whispers to me, "Is there anyone sane in this country?"

Tired of this bizarre parade of oratory and hoping to capture the mood of the campaign's final days, I drive with friends to the middle-class neighborhood of Beit Hakerem. While they get busy distributing literature for Meretz, the human rights, pro-peace party, I wander around to look for those all-important undecided voters. The ones I've interviewed since I've come here have each said they'd have chosen Rabin over Netanyahu, but have decided on Bibi over Peres. Each repeats some variant of "I can't relate to Peres," or "I'll shut my eyes and pull for Bibi."

Near a shopping strip, I meet a woman who says that she, just this hour, made up her mind . . . for Netanyahu. She's standing with her father who grew up in the 1920s and 1930s in Jerusalem's Old City with "Arab neighbors." He's for Peres, she says, "because he knows the Arabs. But we don't."

"Why Bibi?" I ask.

"Because then the peace process will slow down. And we'll have more time to create trust between us. Our generation needs to meet Arabs. If the process goes slowly, we can educate our kids and their kids about each other." Just as I'm about to argue that speed (Peres's line from the day of the Handshake: "You don't leap over a chasm in two steps") would help forge such connections, she wards me off. "Please," she says, "I've just made up my mind. I don't want to think it over again." Her father looks at me ruefully, shrugging, "What can I do? She has her own beliefs."

I drive back downtown to the Holiday Inn, a newly rebuilt skyscraper hotel in modern Jerusalem. The journalists cram into an airless basement as more candidates for the many Knesset parties are due to speak. Jerusalem's new Likud mayor, Ehud Olmert, is debating Labor Minister of Health Ephraim Sneh. Olmert's detractors refer to him as "the snake." Up close, I can see why. He acts nonchalant, yet with his nimble mind and clever tongue, he can shift an argument with a mere vocal intonation. His description of Orient House in East Jerusalem, for example, the PLO meeting place since Oslo, conjures the image of a hotbed for gun-toting terrorists, not the shabbily elegant house frequented by upper-crust East Jerusalem Palestinians—the place where they greet visiting dignitaries, hold meetings and invite the press. Labor Minister Sneh offers a limp response, as if Orient House *is* built of dynamite.

During a break I go upstairs to the lobby for coffee. Fresh air is blowing in through the front doors, making me feel more alert than I was down in the stifling basement. The lobby cafe is crowded and merry. At a nearby table I watch a group of ten intense Sephardic men who are studying piles of paper spread out before them. They look unkempt, as if they haven't slept, or like gamblers after an all-night session. Smoking like mad and guzzling coffee, they work at their littered table, tallying numbers. My guess is that they're campaign workers for the Likud. I know all too well how the Labor and Meretz Ashkenazim look down on them, the *frechim*—a racial slur I struggled to understand during my relationship with Shuki.

Loosely translated, *frechim* means "primitive," and is used to refer to families who emigrated from North Africa or the Orient, the ones considered uneducated, who are still second-class citizens. When I was living with Shuki, this was a subculture I grew to know intimately. So I'm well acquainted with the Sephardic point of view—how they see us Ashkenazim, with our airs of superiority, as infuriatingly condescending. While "we" go off to the university, "they" try to make a living by driving tourists, save to buy taxi medallions, then often gamble their bounty away and are forced to begin all over again. Taxi drivers, restaurant workers, grocers and gofers, these Israelis embody the energy that makes Israel feel so alive. They don't benefit economically from the peace process; they don't create computer software of women undulating at the hip in front of Masada. Instead, they take tourists to the Masada of "never again."

Though Shuki and I fought over the Palestinians, what most fueled his rage was what he saw as my Ashkenazi privilege and my friends' denigration of him. As I watch these men working furiously over their papers, I remember how Shuki always felt on edge when he was with my friends. He imagined, correctly as it turned out, that they saw him as unworthy of or attempting to con me. I'm well versed in the rage of the Sephardim against us, the Ashkenazim.

One man at the next table has a soft, vulnerable face. When he gets up and passes by me, I say politely, "It's none of my business, but what are you guys doing?" To my surprise he snaps, "Exactly. None of your business," as his cohorts glare. I'm flashing back to my fights with Shuki as this group leaves the hotel, driving off in a huge white van with Mayor Olmert. I see their smiles and hearty backslaps as a bad omen.

Down in the airtight basement again, a poised woman outlines the platform of her "Third Way" party, a group whose main focus is on the Golan Heights. She says that her people are ready to work with either Labor or Likud, whichever party will assure that no negotiations with Syria are implemented. Next, a long-winded Natan Sharansky aide (from Yisrael B'Aliyah, the Russian immigrant party) who's from Canada, not Russia, begins speaking. He goes on far past his allotted ten minutes, meandering from his political point: that 65 percent of Russian immigrants who have Ph.D.s or M.D.s are still relegated to menial work. Some who directed hospitals in the Ukraine or Moscow now collect urine samples, even after years of living here. Then he takes a long detour about his own life in America and Canada as we journalists drop all pretense of note-taking.

Finally, Naomi Chazan takes the stage. A powerful speaker, she's especially passionate tonight. A native-born Israeli and professor at Hebrew University, she was elected to the Knesset in 1992 from Meretz. Chazan is widely admired for being articulate and unusually cogent. Her first words wake up the room. "I'm sorry the candidates for prime minister have blurred their boundaries because the differences between Labor and Likud—between Peres and Netanyahu—are vast," she begins. She then delineates what Meretz stands for: peace and justice for Palestinians (and for Israeli Arabs as well), equality for women (Jewish *and* Arab) and social justice for the Sephardim. Listening, I find myself wishing *she* was running for prime minister. Increasingly, I'm aware of how ineffectual Peres's campaign is. His Labor party has mismanaged him, falling into the trap of not disputing the Likud's Arab-bashing. Peres has refused to educate voters and has avoided any discussion of Rabin's legacy and all that they shared. Their campaign doesn't explain *why* Rabin changed his point of view, thereby changing Israel.

When the panel breaks up, I rush to catch up with Naomi Chazan. I want to tell her how much her words have energized and given me a needed perspective. I tell her how much I always learn from her, adding that I wish Peres could publicly generate what she does—seemingly without effort. I'm smiling with praise but she doesn't look at me, though we've met many times. She looks down while vigorously inhaling on her cigarette: "Peres has my vote and your vote. He talks the way he does to win the seven percent who are undecided," she says, talking to the floor. But, I wonder, how can the undecided decide if Peres won't speak out? Chazan doesn't answer; she walks away.

As I drive toward East Jerusalem, I'm wondering about those on the left whose positions don't seem to mesh with their attitudes. However brilliant Naomi Chazan is about social justice, if she's snobbish toward me, how much do such words mean? I then ponder the rampant racism of Bibi's new slogan: "Bibi is good for the Jews." This is *not* countered by Labor or Meretz, though these parties are in the forefront of the coalition with Israeli Arabs, in partnership with Arafat and the Palestinians in the territories. Establishment liberals or leftists haven't spoken out during this campaign. By withholding their views, they add credibility to the Likud's fear-mongering.

I arrive in East Jerusalem to the loud drone of helicopters overhead. I imagine how the election would look from up there, high above. What I see is that this vote is being held with guns pointed at the Arabs all around us—the territories are clamped shut; the "mistaken" bombing of Qana, that senseless bloodbath. Something is very wrong with this picture. Why was Peres withdrawn during his TV debate, when, in person, he has a genius for opening minds? The few breakfasts for the foreign press I've attended with him were filled with his insights about Mideast realities. A memorable speech is one he uttered early one morning, over a year ago. "In five years (or in ten, if we're very lucky), Iran and Iraq will have nuclear and biological weapons. We'd be wise to shore up our allegiances with the Palestinians now; if we drag out negotiations and stall in making compromises, Israel will be far more vulnerable to future war. This nitpicking with Palestinians—where each detail is treated as life-threatening—is not in our interest. It's utterly counterproductive because *time is not on our side.* We will look back at this period as one of tiny skirmishes, once Iran begins aiming sophisticated weapons our way. If we hold to that vision, we'd wrap up negotiations with Arafat and his people in no time. It's easy to make deals when Israelis feel urgent. But that urgency is *not* easy to create." The man who spoke these words is sleeping, or worse, through this election. I don't feel his presence but his absence. "Peres would lose if he ran against himself," one of my cynical friends has commented.

On Salah el-Din Street, I meet Achmed and a friend who arrive from an out-lying Arab town. It's good to be with him, to be here in this East Jerusalem mul-ticultural cafe, a meeting place for artists, writers and filmmakers from both sides. We order hummus and tahini downstairs where a Jewish jazz pianist, a close friend of Judith's, is playing. I relax into the music, the simple beauty, the bohemian ambiance and our conversation. With Achmed and his friend, talk is soft; they are so patient, I think. I'm remembering what James Hillman wrote, long ago: "The true revolutionary is he or she who stays true to depression." Those words puzzled me and came alive only after repeated visits to the West Bank, seeing how Palestinians are loyal to suffering. However politically mad-dening or suicidal is their stoical acceptance of grief, in person it allows for shared soulfulness. They know that you're sad too, whoever you are. This way of bearing ill fate affects me powerfully. It's not necessary to be "on" with them. I settle into myself tonight, as so often in the past, finding the tone of their soft voices an invitation to enter all the hidden layers of myself. I tell Achmed what I've been thinking. He says we should order our food.

While enveloped in kindness in this small East Jerusalem cafe, for the thou-sandth time, I think how Israelis are great at generating joy, are able to usher anyone who's willing into the upbeat, manic side of life, whereas most Pales-tinians nourish an interiority, a sensitivity to pain that slows time down, that lengthens any given moment. After all the politics, harangues, irrelevancies, slogans and stress of this election, tonight's ambiance is a gift I savor. Achmed says, "It's so good to see you relax. It's like the old days, when you lived here. These short trips, all jet lag; they can't keep up; I've found a school for you to look at for Eliza." He hands me a paper that's clearly written, stating a direc-tor's name, the number of students in each class at a learning program for dyslexia. It's in the West Bank; Arabic is spoken in the school. Most unrealis-tic, but so thoughtful of him. Now I relax into food, music, friendship. The best things in life aren't free, but they aren't expensive either, I think, sitting in the rich poverty of East Jerusalem. Only later will I realize that not hearing a word about the elections was not a good sign, was a sign that the Israeli Pales-tinians would sit out this vote.

Two days later I'm back in Israel proper, surrounded by manic conversa-tions on election day. Peres is safely ahead in the polls and there's a wild holi-day feeling afloat. After voting, many Israelis swim or sit outside, chatting in cafes. In my favorite hangout, Cafe Moment on Azza Street, the customers cluster at street-side tables and share hilarious Bibi stories. This is the fun of Is-rael; strangers are not strangers for long. Though I learned this on my first week here, I've gotten better at using this pandemic friendliness while working as a journalist. Today is a perfect example of such instantaneous intimacy. The sun is blazing; we're pulling open our umbrellas as we listen to a man who knows firsthand about a fiasco over an apartment Bibi bought on this very street. The story, true or not I never verify, though I've heard bits of it all week: During massive renovations on his new apartment, a floor caved in and destroyed his downstairs neighbors' ceiling. Bibi refused to pay the damages so the neighbor took him to court, only to find that he had a long line of similar lawsuits. "He's the cheapest man in this country," the storyteller says. The phrase creates laughter, since to be the cheapest person in Israel is a feat.

Bibi anecdotes, not unlike Dan Quayle jokes, feed on themselves and give a mildly malicious comfort to those of us who fear him, which includes everyone at this leftish, hip cafe. Talia, a beautiful woman who has typical Israeli features (jet black hair, sparkling black eyes, a thin face and lively manner), says that she grew up with him, went to the same schools and often attended parties at his house. She has everyone's attention. We're leaning over the table, all eager to catch every word. Talia says that though he did obtain his much touted degree from MIT and is supposedly academically smart like his erudite dad, a writer, he didn't have life smarts in elementary school. "No one thought of him as especially bright," she says, "not when compared to his svelte, to-die-for older brother, Yoni." Talia pauses; she seems to be recollecting Yoni's beauty.

"Bibi was the social dyslexic," she continues. "Bumbling, awkward, *not* quick-witted. It was Yoni who was facile and funny, the really brilliant one. Only after Yoni's death [he was the only Israeli killed leading a raid to free highjacked Israelis at Entebbe, Uganda, in 1976] did Bibi build his career on his brother's memory." As we part ways, I realize that we've been dissecting the least-known Israeli politician for hours, but that no one has mentioned that *he might win.* Were we avoiding the coming reality? Is this a sign? I tell myself to stop looking for omens, for we'll know soon enough. Anyway, today wasn't about politics; it was about enjoying typical Israeli gossip on a gorgeous day.

The polls close at 9 P.M. At the last minute, I decide not to join the crowds at the Likud or Labor headquarters in Tel Aviv, but to watch the election at the home of Shimon's best friend, Eitan, who has a lavish apartment in the German Colony, a well-heeled and charming neighborhood. In his living room there are three televisions going at once: Israel's Channel 1 (Haim Yavin), Israel's Channel 2 (Gadi Sukenik) and CNN, which translates the others and then adds its own coverage. Tonight's host is Christiane Amanpour, who's here in Tel Aviv.

At precisely 10 P.M., the results are announced based on exit polls, much like in the States. Peres is the winner. Within minutes, anchormen on both Israeli stations interview Yossi Beilin and Yossi Sarid, the Labor and Meretz leaders, respectively. They're discussing the makeup of the new cabinet, the composition of the just-elected Knesset. Despite large votes for the small, anti-peace parties, the peace process still has enough advocates elected and so will be on track. Only Christiane Amanpour keeps insisting that the full vote is not in. I find her attitude odd. Aren't these sample polls known to be definitive?

At Eitan's house everyone is relieved by the results. Yet even after Peres has won, there's an emotional dullness at the center of the room. Why are we not euphoric? Maybe because the race was so close? Maybe because we're all remembering the last election and are grieving for Rabin?

At midnight everyone leaves. Tomorrow there's work for the adults, school for the kids. But in Shimon and Daphie's guest room, I can't move away from or turn off the TV, even after everyone else in the house has gone to bed. I'm mesmerized by the colorful graphs for Knesset seats, by the pie-shaped blue and red circle that's almost evenly split between Netanyahu and Peres. Peres keeps his lead, as expected. Commentators, professors and politicians are talking faster than usual in Hebrew. I can't grasp a word they say, but I watch their expressions and keep an eye on the circular graph: red representing Peres's votes; blue, Bibi's.

At 3:30 A.M., I see the proportions have shifted. Peres's red grows slightly smaller as Netanyahu's blue eats into the Labor half of the pie. Is this a temporary bump? The Haredim vote just in? Or could this be the upheaval I've intuited since the hour I arrived? CNN has long been off the air vis-à-vis these elections, so I race outside, barefoot, into a warm Jerusalem night. Needing to talk to someone, I jump into my aged blue Renault and drive to an all-night market. The guys inside are shouting as I enter, "We've won! Bibi's in!"

Equally certain are a group of teenagers walking along the Tayelet before dawn. As the sun rises, Likud youngsters near the Knesset confirm that it's an upset, that Bibi's won, if only by a slight margin. Then they tell me why Bibi smiled at his loss last night, why he didn't concede the election. (What he said, grinning widely, was "it's not over till it's over.") Now, I learn that he knew the ultra-Orthodox had executed a plan to trick the pollsters, to purposely lie about voting for Peres in order to make his own victory more dramatic and more crushing for Peres's supporters. Driving around Jerusalem at dawn, I'm in shock. I also know that in less than an hour, half the country will wake to painful chagrin, the other half to euphoric joy.

Sure enough, with morning, we who've lost enter the first stage of grief—

denial. We use nearly identical words: "Maybe it won't be so bad. . . . Remember Menachem Begin and the Sinai. . . . Maybe the right wing can finish the peace that Rabin and Peres started. . . . Bibi loves power; he won't do what he claimed in the campaign; he won't be crazy enough to start a new Intifada or build new settlements, as he promised. . . . He can't respond violently to every Palestinian flare-up. . . . Maybe he'll dump Ariel Sharon and withdraw from Hebron. . . . Ex-Minister of Defense Moshe Arens isn't half bad. . . . Dan Meridor is in Likud; he's good . . . the Likud has some wise men. . . . David Levy for foreign minister? . . . Harmless, he'll just go to Paris for haircuts. . . . Netanyahu's no fool," we assure each other; "surely he'd rather hang out with Clinton and powerful sheikhs than with the ultra-religious Haredim. . . . He's secular, four marriages before age forty."

But we who are so smart are not so smart this morning. My friends and cafe mates are spinning scenarios, even as we ask each other, "Are we in denial? Are we rationalizing?" In a few days most will not remember what they've said today. I drop in to visit Jon and Anna Immanuel and find them sitting out on their terrace, annoyed by TVs blasting louder than usual from apartments below them, inhabited by Russian immigrants. In his meticulous, ironic tone, Jon asks, "I gave our Russian neighbors some potted plants a few months ago, with one condition. That they water them every day. They did, until today. Could they feel so empowered by winning seven Knesset seats that now they won't deign to water our Anglo plants? Is that possible? In only one day?"

We all laugh. "Yes, it is," someone says.

Alison, politically active in Meretz, counted votes at the polls all during the night. In her kitchen, she looks dazed. "It was sweet sitting among the different social groups while tallying the ballots. It was interesting to meet the other Israelis. They weren't hostile or crazy, nothing like the extreme settlers. It was a good vibe. Maybe the right wing and the Likud need to play out their scenarios for a couple of years. I bet they'll come around," she says. Three days later she only dimly remembers saying this, is worried sick about her teenaged son in the army, afraid that the West Bank will go up in flames because the Palestinians will lose all hope.

During the last hours before I pack up to leave, I walk around Jerusalem. And what I see is a complete upheaval in consciousness, a reversal not only of power, but of mood. Imagine walking around Manhattan and seeing the working poor *not* trudging off subways, exhausted, but singing in the streets—while those of us with classier jobs are sitting along park benches, morose and dejected. Picture this and you'll glimpse what I see tonight.

Yet even in shock, something about this turnabout, this seesaw in destinies seems . . . fair. Why? Because we were so busy trying to make sure that the Palestinians got a better deal that we forgot to be fair to a whole class of Israelis—those without our leisure, our access to education, our more comfortable homes. And, mostly, those who aren't free to live a life of the mind, to see everything from eight or ten angles—that greatest of luxuries. We've been arrogant, I think, as I walk in and out of Sephardic-owned groceries, knowing that our fantasies of a multicultural life have neglected a large culture that's right in our midst. And now we've lost to them and had better begin getting to know these "other Israelis."

Anna drops in just before I leave for the airport to offer me a novel for the airplane. A novel? I look at her in amazement. What storyteller, what Scheherazade or Tolstoy could spin a tale equal to the dramas unfolding around us on this tiny spot of magical land? What writer could dream up these scenes and this cast of characters: The Haredim with their hundred-year-old *rebbe* dispensing religious orders to vote for Bibi? Russian immigrant doctors turned janitors and voting for the Likud? The Ethiopian Jews, recently enraged to find their blood was dumped from the national blood bank? What scenario could compare to the Mizrachi (Sephardic) Jews from Arab countries who look most like the Arabs but hate them fiercely? Or the bitter rivalries among tiny Israeli Arab political factions?

Nothing I read tonight could hold a candle to this living plot: the Chinese torture of a sure win at midnight, upturned at dawn . . . the view of Shimon Peres, slumped in his dark-windowed, bulletproof car, while Bibi, the man who was a joke yesterday, is raising his arms in an awkward Nixonian V . . . the news, repeated hourly, that Rabin's assassin, Yigal Amir, who cast his vote in 1995 with his gun, was first on line in prison to vote by ballot . . . and this denouement: that millions in the Mideast will have radically altered lives because of *a few thousand Israeli votes.*

Just before I leave, I stop at another grocery store to buy Turkish coffee to spice up my life in the States. The owners, shoppers and errand boys here all are beaming. We think they're dead wrong, yet (what stage of grief is this?) it's fascinating and important to see how they feel, which is exactly how many of us felt while watching the Handshake on the White House lawn: victorious. To know that we're about to face emotions they've endured: horror, dread, our world coming apart. I watch as if it's a movie (if this is denial, it's also an imaginative opening) how in this moment, when so many on the Israeli streets are feeling joyous, I can't yet feel defeated. I'm too absorbed by the spectacle of those we kept invisible—the Sephardim, the Russian immigrants, the Ethiopians, the working poor—all of whom are coming joyously into visibility, feeling, a new power. I think of Shuki and his friends' exclusion from the university and from select positions in every area of life here, and seeing the happiness around me, part of me thinks: Good for them. And then my mind opens to this insight, for what it's worth: that the way I briefly felt diminished by Naomi Chazan was the barest taste of what these people chronically feel—invisible.

The cabdrivers, postal workers and shopkeepers voted not only against peace but against their second-class position in Israeli society. I don't pretend to understand all the nuances, but I do intuit the social dynamic. For the ideological settlers did not throw this election. Who threw this election were the Haredim, Russian immigrants, core Likudniks. However democratically, we've just elected a fundamentalist Knesset and a prime minister who is the first ever to win in a direct election, which gives him more staying power than any prime minister in Israeli history. In addition, the religious defeated us secular Jews in Jerusalem, making this city increasingly, and obviously, ultra-Orthodox. Why didn't we focus on all these voters? The ones who don't reap benefits from any peace process? Why were we so myopic? Why didn't we see it's *we* who infuriate the current winners and that Peres, who's viewed as the quintessential Ashkenazic intellectual, represents *us?*

• • •

My forty-something cabdriver doesn't speak any English but whistles all the way to Ben-Gurion Airport. He's the kind of guy who would usually have music blaring and drive like a maniac. How can I convey the poignancy of his soft musical sounds, his sweet reverie as he's driving in the middle of the night toward my 2 A.M. flight? As he's trilling his tunes, I can feel all the layers that constitute these melodies: self-esteem, his world set right, Bibi! We pull up to Ben-Gurion Airport and he asks someone to translate: "Tell her this is the first time in my whole life that I know *I'm* the real Israeli."

On line at the airport, I find out that the American black-hatted Haredim have bought out first class. Only four of them are here, but they've booked every seat. They don't want anyone else to share their cabin. The thought occurs: Did *they* buy this election?

Behind me, two Sephardic *yoradim* (Israelis who've moved abroad) wearing gold necklaces and bracelets are hugging repeatedly, saying, "We did it, we did it, we did it."

It's only we in business class who are, for once, mute. There's no small talk; there's no talk at all. Since the final tally still isn't in (the mail-in votes haven't been counted) and since we did not anticipate this upset, we can't yet digest it. We simply stare at each other.

At 2 A.M. we board the plane. Over the loudspeaker the pilot is asking, "Will Passenger Isachoff please come to the front?"

Bright lights are on inside the plane, the only one lit up on this airstrip. "Will Passenger Isachoff please come to the front of the plane?" the pilot repeats at two-minute intervals. Finally, after 3 A.M., comes the inevitable, "We have the bags of a passenger who did not show up. We must get them off the plane before takeoff." The jet doors open. Flight attendants stand on the stairs and allow us passengers to converge out there as well. We all welcome the fresh air as we realize that if Passenger Isachoff did not show up, we have a long wait ahead. El Al security must pull thousands of suitcases to locate, and remove, those tagged with that name. This search will be relentless; the possibility that the bags belong to a terrorist makes removing them essential.

Ten of us stand outside on the rickety stairs of the plane. Each has his or her take on the delay. A sexy Israeli woman—high heels, slinky dress—is furious at the idea of missing *Shabbat* in Los Angeles. She insists to the flight attendants that we take off immediately.

"But wouldn't God prefer you alive on *Shabbat*?" I ask. "They're only trying to protect us."

A rotund man wearing a *kippah* and beard fully agrees. "She's a *real* Jew," he says, winking at me. "A real Jew?" a man so slim he's nearly invisible under his black fur hat derisively retorts. "I bet she doesn't even keep *Shabbat*."

"I light candles," I say meekly.

"You see," the tiny Orthodox man pounces, "she's *not* a real Jew."

The hefty scholar admonishes him. "Please. Please don't talk like that to *anyone*; let's be polite." He smiles an apology my way.

"Isachoff," a diamond dealer from Belgium asks the steward, whose hair is blowing in the wind, "is this person male or female?" Another passenger chimes in, "Orthodox or secular?" Another asks, "Sephardi or Ashkenazi?" Finally, someone jokes, "Well, is 'it' an Arab or a Jew?"

We all know that the steward has no more idea about Isachoff than we do, but somehow all of us, seculars and observant, Haredim and journalists, Sephardim and Ashkenazim, need this playful banter and laughing, these catch phrases that succinctly capture, and dispel, the main themes of political life here. Our mood lightens. Dawn rises. The bomb scare has shifted us off the election, given us a chance to connect inside the great Israeli disconnect. It's good to be together in something that's not as heated as politics. The missing Isachoff has helped us to cut through stereotypes.

Meanwhile, endless bags are being unloaded. It's 4:30 A.M. It's 5:30 A.M. At six, dawn turns to bright morning and the plane takes off. Some are snoring before liftoff; others, no matter how sleep-deprived, begin election analyses that spread across, and up and down, the aisles. Hardly any of us in our section are pro-Likud, and our talk carries the depressive weight of loss, though the final results haven't been tallied, as we repeat—the army votes aren't in, nor are those from the sick in hospitals. We know what we don't yet admit, that the implications of this election will take a long time to sort out.

We arrive at New York's JFK Airport eleven hours later, where it's still early Friday morning. After getting my bag, I leave the terminal. There I see a driver holding a huge black sign that reads ISACHOFF. I rush to assure him that she or he is definitely, positively, without question, Not On This Flight. Finally convinced, he agrees to drive me to La Guardia Airport to catch my shuttle flight to Boston.

It's in his car that I hear, on National Public Radio, Linda Gradstein's so familiar, no-nonsense voice. She's announcing the final election tally: "*Shabbat* is descending on Jerusalem," she says. "Bibi Netanyahu has just been declared the new prime minister of Israel, an election he won by 30,000 votes."

I become hysterical while Gradstein speaks, as if this really *is* news to me. The driver turns around and asks, "You all right, lady? You okay?"

CHAPTER TWENTY

Sadness in Ramallah

It's summer in Israel. Shortly after I arrive with Eliza for six weeks, I walk around, shocked to see posters of Netanyahu hanging everywhere. His enlarged photograph is displayed in shops, in every official building, in grocery stores, banks, travel agencies. A chilling sight, especially since it feels as if everyone left of center, or in the center, has turned his and her back on internal Israeli politics and on what's going on in the Palestinian world as well. This summer feels like the end of something precious, though there's little news, and unusually glorious weather.

I visit my friend Seffi Elon at his office. He's a lawyer from a prominent left- and right-wing judicial family, the only one of five sons whose politics aren't advertised. My guess is that he voted for Bibi. Yet I find him burrowed inside thick legal texts, talking out loud to himself while flipping through pages. He's investigating how Netanyahu can be brought down. He says, though I didn't ask, "There are only two ways to impeach a prime minister in a direct election." Closing his books, he sighs, "It's nearly impossible for this government to fall. Because in this unique situation, the entire Knesset, not just the majority, would have to vote themselves out of office to get rid of him."

The new prime minister's budget cuts are creating ripples of rage. Netanyahu doubled bus fares, cut the long-established army stipend, limited access to health care—moves that affect the daily lives of his working-class supporters. That he did this instantly, before flying to the States to curry favor with his wealthy U.S. friends, is not lost on his constituents. And of those committed to the peace process? I ask a woman I know as we pass each other in a cafe on Ben Yehuda. "What's the focus these days?"

"It's the same conversation everywhere," she says.

"Politics or personal?"

"Politics are too sickening now," she says, laughing. "We're back to men."

I reflect that the personal *is* more prominent these days. Three couples I know, including Daphie and Shimon, are getting divorced. Of course, their schisms have nothing to do with this election, but the intense focus on the merely personal does.

Netanyahu's plans, unstated but ominous for the peace process, affect everyone. His words and actions, and lack of actions, fill most Israelis I know with anxiety, if not dread. The quiet of this summer is carrying within it a twilight sense of doom.

Eliza and I are staying with Sara, who is spending much of her time this July covering Bibi. She's been at his office for hours, day after day, watching him get interviewed, interviewing him herself and has taken visiting film crews from BBC, ABC and NBC to his office. "So, what's he really like?" I ask her.

She is not energetic this Friday night, but is depleted. "He's not pure evil," she says finally, "but he's full of words, a pro of an actor. That makes it hard to get beneath his talk, hard to get a read on him." She pauses. "But he gives himself away. For instance, he didn't use the word 'Palestinian,' not once this week—only 'Arab.' . . . It's as if he single-mindedly went after power without thinking what he'd do if he achieved it. He seems rigid. Enthralled to his crazed constituents. Maybe crazed himself. If not crazy—he may not be—that is one confused, concealed man."

Later, when she thinks I'm asleep on her couch, I'm astonished to see her walking quietly into her kitchen. There, she ferrets around for her grandmother's silver candelabras and places them in a corner of her kitchen. After lighting candles she sings under her breath in Hebrew, waving her arms to usher in the *Shabbat, "Shekinah."* I sit up to watch my secular friend, remembering her final words at dinner: "God help us."

Judith, too, seems different. She is not her usual energetic self, working through thin and thin for coexistence. She's especially disappointed because a planned event in Nablus was just canceled. It was going to be the usual face-to-face meetings, Israelis and Palestinians together, sharing a vision, creating a common bond. Today when I visit her is the day that event was to take place; she describes how at the last moment, in a way that has become "eerily familiar," the get-together was disrupted. This happens so often, she says, whether under Israeli occupation or now, under the Palestinian Authority, that "it's truly uncanny."

"We have weeks of calm; then violence erupts just when we're about to create a positive event. Why do our projects *always* get canceled and *always* at the last possible moment?" Yesterday, she tells me, a boy was beaten harshly by the Palestinian Authority. Word went out that the residents of Nablus were

upset, that the city was too wildly unsettled and too combustible for the Israelis to visit. But there's always a reason to cancel, it seems.

She tells me that New Age work, specifically Reiki Healing Touch, is now
the rage up in Nablus; it's a way to help pregnant women and traumatized ex-
prisoners, and is soothing for hardworking activists, too. She's excited about
this. I think back to something she mentioned long ago, in passing—that as a
youngster in Massachusetts in the 1950s, she didn't identify with Anne Frank,
like most of us, but with the righteous Gentiles who protected endangered
Jews.

As she speaks, I realize that her heart is, most of all, absorbed with justice.
She's happy at the incremental successes, defeated when plans don't pan out,
as so often they don't. Increasingly, I see her as one of the all-too-rare righteous Jews living in Israel. She gives weeks at a time to grassroots projects with
Palestinians from all over the West Bank, travels back and forth to build hope
on the ground. Along with a few colleagues, she does this without fanfare, for
no financial gain. Even though it's often frustrating, for Judith the reward is all
in the work she's been doing, as intensely since the election, despite the regres-
sive officialspeak. Her group believes in creating a context for hope; they ignore, as best they can, whatever is hopeless, negative or abstract.

No matter how horrid the new cabinet, Judith and the other Rapprochement
leaders are concentrated on keeping the possibility of peace alive between
"Palestine and Israel, Two States Free and Secure," as their slogan puts it.

I suggest that we spend the day in Ramallah, the Palestinian city closest to
Jerusalem. We've both heard that Ramallah is thriving, rising from the dust of
occupation into a lively cultural center. Neither of us has been there in a long
time. Ramallah is also where the acclaimed filmmaker Rashid Masharawi is
shooting his new movie. And tonight, his recently released *Haifa* (which I saw
last week at the Jerusalem Film Festival, where it won all top prizes) will debut
at el-Walid, the only movie theater in the West Bank. I call the filmmaker and
schedule an interview with him for 2 P.M. We travel there from East Jerusalem
with Hassan, a Palestinian cabdriver.

We find the filmmaker standing in the middle of a stark, dilapidated room,
wearing a rumpled T-shirt and worn pants. At first, assuming he's a handyman
or office assistant, I peer behind him, a mistake he catches. With a wry smile,
he ushers us to his desk. Sitting across from him I notice his wild green-blue
eyes; they remind me of the light permeating the sky in his movie.

Had I expected that because he's a genius, he'd be wearing a silk jacket,
have rows of secretaries and serve Evian? He's direct, no-nonsense, a quintessential Palestinian. Behind his desk, a few posters of his earlier films are tacked

onto peeling walls. He gives the impression that he has no time to waste on trivia. In response to our questions, he replies that he grew up in the Shakti refugee camp in Gaza and that despite offers to move abroad, he won't leave his people, his home or his work, that he travels abroad only for his films' gala openings.

He needs to live among his people, he says, to participate in their consciousness—that peculiar mix of simplicity and complexity, certainty and confusion, action and inaction *(samudi)*, languor and deluded desire. He attempts to capture all that as well as their fateful stoicism in his films. What Rashid has created in *Haifa* is a portrait of a people living in a nether world. I say that I assumed he lived elsewhere, that it didn't seem possible to create art out of such suffering, except from a great distance.

Was he at the West Jerusalem Cinémathèque? I ask. Yes, he was. He admits that he, too, was dazzled by his own cinematography, by the wonderful desert light. He says that capturing that brightness was his aim, carried out with painstaking deliberation. He chose the time of day and the exact location (outside Jericho) in which to shoot. He sums up for Judith the eight main characters in the film who live in a world with no hope, inhabiting crazed dreams and demented delusions. At the heart of the story is a man named Haifa. He is certifiably mad, wonderfully eccentric and, until his own personal breakdown, incredibly kind. Every character, however distorted, is beautiful in Rashid's hands, as I say to Judith.

"To do what I do," Rashid says, "I have to tune out all day-to-day political developments." He explains that to stay loyal to the deeper currents of feeling among his people—so long dispossessed of land, clarity and justice—he has to avoid distractions, especially the soap-opera news. If he were to fall into the daily morass, the ups and downs, he'd lose that ethereal narrative that he's after. Judith asks him who has most influenced his work. He answers, without modesty or bragging, that no one else attempts what he does. He can admire or learn from other filmmakers' work, but he has no model for his own.

I'm studying his brochures while Rashid and Judith begin to talk. I'm glad because it seems to me they have much in common. He's picked up this likeness. I listen as the righteous Jew and the righteous Palestinian talk with an undercurrent of kinship passing between them. As we stand to leave, Rashid tells us there won't be English or Hebrew subtitles during tonight's showing—that this will be a first run for the ordinary Palestinians that the film depicts. Looking at Judith, he says that meeting her has been his privilege.

Judith and I spend the late afternoon in a coffee shop on Ramallah's main downtown street. What I've imagined, reading about the new Ramallah, doesn't match today's experience. The streets are teeming. Everyone who's rushing around us seems pressured, poor, hot or ill-tempered. The atmosphere is honky-tonk, smelly, run-down. "Not a renaissance, but a slum," I say to Judith, who is also being brought down here, just the opposite of what I was hoping for her. There are no Israeli soldiers in sight, but there's no joy either. "It's no different than Gaza," Rashid had said. "They're both just occupation by . . . ," he searched for his word, "remote control," he finally said dryly.

Our taxi driver, Hassan, an Israeli Arab fluent in Hebrew, agrees to watch the film with us. He will translate the Arabic into Hebrew for Judith (neither of them has seen it). With my rave reviews they begin to get excited. But, to our chagrin, the theater, like the town itself, is a terrible disappointment. It's nearly empty on opening night, and is dirty and desolate. For unknown reasons, no one is allowed to sit downstairs, where comfortable movie seats are clearly visible. The few of us who've come are ushered upstairs to a small mezzanine where rickety chairs have been set up.

As soon as the film begins, I'm horrified to see that the screen, not much larger than a large television set, is terribly damaged—as if it's drenched in oil. There are only a few spots unsullied enough to let the original colors shine through. The glowing light of the film as seen in West Jerusalem is nearly obliterated here. After minutes of frustration, I leave Hassan to translate for Judith and go to sit on the theater's chipped, dirty steps. I'm hoping for someone to talk with.

Within minutes, a young man in his mid-twenties, who hesitantly gives his first name, George, joins me. He's in charge of selling Coca-Cola tonight. Now that the film has already begun, George is free to talk. He speaks English, as many in downtown Ramallah do not, which he has learned over the past two years when doing menial work for an uncle in Great Britain. George says that he's just returned to Ramallah, and so has "new eyes" for his hometown. Then he earnestly (if not fully consciously) begins expressing the contradictions of this time.

His words echo what many other Palestinians have said since the Israeli elections, but tonight I'm unusually alert, or he's unusually clear, and so I hear him. As he speaks, I remember how, long ago, during my very first week here, I discovered that finding out what's really going on, whether in Israel or "Palestine," is easier here than elsewhere because everyone you meet is part of the story. In this regard, George is a real find. He opens by saying, "Netanyahu is better than Peres or Rabin," as we share a soda on the dirty stairs. "They all think the same way. But Netanyahu gives it to us straight. He says openly that there'll be no Palestinian state, *not ever*. No hope for us even in

East Jerusalem, *not ever.* Finally, we have an Israeli leader who says what they *all* mean. We know he'll steal more of our land for Jewish settlements. But at least he says so. He's reopened some closures, which allows more Palestinians to get work—building the settlements, building our own demise. But to work is good."

George stops to check me out. Seeing that I'm with him, that I am listening fully, he continues, "We all need work. Our people are starving, as you must know. They pay us Arabs so little, and even so, it's only the lucky ones who find jobs. Our people work twelve-hour shifts, seven days a week, while even the poorest Jews get Saturday off, work seven or eight hours during the week and for six times the pay."

"But it's worth it?"

He nods. "Of course. We're worse off today, worse off than *ever.* People dig in garbage for food. I watch them doing that, embarrassed; usually it is in the middle of the night. Some who are healthy, maybe you read about this, sell their own kidneys to rich Jews. Is that or is that not horrible?"

He runs to check his soda counter, then returns. "We need money, not ideals. It's ideals that make Hamas blow up Israel. And if they start doing that again, I tell you, that will be the end of us. We can't live on false hopes, on distorted ideals." (Ironically, the movie that is playing not ten feet away from us is about what results from delusions.) "We have a serious problem with the Hamas, their bombings. It's desperate, really desperate, far worse than when I left in '94. Everywhere . . . in Gaza, in Nablus and especially in Hebron—very bad." George bows his head.

"You see, I'll tell you the real problem." He's not staring at the stairs now, but directly at me. "It's that we lost so many during the Intifada. We don't want to bury any more of our people. We don't want more deaths." He pauses, as if choking back tears, then says, "Listen, I know what I'm saying; I lost my brother and my father." We're quiet for a few minutes. Kids wander in and out of the lobby.

When they leave, I say, "You're very tired, your people?"

He looks at me, then through me. "Exactly. We are so tired."

Something in our talk shifts his energy. He leans close to me. "If we really all joined hands, all Palestinians, all of us here, then we could really make something," he says.

"Something violent or nonviolent?" I ask, seeing the fire in his eyes.

"Violence, total violence," he answers. I sense what he feels and why. With no hope for land, no working economy, without a sliver of a dream left inside this "remote control" occupation, a death wish arises, a pull toward a Palestinian Masada. I've seen how this undertow exists alongside the daily grind—most Palestinians scrounging to merely exist, eat, survive.

Kids run back into the building. The movie is almost over and they're trying to get in for free. I hear them arguing with George in Arabic; after all, there's only a half hour left. "Not allowed," George retorts (in Arabic to them, in English to me). Why are you so hard on them? I ask. "But that's my *job*," he mumbles. "My job," don't I see?

Other groups of boys, young teens, now rush in, empty their pockets, pool their shekels, begging for a reduction. George counts, nods, and up they go. Still others are turned away. These kids seem lacking in confidence. I see their little bodies puffed up, but I don't see any fight in them, nor any focus. They seem insecure, almost disfigured—what was not true during the Intifada, nor at the height of the peace process. Maybe I'm seeing bleakly in these bleak surroundings, with George's words in my ears. Yet as more kids—all boys ages eleven to fourteen come and go—I do see a vacancy in their eyes. I have never seen teenaged boys in the territories look so nakedly vulnerable.

Into the lobby stroll two men in their early sixties. One is tall and appears to be eminent. There's something stately in his posture. His friend is very short. The first says, "I haven't been to a film in twenty-five years." We talk of Rashid Masharawi, whom they revere as "a genius." But they haven't come to see this film. They've just stopped by on their evening stroll. When George sees them, he runs back upstairs. Now, the men stand above me as we agree that the recent Israeli election is the end of an era.

One of them says, "I hear Netanyahu skipped off to Paris last weekend, that a direct deal with Lebanon bypassing Syria is on the table." But right beneath his words is the feeling we all share, "Who cares?" or "To what end are we discussing this?" During the Rabin-Peres years, this kind of detail, however ambiguous or gloomy, would carry energy. Most Palestinians follow politics so carefully that outsiders who visit with them are often, within minutes, inside a joint passion that melts mistrust. Once absorbed in trading opinions and analyses, in poring over the latest developments, we bonded.

It's different tonight. Tonight our talk carries the pathos of idle chatter, a substrate of mutual despair. These men well know what George may not: that there was a process in motion, that the difference between Shimon Peres and Bibi Netanyahu is immense. The fact that we share such knowledge doesn't animate us. On the contrary, it mires us in depression.

The film has ended. I see Judith and Hassan walking slowly downstairs. Youngsters are rushing by them, leaping three steps at a time on either side of them. Not one looks elated, as the audience did in West Jerusalem, where we all stood, applauding, when *Haifa* ended. At that festival this portrait of Palestinian madness, suffering and poignant love was at a remove from the people it depicted. Here in Ramallah, the film is not the same. The lives of the audience and those on the screen are too closely entwined. What was Chekhovian in one context is like Jean-Paul Sartre's *No Exit* or Samuel Beckett's imprisoned consciousness here. If they do go to the movies, Palestinians want to escape from suffering, not be overwhelmed by more of it. They want to be, as Rashid's brochure for *Haifa* said, *"There, not here."*

On the near-deserted street, it's midnight when we exit and then spot Sami Kilani emerging from the theater right after we do, along with his wife and three kids. They've driven down from their home in Nablus after finding out that the dialogue festival was canceled. One look at their faces and it's clear they've found this movie hard to take. This might be an awkward moment except for Sami and Judith's close friendship, two pillars of coexistence work, the sponsors of the just-canceled Nablus event. Each is amazed to find the other here in Ramallah, far from their respective homes. They speak in the shorthand of old, close friends. He politely turns to me and Hassan. "It's very bad," he says, meaning Nablus, meaning the potential for riots, the closure's effects, referring to all that's happened since Netanyahu's election.

I've come to appreciate how much Sami Kilani's mobile face can express a range of emotions, though he's always courteous. "You don't need to explain," I suggest. "Because it's written all over your face." He smiles, his eyes locked in melancholy.

Judith, Hassan and I drive back to East Jerusalem. "Israeli drivers have nothing on Palestinians," I remark as cars whiz by, cutting each other off, using no turn signals, honking like mad. Hassan remains calm and steady at the wheel, as Judith and I begin to relax in the backseat. She says quietly, "It was embarrassing to see such poverty and confusion up on that screen while sitting in the midst of it. If I were Palestinian, that movie would not give me a lift."

I see her point. "It was no *Fiddler on the Roof*," I agree.

"Imagine," she continues, "seeing your collective soul as so maimed, so crazed. That must be utterly depressing." We're talking about the way *Haifa* was beautiful in West Jerusalem and unbearable in Ramallah as we arrive in East Jerusalem and pick up my car. We're quiet, pondering this strange day—the poverty, the way Rashid's film mirrored the wretchedness of downtown Ramallah. I'm also thinking about all that George gave voice to, imagining the turmoil in Nablus. My car seems filled with sad images as all that we say and don't say floats between us until I drop Judith at her home.

It's almost 1 A.M. I pull up to a new cafe run by Orthodox Jews on Emek

Refaim, a main street in residential Jerusalem. There I sit down at an outdoor table. Israeli night life often begins at midnight; all around me are groups of all ages, sitting relaxed, enjoying friendly conversations. There's a soft summer breeze. "Mom, what happened? Emek Refaim looks like Madison Avenue," Eliza, now eleven, observed recently. She's right. The German Colony in Jerusalem is not only far more luxurious than Ramallah (that goes without saying) but has become gentrified in just a few years.

Tonight, for the first time, I feel like caving in—not to hopelessness about peace, but to hopelessness about my own involvement. I'm tempted to write in my journal, "No more West Bank. No more Palestinian inquiries. No more searching for slim rays of hope." I look around and see, in this large outdoor cafe, Israelis who are able to tune out what's going on in the territories.

Even the best, most moral and soulful activists have, rightly so, many other dimensions to their lives: kids, family, culture, religion, work, homes to run. On the other hand, I, who am not Israeli, have taken the peace process too much to heart, have hoped too much, have been—an accusation I've resisted for years—too invested in this particular round of peace, its pace.

Now the obvious occurs. Why should I be so obsessed by the situation, especially when it's clearly about to go into reverse gear? When there was more hope, it was a privilege to go out on the edge, to cross the Green Line. But what or who does my current sadness serve? I hate thinking this way, but I am defeated tonight. I don't feel afraid in the West Bank anymore. It's not about fear. It's about the slowness, the reversals, the current vortex of despair. Which is not to say that there is no hope. It's that, for now, I have to wonder why I travel so far, usually for short visits, to feel so utterly useless. I can hear my grandmother, wagging her gnarled finger, saying, "What's it your business, to help the Arabs?"

The Americans who sat across from me on the plane happen to be seated at the next table. Their Bar Mitzvah must be over and I notice that they're tipsy. They shout for me to join them, as if we're old friends. They have no idea that we are not inhabiting the same Israel tonight. As soon as I know this, it's an image that isolates me. I'm not Israeli; I'm not Palestinian. I'm no longer like most American Jews either. I've seen too much. A terribly lonely feeling rises up in me, as I sense that in this cafe and on this street, very few have any sense of Ramallah or Nablus. For those who do know, the Palestinian problem is lively fodder for debate or conversation. For many, it's not personally wrenching, and I respect that. I respect the quest for pleasure.

Today was the antithesis of hope. I console myself that a few Intifada stones thrown at his car was why Thomas L. Friedman, who lived through the terrible war in Beirut, knew he had to leave the Middle East. It can be something seemingly small, a minor incident that can turn off anyone's passion for studying life here. Tears fall on the page as I write in my notebook. Anyone looking my way would think I am mourning a lost love. They'd be right.

My waiter, who wears a *kippah,* is in his mid-twenties. He kneels beside me. His voice is soft and comforting. I say I'm exhausted from a day in Ramallah. He nods. "I know it's terrible there," he says. "You should eat. Let's work on your meal. Come, we'll figure it out together."

After we do, I ask him, "Were you stationed there?"

"For a month," he says. "It was very hard."

"It's so sad," I say. "Yes," he nods slowly. "But that's their fate. It can't be any other way; it won't ever be different for them." For once I don't argue with this view. With Netanyahu's new government, peace activism will be more important than ever, but on the Israeli side there are so few. And who really knows what goes on inside the Palestinian world? Both peoples wish for more Israeli generosity, but we can't bring Rabin back from the dead or wish Netanyahu away.

I pay my bill. This nameless waiter doesn't stop conferring gentle attention upon me even though my meal is long over. When I stand to leave, he says in a tender voice, "Go home very, very slowly. Everything will *not* be okay, but you must be very careful with yourself." He's right, I think, marveling at his wisdom, his solicitous tone. His is not a typical Israeli voice, not the way Palestinians say goodbye, surely not the tone now dominating the Bar Mitzvah gang, still partying in loud English at the next table. Yet his are the words I most need. And I do go home.

•   •   •

It is weeks later. I have returned to Boston, and in mid-September the worst fears come to pass. On CNN, I see armed Israeli soldiers fighting against armed Palestinian police at a tunnel under the al-Aqsa Mosque in Jerusalem. This violence is unprecedented, as is the fact that for the first time since the Oslo Accords, Israeli troops reenter Nablus, Gaza and Ramallah. Eliza watches TV with me and is worried about her friends. "How will Tal and Michal stay safe?" she asks. I assure her that they'll stay home, or that their schools will have guards. I answer her distractedly, holding her hand, thinking how this was not inevitable. As we watch shots ringing out I remember all those vague fears from this past summer. What was to come no one could say for sure. Now we can.

CHAPTER TWENTY-ONE

A Place Named Israel;
a Place Named Palestine

An Englishwoman, an old friend and a wonderfully accomplished writer, tells me that she always makes a final trip to the site of any book she's written. It's a way to wind down, she says. She suggests I do the same, return to Israel with an entirely different aim than usual. I'm to go and "gather the visuals," she says. I don't know what she means.

She explains, "You pretend you're a painter or a photographer. Not a writer, not a journalist and certainly not someone who delves into everyone else's mess." We laugh at that. "Then you focus on the visual environment, noticing sights you've missed, anything at all: a flower bed, a bird, a patch of bushes. Or you capture the aromas and sounds. But only the sounds of music, of instruments or prayers. You listen and write about the animals, the birds, the wind. No people! No talk! People are far too crazy. You're going for the aesthetics, not politics. Now doesn't that sound like pure joy?" Before I can answer, she adds, "And in your beautiful Middle East, of all sensual places. You'll return with notes, with visual flesh that will feed the work."

I try to understand. "I'll be a camera, an eye, and turn off my mind?" I ask.

"A camera. An eye. That's the spirit," she assures me. "That's it precisely."

And so, in mid-March 1997, I'm again flying the six thousand miles to Jerusalem. Eliza, sitting next to me, is excited to see her friends during this spring break. I'm excited too—ready to become that camera. Instead of the usual clashing narratives, I'll capture the light shifting over the desert terrain, the stones glistening at noon or dulling at dusk and the olive trees, each branch and root unique as a fingerprint. I look down at my empty notebooks, knowing they'll be filled not with the fury of human distress, but with alleyways, trees, courtyards, stars, the ever-shifting Jerusalem sky.

The customs room at Ben-Gurion Airport has eight long lines, each one moving at the speed of the continental drift. So we make a quick about-face and sit outside on a low sandstone step. It's warmer than New York, if far from hot, and it's windy. I breathe in this air, thrilled, as always, to be back on the land, *ba'aretz*.

Eliza is chatting while I fish out a notebook and study the Israeli flag. It's flying at half-mast—I don't know why—and is whiplashed by gusting winds. I practice capturing it, write: "Blue Star of David. White background. Blue stripes—two." These words sound stilted, and I pause. As I do, the phrase "Named Israel, Named Palestine" leaps from my pen and repeats in my mind, rhythmic as a drumbeat—illogical but evocative.

"Named Israel, Named Palestine." Maybe the one name needs the other in order to redeem both? Soon we're riding in a tourist van toward Jerusalem. As usual, Eliza is visually engrossed. Staring from her rear window, she's no doubt seeing with ease whatever it is I'm ducking and craning to catch as we whiz past. "Clumps of thin pines," I jot. Then: "Lolling green hills; speckled sand." Approaching Jerusalem, I scrawl: "Stone hills, sliced thin, dirt." As I write this last word, I realize this visual task is going to be far harder than anticipated.

We arrive at the Laromme Hotel to find the lobby filled with Israeli and Palestinian politicians. The Palestinians look unusually grim. At the reception desk, I discover why: We've arrived the night before Israeli bulldozers are scheduled to begin digging into land that's said to be in Jerusalem though it's located many miles away, past Bethlehem and Beit Sahur, above the city of Beit Jalla. It's a hilltop that the Palestinians call Jabal Abu Ghaneem; the Israelis (and the international press) call it Har Homa. Whatever the name, it's a lone hill where Netanyahu just declared his government intends to build 6,500 co-ops for Jewish settlers. "This hill that hasn't seen human habitation since Joshua entered the Promised Land," is how Jon Immanuel describes it in today's *Jerusalem Post.*

Up in our room, I flop on a bed and reread Jon's op-ed piece. I know most Israeli and foreign Jews might brand him pro-Palestinian—typecasting that's laughable. My English-Israeli friend is as patriotic a Zionist as I know. But obviously, he's gotten an education while covering the territories as a journalist. He visits Palestinian homes and workplaces, enters shops and refugee camps, hangs out in offices and on street corners, places that 99.9 percent of Israeli and American Jews never go near.

I remember how, on the morning we met four years ago, Jon saw no problem with occupation. He didn't believe in gratuitous Israeli violence. About human rights abuses, he said, "I don't tear my hair out over them, because we must never give Palestinians the idea that their violence will work." Now he has written:

> *No government can give in to threats of violence. Yet the threat lies in the situation this government has created. Nobody was about to grab this area from Israel. . . . But without visible gain, this [Israeli] government is tempting violence. . . . It is not true that anywhere Israel builds the Palestinians will cry, "Provocation!" . . . Psychiatrists point out that nothing appeals more to the lonely lunatic than mass murder. . . . What psychiatrists fail to explain is why an ostensibly sane government would go out of its way to create an open season for lunatics. (Jerusalem Post, March 17, 1997)*

I've never heard Jon speak or write so clearly against Israeli policy; soon I'm surfing TV channels, shifting from Israeli Channel 1 to Channel 2 to CNN, thinking that my plan to re-create minarets and church gargoyles, to paint an apolitical land in words, will have to wait, for, by chance, I've arrived at a critical moment. Every channel shows images of bulldozers, large yellow ones with the German word *Leibherr* stamped on each. Then there are images of Israeli soldiers on high alert, their long sniper guns pointed at Har Homa, already "a closed military zone."

For a few seconds, the cameras scan an adjacent hilltop, windswept and wet, where a group of moderate Palestinians and Jews are standing in protest. The camera zooms to Faisal Husseini, whose distinguished Palestinian family has lived in Jerusalem for three centuries. He says, in a soft voice, that nonviolent resistance is crucial. He warns that if the bulldozers aren't turned back, they will upset more than land. "Much more," he assures the audience. Just as I'm gazing at this scene, Shimon and his daughter, Tal, race in.

The girls rush out to the large terrace. Shimon embraces me, then collapses into a chair, mumbling that most Israelis he knows are disgusted by this action. He switches on the radio, where we listen until jet lag tosses me into a numbing sleep. When I wake, Eliza is sprawled out beside me; the clock's digital red is blinking: 3:00 A.M.

I walk onto the terrace. Beyond the awning, I feel gusts of rain and hear thunder in the distance. Flashes of lightning illuminate the Old City's gap-toothed walls. Sopping wet, I tiptoe back inside, swiveling the TV, turned very low, away from the bed. While waiting for the morning news, hours away, I read Martin Buber and other early Zionists in *A Land of Two Peoples,* a book edited by one of the first Israelis I met in 1991, Paul Mendes-Flohr. Each chapter is composed of excerpts from authors writing about Jewish relations with the "indigenous peoples." Culled from the last century and ending in the 1940s, their words apply with amazing relevance directly to what's happening today. In 1891, Ahad Ha'am writes: "Outside the Land of Israel, we . . . believe that all Arabs are wild sons of the desert, too dull to see and understand what is happening. But the Arabs, like all Semites, have keen intelligence. . . . As our people's life encroaches on theirs they will not yield so easily." I ponder this, then find a quote from a Zionist named Moshe Smilansky. In 1913 he writes:

We, who are so close to the Arabs in terms of race and blood, remain foreign to them. It's their enemies, those who constantly await their downfall . . . who gain their confidence and are admitted into the intimate aspects of their lives. During these thirty years, it's not they who've remained alien to us, but we to them. This country is full of Arab memories.

I'm surprised to see David Ben-Gurion in 1930 asserting:

For hundreds of years large numbers of Arabs have lived in Palestine. Their fathers and fathers' fathers were born here. Palestine is their country where they want to live. We must accept this fact with love.

It's Martin Buber's words from the 1920s that touch me most. He exhorts future generations of Jews to create our own state while working to include, not alienate, Palestinian Arabs. This daunting task is one he predicts we will ignore at our great peril. Religion and what it teaches about right and wrong is inextricable, he believes, from the mess of politics, the work of coexistence. I'm underlining his sentences like mad, amazed that Buber, so long ago, predicted exactly what's facing us today, and that he was so prescient about how to avoid it.

He suggests that Jews of Palestine must marshal all the spiritual energy possible in order to "reach the possibilities of truth and justice in any particular hour," then admonishes future Zionists to resist globalizing any particular conflict, suggesting that we (you and I and they) view each situation "as a newborn child, with a new face, never seen before, never to be seen again." He ends with a prayer for the coming generations to retain the wisdom that the "Palestinian problem" is also our own and so belongs *inside mutual dialogue* rather than in debates among ourselves or left inside drifting abstractions. Buber urges that we, the future generations, work to create and sustain direct Jewish-Arabic encounters. He counsels that this will be the only way toward reconciliation.

When I look up, I see the rain has stopped. A gray dawn is spreading its gloomy light over this stone city. I step back out to the terrace, trying again to capture the "visuals." Yet nothing I see compares to the high-voltage events of this past week. Not only the bulldozers at Har Homa, but the murders of seven Israeli schoolgirls four days before we arrived. A crazed Jordanian terrorist killed them when they were on a field trip with their eighth-grade class in an area close to our mutual border. This incident, as Shimon has told me, was given round-the-clock media coverage. King Hussein made condolence calls in the Israeli town of Beit Shemesh—literally down on bended knees inside the homes of the bereaved. He expressed his pain, the sense of responsibility he feels, asked forgiveness from families in wild grief.

Hussein's action warmed Israeli hearts and was reminiscent, for most, of Egyptian president Anwar Sadat's visit to Jerusalem in 1977, but with this telling difference: Sadat's visit led Begin to negotiate with Egypt and ultimately to cede the Sinai for peace. In contrast, nothing King Hussein, our closest Arab ally, says or does seems to deter Netanyahu from seizing a lone hilltop.

With morning come more TV images: medical assistants working overtime at the largest East Jerusalem hospital, Al Makasset, refrigerating blood for the thousands expected to be injured in the upcoming, inevitable riots. Close-ups of doctors counting pints donated, of nurses readying extra cots, are shown. Then the scene switches to row upon row of Israeli battalions now assembled at the "borders." (What borders? Looking around Jerusalem what's obvious is the porousness between Jews in Israel and Palestinian Arabs.) An anchorman ends his report with the prediction that despite massive pressures against this action from the Israeli left, from Palestinian moderates *and* from the international community, Netanyahu will not waver, but will begin upturning land later today.

On the terrace, I'm pacing in anxiety. I know that this hill and those bulldozers may seem minor to many Jews. But violence is guaranteed to erupt over Har Homa, as Palestinians once again come up against the reality that Israel doesn't want to negotiate with them but to dominate—and invade—their land. For many Israelis the resulting upheavals will only confirm their preconception that the Arabs simply hate us. They won't see that Netanyahu has a direct hand in this debacle, won't understand why land expropriations so inflame our neighbors. For many the world over, virulent protests will solidify their stereotypes of Arabs as Jew-hating killers. Stone-throwing (or much worse) won't help anyone out in CNN-land to know how much Netanyahu's politics of humiliation and provocation have increased Palestinian despair, fueling the desire for revenge, creating more potential terrorists. Or that, with few exceptions (the withdrawal from part of Hebron is the primary one), virtually everything this prime minister does breaks with both the letter and spirit of Oslo. Images of those bulldozers fill me with rage, horror, fury. What must they be doing to the Palestinians?

From the terrace, I turn to face Jabotinsky Street. There I see what I'd somehow missed earlier. Directly across the street is the apartment where I lived for years. I gaze at "my" picture windows, remember writing long essays in that room about the growing trajectory toward peace under Yitzhak Rabin. Another window ledge held my fax, from which I sent reports and updates to New York. I begin shooting photographs of the windows just as a woman wearing a dark blue head scarf opens "my" silky white curtains. This sight evokes a cold nostalgia in me, a sense that all that has happened recently took place in a distant time, a foreign culture. For today's bulldozers may prove to be the pivotal reversal of all that we worked for, costing Israel not only relations with the Palestinians but also with the hard-won diplomatic recognition from most Arab nations. Diplomatic ties and cross-cultural treaties, once uniformly described as irreversible, may indeed reverse, becoming an insignificant blip on history's fickle screen. A horrid thought, especially as the Palestinians are—all propaganda to the contrary—potentially still our closest allies here in the Mideast.

Turning 180 degrees I scan from the far side of this terrace the settlements of Ma'ale Adumim. They seem to have doubled in number since last I looked. Their boxy shapes are built in the style planned for Jewish apartments on Abu Ghaneem. They look menacing and I think, We're mangling land, mangling architecture, mangling peace—to what end? Why not leave the Palestinians their own sunsets and moonscapes when we in Israel have an abundance of ours? I shift again, face the Judean mountains and then Jordan, beyond the Dead Sea, which is visible in the distance. Of course, Abu Ghaneem, or Har Homa, call it what you will, isn't visible from this high roof. It's as integral to Jerusalem as Buffalo is to Manhattan. No "legal" sales from exiled or money-hungry Arabs to fundamentalist Jews will ever make that land truly ours. What's happened to that hard-won leap of faith, the peace process?

What the early Zionists saw with clarity is invisible to many, if not most, modern Israelis: That Palestinians are due respect. That there are millions of them with a legacy to this land dating back *thirteen centuries*. (*"This country is full of Arab memories"*) . . . I walk inside to check on Eliza. She's still sleeping, and just as I cover her, Shimon walks in. Together we tiptoe outside to sit on two wet porch chairs. Shimon, who's usually calm, is jumbled this morning. He says that he's going through an emotional roller coaster and feels more disoriented than ever before in his life.

I ask why. First he reminisces about growing up on Kibbutz Ein Gev, fighting for Israel, as unquestioningly loyal as were his parents, who helped found and sustain this country, who both died fighting for it. He grows quiet, then blurts out that since Netanyahu's election, and now with Har Homa, his feelings for Israel border on disgust. We sit in silence. Then he says, "Netanyahu and the Israelis who support him make me sick. They're cruel; they're bullying and they're—" He searches for the English word. "Megalomaniacs." His face contorts as he continues in his halting speech. "I . . . look at . . . our flag. It represents the only world . . . I've ever known or loved. And . . . it seems . . . ugly." I think back to the moment at the airport, to the words that arose as *I* looked at the flag. Shimon goes on to say, "If Netanyahu digs . . . into Har Homa . . . I swear . . . I'll buy a one-way ticket . . . I'm out of here."

I argue that protest and action are more important, and suggest that he start attending the dialogue meetings in Beit Sahur, but Shimon shakes his head. He can't imagine crossing the Green Line, which lives in his mind as a *black* line, signifying death and danger, as it does for most Israelis. Most are afraid to go to the West Bank; they assume that life over there is synonymous with what's shown nightly on TV, a stone-throwing, anti-Israel locale. Shimon then agrees to watch Eliza as I drive to see Judith in Abu Tor.

Her car pulls up right after mine. She's been at the protest demonstration, watched from that adjacent hillside as the bulldozers began upturning land and trees at 2 P.M. on the dot. Sitting at the kitchen table in her Orthodox home, I say I want to go there, to see for myself. She insists that's impossible today, that the area is surrounded by soldiers and is a closed military zone, for now. In a monotone, she says that the only way to get to the peace protesters' tent is to wait until tomorrow night. Then I can travel with Abu Rami, the Palestinian bus driver who usually takes us to Beit Sahur dialogue meetings. He's using back routes we don't know, she says. Then she adds that the protesters have new neighbors: Israeli soldiers have just taken over a stone hut that's situated between the two hills, on *undisputed* land. She watched them shattering windowpanes and pointing their guns toward the lone peace tent, thirty feet away.

With this vision, I leave Judith to pick up Eliza. She's awake and eager for me to take her down to Moshav Beit Zayit, where Sara and her children live. Once inside this bucolic village, a ten-minute ride down the Jerusalem–Tel Aviv highway, we pass carefully tended houses, flowering trees and bushes, dogs and cats and quiet. At Sara's house, a babysitter tells us that she has just left to cover the riots that are already breaking out in Hebron. Sara's daughter, Michal, runs to greet Eliza; the two girls fly, a tiny, colorful tornado, toward the playroom. I drive back to Jerusalem to catch the 8 P.M. nightly news with friends. On Channel 1 is Jerusalem's mayor, Ehud Olmert, the man reputed to be upstaging and trying to replace Netanyahu. He's eating a chocolate-covered doughnut at the brand-new Dunkin' Donuts which opened today in downtown Jerusalem. Giving his Cheshire grin to the cameras, Olmert announces that "very soon" an identical shop will open "on top of Har Homa." He adds that these American imports taste so good that he can't wait for that construction to eat one there. Holding up a half-eaten doughnut, while chomping on another, he crows, *"Ze tov meod"* (it's very good), grinning again.

The next night I go to the intersection of Hebron and Rivka Streets at 5:45 P.M. There I join fifty Israeli and foreign Jews for the bus ride to the peace camp. Abu Rami, a gruff cigarette smoker with incongruously gentle eyes, closes the bus doors and we're off. He avoids the Bethlehem Checkpoint two miles down the road ("Closed," he says), taking a circuitous route instead. He bumps over thistled fields, swerves through hidden alleyways, drives into and through someone's backyard until, all of us dizzy from zigzagging curves, we reach the base of the road that leads up to the hill. What should have taken fifteen minutes has tonight taken an hour. Abu Rami applies his brakes to applause and we all jump out. It's only now that I see Abu Ghaneem is more than a hilltop; it's a mountain. We, Israelis, Americans and European Jews—secular and religious; new or old hands at dialogue—rush uphill in the darkness.

The night is clear. The stony mountain path is filled with scents of thyme and zatar. We exclaim over the beauty of this pristine terrain, glad to be far above Israeli cities with their barking bad news and above Palestinian towns filling with a violence not seen since the late 1980s. Under the moonlight, we trip over tiny shrubs, inhale acacia air and point out swirling van Gogh–like stars. I watch as the boots and sneakers of the others pirouette over boulders in a climb to the mountaintop. Walking slowly, I'm the last to arrive.

And here I see more than a hundred Palestinians and Jews mingling around a fire whose light is reflected in their glowing eyes. We sit cross-legged on the ground, or lower ourselves onto small stools as the flames leap above us. Even among strangers, there's a flurry of handshakes and the sounds of *"Ahlan, Ahlan"* (Greetings) in Arabic. This simplicity and human warmth is in such contrast to the turmoil raging below that everyone is smiling.

Veronica Cohen asks, "Who wants to go first?" as one Israeli and one Palestinian volunteer to translate from the English always used at our meetings. An unusually tall Palestinian man, in his late fifties, speaks. He begins by saying that he plans to live here at this peace camp full-time. Violence was once his credo, he admits. But years ago he renounced that for nonviolent action and dialogue. No matter what Netanyahu does, "nothing, but nothing" will ever again provoke him into savagery. He points to the sky and says, "When it gets very dark, do you see how the stars shine so much brighter?"

Such poetry may speak to this starry night and to our hopes, but these words make no sense to an elderly Palestinian man. He says that killing civilians is abhorrent to him but he believes Netanyahu's actions will make "the crazed go even crazier." That there will be killing. Turning to the poet, he asks, "Your stars, how will they help with that?" A Jewish woman in her thirties agrees. If she were Palestinian, she too might become violent at the sight of her land being taken and her people in such misery.

An old Jewish man, a Holocaust survivor, disagrees: "No. You never turn to violence. What we need are more Palestinians and Israelis to join this nonviolent resistance. If we create a huge tent city here, that'll bring down the neighborhood. [Laughter all around.] Those settlers won't consider 'Har Homa' so desirable, not with thousands of us living right next door." The next speaker, a middle-aged Palestinian, finds nothing to laugh about. "Even if hundreds of thousands of us committed to coming here, you know the Israeli Defense Forces would find an excuse to close us down." He gestures toward the hut where the Israeli soldiers and their guns are clearly silhouetted. "Violence is evil and violence is inevitable."

An older Israeli woman asks a powerful question: "We Israelis are free to live in Jerusalem. But what is it like for you—you who have little or no access to Jerusalem while living so near the bulldozers?" She's answered by a hoarse-voiced, slim Palestinian man: "I'll tell you what's worst. The lies. The whole world is hooked to CNN. They slant all their stories toward you Israelis. But they remain deaf to our reality. That's most maddening. To live a story that no one in power emphasizes while Israeli distortions and pain *always* make world headlines. Do they ever show the soldiers or settlers taunting or killing *our* people? They describe a settler who kills as 'a seminary student,' but if a single Israeli is killed, we're *all* branded as 'terrorists'; *all* of us go unnamed; *all* of us are suspects."

I'm thinking of the Hebron massacre in 1994. Walking around that city after the slain were buried, I had watched the 450 downtown settlers dancing in celebration of their killer, Dr. Baruch Goldstein, while hundreds of thousands of Hebron's Palestinians were locked inside their homes for four weeks—the victims punished—a scene I wouldn't have believed had I not seen it. It was in Hebron that I committed myself to dialogue precisely because I agree with this man's point. The Palestinian story *is* the one less broadcast, the one underreported. Those distant days spent in the West Bank have brought me into this moment, where the subject is still violence.

We all agree that if one Israeli gets killed, the street will line up for, not against, Netanyahu's policies, that Arab violence is political suicide. We wonder how Arafat can keep a lid on everyone, especially with so little since Oslo that's positive—emotionally and economically—to hold out to his people. "Arafat can't control every single soul," a Palestinian woman says, as we all nod in agreement. "He's certainly not your best leader," an Israeli woman says. Again, everyone nods.

An elderly man with a red-checkered kaffiyeh wrapped over his head, draped along his wizened face, repeats: "Those two. Our so-called leaders. What did we Palestinians and you Israelis do to deserve *them?*" Ghassan Andoni, leader of the Beit Sahur group, asks: "Please. Can you tell me why more Israelis aren't up here? Don't they understand our daily reality? Tell me, why do those who say that they care about what we endure, who know that our two peoples' fates are entwined—why do *they* refuse to come?"

I talk of Shimon, of the "silent Israeli minority or majority" (I'm not sure which) who do care but won't come up here because they're afraid. And part of their fear, I think to myself, has to do with the press and what they choose to cover; the press corps, who, for example, aren't here. They're pouring into the sewers of war spreading from Hebron to Bethlehem, from Ramallah to Nablus. During this past night, Israeli tanks were repositioned to enter the West Bank in case the Palestinian police can't or won't control their crowds.

Once inside, the Israeli soldiers will presumably do surveillance, roughing up anyone they consider a potential terrorist. I first heard about that typical, brutal strategy from Mohammed in the Deheishe refugee camp in 1992, when the honesty of his demeanor and the vividness of his descriptions started me on this long journey into the Palestinian world. Then, I wasn't fully convinced that what he described was true, although seeing those four Israeli soldiers storm the house in which we were talking certainly helped to establish his credibility. I've since learned that what he said about Israeli methods of interrogation *is* true, though that's another matter that doesn't get on-air press coverage. I make a mental note to call Mohammed as well as Achmed, still my closest Palestinian friend. They should come up here, too.

• • •

Early the next afternoon, a Friday, a terrorist bomb goes off in Tel Aviv at the Apropos, an upscale cafe. This horrible event surprises no one I know. The only question was where the violence would happen and how many would be killed. The murderer strikes at two in the afternoon—the same time as the bulldozers. Is this coincidental? It's the day before Purim. Gruesome details are given nonstop coverage on Israeli and international TV. Israeli stations repeat the same few images: The injured and maimed are shown along with reports that three women are dead. Those hurt seem plucked straight from central casting. Fifty, a hundred times, we see a curly-haired six-month-old, her Purim costume in tatters as she's lifted into a waiting ambulance. The voice-over repeats that her thirty-two-year-old mother, a lawyer, was murdered. Then endless replays show every Jew's archetypal aunt, her face and arms bloodied, screaming in Hebrew as she's carried away on a stretcher.

The "visual flesh" I came for are now literally and sickeningly shown—the tidal wave of broken glass, splintered wood, blasted tabletops, human remains—all accompanied by Netanyahu's pronouncement that Arafat is to blame, that he gave a "green light" to this violence. I watch this carnage while calculating how it will play to the Israeli street, how these films will feed Netanyahu's mantra: "Zero tolerance for violence." With maimed and murdered Jews so vividly depicted on the air, no one dares to say outright (on CNN or Israeli TV) that Netanyahu has had a large hand in this round of violence.

Viewers are given little idea what Abu Ghaneem or land in general means to Palestinians or how powerless most of them feel. Those who do understand Netanyahu's culpability, who have some inkling of Palestinian reality, are profoundly uneasy now. Shimon, my icon of the quintessential Israeli, is rattled. "There's no one to trust," he says. On the phone, Judith sighs, "Back to settlements and bombs."

As *Shabbat* closes in, I careen down the highway to Beit Zayit, arriving minutes before Sara pulls in from Hebron. As we make dinner for our kids, we listen to which videos they watched, how they arranged toys in a tree house. Only after eating, dishes and laundry, after orchestrating their baths, do we two adults step outside to sit under a weeping willow tree. The lights of Jerusalem hang above us, like a brightly lit chandelier.

Sara describes her day in Hebron—how rubber bullets, stones, tear gas and Molotov cocktails were thrown back and forth inside a narrow alleyway. Today was the fiercest explosion she's witnessed since the height of the Intifada, maybe worse. She rolls up her sleeves to show me where a stone bruised her elbow. She caught a huge dose of tear gas and already has a wicked cold.

Sara's oldest son, sister and parents all live in Tel Aviv. I ask if the bomb blast that went off at the Apropos, close to their apartments, makes her more sympathetic to Netanyahu's pronouncements. She shakes her head firmly, no.

The next day, the Tel Aviv terrorist is identified. He wasn't from Arafat's Hebron, but lived in a section still under Israeli control. Nonetheless, blame for Arafat's "green light" is still the "master narrative" circling the globe. Since it's *Shabbat*, we stay home with the kids. I reread *Ha'aretz* columnist

Danny Rubinstein's book *The People of Nowhere,* published in 1991, an account of what land means to Palestinians. He details the 1948 generation's attachment to their lost plots of inherited earth, their destroyed homes. "If removed from her house in the village, even if by a few kilometers, a woman was in exile," he writes. He tells how an olive or lemon tree growing in the ancestral yard became part of the family's personal identity. What can we wandering Jews, longing for a land we left centuries ago, know of such a howling state of exile because a stone wall or one olive tree is gone, or simply moved?

In the evening we turn on the TV. Each young Palestinian face looks dark with hatred. This is selective journalism. Just to make sure we get the point, the telecast repeats Hamas bulletins warning of more reprisals. Sara and I debate whether or not she will wear a bulletproof vest or carry a gas mask as other journalists have begun to do for the first time.

On Sunday, a weekday in Israel, we leave the kids under "house arrest." They're bored but safe in Beit Zayit, as Sara heads out to cover the day's riots that are spreading to every city and town in the West Bank. I head up to Jerusalem, where I'll later meet Judith to go on another trip to the hill adjacent to Har Homa/Abu Ghaneem. I have time to wander around Jerusalem. I stop and chat with acquaintances and friendly strangers. Every discussion concerns "Har Homa." I hear identical phrases from a bookstore owner, two cabdrivers, an electronics whiz kid, a rental-car saleswoman: "It's our land and we can do whatever we want." Or: "Give an Arab an inch, he'll take a mile." I brush past these familiar words. Then, ambling past the Khan Theater, I discover that the Fourth International Poets Conference has convened here, only blocks from Judith's house in Abu Tor. I enter the rounded arches and sit in the open stone courtyard.

Here I see poets and readers from all over the globe. Some are waiting for the next reading to begin; others are reading aloud to each other. These bohemians, artists and intellectuals seem to inhabit a parallel universe, one in which making art is disconnected from the mess of politics. Everyone I see is relaxing inside this summer art scene. The few Israeli poets I know, long in favor of a two-state solution, try to dissuade me from going to the West Bank tonight. At first casually, then more urgently, each says, "Don't get so involved." Even Danny Rubinstein suggests I don't go.

Puzzled, I drive the few blocks to Abu Tor to pick up Judith. I'm early. She's busy making dinner with her four kids. I go outside to her backyard, where her husband, Jeff—a novelist, book reviewer and translator—is lying on a long canvas lounge chair. I watch while he pats their large black dog. Nearby, I spot a black cat with bright yellow eyes sitting curled in a patch of waning sun.

Soon, the Greens' youngest daughter, Hannah, aged twelve (straight-backed, politically engaged, the child I joke will be prime minister one day, a "joke" I fully believe), walks out to talk to her dad. She's wearing all black—a T-shirt, a long skirt. My eyes wander from the dog to the cat to the girl, seeing a silky blackness slithering from one to another, like a line from a poem.

I'm relaxed for the first time since my return to Israel. Lulled by the loveliness of the views of the Judean hills, of the olive, pomegranate and peach trees hanging overhead, I sink into some alpha zone, a tranquillity that's eluded me for the past nine days. From this wonderfully pleasant spot, those tents and firelight and discussions up on the mountaintop seem as distant as Siberia. I don't want to go, I say to Jeff, who raises an eyebrow in complete understanding. But shortly, Judith steps outside, signaling that it's time to leave. I hesitate. Finally, my fear of letting her down mixes with echoes from Buber's essays (his call to enter politics, to create dialogue with the Palestinians) and I rise slowly, waving a hesitant goodbye to Jeff, who laughs. He nods at Judith and says, "I'm lucky. *She* goes for me."

The minute we arrive at our regular bus stop and join the crowd of Israelis waiting to make the trip, my inertia lifts. Everyone is talking. I tell Uri Avnery, a grandfather of coexistence work, that each call I made to encourage Israelis to join us tonight was futile. Every friend or acquaintance gave one or another excuse about not being able to come: a cold, a headache, no babysitter, on and on. Uri nods. He's worked against this Israeli passivity toward political action all his life. Only Shimon, a gardener at the Israel Museum, whose Arab workers are under closure, has given me a tentative maybe. Now, I'm startled to see him strolling toward us. Bringing a new sabra into dialogue is so rare; it's like carrying a fragile jewel. We all reach out to include him, but on the bus he's withdrawn, refusing to participate in the lively chatter that fills the aisles. I watch him staring from the bus windows at the West Bank.

We arrive to find that more than eighty Palestinians and Israelis now living full-time on this mountaintop. Overnight this place has become a village. Many locals visit daily, bringing food and supplies. A section has been cleared for a parking lot, which tonight is completely filled. An Israeli tent is being set up along with a huge Rapprochement sign: "WE WANT PEACE BETWEEN PALESTINE AND ISRAEL—EACH FREE AND SECURE." The words are written in English, in thick blue Hebrew block print, in red and green Arabic script. More tents are being carried up as the townspeople arrive with food for dinner.

Because daylight savings time began yesterday, I'm now, for the first time, able to see the hills and towns around us. The green hill of "Har Homa" is very close. Four yellow bulldozers sit there, motionless as statues. As I study them, the lights of Beit Jalla blink on below. The sky flushes rose, then pale orange.

I spot Achmed exiting from a car. The feelings we exchange when looking into each other's eyes are a testament to our long bond. We move away from the group to sit together off to the side of tonight's low fire. We see the man who talked so poetically last week ("When it gets dark, the stars shine brighter"). We gaze at him as he rides up astride a colorfully adorned donkey; he's draped from neck to ankle in a brown blanket. "A Palestinian Ichabod Crane," I joke. Achmed shakes his head. "No," he whispers, saying that the man I thought a quixotic poet is a very high Palestinian official named Salah Ta'amari. "He's a beloved Palestinian leader, a man likely to succeed Arafat in a democratically held election." Looking at him now, I realize I have seen him at official Palestinian events and on television.

He leaps off his donkey, ties it under six Palestinian flags—green, red, white and black—that are staked into the mountain's hard ground. Each flag flaps in tonight's surprisingly strong winds. "Named Israel, Named Palestine" recurs in my mind as Achmed and I join the others who bundle together in the unexpected cold. An American flag is flying in honor of a Jewish couple who, after catching fifteen seconds of Faisal Husseini on CNN, have flown here from California to participate. Around tonight's small fire, we rub against each other for warmth. A Palestinian girl of fourteen flops onto my lap to warm herself. I burrow my numb hands inside her thick, spongy hair. She hugs me, crying over the memory of her father's arrest. Then she whispers that she can't concentrate at school because her life is too hard. To my surprise, she then points out her dad, who's sitting erect, directly across from us on the far side of the fire. Her tears had led me to believe he was locked in prison or dead. I tell her how much I wish my dad were alive, saying that we all suffer, that I find studying hard is a good way to rise above sadness.

Our meeting is interrupted by the constant ringing of cell phones. Everyone checks his or her pockets. This comical anachronism is the only clue that we're meeting in the late 1990s and not in biblical times. Ghassan Andoni opens the meeting. I hope that Shimon, whom I've neglected while talking with Achmed, is catching the spirit. A second speaker says he thinks we have only one week before all-out war. Another Palestinian disagrees: "I'm hopeful. We will succeed. We will stop both Israeli and Arab madness with this peace camp. This is the only creative option."

Veronica announces that we have a veteran of peace work here tonight. In deference to his long years of work, we'll allot more time than is usual to Uri

Avnery. He begins: "It's a moving experience, sitting under the stars of our common homeland. We here know that we will either live together or die together. We all agree we must have two states, Israel and Palestine, with a common capital in Jerusalem." Seeing that he has everyone's attention, he continues. "This mountain symbolizes peace. We must convince others that this is the way. We need media attention focused on what *we* represent instead of continually broadcasting scenes that feed hopelessness. It's not enough to sit here with beautiful feelings, knowing that we are in the right. We must encourage many others to join us."

The Palestinians listen attentively until bone-chilling winds force us to scatter into tents, each equipped with a gas heater, to continue our discussions. I linger outside, talking to a few people sitting around the dying embers of the fire.

Only on the bus ride back down do I learn of Shimon's beginner's bad luck. He was the only Israeli in a tent surrounded by Arabs, all of whom were new to dialogue. They berated Israel and the occupation. "The same thing I hear from my workers every day," Shimon says. We try to assure him that Palestinians new to dialogue focus automatically on a litany of Israeli wrongs and Palestinian wounds—the last thing any Israeli who shows up for reconciliation wants to hear. Shimon felt trapped and bored, but . . . he'll be back. He's glimpsed that active participation is "way better than passively watching TV." Later, in private, he confesses that he endured a surge of anxiety bordering on panic on the bus ride up.

Back at the Laromme Hotel, dreams of tanks, guns and warring bedlam toss me about much of the night. In the lobby the next morning, the front desk has a spread of today's *Jerusalem Post*. Its headlines blast of war and the front-page photographs show bloodied Palestinians in Hebron. What seemed all-powerful last night once again shifts to the margins. But it's now that I see, perhaps for the first time, that grassroots organizers and activists pay no attention to daily riots or the daily press. What they attend to is a different dimension, far from what most concerns the journalists and politicians. Right now, all the peace people I know are working around the clock to prepare for an event, scheduled for next Thursday on the mountain—six days off. This peace celebration will include Palestinian and Israeli children, a gesture toward the future of our two peoples. For the first time, I join their work directly. I contact friends, acquaintances and strangers. I feel victorious when most of my journalist friends agree to come, each with the proviso, "Only if nothing else huge happens that day."

My personal problem is the usual one, that in order to join them, I'll have to stay an extra five days, sending Eliza back to school in the U.S. with a friend booked on our return flight. My daughter reluctantly agrees, only after assurances that *this time* I'll keep my word and arrive home early Friday "before school." "Promise?" she looks at me sternly, knowing how often I slip in, or try to, an extra day, if not more. "No question!" I promise.

The morning of the event, I wake early. Only at this last minute does it dawn on me that we'll be traveling to the mountain at the most dangerous time, midday. What I've been pressuring others to do now alarms me since I know that the *shabab* (Palestinian fighters) keep strict hours, flooding the streets with violence from noon till 5 P.M. Imagining dying in a crossfire, with Eliza halfway around the world, fuels my panic. I can't get killed when she's so far away, I think (as if it's okay to die while she's here in Beit Zayit). At noon I'm on the bus to the peace camp. I sit next to Uri Avnery, whose face clouds over after we pass the Bethlehem Checkpoint. Even he suggests that, without a single Palestinian on board, we aren't safe.

When I see a cadre of Palestinian police I lean out the bus window and frantically wave. I feel a special rapport with these men, having profiled some on the week they arrived back into Jericho and Gaza. As usual, they warm to us "Peace Jews," which is how they refer to us. They are glad to help. I motion to one man with a thick black mustache and gleaming eyes to please, please hop on board. But they all insist on doing something better; they'll escort us by car through the riots—except that there are no riots. In our ten-minute ride to the mountain, we see nothing but sheep, flowers, sunny hillsides and bucolic towns.

We are greeted by a smiling Salah Ta'amari, the Palestinian official Achmed identified for me. "See, we brought you a perfect day," he says. I look up and around. The sun is directly overhead in a perfect, cloudless, cerulean sky. I've never been here at midday, have never seen just how Arab this neighborhood is. All around and below us are Palestinian villages and towns between which lie huge white wheat fields that alternate with equally large rectangular green farmland, a checkerboard pattern that stretches all the way to the distant horizon. Beneath this hilltop are Arab homes, Arab villages, Arab architecture, Arab agriculture, Arab sheep and goats.

By three in the afternoon, more than five hundred Palestinians and Israelis, including seventy children, are moving about in gleeful friendliness. I shoot film, capture "the visuals," which are what I came for in the first place. My photographs document the gorgeous, untrammeled land and the infinite variety of faces among the assembled. I aim my camera at Palestinian women dressed in suits, stockings and high heels, who look as if they're about to stroll down Fifth Avenue; at Palestinian men in torn T-shirts and tattered pants; at Greek Orthodox priests in high-top birettas, long black cassocks and large gold crosses lying on their chests. Many Palestinians are here because Abu Ghaneem is near to their homes. Most of the locals have never met Jews before. Yet they greet us warmly—us secular and Orthodox, men and women, old and young, religiously attired and bohemian, Holocaust survivors and young babies. All of us are embraced.

The only official Israelis in sight are the soldiers pacing in the stone hut yards from where the kids, Palestinian and Israeli, ages seven to fourteen, sit. Rachel Avnery and several other prominent Israeli educators are here, keeping the children focused on their sketching, giving words of reassurance when three soldiers suddenly object that the kids "have crossed the white line." What white line? One soldier points to a tiny demarcation, nearly invisible, that he's drawn with a stick into the ground. That's a new one, I think, seeing that nothing they say can ruin this group's high spirits.

Very few journalists show up. Of the many I've invited, only Jon Immanuel comes. Though his presence is welcome, I'm disappointed that more do not arrive. A freelance journalist from London says that something horrible is brewing down in Bethlehem. Other foreign photojournalists and newsmen and women confirm this. I watch as they join the infectious partying. I have brief conversations with dozens of people, including a funny exchange with Salah Ta'amari, who, I've recently learned, is married to a Jordanian princess. I watch him talking to his constituents. He wears a blue woolen cap under which his face is sunburnt bright after twenty days living up here full-time. I say, "First I thought you were a weird poet, then I find you're a famous politician. And now I learn that you're married to a princess." He's busy orchestrating crowds, but he winks at me, saying in a tone of wry intimacy, "Not a princess, a queen. Try being married to a queen!"

Soon after, he is the opening speaker at the press conference that has been scheduled to draw attention to events here. Although every other speaker who follows him tries to convey lyricism, humor and history, it's Salah who's the most passionate and inspiring. The press conference goes off so well that I'm confident that, this time at least, the world will see another, better side to Israeli-Palestinian relations, and will understand the importance of direct encounters for creating peace on the ground.

I've happened upon the "visuals" that I came for and then some; one could call this day a politics of beauty. Of all I've seen these last six years in scenic Israel, in the lilting West Bank hills, in crowded Gaza, today, without question, is the most purely pictorial. Long-haired and poised Palestinian girls wear ankle-length, traditional black dresses spangled with gold tassels that leap up and down as they perform a dance. Israeli children, most of the boys in *kippot,* watch them, wide-eyed, as other children bend over, intently drawing and painting together, trying to capture the sights. One old man in a kaffiyeh is in tears as he stands above them. Statuesque Palestinian women look on with pride.

I move a few feet back to sit with three grandmothers from Beit Jalla. Holding hands, we exclaim over the scenery, the peace signs and posters on display in front of the "art" tent. We describe our children, exchanging photographs and phone numbers. Despite the Israeli soldiers who again warn us, this time about how many tents we're allowed to set up here, on land owned by residents of Beit Jalla, still more tents are being assembled. Everywhere I look I see people talking.

By 5 P.M., a planning session begins along the largest picnic table. Israeli and Palestinian Rapprochement leaders are discussing which writers, musicians, poets and painters they'll invite here in the coming weeks. While the organizers do their work, my only thought is, I don't want to leave. Up here, this day of discussion and food, music and art and friendship, ushered in partly by the official Handshake, is the real mutual recognitions in action. The spectacular vistas and the mountain air enhance an ambiance that suggests—if I didn't know better—that we've already solved the great, mysterious, monstrous, never-ending Israeli-Palestinian conflict. What eludes the politicians is embodied and embraced all around me. From inside this day I see the ideal Mideast future.

As the sunset paints the surrounding hills a watercolor golden peach, then dims into darker, apricot hues, Hillel Bardin yells, "Hurry, if you're taking the bus!" I hug a calm Israeli named Sa'adia, who plans to stay up here for months. I feel a surge of envy as I watch others who also plan to stay. They begin to unroll sleeping bags or tuck backpacks into their tents. Then they sit close together relishing tonight's spectacular sunset.

Hillel shouts again, to the sound of the bus motor revving up. I have a plane to catch, a child to rejoin. Others also have family, work or children needing dinner or help with homework tonight. Those who are staying here have broken with all such routines. I stand immobilized, calculating how to get a few more days (and what exactly I'd say to Eliza) when Salah Ta'amari, as if overhearing my thoughts, stops nearby. He studies my face and says, "Do it." He pauses. "Stay. You know this is the real peace." He's right. That other, the official process—the one endlessly discussed and debated, signed and unsigned, that "almost," "on the verge," "not quite," "distant," "impossible" peace with its blatant failures—is upturned here, where coexistence seems easy, has already happened.

Until today, I've been faithful to capturing the official events, intent on getting the news and dialogue as exactly as I'm able, trying to erase warped stereotypes on the page. For the last six years I've lived to describe such scenes, what today I've been simply living. For more than a split second, I stand completely still and do not move to get onto that bus.

On the ride down, I hear Judith mention that coverage of this day will be shown on BBC at eight. Someone else says, "Also on CNN and on Israel's Channel 1." It's almost 8 P.M. now. I rush to Shimon's apartment. He has a satellite dish that will give me a perfect picture of what the cameras have captured.

But this day gets exactly three seconds on each station. They show only shots of the kids' heads (Muslim shawls and *kippot*) as they sit drawing. These children could be anywhere in scenes that look almost bland. And that's all that's shown on every station, the tiniest slice of this day: not the press conference, not the hillside's views, no shots of the huge group sharing in one spirit. Even on supposedly liberal Israeli TV, our day is flattened, robbed of all color and life, derided by a TV anchorman as "attended by the usual handful of left-wing Israelis." These words are followed by a full two minutes of stone-throwing in Ramallah, then a funeral for peace in Bethlehem where Palestinian men carry a coffin that's covered with dead doves.

I rush back to the Laromme's lobby to pack. It is here that I finally understand the real impact of today's event. For as soon as I enter the lobby, after only seven hours on top of Abu Ghaneem, it looks strange to see only Jews milling about, instead of that heady mixture of Jews and Palestinians, interconnected in such ease.

I'm off to the airport. The shuttle bus to El Al's flight 001, the nightly 1 A.M. plane to New York, is full. Boys in their twenties, dressed all in black—from hat to shoe—with perfectly curled *peyot,* fly past us, rushing to grab seats. I'm standing next to a couple, actors from Tel Aviv: aging and glamorous, all cheekbones and dazzle. Too rushed to change clothes, I'm still wearing sweatpants which are dusty from this day on the mountaintop. We notice that Yossi Sarid, the leading minister from Meretz, the peace party, is sitting silent, right next to Dore Gold, a Netanyahu advisor, the man about to become Israel's ambassador to the United Nations. The bus jostles their thighs together. Each stares straight ahead. Not a word passes between them.

"Could you dream up this cast of characters?" I ask the actor couple. They laugh and look around at Jewish businessmen, diamond merchants, the yeshiva students, before we settle our eyes on the two politicians—far left and far right—locked in their mirrored stoicism.

As always, this land I love is a world as impossible to fully decode as it is unbearable to leave—this theater of incongruous, gruff, sexy, close-minded, religious, secular, cruel, funny and excitable characters. This drama has everything but an ending, I think. Whatever the next chapter brings for these two countries—one named Israel and the other, officially or not, named Palestine—I can't know. I can only hope that it will be happier than the current one.

As I board the plane, I have an ominous premonition: that I won't be back, that I won't, for reasons I can't now fathom, participate in all the surprises that await everyone in this region.

Acknowledgments

One must, above all, thank one's own dogged determination to capture the subject that holds one in thrall. That is what got this book going and got it finished. Central to my persistence in writing and rewriting was all that I witnessed and lived through during my years in Jerusalem.

It is also true that one cannot go it alone. Great thanks are due to these friends who read, commented and improved on the manuscript: Beth Rashbaum, Sara Blackburn, Denise Fletcher, Helen Kritzler, Ed Kritzler, Jerri Udelson, Susannah Greenberg and Holly Grano. For wise writerly advice: Eva Fogelman, Jeff Green, Anna Immanuel, Jon Immanuel, James Hillman, Frank Rose, Michael Koran and Marjorie Saunders Levenson. For moral support and wonderful conversations: Judith Green, Achmed Mashall, Hali Weiss, Jesse Rosenthal, Harold Bobroff, Sara Rabinovitz, Bea Bookchin, Said Saber, Jean Travillion and, most especially, Maria Leal. For all-around expertise: Howard Siegal.

To those in the Mideast who inspired me to tell their stories—some of whom have asked that their names be changed; most of whom did not.

To Thomas L. Friedman, whose book *From Beirut to Jerusalem* was an abiding inspiration.

To my daughter, Eliza Orange, for her (exasperated) patience. ("Didn't you finish that book last year? You're writing that same book, again? Mom!") And in thanks for her humorous company and many title suggestions.

To Michael Lerner, who introduced me to Israel, and to Alice Chasan, who edited versions of several of the chapters when published in the magazine *Tikkun*.

This book would not have seen light of day without my agent, Joy Harris, trouble-shooter extraordinaire. And her fabulous staff, Kassandra Duane and Leslie Daniels.

In gratitude to my tireless and scrupulous editor, Alice Mayhew, who showed me *why* less is more and so how to keep a plot moving *forward*.

To her wonderful assistant Ana DeBevoise, a voice that lit this writer's darkness. In gratitude to Cindy Hamel, organized publicist and friend to this book.

And to those copy editors at Simon & Schuster who made certain that Khalid did not devolve into Khilada along the way.

Index